Notes on Grammar

ALSO BY DEE ANN HOLISKY

Aspect and Georgian Medial Verbs

IN COLLABORATION WITH
KATHY TRUMP AND SHERRY TRECHER

Walk, Amble, Stroll, Level 1
Walk, Amble, Stroll, Level 2

NOTES ON GRAMMAR

DEE ANN HOLISKY

ORCHISES
WASHINGTON
1997

Copyright 1997 © Dee Ann Holisky

Library of Congress Cataloging-in-Publication Data

Holisky, Dee Ann.
    Notes on grammar / Dee Ann Holisky
        p.   cm.
    Includes bibliographical references and index.
    ISBN 0-914061-31-3 : $49.95
    1. Grammar, Comparative and general. 2. English language—
Textbooks for foreign speakers. I. Title
    P201.H7 1997
    415—DC20   92-28791
                                                                     CIP

Manufactured in the United States of America

Orchises Press
P. O. Box 20602
Alexandria
Virginia
22320-1602

G 6 E 4 C 2 A

To my Linguistics Professors
at the University of Chicago

*With the hope that they are not dismayed
by the practical use to which I have put
the theoretical concepts they taught me.*

TABLE OF CONTENTS

i

PREFACE

As suggested by the title *Notes on Grammar*, this book began as notes for a class on English grammar. At first they were lecture notes intended to supplement missing or inadequate sections of textbooks, but over time they grew into ever longer handouts and then, chapters of a book. As also suggested by the title, this is not a reference grammar; in fact, many subjects are treated only in passing. Rather than striving for completeness, I have attempted to give readers a systematic foundation for the descriptive study of English grammar and have chosen to cover topics that represent my own areas of interest and those of importance to English teachers, especially ESL teachers. I have tried to discuss grammar in a way that is accessible to people with a limited knowledge of linguistics. At the same time, in the descriptive analyses, I have attempted to be sensitive to current theoretical concerns so that this book can serve as a background for students who will go on to more advanced work in syntactic theory. One of my students has called it pre-syntax. It could be used as a text in a class on English grammar or for self-study.

In the sixteen years I have worked on this book, I have benefited from the help of many people, first among them my students. They presented me with the challenge of making sense of English grammar and provided me with most valuable criticisms of everything from incoherent explanations to faulty examples. I also owe a significant debt to Roger Lathbury, who nudged me into thinking of earlier versions of this as a book and who has waited more or less patiently for a long time, to Anne Farley and Charlie Jones, who piloted earlier versions in their classes, and to Stephanie Buchner for help with editing. Finally, I thank Steven Weinberger and Marshall and Gena for the many ways they support my work and most especially Charlie for his invaluable contributions to both the content and the form of this book.

iii

ABBREVIATIONS

A	Adjective
Adv	Adverb
Advbl	Adverbial
C	Complementizer
Con	Conjunction
CP	Complementizer Phrase
Dir	Direct
Gen	Genitive
Ind	Indirect
Inf	Infinitive
Int	Intensifier
IQ	Indirect Question
Mod	Modifier
N	Noun
Obj	Object
P	Preposition or Phrase
Par	Particle
Part	Participle
Pass	Passive
Pres	Present
PIP	Place Phrase
PNG	Postnominal Genitive
Pred	Predicate
Prep	Prepositional
Pro	Pro-form
Rel	Relative
S	Clause
Sg	Singular
TP	Time Phrase
V	Verb
XP	Phrase with member of word class X as head (X = N, V, etc.)

UNIT I

UNITS OF GRAMMAR: WORDS, PHRASES, CLAUSES

STUDYING GRAMMAR is like studying a foreign language. There are new words to learn and new concepts to master. The goal of Unit I is to introduce the words and concepts necessary for any intelligent discussion of grammar. Some are familiar and some will be new, but even familiar words will be used in unfamiliar ways.

Each chapter of Unit I deals with a major unit of grammar. In Chapter 1 words and word classes (the parts of speech) are discussed. In Chapter 2 the focus is on phrases. There is an extended discussion of the overall architecture of phrases and an explanation of the strategy to be followed in exploring phrases.

In Chapter 3 the major elements that make up clauses (subject, verb, direct object, etc.) are discussed, and the notion of a basic clause is introduced. The syntax of all clauses is described in terms of basic clauses. At the end of Chapter 3 there is a brief discussion of the typology of clauses and the main functions of subordinate clauses.

Unit I concludes with a brief summary of the units of grammar that are used in this book. It may be helpful to refer to this list from time to time.

1

1

WORD CLASSES, OR
THE PARTS OF SPEECH

CONSIDER THE SENTENCE IN (1), found on a chopstick wrapper. It is ungrammatical, as indicated by the asterisk ("*") at the beginning.

(1)   *Please try ... Chinese food with Chopsticks, the traditional and typical of Chinese glorious history and cultural.

The problem in (1) is that words which are adjectives (*traditional*, *typical*, and *cultural*) are used in ways that English native speakers would use only nouns. For instance, only nouns combine with the definite article *the*. Since the words *table* and *house* are nouns, the combinations *the table* and *the house* are grammatical. But since the words *traditional* and *typical* are adjectives, not nouns, the combinations **the traditional* and **the typical* are not.

In addition, nouns (more accurately, the phrases that nouns head) are used as objects of prepositions like *of*. Since *rice* and *culture* are nouns, *of rice* and *of culture* are grammatical. Since *cultural* is an adjective, **of cultural* is not. Adjectives (more accurately, the phrases that adjectives head) cannot be the object of a preposition.

The errors in sentence (1) exemplify an important aspect of grammar: there are distinct classes of words, and members of different classes have different grammatical properties. In this chapter we will explore the word classes of English and their grammatical properties. We begin first with a look at how traditional grammars have treated word classes.

3

CHAPTER 1

1. TRADITIONAL CLASSIFICATIONS

In traditional treatments of English, words are divided into classes called the parts of speech, a classification that is usually central to the description. The number of classes varies, but eight is often considered the magic number, as in the fairly typical list given in (2).

(2)   Noun
      Pronoun
      Verb
      Adjective
      Adverb
      Preposition
      Conjunction
      Interjection

   The parts of speech have a very long history. They appear in the first grammar of Latin written in English (Lily and Colet 1970), published in 1549. This work, known as "Lily's grammar," remained in wide use for 400 years and influenced many writers, including Ben Johnson, who published *English Grammar* in 1641 in which he added a ninth part, the article.

   English grammarians continued to use the Latin-based parts of speech, but their lists varied in number from two to nine. By the 1760s grammarians had fixed on the eight parts listed in (2). There is in fact nothing magic about eight, and linguists today would argue that we must recognize a larger number of word classes.

   This brief history tells us little about the justification for dividing words into parts of speech and provides no rationale for deciding how many "parts" are necessary. In order to do this, we need first to consider how word classes are to be defined.

2. DEFINING THE PARTS OF SPEECH

2.1 Traditional Definitions

A look at many grammar books would produce a list of definitions similar to that in (3).

(3) Traditional Definitions of the Parts of Speech

Noun:	is the name of a person, place, or thing.
Pronoun:	is used in place of a noun.
Verb:	denotes an action or a state of being.
Adjective:	modifies a noun or pronoun.
Adverb:	modifies a verb, adjective, or another adverb.
Preposition:	indicates a relation between the noun or pronoun it governs and another word.
Conjunction:	joins together sentences or parts of sentences.
Interjection:	is an outcry which expresses pain, anger, pleasure, or some other emotion. (*Ouch! Oh!*)

Note that the definitions are of two kinds: Nouns and verbs are defined in terms of their meanings, while adjectives, adverbs, and prepositions are defined in terms of their functions (e.g. modifying and relating). Definitions based on meaning and function are problematic when it comes to classifying words. Sometimes it is difficult to apply the definitions because they are too vague, and sometimes the definitions are at odds with each other.

As anyone who has tried to teach the parts of speech knows, the meaning-based definitions of noun and verb are often hard to apply because they are expressed in terms of everyday notions like "thing" and "action." Take the definition of noun, for example. ("A noun is the name of a person, place, or thing.") Person and place are fairly easy to understand, but what does the word "thing" include? If *thing* means "physical object", there are many entities which are not physical objects which would (incorrectly) be excluded from the class of nouns, including *fact, idea, culture, linguistics, justice.*

If "thing" includes abstract entities, then it becomes so vague that it is difficult to determine whether a word names a thing or not. Consider the word *red*. Isn't *red* the name of a color and isn't a color a thing? This reasoning makes the word *red* a noun. But *red* can modify a noun (as in *the red house*), which makes it an adjective. What about the word *destruction*? Traditional classifications consider it a noun, but does it make sense to say that destruction is a thing? It names an action, which would (incorrectly) make it a verb and not a noun.

In fact, though most names of people, places, and things (whether concrete or abstract) *are* nouns, nouns can have many other kinds of meaning as well, as shown in (4).

(4) (a) an action: the *destruction* of the city
     (b) an event: a long *meeting,* a *party*
     (c) a quality: *happiness, intelligence*
     (d) a path: the *way* to San Jose
     (e) a measurement in space: five *miles*
     (f) a measurement in time: six *hours*
     (g) no meaning at all: kick the *bucket,* pull my *leg*

The fact that nouns can name actions underscores the inadequacy of the meaning-based definition of verbs as well. ("A verb denotes an action or a state of being.") Not all words that name actions are verbs, and, moreover, many verbs do not name actions, as shown in (5), a list of kinds of meaning that verbs can express.

(5) (a) a state of being: She *is* nice. God *exists.*
     (b) a mental or emotional state: She *knows* French.
                                              They *like* caviar.
     (c) possession: We *own* a house in Florida.
                                              They *have* three cars.
     (d) a relation among things: Two plus two *equals* four.
                                              The evidence *falsifies* the theory.
                                              The exception *proves* the rule.
     (e) a position or location: The house *stands* on the corner.
                                              A canal *runs* through town.
     (f) a cognitive process: I *think* about grammar.
                                              They *decided* to go.
     (g) no meaning at all: *kick* the bucket, *pull* my leg

The diversity of meanings expressed by nouns and verbs leads us to reject meaning-based definitions. They clash not only with each other, but with the function-based definitions for the other parts of speech. In sum, the traditional definitions do not provide clear criteria that allow us to assign words to word classes in an unambiguous way. Some change is in order.

2.2 New Definitions

The traditional definitions fail because they are couched in terms of meanings and functions. Before we turn to new definitions, however, we should understand why a classification like the parts of speech is necessary in the first place.

We need to distinguish between words like *destroy* and *destruction* because they have different grammatical properties, including both morphological properties (e.g. they are inflected differently) and syntactic properties (e.g. they combine with different classes of words), as shown in (6) and (7). (Remember that an asterisk ("*") means the word or phrase is not grammatical.)

(6)   (a) The verb *destroy*
             takes suffixes *-(e)d* and *-ing* (*destroyed, destroying*)
             combines with a noun phrase to form a verb phrase
             (*destroy* [*the city*])

        (b) The noun *destruction*
             does not take suffixes *-(e)d* and *-ing*
                (**destructioned*, **destructioning*)
             does not combine with a noun phrase (**destruction* [*the city*])

(7)   (a) The noun *destruction*
             has singular and plural forms (*one destruction, two destructions*)
             combines with *the* to form a noun phrase (*the destruction*)
             combines with prepositional phrase with *of*
                (*destruction* [*of the city*])

        (b) The verb *destroy*
             does not have singular and plural forms
                (**one destroy*, **two destroys*)
             does not combine with *the* (**the destroy*)
             does not combine with PP with *of* (**destroy* [*of the city*])

In this view, verbs are words with verb-like behavior; nouns are words with noun-like behavior. That is, words that have the same grammatical properties belong to the same word class. From now on, instead of calling the different classes "parts of speech" we will use the term "word classes" to emphasize the new approach. The following three points are basic to this approach.

Grammatical properties. The definitions of word classes are based on the shared grammatical properties of the words. These grammatical properties include facts about both morphology and syntax, as in (8) and (9).

(8)   Some *Morphological* Properties of Different Word Classes
       Verbs have forms with the suffixes *-(e)d* and *-ing*
       Verbs take the suffix *-able* to form adjectives (*read, readable*)
       Nouns have singular and plural forms (*girl, girls*)
       Adjectives take the suffixes *-er, -est* (*redder, reddest*)

(9)   Some *Syntactic* Properties of Different Word Classes
       Nouns combine with articles to form noun phrases
              (*the* plus *dog* forms *the dog*)
       Verbs combine with noun phrases to form verb phrases
              (*destroy* plus [*the city*] gives *destroy the city*)
       Adjectives combine with intensifiers (degree words)
              (*very* plus *hot* forms *very hot*)

Cluster approach. The traditional definitions which were criticized above involved a single criterion. The approach taken here is different in that the definitions involve a cluster of properties and do not apply in an all or nothing way. For a given word, some of the properties of the word class will apply, while others may not. For example, not all nouns have the properties mentioned above. Some nouns do not have singular and plural forms, as in (10), while others do not combine with articles, as in (11).

(10)   Nouns with no plural form (Noncount Nouns)
       Singular: furniture   Plural: *furnitures
                    information   *informations
                    sincerity   *sincerities

(11)   Nouns that do not combine with an article (Proper Nouns)
       Peter   *the Peter
       Boston   *the Boston
       France   *the France

The cluster approach allows us to define nouns in terms of their grammatical properties, but to recognize at the same time that not all nouns will have all of the properties that comprise the definition.

Subclasses. A third important point is that there are distinct subclasses within each of the major word classes. The subclasses arise because words behave differently with respect to the defining properties of the class, as shown above. Since not all nouns have singular and plural forms, this leads to two subclasses, called count and noncount nouns.

(12)   (a) Count nouns: Have singular and plural forms.
       (b) Noncount nouns: Do not have plural forms.

Other word classes have subclasses as well. For instance, though words that take the suffix -ing are verbs, there are a few verbs which don't (*may-ing, *must-ing), namely members of the subclass of modal verbs. As mentioned in (9), adjectives take the suffix -er; that is, more generally speaking, they can be compared (red, redder; beautiful, more beautiful). There are, however, some adjectives which don't have comparative forms, the subclass of nongradable adjectives (gigantic, ?more gigantic; unique, ?more unique).

3. OPEN AND CLOSED WORD CLASSES

Word classes may be open or closed. Open word classes are very large and open-ended, with new members easily added either by productive word formation rules or by borrowing. The open word classes are nouns, verbs, adjectives, adverbs, and, to a lesser extent, intensifiers (degree words). Closed word classes, by contrast, contain a limited number of items. They are highly resistant to the addition of new members, and there are no word formation rules that create new members. The terms open and closed can be applied also to subclasses: the class of verbs is an open class, but the subclass of auxiliary verbs is a closed class. The closed word classes include the familiar classes of prepositions and conjunctions, and other, less familiar ones, including articles, demonstratives, pro-forms, and complementizers.

Articles and demonstratives are two very small closed word classes whose members are listed in (13). They function as determiners (see 4.2 and Chapter 29).

(13)   (a) Articles: a/an, the
       (b) Demonstratives: this, that, these, those

Proforms are a closed class whose members cross-cut all syntactic categories. Their function is to replace various types of phrases, including noun phrases, verb phrases, place phrases, and clauses (also known as complementizer phrases), as in (14), where the proforms are in italics.

(14)   (a) The princess came into the room, and everyone stared at *her*.
            (*her* = [the princess], a noun phrase)
       (b) I like grammar and they *do*, too.
            (*do* = [like grammar], a verb phrase)
       (c) My sister lives in Paris, but I've never been *there*.
            (*there* = [in Paris], a place phrase)
       (d) You say that you like me, but I doubt *it*.
            (*it* = [that you like me], a clause (or complementizer phrase))

Some proforms are the pronouns of traditional grammar, and in this book, the term "pronoun" will be used for those proforms that replace noun phrases, including the subclasses listed in (15).

(15)   Some Pronoun Subclasses
       (a) Personal pronouns: I/me, you, she/her, he/him, it
                                    we/us, you, they/them
       (b) Reflexive pronouns: myself, yourself, herself, himself, itself
                                    ourselves, yourselves, themselves
       (c) Genitive pronouns: my/mine, your/yours, his, her/hers …
       (d) Indefinite pronouns: someone, somebody, something, some …
                                    anyone, anybody, anything, any …
       (e) Negative pronouns: no one, nobody, nothing, none …

WH-words are a subclass of proforms that are found in a number of special syntactic constructions, including content questions and relative clauses, as in (16). In addition to WH-words, there are WH-phrases; we will refer to the class as WH-expressions. Some common ones are listed in (17), and constructions which require them are discussed in Chapters 23-25.

(16) (a) Content Questions: *Who* did that?
                                 Where did they go?
      (b) Relative Clauses: We know the boy [*who* did that].
                                 I saw the place [*where* he died].

(17) WH-expressions
      who, whom, what, which, whose ...
      what kind of, how much, how many ...
      where, when, how, why, whether ...

As the name indicates, this class contains words which begin with the letters <wh> (pronounced [w] in some words and [h] in others) and one word which begins with the letter <h> (pronounced [h]) (*how*).

The closed class of complementizers includes *that, for,* and the subordinating conjunctions of traditional grammar (*because, since, if, whether,* etc.). Complementizers combine with clauses and serve to mark them as subordinate; the resulting constituent is a complementizer phrase. In (18) the complementizer is in italics, the clause and resulting complementizer phrase in square brackets.

(18) (a) Students believe [*that* [syntax is fun]].
      (b) [*For* [Malcom to praise you in public]] is embarrassing.
      (c) I'll help [*because* [you asked so nicely]].
      (d) [*If* [it rains]] they won't go to the ballgame.

4. CASE STUDY IN WORD CLASSES:
A DEFINITION FOR NOUNS

In this section we use what we have learned to construct a definition for nouns that draws on their morphological and syntactic properties.

4.1 Morphological Properties

In terms of inflectional morphology, nouns have singular and plural forms. The plural is formed with the suffix /s/ written <s> or <es>. (Phonetic forms of this suffix are discussed in Chapter 26.)

(19)   Singular   Plural
       one cat   two cat-s
       one culture   two culture-s
       one bus   two bus-es

Many descriptions of English say that nouns have possessive forms too, but the so-called "possessive suffix" attaches to noun phrases, not to nouns. It is called a genitive in this book and is discussed in Chapter 30.

There are many rules of derivational morphology that help identify nouns. First of all, there are rules which form nouns from members of other word classes. Although not without exception, a word with one of these suffixes is highly likely to be a noun.

(20)   (a)   Nouns naming people are formed from some verbs
             by adding the suffix *-(e)r*
             Verb   →   Noun
             play   play-er
             read   read-er
             teach   teach-er

       (b)   Abstract nouns can be formed from some verbs
             by adding the suffix *-ment*
             Verb   →   Noun
             amuse   amuse-ment
             arrange   arrange-ment
             disappoint   disappoint-ment

       (c)   Abstract nouns can be formed from adjectives
             by adding the suffix *-ness*
             Adjective   →   Noun
             bright   bright-ness
             kind   kind-ness
             mean   mean-ness

In addition to rules which are used to form nouns, there are rules which apply to nouns. These too are part of the morphological pattern of nouns and can be used as evidence that a word is a noun.

(21)   (a)   Adjectives can be formed from nouns with the suffix -*ic*
            Noun   —>   Adjective
            atom   atom-ic
            despot   despot-ic
            idiot   idiot-ic

       (b)   Adjectives can be formed from nouns with the suffix -*ish*
            Noun   —>   Adjective
            book   book-ish
            boy   boy-ish
            girl   girl-ish

4.2   Syntactic Properties

An important syntactic property of a noun is that it serves as the head of a noun phrase (abbreviated NP). A major function of NPs is that they combine with verb phrases (VPs) to form clauses. (See Chapter 2.)

(22)   Noun Phrase   + Verb Phrase   —→   Clause
       the team   went home   The team went home.
       a house   burned down   A house burned down.

A second property of nouns is that they combine with determiners to form NPs. (Determiners include articles, demonstratives, quantifiers, and genitive NPs (see Chapters 29, 30).) Nouns can also be modified by constituents of various syntactic categories, including adjectives (or adjective phrases) and relative clauses, among others.

(23)   (a)   Adjective   +   Noun
            smart   people
            really terrible   destruction
            nearly extinct   culture

(b) Noun   +   Relative Clause
    people   who I know
    cats   which live in my yard
    book   that was lost

Exercise 1

Following the model for nouns in Section 4, construct definitions for the word classes listed below. Try to include two morphological properties and two syntactic properties for each class, though not all classes have distinctive morphological properties.

Word Classes: Verbs, Adjectives, Adverbs, Prepositions, Conjunctions

Exercise 2

Identify the word class of the italicized words in the following sentences. Be prepared to give a reason for your answer. If the word belongs to a major subclass, name it as well.

1.   *Is* your *boss* looking *for* a new office manager?
2.   *Those* children are disturbing *us* with their *loud* music.
3.   *Sally's* ideas were *thoughtlessly* dismissed *by* that idiot.
4.   Do *you* approve *of* the *new* plan *or* would you rather keep *the* old one?
5.   A: *Who* will go *downtown* with me?
     B: Not me. I've been *there* already *today*.
6.   *We* are *extremely* happy *that* you *have* won the *lottery*.
7.   *Unfortunately*, we *arrived* late, *and* my sister was *furious*.
8.   *Your* mother looked *at* us very *oddly*, then *suddenly*, she *started* to laugh. Then *everyone* was anxious *for* us to leave.
9.   Some *people* reported that the reception *in* the garden was *quite* lovely, *but* I wouldn't *agree* with *that*.
10. *After* he threw *up*, they *reluctantly* decided to go *to* the   *emergency* room.

Exercise 3

Often different words have the same root or even the same phonetic form. Identify the word class of each italicized word.

1. Bring me the *mop*, and I'll *mop* up this mess.
2. *Concerning* today's meeting, I have a *concern* that unfortunately *concerns* all of you.
3. On this *round* of the competition, the task is to *round* off each number to the nearest 10. Then identify each *round* object in the picture by drawing a circle *around* it.
4. Don't make a *sound* until we have a chance to *sound* out our clients about this very *sound* proposal. We are afraid of being *soundly* defeated if someone *sounds* off in an *unsound* way.
5. Her *interest* in this very *interesting* mystery was heightened when she discovered who the *interested* parties were. *Interestingly*, even that revelation failed to *interest* her *uninterested* partner.
6. It may be *mean* of me, but his message was *meaningless*. I *mean*, I didn't get his *meaning*.

Exercise 4

Strong evidence that words are not put into word classes on the basis of their meanings comes from "made up words." Identify the word class of the italicized words in the following passage from "Jabberwocky" by Lewis Carroll (1960:191). How can you do this if you don't know what they mean? Are the italicized words members of open or closed word classes?

'Twas *brillig*, and the *slithy toves*
Did *gyre* and *gimble* in the *wabe*:
All mimsy were the *borogoves*,
And the *mome raths outgrabe*.

Exercise 5 For Discussion

Do students learning English as a second language need to know about different word classes? Do they need to be taught about the different word classes of English? Do students from some language backgrounds have more difficulty with this area of English grammar than students from other language backgrounds?

2
PHRASES

AS DISCUSSED IN CHAPTER 1, word classes are defined in terms of their grammatical properties. In this chapter we will explore one important property of word classes, the phrases they form. Each word class forms a distinct type of phrase; i.e. verbs form verb phrases, nouns form noun phrases, and so on. The phrases we will discuss here are listed in (1). (The abbreviations are to be read as acronyms, i.e. by naming the letters.)

(1)

Word Class	Phrase Type	Abbreviation
verb	verb phrase	VP
noun	noun phrase	NP
adjective	adjective phrase	AP
preposition	prepositional phrase	PP
complementizer	complementizer phrase	CP

In addition, there are a few phrase types which are not defined in terms of a word class, but in terms of their semantic function. Of these, the most important are phrases that denote place and time, which function as adverbials.

(2)

Phrase Type	Abbreviation
place phrase	PIP
time phrase	TP

Phrase types are discussed individually in later chapters, but in this chapter we discuss phrases in general, beginning in Section 1 by considering the overall architecture of phrases. In Section 2, we present tests for the major phrase types, and in Section 3, discuss the syntax of conjoined phrases.

16

1. INVESTIGATING PHRASES

There are two important aspects to understanding any phrase. First, we want to know what the phrase is composed of, or its internal syntax. Second, we want to know how it is used (e.g. what positions it can occur in), or its external syntax.

1.1 Internal Syntax

The phrases listed in (1) and (2) differ in the details of their internal syntax. For example, noun phrases contain a noun, verb phrases, a verb, and so on. Though the details differ, there are important generalizations to make about the internal syntax of all phrases.

The head and its complements. Every phrase has two levels: The upper level is like a hook on which different kinds of words or phrases can be hung, while the lower level contains the words and phrases which make up the phrase. The single most important element in the lower level, and the only obligatory element, is the head. The head of a noun phrase is a noun, the head of a verb phrase is a verb, and so on. We connect the head with its phrase by a straight line, as illustrated in (3).

(3)   Phrase Level: NP   VP   AP
                          | | |
        Head: N   V   Adj

Examples of phrases containing a single word are given in (4). The words in parentheses give a context for these one-word phrases.

(4)   (a) NP   *people*   (are funny)
                   chocolate   (is fattening)

       (b) VP   (the baby)   *cried*
                   (my gerbil)   *died*

       (c) AP   (people are)   *funny*
                   (that house is)   *big*

Besides being the only obligatory element, the head of a phrase also determines what other elements are possible. That is, the head dictates the internal syntax of the phrase. Let's see how this works by looking at a few verbs and the phrases they occur in.

Some verbs, such as *cry* and *die* in (4)(b), can occur alone in a verb phrase. They don't imply the existence of anything else, and they don't require any other elements in the phrase. Other verbs, such as *kiss* and *love*, do not necessarily occur alone in a verb phrase. Because of their meanings, they imply the existence of other persons or things, which may be expressed in an accompanying noun phrase, as in (5). (The noun phrases are in square brackets.) (As above, the words in parentheses indicate a context in which the verb phrases might be used.)

(5)   Verb Phrase
    (a) (the old woman)   *kissed* [her son]
    (b) (all children)   *love* [their parents]
    (c) (the policeman)   *shot* [a sniper]

The noun phrases which accompany the verbs in (5) are known as complements. A complement provides information about things whose existence is implied by the head. For example, the verb *kiss* implies that someone gets kissed, expressed in (5)(a) by the noun phrase *her son*. The verb *love* implies the existence of someone who receives love, expressed in (5)(b) by the noun phrase *their parents*, and so on.

Not all complements of verbs are noun phrases. As we shall see in Chapter 10, different verbs require complements of different syntactic categories; some verbs require more than one complement.

Words in other word classes can have complements as well. Again, the presence of a complement and the form it takes are determined by the particular word (lexical item) which is the head of the phrase, as in (6) - (8). (The heads of the phrases are in italics; the complements are in square brackets.)

(6)   Prepositions with NP Complements
    (a) (we read books)   *about* [linguistics]
    (b) (Mary had a fight)   *with* [her mother]

(7)   Nouns with PP Complements
    (a) (we have)   *discussions* [about linguistics]
    (b) (I like)   *pictures* [of children]

(8)   Adjectives with PP Complements
    (a) (she is)   *fond* [of children]
    (b) (we are)   *unhappy* [about your decision]

To summarize, a phrase consists of an obligatory head and possibly some complements. The presence of complements and the forms they take are determined entirely by the particular word that is the head of the phrase.

When we represent the structure of a phrase which contains a complement, we connect the complement to the phrase by a straight line, as in (9). In English complements always follow the head.

(9)   Phrase Level:

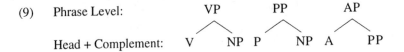

Labeled tree diagrams for a few phrases are given in (10). Note that in drawing tree diagrams, a triangle can be used as an abbreviation. For instance, a triangle is used to abbreviate NPs in (10) since we have not yet discussed how to represent their internal structure.

(10)

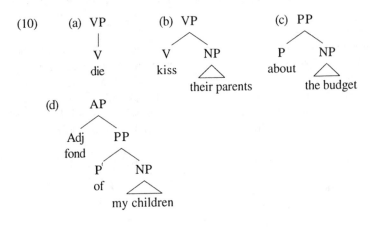

Modifiers. In addition to heads and complements, phrases can contain modifiers, which add optional information that describes the head (or the head plus complements). When investigating the internal syntax of a phrase, therefore, it is necessary to determine the syntactic categories of its modifiers and the position they occur in. For instance, verb phrases are modified by adverbs or prepositional phrases, which follow the verb phrase, as in (11) and (12), while nouns are modified by, among other things, adjectives, which precede, as in (13). (The modifiers are in square brackets.)

(11)   Adverb Modifying a Verb Phrase
        (a)   (the baby)   *slept* [quietly]
        (b)   (he)   *left* [immediately]

(12)   Prepositional Phrase Modifying a Verb Phrase
        (a)   (the baby)   *slept* [in her crib]
        (b)   (my gerbil)   *died* [during the night]

(13)   Adjective Modifying a Noun
        (a)   [happy] *child*
        (b)   [big] *house*
        (c)   [complicated] *ideas*

Except for these brief observations, we postpone discussion of modifiers until later chapters. (See especially Chapters 4-7, 24, 27, and 28.)

1.2 External Syntax

When we investigate the external syntax of a phrase, we look at how the phrase is used. We examine how it "hooks into" larger structures by considering the kinds of constituents it combines with and the syntactic category of the phrases that result. Consider, for example, noun phrases, which combine with verb phrases to form clauses. NPs which have this function are so important that they have the special name of subject, as in (14).

(14)   NP Subject VP
        my mother   lives in New York
        Sally   kissed her husband
        they   painted the barn red

(c) [very foolish]
(d) (she) seems [fond of children]
(e) (they) seem [able to manage]
(f) (they) seem [very foolish]

The phrases of (20), however, cannot combine with *seem*, and we conclude that they are not APs. What kinds of phrases are they?

(20)   ???
    (a) [liked children]
    (b) [a big fool]
    (c) (she) *seems [liked children]
    (d) (he) *seems [a big fool]

2.3 Noun Phrases

We saw in 2.1 that NPs combine with VPs to form clauses. We can use this fact as a test for NPs. If we have a phrase that we know is a VP and in combination with an unknown phrase it forms a clause, the unknown phrase is a NP, as in (21).

(21)   ???   +   VP
    (a) [the enemy] destroyed the city
    (b) [that dog]   barked
    (c) [your idea]   seems very foolish

This test can be used to identify different types of NPs. For example, (21) shows that a NP can consist of a determiner and a common noun, while (22) and (23) show that a NP can consist of just a proper noun or just a pronoun. These NPs are diagrammed as in (24). (To simplify tree diagrams, in this book the labels in parentheses will often be omitted.)

(22)   ???   +   VP
    (a) [Alexander] destroyed the city
    (b) [Cable]   loved children
    (c) [Duluth]   is on the shores of Lake Superior

(23)   ???   +   VP
     (a) [they]   destroyed the city
     (b) [I]   loved children
     (c) [someone]   has to be responsible

(24) (a)   NP   (b) NP   (c) NP

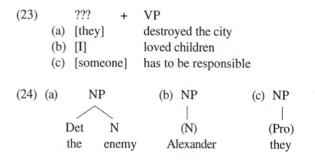

         Det   N   (N)   (Pro)
         the   enemy   Alexander   they

3. CONJOINED PHRASES

Conjoined phrases have a special structure. They consist of two or more constituents of the same syntactic category, often with a conjunction *(and, but, or)* between the last two. In (25) the conjoined phrases are in square brackets.

(25)   (a)   [A rotten apple, two grapes, and some carrots] were lying on
             the kitchen counter.
       (b)   The gardener [planted some roses and watered the grass].
       (c)   It was a [very sunny but rather cool] Sunday.

A conjoined phrase can consist of words or phrases of any type, as long as they are all of the same syntactic category (all Ns, all NPs, all VPs, etc.). In (25)(a) the conjoined phrases are NPs; in (25)(b) they are VPs; and in (25)(c) they are APs. The phrase that results from conjoining belongs to the same syntactic category as the individual conjuncts, as shown in (26).

(26) (a)   NP

                NP   NP   Con   NP

             a rotten   two   and   some
              apple   grapes   carrots

(26) (b)

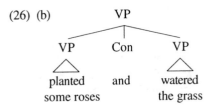

To summarize, this chapter has focused on the phrase, an important unit of grammar. The most important element of a phrase is known as its head, and a phrase can consist of only a head or of a head plus complements and/or modifiers. The major phrase types in English were introduced, along with simple tests for identifying them. The analysis of a phrase should include a description of both its internal and external syntax. Any type of phrase can be conjoined with other phrases of the same category to form a phrase of the same syntactic category. That is, NPs combine to form conjoined NPs, VPs combine to form conjoined VPs, and so on.

Exercise 1
In this chapter some simple tests for identifying the major phrasal categories of English were given. In your own words, state a test for a VP, for an NP, and for an AP.

Exercise 2
In the sentences below, identify the syntactic category of the constituents in square brackets.

1. [The pretty kittens] were adopted [by a neighbor].
2. You should [study French].
3. [A girl I knew in college] became [quite famous].
4. The baby [was sleeping quietly].
5. We were surprised [that the choir sang so well].
6. Take this pill [every day].
7. [We] need to take a long vacation [in the mountains].
8. [The passengers and their guests] should proceed directly [to the gate].
9. Before they [can collect their allowance], they must [clean up the kitchen and wash the floors].

10. This car is [very small and terribly dirty].

Exercise 3

For each word or phrase listed below, state whether it can be a verb phrase, an adjective phrase, or a noun phrase. More than one may be possible. In each case, give a reason for your answer. (The head of each phrase is in italics.)

1. *paintings* of their children
2. *amused* by their jokes
3. *look* at the scenery
4. *prepare* for winter
5. the *reason* for his departure
6. *walks* along the river
7. *people*
8. *sighs*
9. *teacher*
10. *bored*

Exercise 4

For further practice in describing the external syntax of phrases, examine the following sentences, which contain adjective phrases (in square brackets). For each, state the syntactic category of the constituent(s) the adjective phrase combines with and of the resulting phrase.

Example: The lake seems [quiet].
Answer: The adjective phrase [*quiet*] combines with the verb *seems* to form a verb phrase [*seems* [*quiet*]].

1. That girl is [very tall].
2. [Very naughty] children should be disciplined.
3. Your sister looks [rather silly].
4. My neighbors painted their house [bright pink].

Exercise 5

Examine the following sentences, which contain prepositional phrases (in square brackets). For each, state the syntactic category of the constituent(s) the prepositional phrase has combined with and of the resulting phrase.

Example: We stared [at the beautiful sunset].
Answer: The prepositional phrase [*at the beautiful sunset*] combines
           with the verb *stared* to form a VP [*stared* [*at the beautiful*
           sunset]].

1.   The teacher agreed [with her students].
2.   He is afraid [of snakes].
3.   The baby pointed [to the clown].
4.   They like arguments [about syntax].
5.   Discussions [with John] are always fruitless.
6.   Those people are crazy [about the theater].
7.   She slipped the paper [under the door].

Exercise 6
Draw labeled tree diagrams for each of the following phrases, following the
examples in (10), (24), and (26).

1.   eat the cookies
2.   love their children
3.   for Mary
4.   talked about the president
5   aware of your concerns
6.   her ideas and his money
7.   with her ideas and his money
8.   a book and a newspaper
9.   buy a book and a newspaper
10.   seem happy about the evaluation but concerned by his reaction

Exercise 7   For Discussion
Do speakers of English need to know about different types of phrases? Do
learners of English need to be taught about phrases? If so, what should they
be taught and how should it be taught?

3

INTRODUCTION TO CLAUSES

IN MANY WAYS the most important syntactic unit for grammatical analysis is the clause. Clauses come in a wide variety of forms and have a number of different functions. In this chapter we will explore in a very general way the internal and external syntax of clauses.

In the first section, the main elements of the clause from a functional point of view are presented. In future chapters knowledge of these elements (e.g. subject, object, adverbial) will be assumed. In the second section, the notion of a basic clause is introduced, while in the third, which contains a typology of clauses, the variety of forms that non-basic clauses have is presented. This serves as an introduction to the internal syntax of clauses. In the fourth and final section, the functions of subordinate clauses are listed. This brief look at the ways that clauses are used is an introduction to their external syntax.

1. ELEMENTS OF THE CLAUSE

In terms of internal syntax, a clause consists of two phrases—a noun phrase followed by a verb phrase.

(1)   NP   VP
     (a) John   left
     (b) the girls   went to sleep
     (c) some children   put the books away

We represent the structure of a clause with two levels, in the same way we represent the structure of a phrase. The upper level is the clause level, with the symbol 'S' for clause, the hook on which are hung the NP and VP.

(2)   S
          ⟋   ⟍
      NP   VP

In later chapters we will examine the internal syntax of NPs and VPs, but at this time, we want to look at the clause from a different perspective, by considering the most important functional elements of the clause: verb, subject, object, predicate noun phrase, and adverbial.

1.1 Verb
The verb is the most central element of the clause. Its centrality can be seen, first of all, in that it is the only obligatory element; some clauses consist of only a verb (*Stop! Look ! Listen!*). Secondly, the verb determines what other constituents will occur in the clause (see Chapter 10). Thirdly, the *form* of the verb is important to the external syntax of the clause (i.e. to how the clause can be used). Clauses whose head is a finite verb form are called finite clauses, while clauses whose head is a nonfinite verb form are nonfinite clauses, as in (3), where the nonfinite clauses are in square brackets. (Verb forms are discussed in Chapter 8.)

(3)   (a) Finite Clause: Sue *wrote* a letter.
             Nonfinite: I prefer [for her to *write* the letter].
       (b) Finite: Sam *swam* the English Channel.
             Nonfinite: [Sam's *swimming* the Channel] surprised me.
       (c) Finite: My father *walks* a mile every day.
             Nonfinite: I insist [that he *walk* a mile every day]

1.2 Subject
As already noted, we give the special name of subject to the NP which combines with a VP to form a clause. (Subjects and objects which are not NPs are discussed in Unit V.)

(4)   S
          ⟋   ⟍
      NP   VP
      └────┘

      subject

The subject of a clause has special properties. First, it determines agreement with a verb in the present tense: If the subject is third person and singular, a special form of the verb, called the 3rd singular form, is used. If the subject is third person and plural or any other person, the general present form is used.

(5)   Third Singular Subject   Other Subjects
           3rd singular verb form   General present verb form
    (a)   John *works* hard.   I *work* hard. You *work* hard.
    (b)   Sally *loves* him.   I *love* him. We *love* him.
    (c)   Mother *walks* slowly.   You *walk* fast. They *walk* fast.

Second, it is the subject which changes position as we go from a declarative to an interrogative, as shown in (6). (The subjects are in square brackets.) This process, called inversion, is discussed in Chapter 9.

(6)   Declarative   Interrogative
    (a)   [That doctor] is nice.   Is [that doctor] nice?
    (b)   [They] will call soon.   Will [they] call soon?
    (c)   [The children] are sleeping.   Are [the children] sleeping?
    (d)   [My three sisters] have left.   Have [my three sisters] left?

Third, in tag questions like those in (7), the pronoun in the tag agrees in number and gender with the subject. (Both the pronoun in the tag and the antecedent subject are in brackets.)

(7)   (a)   [That doctor] is nice, isn't [she]?
       (b)   [Your uncle] will call soon, won't [he]?
       (c)   [The children] are sleeping, aren't [they]?

Formal versus functional categories. Before leaving this discussion, it may be useful to point out a general difference between formal categories and functional ones. Formal categories are defined in terms of "how they are formed," while functional categories are defined in terms of "what they do." This is precisely the difference between the category noun phrase and the category subject. NP is a formal syntactic category; a phrase is a NP if its head is a noun or pronoun. The phrases in (8) are all NPs because of their form, and they will remain NPs regardless of how they are used in a clause.

(8) (a) that doctor
     (b) your uncle
     (c) John
     (d) everyone

Subject, on the other hand, is a function which is filled by a NP in a clause. The NPs in (8) are not subjects because a NP can only be a subject with respect to its use in a particular clause. In (9) the NPs in square brackets are subjects; in (10) they are objects, discussed in the following section.

(9) (a) [That doctor] left suddenly.
     (b) [Your uncle] can sing very well.
     (c) [John] got married.
     (d) [Everyone] is bothering me.

(10) (a) Mary called [that doctor].
     (b) I love [your uncle].
     (c) We sent [John] some money.
     (d) I saw [everyone] just yesterday.

1.3 Objects
As we saw in Chapter 2, verbs combine with NPs to form VPs. But they do so in two different ways: Some verbs take an argument NP, while others take a predicate NP.

An argument NP is used to refer to (to pick out) something which is distinct from the other entities mentioned in the sentence. Subjects, for example, are usually argument NPs. Argument NPs which combine with verbs to form VPs are given the special name of object. If there is one object, it is a direct object, as in (11).

(11)   Verb   Direct Object
     (a) saw   your children
     (b) kissed   her mother
     (c) touched   the dog

If there are two objects, the first one is an indirect object and the second, a direct object. The two object NPs refer to two different things. They are both argument noun phrases.

(12)   Verb   Indirect Object   Direct Object
     (a) gave   her mother   a kiss
     (b) sent   the children   Christmas presents
     (c) threw   the catcher   the ball

1.4 Predicate Noun Phrase

A predicate noun phrase is not used to refer to a distinct entity; it is used to say something about an argument NP. The NPs in square brackets in (13) are predicate NPs.

(13)   (a)   That woman over there is [a very good friend of mine].
        (b)   Your children are [extremely talented musicians].
        (c)   My daughter became [a doctor].

In (13)(c) the subject NP *my daughter* is used to refer to a specific person; it is an argument NP. The predicate NP *a doctor*, on the other hand, doesn't refer to anyone, but is used to describe the subject NP.

1.5 Adverbials

Adverbials, the last major clause element, are modifiers of VPs or clauses. (They also function as modifiers of nouns, a function not considered here but taken up in Chapter 28.) Adverbials belong to various syntactic categories, namely adverbs, PPs, CPs, or even NPs. What adverbials have in common is the fact that they express semantic categories such as time, place, manner, reason, and so on. (See Chapter 4.) (The adverbials in (14) are in square brackets.)

(14)   (a)   She arrived [yesterday] [at 4:00].
        (b)   The baby was sleeping [in her crib].
        (c)   Dora was singing [cheerfully].
        (d)   She was happy [because her sister had arrived].
        (e)   [Unfortunately], the dog got lost [last night].

The sentences of (14) would be grammatical, though less informative, without the optional adverbials. Adverbials are required by some verbs, though, as discussed in Chapter 10.

Two other properties of adverbials make them quite different from other clause elements. First, there may be several adverbials per clause, with no upward limit on the number. In contrast, a single clause may have only one finite verb, one subject, one direct object, and one indirect object. Second, some adverbials can occur in a number of possible positions in the clause. Other clause elements do not have this mobility.

(15) (a) I [usually] have wine with dinner.
      (b) [Usually] I have wine with dinner.

(16) (a) He had stopped the car [suddenly].
      (b) He had [suddenly] stopped the car.
      (c) He [suddenly] had stopped the car.
      (d) [Suddenly], he had stopped the car.

Exercise 1

In each of the following sentences, identify the clause elements by putting a square around the verb, a circle around the subject NP, an "O" over each object NP, and a "P" over each predicate NP. Underline each adverbial.

1. Unfortunately, the cover-up of the scandal had very serious consequences.
2. Sally and I remained very close friends for our whole lives.
3. At the meeting yesterday, they unexpectedly elected an unknown lawyer chairman.
4. The candles dripped very slowly.
5. The only survivors were old people and young children.
6. Howard's neighbor lent him his car while he was in Florida.

---

2. BASIC CLAUSES

One important goal in the study of English grammar is to describe the grammar of clauses. We want to know how they are formed and how they are used in larger syntactic constructions. This is a difficult task, in part because the set of possible clauses is far too large and varied for us to be able to discuss them all at once. Instead, we accord descriptive priority to certain clauses, which we will call basic clauses.

A basic clause can be an independent clause, one that stands alone as a sentence. Most of the clauses in the examples above are basic clauses; others are given in (17). Variants which are not basic are given in (18).

(17)   (a) You are a student.
       (b) I have never seen such a mess.
       (c) The fact that she's lying is obvious.
       (d) Peter called his mother.
       (e) My dog died yesterday.
       (f) My son failed calculus.
       (g) Grandmother opened the door.
       (h) The children did their homework.

(18)   (a) Are you a student?
       (b) Never have I seen such a mess.
       (c) The fact is obvious that she's lying.
       (d) Open the door.
       (e) Peter's calling his mother
       (f) that my dog died yesterday
       (g) because my son failed calculus
       (h) The children did, too.

These sentences illustrate the properties of basic clauses summarized in (19).

(19)   (a) They are declarative (and not interrogative like (18)(a)).
       (b) The entire subject NP (or clause if it is a clause) precedes the
            entire VP. (Non-basic clauses may have variations of this word
            order, e.g. (18)(a), (b), or (c), or may lack a subject NP
            altogether, as the imperative in (18)(d).)

(c) They contain finite verb forms (present or past tense) (and not non-finite forms, as in (18)(e)).

(d) They are not subordinate and thus have no special marking of subordinate status. (In (18)(f) subordinate status is marked by the word *that* , in (18)(g) it is marked by *because.*)

(e) They are complete in the sense that they do not require a special context to be interpreted. (Non-basic clauses may contain pro-forms which require a special context to be interpreted, as in (18)(h), where some previous context is necessary to understand what the pro-form *did* stands for.)

3. A TYPOLOGY OF CLAUSES

Having identified basic clauses as descriptively primary, in this section we turn to the variations in clause structure that are found in non-basic clauses. Independent clauses are basic clauses consisting of an NP and a VP. They are in contrast with subordinate (or dependent) clauses, which show various degrees of "deviation" from this structure. First and foremost, many have an overt marker of their subordinate status, known as a complementizer (abbreviated C). The complementizer and the clause form a syntactic unit, and, because the complementizer determines the *form* of the clause as well as how it can be used, it is the head of the unit, which is for this reason called a complementizer phrase (CP).

(20)   CP

C   S

The complementizer *that* combines with a basic clause (i.e. one that could otherwise stand on its own) to form a CP called a that-clause, discussed in detail in Chapter 20. A tree diagram for (21)(a) is given in (22).

(21) (a) *that* [babies cry]
      (b) *that* [Sam swam the channel]
      (c) *that* [my father walks a mile every day]

(22)

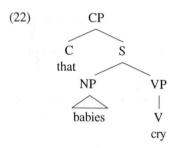

The complementizers *because, since, while,* and *after* (among others), also combine with basic clauses, as in (23). Though these words are called subordinating conjunctions in traditional grammar, they are complementizers because they serve to mark a clause as subordinate. Subordinate clauses with these complementizers function as adverbials, discussed further in Chapter 4.

(23)   (a) *because* [babies cry]
      (b) *since* [my father walks a mile every day]
      (c) *after* [we earn the money]

In addition to the presence of a complementizer, some subordinate clauses show further "deviation" from the structure of basic clauses. The complementizer *for* requires a clause with an infinitive VP, one which has the marker *to* plus a verb in the base form. Such clauses, known as infinitive clauses, are discussed further in Chapter 21.

(24)   (a) *for* [her to write the letter]
      (b) *for* [my mother to help us]
      (c) *for* [you to be good today]

Gerundives show yet further deviation from basic clause structure: The subject NP is in the genitive (see Chapter 30), while the head verb of the VP is the present participle (the *-ing* form).

(25)   NP$_{Gen}$ VP$_{PresPart}$
    (a) Sam's   swimming the Channel
    (b) the people's   protesting the decision yesterday

(c)	the music teacher's	singing off key at the concert
(d)	her	writing the letter to the dean

Gerundives are odd because they lack a complementizer and have the external syntax of a NP and not of a clause. Nonetheless, they have the internal structure of a clause and so are included here. Gerundives are discussed further in Chapter 22.

A final type of subordinate clause consists of a complementizer that is a WH-constituent (a phrase containing a WH-form) and an incomplete clause; the clause is missing a phrase of the same syntactic category as the WH-constituent. In the WH-clauses of (26), a blank line indicates the position of the missing phrase.

(26) (a) who [my little brother bit ___]
 (b) what [you ate ___]
 (c) whose father [they were talking about ___]
 (d) where [we put the money ___]

We account for the structure of WH-clauses by means of a syntactic rule known as WH-movement. We assume that the WH-constituent is originally within the clause and is moved into complementizer position by WH-movement. (See Chapter 23.)

There are other types of nonfinite subordinate clauses, all more minor than these. For instance, there are structures which have some of the properties of clauses, but which lack verbs, as in (27). (The verbless clauses have been set off by square brackets.) These "verbless clauses" are sufficiently rare and stylistically marked that we will not discuss them here.

(27) (a) 73 people have drowned, [many of them children].
 (b) She marched briskly up the hill, [the blanket across her shoulder].
 (c) [With the tree now tall], we get a lot more shade.

A summary of the variations in the internal structure of clauses is given in (28).

(28)   CLAUSES

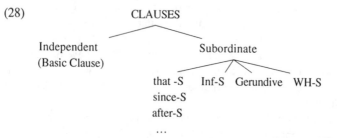

Independent   Subordinate
(Basic Clause)
                     that -S   Inf-S   Gerundive   WH-S
                     since-S
                     after-S
                        ...

4. EXTERNAL SYNTAX OF SUBORDINATE CLAUSES

In this section, we turn to the ways in which clauses fit into other syntactic units, a look at their external syntax. Independent clauses, which stand alone as sentences, do not combine with any other constituent. Subordinate clauses, on the other hand, are used in three main ways: They can be nominal, adverbial, or relative.

4.1 Nominal Clauses
A nominal clause occurs in some of the positions that an NP does. For example, it can combine with a VP to form a S (i.e. it is a subject) or with a V to form a VP (i.e. it is an object).

(29)   Nominal Clause as Subject
       (a) [That babies cry] is disturbing.
       (b) [For her to write the letter now] would be rude.
       (c) [Sam's swimming the Channel] surprised everyone.
       (d) [What you ate] was rotten.

(30)   Nominal Clause as Direct Object
       (a) I know [that babies cry].
       (b) I prefer [for her to write the letter].
       (c) They regretted [Sam's swimming the Channel].
       (d) We ate [what you ate].

As the examples in (29) and (30) show, clauses of different forms may occur in NP function. The nominal clauses in (29)(a) and (30)(a) are that-clauses; in (b) they are infinitive clauses; in (c) they are gerundives, and in (d) they are WH-clauses. As these sentences demonstrate, there is unfortunately no simple match between the internal and external syntax of a clause.

4.2 Adverbial Clauses

An adverbial clause functions like an adverbial within another clause, modifying a VP or a clause. Common meanings expressed by adverbial clauses include time, place, reason, manner, and condition, as in (31).

(31) (a) Time: He left [before I did].
      (b) Place: I want to live [wherever you do].
      (c) Reason: She was crying [because you hit her].
      (d) Condition: [If you're nice] I'll invite you to my house.

4.3. Relative Clauses

A relative clause functions as a modifier within a NP. (In some grammar books these are called adjective clauses.) (See Chapter 24.)

(32) (a) The girl [who my little brother bit] is crying.
      (b) I know the man [that they were talking about].

This overview does not exhaust the functions of subordinate clauses, but the remaining functions are more minor and will not be treated in this book.

Exercise 2
Put square brackets around each subordinate clause in the following sentences. State whether it is finite or non-finite and whether it is a that-S, a WH-S, an Inf-S, or a gerundive. Give the function of the subordinate clause, stating whether it is nominal, adverbial, or relative.

1. I know what I know, so don't bug me about evidence.
2. Because it has been so cold, I believe that it won't snow this week.
3. The teachers that work in this school don't like your whistling during the lectures.
4. For you to complain about the service here, after they gave you every special consideration, is what I call nerve!
5. That the parents went to Mexico and left their children home alone surprised no one who knew them well.

Exercise 3
Give tree diagrams for the following phrases and sentences.

1. Mary loves John.
2. She became a doctor.
3. that Mary loves John
4. if she becomes a doctor
5. after they arrive, but before she leaves
6. I know you and you know me.
7. that I know you and you know me

SUMMARY:
THE UNITS OF GRAMMAR

1.   WORD CLASSES   SOME SUBCLASSES

    Verb   lexical, auxiliary, modal auxiliary
                          transitive, intransitive, ditransitive ...

    Noun   proper, common; count, noncount
    Adjective   gradable, nongradable
    Adverb   place, time, manner ...
    Intensifier   amplifer, downtoner
    Focusing word
    Preposition   transitive, intransitive (= particle)
    Conjunction
    Article
    Demonstrative
    Complementizer
    Interjection
    Proform   pronoun, WH-expression,
                          proverb, proplace phrase ...

2.   PHRASES   SUBTYPES

    VP   verb phrase   InfVP, PassiveVP
    NP   noun phrase
    AP   adjective phrase
    PP   prepositional phrase
    CP   complementizer phrase
    PlP   place phrase
    TP   time phrase

41

[illegible] SYNTAX OF CLAUSES

	Complementizer	Clause Form	
[illegible]ause	(none)	NP	VP
That-S	that	NP	VP
Inf-S	for	NP	InfVP
Gerundive	(none)	NP_{Gen}	$VP_{PresPart}$
WH-S	WH-phrase	S	
	(C = XP, a phrase containing WH-expression; S is missing a phrase of the same syntactic category as XP)		

4. EXTERNAL SYNTAX OF CLAUSES

independent	(function as a sentence)
nominal	(function as an NP)
adverbial	(function as an adverbial)
relative	(function as a modifier in an NP)

5. FUNCTIONAL CATEGORIES

Within phrases:	head, complement, modifier, determiner, intensifier
Within clauses:	subject, verb, object, predicate NP, adverbial

UNIT II

ADVERBIALS, PREPOSITIONS, AND PARTICLES

IN UNIT II WE EXAMINE adverbials, which serve as modifiers of phrases and clauses. In Chapter 4 we look more closely at the range of constituents that function as adverbials, including the word class of adverbs. Along the way we introduce two new word classes, intensifiers and focusing words.

In Chapter 5 we turn to the class of prepositions. Some prepositions occur with complements, while others do not, and we adopt the term "particle" to refer to prepositions that do not occur with a complement. We continue the exploration of modifiers by looking at the syntax and semantics of prepositional phrases used as modifiers. (Their use as complements is discussed in Unit III.)

The two final chapters of Unit II are a case study of one type of modifier, time phrases.

4

ADVERBIALS, ADVERBS, INTENSIFIERS, FOCUSING WORDS

THE TERM ADVERBIAL refers to a functional element within a clause, while the term adverb refers to a word class. Adverbs function as adverbials, but the picture is complicated by the fact that there are other types of adverbials as well. This chapter is devoted to exploring some properties of these overlapping units of grammar. Along the way we will identify two new word classes, intensifiers and focusing words.

1. ADVERBIALS

As discussed in Chapter 3, if you strip away the subject, verb, objects, etc. from a simple sentence, the constituents that are left are adverbials. In (1) the adverbials are in square brackets.

(1) (a) I sent my mother a package [yesterday] [for her birthday].
     (b) [Fortunately], we finished the project [at home] [last night].
     (c) The little girl [faithfully] brushes her teeth [every day] [with a metal brush].
     (d) [Frankly], I am sick of you [because you are so obnoxious].
     (e) [In addition], you have to sit [here] [for one more hour].
     (f) The party [on the beach] was a big success.
     (g) [If you're nice], I'll lend you my shirt [from The Gap].

As shown in (1), adverbials are from different syntactic categories, including adverbs (*fortunately, faithfully*), PPs (*for her birthday, on the beach*), NPs (*last night, every day*), and CPs (*because you are so obnoxious, if you're nice*). In this section we will discuss first the syntax of adverbials, showing how they fit into the structure of sentences, and second, some of the many semantic categories they express.

1.1 The Syntax of Adverbials

Adverbials modify VPs and clauses. (Though they also modify nouns, we postpone examination of this function until Chapter 28.) Adverbial modifiers combine with the constituent they modify and form a constituent of the same syntactic category. Though it is a complicated matter to state all the possible positions of adverbial modifiers, generally speaking, we can say that position depends on the constituent being modified: Modifiers of clauses tend to precede the clause and may on occasion follow it, while modifiers of VPs most often follow, as shown schematically in (2).

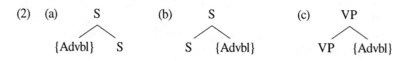

Since tree diagrams represent syntactic and not functional categories, the label "adverbial" is *not* used when diagraming particular sentences. Rather, the adverbial constituent is labeled with its syntactic category (e.g. Adv, PP, NP, CP), as in (3).

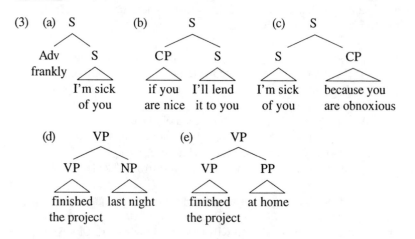

A phrase or clause that contains an adverbial modifier can be modified by another adverbial. Multiple modifiers are "stacked," as shown in (4).

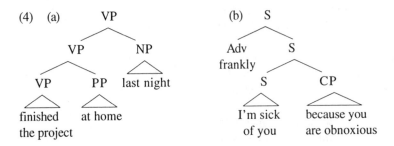

1.2 The Semantics of Adverbials

Adverbials express an amazing range of semantic categories. Following Quirk (1985: Chapter 8) we divide them into three groups—adjuncts, disjuncts, and conjuncts. This classification is based on the degree to which the adverbial is integrated into clause structure and makes it easier to characterize their meanings.

Adjuncts. Adjuncts are adverbials that are tightly integrated into clause structure, which can be seen in the fact that they can serve as the focus of questions. The answer to a question with *where, when, how,* or *why* will be an adjunct. In (5) the adjuncts are in square brackets.

(5) (a) We took a vacation [in France] [last year].
     (b) They [carefully] signed their names [at the bottom] [with a pen].
     (c) We [always] call Mother [on Sundays] [if we have time].
     (d) They baked a cake [for their boss] [on his birthday].

Syntactically, adjuncts are most often modifiers of VPs, but they can also modify clauses or nouns (see Chapter 28). Semantically, they express information about the circumstances surrounding a state or event, including the place, time, manner, etc. semantic categories often associated with the word class of adverbs. A list of the subcategories of adjuncts with examples is given in the appendix.

Disjuncts. Disjuncts are clause modifiers that are peripheral to both the structure and the meaning of the clause. Appearing most often in initial position, their peripheral status can be seen in the fact that they are usually set off with commas in writing and intonation pauses in speaking.

(6)   (a) *Frankly*, I am sick of you.
       (b) *Obviously*, you are mistaken.
       (c) *In all seriousness*, you should get a haircut.

Semantically, disjuncts convey the speaker's commentary on the sentence. In using certain disjuncts, the speaker comments on its truth value or expresses some value judgement about it, as in (7) and (8).

(7)   Disjuncts as comments on truth value
       (a) *Obviously*, you are mistaken.
       (b) *Supposedly*, I have the day off.
       (c) The president will *definitely* resign tomorrow.

(8)   Disjuncts as expressions of a value judgement
       (a) *Surprisingly,* they didn't call yesterday.
       (b) *Unfortunately,* I didn't pass geometry class.
       (c) The politician *unwisely* accepted a large contribution from a foreign government, but now he has *sensibly* returned it.

With other disjuncts, the speaker comments on the conditions under which he or she is speaking (*seriously, literally, metaphorically speaking*, etc.). Such disjuncts draw attention to how the message is packaged, sometimes to the form of the utterance itself. Clauses that express hypothetical conditions are also disjuncts. (Additional examples are given in the appendix.)

(9)   Disjuncts as comments on form
       (a) *Frankly,* I don't know why you put up with them.
       (b) *If I may speak bluntly,* I think you should resign.
       (c) *Confidentially,* I don't like grammar.
       (d) *In all seriousness,* I think you should resign.

Conjuncts. Like disjuncts, conjuncts are clause modifiers that are peripheral to the structure of the clause itself. They also are found most often in initial position, set off from the rest of the clause with a comma in writing and a pause in speaking.

49

ne food was terrible and the waiter was rude.
y were upset, but in addition, the manager seemed
bout their bad experience.
s surprise, their car stalled on the freeway at 1:00 a.m.

8.   y they sent a letter of complaint to the owners and
descri. neir experience in some detail.

Exercise 2

Draw tree diagrams for the sentences in Exercise 1. Use triangles for NPs and other phrases and clauses that do not contain adverbials (as in (3)).

Exercise 3

Describe the ambiguity in the following sentences.

1.   The spy gave the stolen goods to the man on the train.
2.   The police shot the woman with the rifle.

---

2. ADVERBS AND OTHER WORD CLASSES

Of the parts of speech of traditional grammar, adverbs are the most problematic, largely because there is more diversity among words called adverbs than in the other word classes. The "class" has become to some extent a wastebasket because words that do not fit elsewhere have been dumped into it. As a point of reference, it may be useful to begin with a list of words often identified as adverbs, given in (12), which shows typical semantic subsets.

(12)	(a) time	*now, yesterday, soon, later, recently*
	(b) frequency	*often, frequently, always, seldom, rarely*
	(c) place	*here, there, abroad, downtown, northward*
	(d) manner	*slowly, carefully, skillfully*
	(e) means/	*chemically, manually, mechanically,*
	instrument	*microscopically, surgically*
	(f) modal	*perhaps, possibly, probably, necessarily*
	(g) connecting	*however, moreover, nevertheless, so, thus*

(h) degree   *very, pretty, quite, rather, extremely*
(i) other   *not, only, even, ever*

The words in (12)(a) - (g) should be familiar from the first part of the chapter for they all function as adverbials. We take this to be the defining property for the word class: Adverbs are words that function as adverbials. In (12), we find adverbials of all three types; adjuncts in (a) - (e), disjuncts in (f), and conjuncts in (g). (Additional examples can be found in the appendix.)

We can point out two other properties that characterize some adverbs. First, members of subclasses (d), (e), and (f) typically have the suffix *-ly*, which can also be added to adjectives to form new adverbs. Second, some adverbs can appear not only before and after the constituent they modify, but in other positions as well, as shown in (13). Such mobility, mentioned in Chapter 3 as a property of adverbials, is characteristic only of adverbs, in particular of the subclasses in (12)(a), (b), (d) - (f).

(13) (a) We *recently* opened a new account.
      (b) The children will *always* remember this experience.
      (c) He has *finally* reached the summit.
      (d) We can *probably* finish the project by Thursday.

Unlike members of other word classes, only a few adverbs take complements and none have modifiers. For this reason, adverbs rarely form adverb phrases, and we will not posit such a constituent in this book.

The words in (12)(h) and (12)(i) cannot function as adverbials; therefore we do not consider them to be adverbs. They belong to two different word classes, intensifiers (or degree words), and focusing words, which we explore in the remainder of this chapter. The descriptions offered here are sketchy, but the fact that these groups are distinct from adverbs as defined above, both syntactically and semantically, lends support to the view that they constitute separate word classes.

2.1 Intensifiers

Intensifiers express degree, the extent to which someone or something possesses a property or how much of the property there is. Intensifiers combine with constituents from various syntactic categories, including

adjectives, adverbs, VPs, NPs, and PPs, as shown in (14). They form a
constituent of the same category, as shown in (15). Note that unlike
modifiers, many of which follow the constituent they modify, most
intensifiers precede.

(14)   (a)   She was *extremely* helpful.
       (b)   She writes *rather* badly.
       (c)   They *greatly* admire his music.
       (d)   You are *quite* a fool.
       (e)   He ran *right* into the wall.

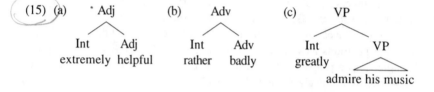

(15) (a)   Adj   (b)   Adv   (c)   VP

         Int   Adj   Int   Adv   Int   VP
      extremely helpful   rather badly   greatly
                                                       admire his music

Intensifiers can be the focus of a question. The WH-expressions *how, how
much,* and *to what extent* are used to ask questions about degree.

(16)   (a)   How tall is she?   She is *rather* tall.
       (b)   How well do you know him?   I know him *slightly*.
       (c)   How much do you miss him?   I miss him *terribly*.

Intensifiers cannot be coordinated (**very and extremely happy*, **rather and
partly intelligent*) and most cannot be intensified (**very extremely happy,
rather somewhat happy), A few intensifiers can be intensified by
reduplication (*very, very tall; terribly, terribly angry*).
   Regardless of the syntactic category being intensified, the constituent
must express a property which is gradable, a property that there can be more
or less of. The function of the intensifier is either to amplify the degree of
the property or to tone it down. Amplifiers are illustrated in (17).

(17)   (a)   Monique is *really* tall.
       (b)   They *greatly* admire his music.
       (c)   She was *completely* overwhelmed.
       (d)   People in this class are *terribly* smart.
       (e)   He thought *very* quickly.

(17)(a) does not just convey that Monique is tall. It conveys that on a scale of tallness, she is at a very high degree. (17)(d) says that on a scale for smartness, people in this class are at the upper end. More generally, when we use a word or phrase that denotes a property that is gradable, we are assuming an implicit scale of intensity for that property. On the scale for tallness, there is a norm for being tall; on the scale of smartness, a norm for being smart, etc. The amplifiers, the intensifiers that amplify, convey that the subject possess a *high degree* of the property, something more than the norm.

Other intensifiers, called downtoners, scale downward. They diminish the effect of the gradable predicate, suggesting a low degree on an implicit scale, something less than an assumed norm, as in (18).

(18) (a) The host was *somewhat* nice.
      (b) They were *slightly* embarrassed.
      (c) She writes *rather* badly.
      (d) They *practically* kicked us out of the bar.

(18)(a) conveys that the host was nice, but the downtoner *somewhat* adds a qualification, as though pulling back a bit from saying he possessed an ordinary or expected degree of niceness. (18)(b) conveys that the subject was embarrassed, but not to a very great degree. Again, there is a pulling back or toning down from an implicit norm of being embarrassed. Common intensifiers are listed in (19).

(19) (a) Amplifiers:
      absolutely, amazingly, completely, deeply, entirely, extremely, greatly, highly, really, sharply, strikingly, surprisingly, terribly, totally, unbelievably, unusually, very

      (b) Downtoners:
      enough (postposed)*; kind of, mildly, partly, pretty, quite, rather, slightly, sort of, somewhat; merely; barely, hardly; practically, all but, virtually*

Exercise 4
The amplifiers in (19)(a) are used with a wide range of words and phrases,
but others have a more restricted sphere of use, and some form a fixed unit,
such as the intensifier-adjective combinations *jet black, sizzling hot,* or
scared stiff (note the postposed amplifier). The amplifier *jet* is used only
with *black*; *sizzling*, only with *hot*. Which adjectives would you pair
with the amplifiers below? Think of two or three other amplifiers which are
restricted to a single adjective or two.

1.	bone	4.	filthy	7.	chock	10.	squeaky
2.	dead	5.	stark	8.	soaking	11.	freezing
3.	stone	6.	fast	9.	wide	12.	piping

Exercise 5
Amplifiers add color or life to the sentence, but as existing amplifiers
become familiar and worn, and thus, less effective, speakers search for new
ways to heighten the effect of an utterance. Interestingly enough, members
of different word classes are recruited as amplifiers. Considering the words
from Exercise 4, which word classes do these words come from: *bone, dead,
filthy, stone, soaking, wide,* and *freezing*?

2.2 Focusing Words

Focusing words form a very small class of words that are used to focus the
content of the utterance in some way. They restrict the application of the
communication exclusively or mainly to the part which is being focused.
They are best illustrated with examples, given in (20) (focusing words are in
italics).

(20) (a) She *merely* hinted that something was amiss.
      (b) I wanted *only* small children for this role.
      (c) The child was *simply* asking what time it is.
      (d) We *particularly* like her original way of putting things.
      (e) *Just* send us your new address, and we will write to you.

In (20)(a) the focus is on the verb *hinted* and the focusing word *merely* restricts the action of the subject to hinting. It implies a contrast between hinting and other possible actions, e.g. giving no information, stating something explicitly, yelling, etc. In (20)(b) focus is on the NP *small children;* the focusing word *only* restricts what is wanted exclusively to small children (as opposed to large children, teenagers, grownups, etc.).

Focusing words can focus on a contituent of any syntactic category, including NPs, verbs, VPs, adverbs, clauses, etc. They usually precede the constituent on which they are focused, as in (20) above, with the constituent in focus marked by intonation. For example, in (21)(a) the focus could be on the VP *wrote Susan last week,* the NP *Susan,* or the adverbial NP *last week,* depending on how it is pronounced. The ambiguity can be resolved by repositioning the focusing word, as in (21)(b) and (c).

(21) (a) The committee only wrote Susan last week.
      (b) The committee wrote only Susan last week.
      (c) The committee wrote Susan only last week.

A few focusing words, including *alone,* follow the constituent in focus.

(22) Everyone was late. Peter *alone* came on time.

Focusing words are unchanging morphologically. They have no particular prefixes or suffixes which would enable us to identify them by their morphology. Syntactically, these words cannot be intensified (**very only,* **rather merely*), and they cannot be coordinated (**chiefly and mostly,* **simply and solely*). (One focusing expression is a fixed (idiomatic) coordination: *purely and simply.*) Unlike intensifiers, focusing words cannot themselves be the focus of a question. Common focusing words are given in (23).

(23) (a) Focus is *exclusively* on the item in focus
          alone, exactly, exclusively, just, merely,
          only, precisely, purely, simply, solely
      (b) Focus is *mainly* on the item in focus
          chiefly, especially, largely, mainly, mostly, notably,
          particularly, in particular, primarily, principally, specifically

(c) Focus is on something which is an addition
     again, also, either, equally, even, further, likewise,
     neither, nor, similarly, too

APPENDIX

These lists of adverbials are adapted from Quirk (1985: Chapter 8).
(Adjuncts of time are discussed in detail in Chapters 6 and 7.)

ADJUNCTS

TYPE	SUBTYPE	EXAMPLES
PLACE	Position	*here, at the store, downtown, in the box, in*
	Direction-to	*here, to the store, downtown, left, away, up*
	Direction-from	*from home, from the store, off the roof, out of the box, out*
TIME	When	*at 4:00, now, today, last year, soon*
	Duration	*instantly, all day, for the summer*
	Frequency	*rarely, monthly, twice a week*
PROCESS	Manner	*carelessly, coldly, loudly, like an expert, with a smile*
	Means	*surgically, on foot, by car, air mail*
	Instrument	*with a knife, microscopically*
CAUSE/ REASON		*because of the rain, on account of your late arrival, freezing from cold, died of starvation*
MOTIVE		*out of fear, for love*
PURPOSE		*for the trip, for the kitchen, to see the lake, because I wanted to*
SOURCE/ORIGIN		*from the store, from my sister, from Chicago*
VIEWPOINT		("If we consider what we are saying from a(n) _____ point of view") *morally, politically, ethnically, linguistically*

DISJUNCTS

•Offer a commentary on the truth of the utterance or express a value
judgement

Express conviction	*admittedly, certainly, definitely, undeniably, clearly, manifestly, obviously*
Express a degree of doubt	*allegedly, conceivably, likely, perhaps, possibly, seemingly, supposedly*

Express the sense in which the speaker judges the utterance

to be true or false	*only apparently, hypothetically, ideally, officially; basically, fundamentally; technically*

Express a value judgement about what is said

*correctly, incorrectly, rightly, wrongly; cleverly, foolishly,
prudently, sensibly, unwisely; amazingly, curiously,
ironically, oddly; appropriately, naturally, predictably;
annoyingly, disturbingly, pleasingly, regrettably;
fortunately, unfortunately, happily, luckily, sadly,
tragically*

•Offer a commentary on the form of the utterance, defining in some sense
the conditions under which the speaker is speaking. (These can usually be
paraphrased by a clause with "I" as the subject and a verb of saying.)

Disjunct	Frankly, he is a slob.
Paraphrase	I tell you frankly, he is a slob.

Disjunct	In all seriousness, I don't like grammar.
Paraphrase	I'm telling you seriously, I don't like grammar.

*candidly, flatly, seriously, truely, truthfully;
confidentially, bluntly, briefly, frankly, simply, in short;
figuratively, generally, in broadest terms, literally,
strictly speaking*

CONJUNCTS

LISTING	*first, second; next, then; finally, last of all; correspondingly, likewise, by the same token; again, also, furthermore, in addition*	
SUMMATIVE	*overall, then, therefore, thus, to conclude*	
APPOSITIVE	*namely, in other words, for example, that is*	
RESULTIVE	*accordingly, consequently, therefore*	
INFERENTIAL	*otherwise, in other words, in that case*	
CONTRASTIVE	Reformulatory:	*better, rather, more precisely*
	Replacive:	*again, rather, better, worse*
	Antithetic:	*conversely, instead, on the contrary, in contrast, on the other hand*
	Concessive:	*anyhow, besides, nonetheless, still, though, in spite of it all, after all, at the same time*
TRANSITIONAL	*incidentally, by the way, meanwhile, in the meantime, eventually*	

5

PREPOSITIONS, PARTICLES, AND PREPOSITIONAL PHRASES

PREPOSITIONS are unquestionably one of the greatest sources of difficulty for learners of English. This is due to many factors, including the existence of a large number of prepositions in English, as compared with other languages, and the fact that prepositional phrases have many different syntactic functions. Contributing to the confusion is the fact that prepositions are used to express a wide variety of adverbial meanings, such as place, time, reason, etc. Often, though, prepositions have no meaning at all, functioning as semantically-empty requirements of verbs or adjectives.

After presenting the properties of prepositions that constitute a definition in Section 1, we turn in Section 2 to the internal syntax of prepositional phrases and in Section 3, to their external syntax. In Section 4 we consider the diversity of meanings that PPs express.

1. A DEFINITION FOR PREPOSITIONS

Because there is great diversity among members of this class, prepositions are difficult to define. Syntactically, members of this class have two properties: First, prepositions are the heads of PPs. They may be the sole constituent of the phrase or may combine with a complement, most commonly a NP (e.g. *in* [*the house*], *for* [*several hours*]). Second, PPs function as the complements of certain verbs, adjectives, and nouns, and as adverbials of all types (see Chapter 4).

Morphologically, there is little to say about prepositions. Unlike members of other major word classes, they do not inflect. Because they constitute a closed word class, there are no rules of derivational morphology which apply to them. Since they are a closed class, though, we can list their members.

1.1 Simple Prepositions

Simple prepositions consist of one word. A rather complete list from Quirk (1985:665-66) is given in (1) (F = formal, AmE = American English, BrE = British English).

(1) Simple — One-word — Prepositions
aboard, about, above, across, after, against, along, alongside, amid (F) *among* (or *amongst* F), *around, as, at, atop* (AmE F), *before, behind, below, beneath, beside, besides, between, beyond, but, by, circa, despite, down, during, except, for, from, in, inside, into, like, minus, near, notwithstanding, of, off, on, onto, opposite, out, outside, over, past, per, plus, round, since, than, through, throughout, till, to, toward* (AmE), *towards* (BrE), *under, underneath, unlike, until, up, upon* (F), *via, vis-à-vis, with, within, without*

The following words, closely related to verbs, also function as prepositions.

(2) *bar, barring, excepting, excluding, save* (F)
concerning, considering, regarding, respecting
following, pending
given, granted, including

A few prepositions are used mainly with numerals: *less, minus, plus, times, over* (e.g. *three times three is nine*).

1.2 Complex Prepositions

The single words in (1) are recognized by most speakers as prepositions, but English also has a large number of multi-word expressions that function as prepositions, called complex prepositions. In two-word sequences, like those of (3), the second word is a preposition from the list in (1), most often *to, of, from, for,* or *with*. (One could also treat these idiomatic expressions as a preposition subcategorized for a PP headed by the second word.)

(3)   Complex — Two-word — Prepositions
    to: *according to, close to, due to, next to, thanks to*
    of: *ahead of, because of, instead of, out of, outside of*
    from: *apart from, aside from, away from...*
    for: *as for, but for, except for...*
    with: *along with, together with*
    others: *up against, as per...*

Three-word prepositions consist of preposition-noun-preposition sequences, as in the examples in (4).

(4)   Complex — Three-word — Prepositions
    in spite of, in front of, in favor of, in view of...
    in comparison with, in common with, in contact with ...
    by dint of, by means of, by way of, by virtue of
    on account of, on behalf of, on pain of
    as far as, in exchange for, in addition to ...

Whether simple or complex, prepositions themselves have one and only one function: They serve as the heads of PPs. In the next two sections we look more closely at their internal and external syntax.

2. THE INTERNAL SYNTAX OF PREPOSITIONAL PHRASES

Like other phrases, PPs contain a head and possibly a complement or an intensifier. All the prepositions listed in Section 1 can occur with a complement; some of the simple prepositions can also be used without a complement. Because prepositions without complements are very important in English syntax, and we need to refer to this subgroup frequently, we give them the special name of particle ("Par") and reserve the term preposition only for prepositions with complements. In the examples in (5) and (6), the prepositions and particles are in italics.

(5)   Preposition (with a Complement)
    (a) They were singing songs *on* the bus.
    (b) She threw the ball *into* the bushes.
    (c) Please call us *during* school hours.

(6)   Particle (without a Complement)
        (a) Mother went *in* silently.
        (b) She threw the ball *up*.
        (c) My sister passed *out*.

Prepositions occur with only one complement, which is most often a NP, as in (7), but it can also be a PP as in (8) or, more rarely, an adverb expressing time or place as in (9).

(7)   NP as Complement of Preposition
        (a) *on* [the bus]
        (b) *during* [school hours]
        (c) *for* [your own good]
        (d) *with* [this large skeleton key]

(8)   PP as Complement of Preposition
        (a) *up* [in the air]
        (b) *down* [from the attic]
        (c) *out* [in the yard]
        (d) *in* [over her head]

(9)   Adverb as Complement of Preposition
        (a) *from* here
        (b) *to* nowhere
        (c) *since* then
        (d) *beyond* downtown

Tree diagrams are given in (10). Since by definition particles do not have complements, there is no internal structure to a constituent with a particle, and we diagram them as in (10)(d).

(10) (a)

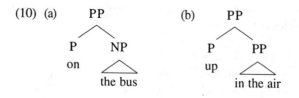

(10)   (c) PP   (d)   Par
                                   in

          P   Adv
        from   here

The complements of prepositions can also be clauses, in particular, gerundives and one kind of WH-clause (a free relative) as in (11) - (12). (See Chapters 22 - 24.)

(11)   Gerundive as Complement of Preposition
        (a) *before* [reaching this conclusion]
        (b) *by* [agreeing to help us]
        (c) because *of* [the baby's incessant crying]

(12)   WH-Clause as Complement of Preposition
        (a) *at* [whatever time you want]
        (b) *with* [what they gave us]
        (c) *from* [what you wrote]
        (d) because *of* [how she reacted to the news]

However, prepositional complements cannot be that-clauses or infinitive clauses, a fact which helps distinguish prepositions from verbs and adjectives. The combination of a verb and a that-clause complement is grammatical, as in (13)(a), while the combination of a preposition (*about*) and a that-clause is not, as in (13)(b). The examples of (14) show a similar pattern with the adjective *surprised*.

(13)   (a) I know [that you are lying].
        (b) *I know *about* [that you are lying].

(14)   (a) They seemed surprised [that the answer was "No"].
        (b) *They seemed surprised *at* [that the answer was "No"].

Finally, a subclass of prepositions take finite clauses as complements. Because they introduce a clause and serve to mark it as subordinate, we consider them to be complementizers. Subordinate clauses with "prepositional" complementizers have the structure in (16).

(15)   (a) They left [*before* [I arrived]].
        (b) I waited [*until* [the lights came back on]].

(16)   CP

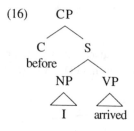

Finally, both PPs and particles combine with intensifiers (see Chapter 4). In the examples in (17), the PPs are in square brackets and the intensifiers in italics. Syntactically, the intensifier precedes the PP or Par and together with it forms a larger PP or Par, as in (18).

(17)   (a) They came [*directly* [from the doctor]].
        (b) The victim died [*just* [after noon]].
        (c) He ran [*right* [into the police]].
        (d) There was garbage *all* over.

(18) (a)   PP   (b)   Par

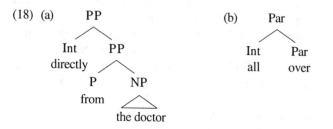

3. THE EXTERNAL SYNTAX OF PREPOSITIONAL PHRASES

In this section we turn to the external syntax of PPs and particles, which function either as adverbial modifers or as complements.

3.1 Prepositional Phrases as Adverbial Modifiers
PPs occur as optional adverbial modifiers, as shown in (19) - (21). (See Chapter 4 on adverbials in general and Chapter 28 on noun modifiers, including PPs.) Tree diagrams are given in (22).

(19)　PP as Modifier of VP
　　　(a)　They were [singing songs [on the bus]].
　　　(b)　I don't like to [work [after dark]].
　　　(c)　Sam [walked home [with a heavy heart]].
　　　(d)　They [baked a cake [for their boss]].

(20)　PP as Modifier of Noun
　　　(a)　the [boys [on the bus]]
　　　(b)　a [party [at midnight]]
　　　(c)　a [story [about polar bears]]

(21)　PP as Modifier of S
　　　(a)　[In all seriousness], I don't like grammar.
　　　(b)　[By the way], this word is misspelled.
　　　(c)　[On the other hand], there are no glaring inconsistencies.

(22)　(a)　　　　　　　VP　　　　　　(b)　　　　　　S

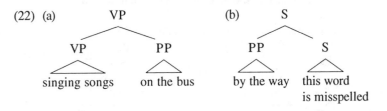

3.2 Prepositional Phrases as Complements
PPs also occur as complements of verbs, adjectives, and nouns. As complements, their existence is implied or required, and the verb, adjective, or noun is subcategorized for a particular preposition, which appears in its subcategorization frame (see Chapters 10 and 11). For example, the verb *rely* is subcategorized for the preposition *on*, the verb *blame* for the preposition *on,* as in (23).

(23)   (a)   I *relied* [on my mother].
       (b)   They *blamed* it [on me].

Two adjectives that take PP complements are *fond* and *happy*, as in (24).
Tree diagrams are given in (25).

(24)   (a)   I am very *fond* [of your mother].
       (b)   We are *happy* [about their proposal].

(25)   (a)

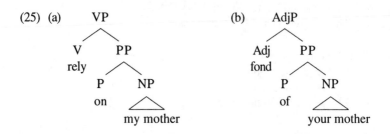

Note the important difference between complements and modifiers: Verbs are
subcategorized for complements, which combine with the verb to form a
VP. Verbs are not subcategorized for modifiers, however, which combine
with a VP. This difference is shown clearly in tree diagrams, as in (26).

(26)   (a)   Modifier of VP   (b)   Complement of V

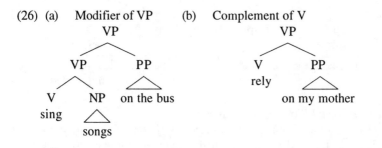

3.3 Particles

Particles do not occur in the same range of positions that PPs do, but are
used most often as complements of verbs, as in (27). These verbs, known as
phrasal verbs, are subcategorized for the particles; the sentences would be
ungrammatical or have a different meaning without them. Phrasal verbs, are
discussed in detail in Chapter 11. Tree diagrams are given in (28).

(27) (a) My sister passed *out.*
      (b) Because they were so far behind, the team gave *up.*
      (c) Please look the number *up.*

(28)   (a)   VP   (b)   VP

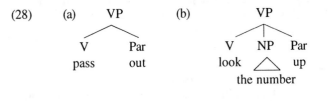

Exercise 1
Give labeled tree diagrams for each of the following sentences, using triangles to abbreviate the internal structure of NPs.

Part A.   PPs as Adverbial Modifiers
1.   We hold staff meetings on Thursday mornings.
2.   The brothers play soccer at the park.
3.   In my opinion, syntax is fun.
4.   She slept on a park bench.
5.   We fixed the leak with some silly putty.
6.   For the last time, my mother went to school in Idaho and my father studied French in Algeria.
7.   The children played basketball for three hours and ate dinner at 6:00.

Part B.   PPs and Particles as Complements
1.   The paper floated down the river.
2.   Your book is up on the shelf.
3.   My uncle ran for president of the neighborhood association.
4.   You seem dissatisfied with the results of the election.
5.   The runaway truck slammed right into the wall.
6.   The baby sat up.
7.   The dog raced out the door and into the yard.
8.   To her surprise, the lights went off and on, the main computer blew up, and the secretary passed out.

4. THE SEMANTICS OF PREPOSITIONAL PHRASES

As already noted, prepositions express a wide variety of meanings. Moreover, the most common prepositions (e.g. *in, out, on, off, up, down,* etc.) seem to be polysemous in the extreme, as a brief look in any dictionary shows. In this section we look at the major meanings expressed by prepositions and the phrases they head.

4.1 Prepositional Phrases as Adverbial Modifiers

It is in their use as adverbial modifiers that we see the range of meanings that prepositions express. Because of the great diversity, it is useful to distinguish two broad, somewhat overlapping categories: adverbial PPs that present circumstantial information and adverbial PPs that give information about semantic roles.

Circumstantial information. Circumstantial information includes information about the circumstances surrounding a state or event, including the time, place, means, purpose, etc. Such information can be optionally added to virtually any clause, as shown in (29).

(29) (a) The butler did it.
      (b) The butler did it in the living room.
      (c) The butler did it in the living room after midnight.
      (d) The butler did it with a knife in the living room after midnight.
      (e) The butler did it with a knife in the living room after midnight
           for the money.

Circumstantial information can be expressed by adverbs, NPs, and CPs (clauses), as well as by prepositions, though many circumstantial categories are expressed primarily by prepositions, as shown in the chart below. Prepositions that express time are discussed in Chapters 6 and 7, a case study of time expressions in English.

CIRCUMSTANTIAL CATEGORY		PREPOSITION	EXAMPLE
Time	when?	*at, on, in*	(see Chapters 6-7)
Place	where?	*in, out, up, down, on, off, at, around, into, out of, past, off (of), to, around*	*She is in the room.* *It is on the table.* *She ran into the room.* *It fell off the table.*
Manner	how?	*in ... manner/way*	*in a friendly manner* *in a rude way* *with a smile on her face*
Means	how?	*by*	*by plane/car/bus/ship* *by phone/fax/mail*
Instrument	with what?	*with, without*	*with a knive* *without using a compass*
Cause/ Reason	why?	*because of* *on account of* *from, of*	*I was fired because of my bad attitude toward work.* *They were freezing from the cold and dying of starvation.*
Motive	why?	*out of* *for*	*They did it out of fear.* *She would kill for love.*
Purpose	why?	*for*	*They prepared carefully for the long journey.*
Intended Target		*at*	*They shot at the dog.* *He aimed the gun at me.*

Semantic roles. Sometimes prepositions are used to express the semantic role of the participants in the event or state. Below are the most common semantic roles and the prepositions used most frequently to express them. Note that semantic roles are expressed not only by PPs, but also by NPs which are subject, direct object, or indirect object. Some semantic roles are complements of a verb. The way a complement is expressed depends on the verb and is indicated in its subcategorization frame (see Chapter 10).

Agent. The agent is the one who performs the action, the initiator of the action. Prototypically, an agent is animate and acts with intention. This role is expressed most often by the subject of a clause when the verb is an activity or event verb (see Chapter 17). In a passive verb phrase (see Chapter 14), the agent may be expressed in a prepositional phrase with *by*.

(30) (a) This mural was painted *by Picasso.*
      (b) A book written *by Chomsky* was stolen from the library.

Recipient. The recipient is a typically human participant who receives the theme, the person to whom the theme goes. (On the theme, see below.) The recipient is expressed by the indirect object if the verb is ditransitive and otherwise most often by the preposition *to.*

(31) (a) Picasso gave this painting *to my mother.*
      (b) The center threw the ball *to the left guard.*

(Note the similarity between this use of *to* and its use as a place adverbial in sentences like *She walked to the store.*)
    Source. The source is the person or place from which the theme comes, often expressed with the preposition *from*. We can also consider the material out of which something is made as expressing a source, albeit of a slightly different kind. This meaning is also expressed with *from* or, more informally, with *out of.*

(32) (a) Sally got this ring *from Jim.*
      (b) Where did you get your TV?   I got it *from Circuit City.*
      (c) This wine is made *from white grapes.*
      (d) I made this collage *from / out of stuff I found in the basement.*

(Note the similarity between this use of *from* and its use as a place adverbial in sentences like *She is walking home from the store.*)
    Benefactive. The benefactive is a typically human participant who benefits in some way from the event. It is expressed with *for.* (This semantic role is closely related to the purpose category discussed above, also expressed with *for.*)

(33) (a) I baked this cake *for Mom.*
      (b) They did this very nice thing *for me.*

A special kind of benefactive is a participant who benefits from an action performed by proxy, where an agent acts in place of someone else.

(34)   I'm working *for Jim* today. It's his wife's birthday and he wanted the day off.

Comitive. The comitive role, expressed by the preposition *with*, names a person with whom one performs the action, someone who does it together with the subject.

(35)   (a)   Kim likes to go shopping *with her mother*.
       (b)   We're going to a movie. Why don't you come *with us?*

Experiencer. The experiencer names a person who experiences, suffers, or feels the emotion named by the verb. There is no preposition that is associated with this role; it is expressed by the direct object of some verbs and the subject of others.

(36)   (a)   The monster frightened *me* with his awful roar.
       (b)   His ideas struck *the professor* as quite original.
       (c)   *The beauty queen* fell in love with a truck driver.

Theme. The theme (sometimes known as the patient) is the thing which is created, affected, changed, or moved by the action of the verb. It is the participant, human or non-human, which undergoes the action. The theme is not expressed by any particular preposition, but is often the direct object of transitive verbs or the subject of *certain* intransitive verbs.

(37)   Theme as direct object
       (a)   They killed *our cat* .
       (b)   We painted *a lovely picture*.

(38)   Theme as subject
       (a)   *Our cat* died.
       (b)   *The picture* hung in our dining room for years.

These are just a few of the more concrete meanings we can attribute to prepositions, though there are many other meanings, more abstract and more difficult to characterize. A summary is given in (39).

(39) PREPOSITION   SEMANTIC ROLE
      by   agent
      to   recipient
      from   source
      for   benefactive
      with   comitive
      —   experiencer
      —   theme — patient, created, affected
                                              changed

4.2 Prepositional Phrases as Complements

In contrast to the diversity of meanings expressed by PPs functioning as adverbial modifiers, prepositions often express *no* meaning when they are complements, functioning as fixed, idiomatic requirements of a verb or adjective. They are required by the syntax, but semantically empty.

For example, the verb *rely* is subcategorized for a PP with *on*. There is no particular meaning associated with the preposition; it is required by the verb. Further examples of semantically empty prepositions are given in (40). Verbs subcategorized for particular prepositions are known as prepositional verbs, discussed in Chapter 11.

(40) (a) They depend *on* us.
      (b) She cared *for* her mother.
      (c) He was referring *to* a well-known paradox.

Exercise 2

Think carefully about the meaning of each sentence below and describe the phrases in brackets in terms of a semantic role or a circumstantial category.

1.   Mother gave a new toy [to the baby].
2.   Father gave [the baby] a bath [in the living room].
3.   [A thief] stole "The Scream" [from a museum in Oslo].
4.   [The rain] destroyed [the crops].
5.   [My daughter] made supper [for me] [last night].
6.   We designed [a beautiful new mural] [for the school].
7.   They sent [the package] directly [to my attorney].
8.   Did you learn anything [from that course]?
9.   I wrote this article [with Kathy] [in January].
10.   [The car] struck [a pedestrian].
11.   My secretary hurt her hand so I typed this letter [for her] [on my computer].
12.   [The garden] is swarming with bees.

Exercise 3

In English, many common prepositions are used to express place, time, and degree (or measurement of some kind). Often the same semantic distinction is expressed by the same preposition in all three domains. For example, the preposition *at* means "a specific point" in place, time, or degree, as shown in (1).

(1)   (a) place   Meet me *at* the corner of 35th and Vine Street.
       (b) time   Meet me *at* 6:00 sharp.
       (c) degree   Water boils *at* 100 degrees centigrade.

Pick two prepositions from the following list and determine if they can be used about place, time, *and* degree. Construct relevant sentences and try to give a general characterization of the meaning of each preposition which holds across all three domains.

Prepositions: *about, above, around, before, below, for, in, over, toward(s), under*

Exercise 4

Prepositions are notoriously polysemous; that is, they have many, many meanings. For example, the *Longman Dictionary of Contemporary English* lists over 10 meanings for the preposition *on*. Pick one or two common prepositions from the list of simple prepositions given at the beginning of this chapter and see how many different meanings are listed for it in a good dictionary. Is each of the meanings possible with a variety of verbs and adjectives, or not? Consider whether any of the meanings are better analyzed as instances of subcategorization (i.e. the preposition is *required* by a particular verb or adjective and used in that meaning *only* with that verb or adjective).

6

TALKING ABOUT TIME
PART 1
TIME-WHEN PHRASES

CAN YOU STATE THE RULE for using *in* and *on* with time expressions? Do you know when a NP can function as a time expression? Do you know how many different categories of time expressions there are in English? There is great variety in the way we talk about time in English, and in the next two chapters we present an overview of the syntax and the semantics of time expressions. In terms of internal syntax, time expressions, like other adverbials, belong to one of these syntactic categories: adverb, PP, NP, or CP (clause), though only expressions of the first three types will be discussed here. For convenience, we refer to all time expressions as TPs (time phrases).

In terms of external syntax, TPs function most often as adjuncts in VPs and NPs and occasionally as complements of verbs. In terms of semantics, they divide into three categories. Some express the *time when* an action takes place, answering the question, "When?"

categories
1. Time when
2. duration
3. frequency

(1) (a) When did they get married?   They got married [in 1987].
     (b) When did she do her homework? She is doing it [right now].
     (c) When will you call us?   We'll call [very soon].

Some TPs express *duration,* the length of time which something lasts, answering the question, "How long?"

(2) (a) How long did he live?   He lived [for 105 years].
     (b) How long will you stay? I'll be staying [all summer].

Still other TPs express the *frequency* with which something occurs, answering the question, "How often?"

(3)   (a) How often do you swim?   I swim [every day].
       (b) How often do you call her?   I call [very rarely].

This chapter is devoted to time-when expressions, and the next, to durational expressions and frequency expressions. The external syntax of all TPs will be treated briefly at the end of the next chapter.

1. THE EXPRESSION OF TIME-WHEN

Time-when expressions answer the questions "When?" or "At what time?"

(4)   (a) When did she see him?   She saw him [yesterday].
       (b) At what time did they wake up?   They woke up [at 4:00 a.m.]
       (c) When will you go to Paris?   We will go [next year].

Before turning to specific time-when expressions, we need to introduce a few concepts. First, time-when expressions denote either a *point* of time or an *interval* of time, a distinction that can be indicated on a time line as in (5).

(5)

       Point: at 4:00 a.m.
                 at this very moment
       Interval: the next morning
                                            next year

In addition, many time-when expressions are understood in terms of their relationship to the time the sentence is uttered, the TU. The TU is always now, i.e. the present, a moment which divides time into past, present, and future, as shown in (6).

(6)
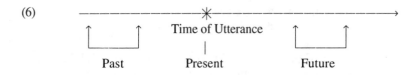

Past TPs show that the time of the situation they modify is *prior to* TU as in (7), while present TPs convey that the time of the situation *includes* TU, as in (8). Future TPs place the time of the situation *after* TU, as in (9).

(7)   (a) They arrived [yesterday].
      (b) She graduated [last year].
      (c) I lost that money [a long time ago].

(8)   (a) She is speaking [now] / [at this very moment].
      (b) We eat out a lot [these days].
      (c) [Nowadays] many people cannot afford health insurance.

(9)   (a) They're leaving [tomorrow].
      (b) I'll call you [next week].
      (c) We must leave [soon].

  Some time-when expressions are understood in terms of their relation to yet *another* time, called the reference time (TR). Time-when expressions indicate time prior to, simultaneous with, or following, a TR.

(10)
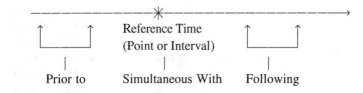

The concept of reference time is illustrated in (11), where TR is established in (11)(a) as 7:00. In (11)(b) the TP indicates that the situation is *simultaneous with* TR, while in (11)(c) the TP indicates that the situation was *prior to* TR. The TP in (11)(d) conveys that the situation *follows* TR.

(11)   (a)   It was already 7:00, and Jason was tired.
        (b)   His cousin arrived [at that very moment].
        (c)   Jason had arrived [five hours earlier].
        (d)   [Later] they both asked to be excused.

The concepts of points versus intervals of time, TU, and TR will be important in the remainder of the chapter, as we examine the semantics of time-when expressions. Time-when expressions that are PPs are discussed in Section 2, those that are NPs in Section 3, and those that are adverbs in Section 4.

2. PREPOSITIONAL PHRASES AS TIME-WHEN EXPRESSIONS

Time-when is frequently expressed by PPs, most commonly with the prepositions *at, on, in,* or *during,* as summarized in Chart 1.

CHART 1. PREPOSITIONAL PHRASES AS TIME-WHEN PHRASES

Preposition	Use With	Examples
at	points of time, including	*at 4:00, at 3:15*
	transitions in the day	*at sunrise, at dusk*
	the word *night*	*at night*
	intervals of time around holidays	*at Easter, at Passover*
on	intervals of time that mention	*on Monday*
	a specific day or include	*on the third day*
	mention of a day	*on December 12, 1943*
		on Saturday night
in	intervals of time less than a day	*in the morning,*
		in the minutes before
		her arrival
	intervals of time more than a day	*in the following week,*
		in January, in 1985
		in the 14th century
during	any interval of time	*during the morning*
		during the day
		during 1985

There are a few clarifications regarding the use of *in* and *on*. Though *in* is generally used with parts of the day (e.g. *in the evening*), if the day itself is mentioned, *on* is used instead (*on Monday evening*). The preposition *on* (and not *in*) is used with parts of the day when they are modified so as to give them unique reference (e.g. *on the morning of her departure, on that very same afternoon, on the night before he was born*). The word *night* is an exception: Although it names a part of the day, it is not used with *in*, but with *at* (*at night* and not **in night*).

To name individual holidays, because they are days, the preposition *on* is used (*on Halloween, on Thanksgiving (Day)*). To denote the interval of time around a holiday, though, *at* is used (*at Christmas* means "the time around Christmas"). This use of *at* is exceptional because it is marking an interval and not a point of time.

In addition to the prepositions in Chart 1, four others denote time-when in a more complex way. Prepositional phrases with *after* or *in* (in a different sense from the use described above) specify an interval of time that is measured forward from a TR to a later point in time. The situation modified by the PP happened, or is to happen, at the conclusion of the interval, as in (12). The temporal relationships in (12)(a) are illustrated on a time line in (13).

(12) (a) He left on Friday and returned [in two days].
       (b) I will write you [in a few years].
       (c) They gave up [after a few minutes].

(13)

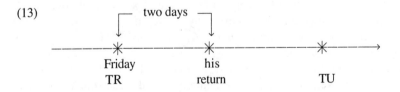

Phrases with *ago*, a preposition that occurs *after* the NP, are used to measure an interval backwards from TU to a point in the past, as in (14). In colloquial American English, the word *back* is used in a similar way (*some time back, a few years back*).

(14)   (a)   I saw him [a few minutes ago].
       (b)   We were in Paris [five years ago].

(15)

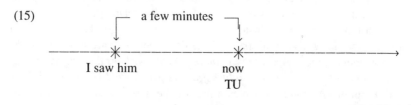

Exercise 1
Name four holidays, including non-American and non-Christian ones, if you know any. Determine whether the generalizations about prepositions and holidays given above hold for them or not.

Exercise 2
Many nouns name intervals of time, including *season, period, interval.* Add four other nouns to this list, using a thesaurus if necessary, and construct NPs with these nouns as head (e.g. *the harvest season, the three-month interval after his death*). Can the NPs you made be used as time-when expressions? Which prepositions from Chart 1 are used?

---

3. NOUN PHRASES AS TIME-WHEN EXPRESSIONS

NPs also function as time-when phrases. In one type, the head noun names a part of the day that is modified by *yesterday, tomorrow,* or the determiner *this* (e.g. *yesterday morning, this evening*). In a second type, the head noun is a unit of time with the determiners *last, this,* or *next*. Like the modifiers *yesterday* and *tomorrow*, the words *last, this*, and *next* are indexed to the time of the utterance and mean roughly, prior to TU, during or including TU, and following TU. Thus, *last Monday* means "on the Monday prior to TU," while *this week* means "in the week that includes TU." These temporal NPs are presented in Chart 2.

CHART 2. NOUN PHRASES AS TIME-WHEN EXPRESSIONS

	Time Unit Part of a Day	Other Unit of Time
Past:	yesterday morning	the last hour
	yesterday afternoon	last Monday
	yesterday evening	last week
	last night	last year
Present:	this morning	this minute
	this afternoon	this week
	this evening	this month
	(adverb: *tonight*)	this year
Future:	tomorrow morning	the next minute
	tomorrow afternoon	next week
	tomorrow evening	next Friday
	tomorrow night	next year

Though NPs with *this* are listed as *present* TPs, they are frequently used with future time reference as well. If one is speaking in the morning, for instance, the NP *this afternoon* will be understood as future. (Note the use of *will* in (16)(a)).

(16) (a) We will stop by to see you [this afternoon].
     (b) We're going to vacation in Washington [this year].

When spoken in the morning, the expression *this afternoon* does not mean "during the afternoon which includes TU" since the speaking takes place in the morning; it conveys something like "during the afternoon closest to TU." The word *later* can be used with any of the expressions with present time reference to emphasize future meaning.

(17) (a) We will stop by to see you [*later* this afternoon].
     (b) We're going to visit Washington [*later* this year].
     (c) I'm going to the office [*later* today].

Present TPs can also be used with past time reference, as in (18) (note the past tense verbs). The word *earlier* can be used along with the TP to emphasize past meaning.

(18) (a) I saw her [this morning] / [*earlier* this morning].
      (b) We finished the project [this month] / [*earlier* this month].
      (c) She went to her office [today] / [*earlier* today].

Exercise 3
Draw the times and events of each sentence on a time line. On each time line mark the TU as well as any relevant TRs. Pay special attention to the time-when expressions in italics.

1.   Mary died on Saturday, June 13th. Sally died *two days later.*
2.   My son graduated from college *four years ago.*
3.   Last night Miss Marbles had a terrible headache. *Earlier in the day* she had lost her purse and *later that afternoon* her dog ran away.
4.   It hadn't rained for a week. *Last Monday* I watered the lawn and *the next day* it rained.
5.   They handed in their papers *earlier this week.*

Exercise 4
If both *this week* and *next week* have future time reference, what is the difference between them? Your answer should also be able to account for the difference between:

this Friday	*next Friday*	(said on a Monday)
this month	*next month*	(said in July)
this year	*next year*	(said in 1996)

---

4. ADVERBS AS TIME-WHEN EXPRESSIONS

There are many, many adverbs which are used to express time-when. It would be an impossible task to treat them all here, so we will look at two subgroups, those indexed to TU and those indexed to some other TR.

4.1 Adverbs Indexed to TU

Adverbs indexed to TU are presented in Chart 3, in which are included PPs and NPs with similar senses. Several subdivisions have been made: Of adverbials with past time reference, some denote the distant past, some denote the recent past, and the rest are relatively neutral. Of the adverbials with present time reference, some code the present as a fairly broad time interval (e.g. *these days, currently*), while others focus more narrowly on the TU (*at this time, at this point*). Of adverbials with future time reference, some refer to the immediate future, some to a near future, and others to merely an eventuality. A few expressions are more neutral about the distance in the future which is involved.

CHART 3. TIME-WHEN EXPRESSIONS
(Indexed to TU)

PAST Prior to TU	PRESENT Including TU	FUTURE After TU
in the past	in the present now	in the future
NP ago		in NP
yesterday	today	tomorrow
yesterday morning	this morning	tomorrow morning
yesterday afternoon	this afternoon	tomorrow afternoon
yesterday evening	this evening	tomorrow evening
last night	tonight	tomorrow night
the day before yesterday		the day after tomorrow
last week	this week	next week
last month	this month	next month
last year	this year	next year
Other Past Adverbials	**Other Present Adverbials**	**Other Future Adverbials**
Distant, Neutral, Recent	Points vs Intervals	Immediate, Near, Neutral, Eventual
(see below)	(see below)	(see below)

PRESENT ADVERBIALS
now

The Present Moment	The Present Epoch
right now	these days
at the moment	nowadays
at this moment/instant	currently
at this point	
at this time	in this day and age
at this point in time	in our time
at the present time	at present

PAST ADVERBIALS

Distant Past	Neutral	Recent Past
a long time ago	before	just now
some time ago	before now	recently
at one time	earlier	latelly
once		of late
sometime back (infml)	not long ago	a short time ago
years ago (infml)	formerly	the other day
ages ago (infml)	previously	only yesterday

in times past
in times gone by
in the old days
in the good old days

In Fairy Tales
long ago
once upon a time

FUTURE ADVERBIALS

Immediate	Near	Neutral
immediately	soon	in the future
at once	shortly	later
right away	before long	in a while
this minute		after a while
this very minute	in the near future	at a later time
any minute (now)	sometime soon	
without delay	directly	after a time
straightaway	presently	by and by
?instantly	in a little while (infml)	
in an instant	in a (little) bit (infml)	
in a second/moment	in a short time	
	just around the corner	
imminently		from now on
		from this moment on
		from this point (on)
		from here on
		from this time forward
		hereafter / henceforth

Eventual		
eventually	someday	
in time	one of these days	
in due time	some/one fine day	
all in good time	sometime	
ultimately	sooner or later	
in the long run		

4.2 Adverbs Indexed to a TR

A second subgroup of adverbs are indexed to a TR which is not the TU, but a time that is assumed or given in the context. Adverbs in this subgroup represent the semantic categories prior to, simultaneous with, and following TR, as illustrated in (19).

(19)   (a)   Suzie graduated from college [in 1978].
        (b)   [Two years earlier] she had been expelled from high school for
               smoking in the bathroom.
        (c)   [A few months later], she enrolled in a GED course and graduated
               with honors.
        (d)   [From then on], her life took a different turn.

(19)(a) establishes as reference time the year 1978. In (19)(b) the phrase
two years earlier measures time back from 1978 and establishes a new TR,
the time she was expelled. In (19)(c), the phrase *a few months later*
measures time forward from the new TR (expulsion from high school) and
establishes still another TR, the time of graduation. The phrase *from then
on* measures time forward from that TR.

   Chart 4 presents some common adverbs in this subgroup, and includes
prepositions and adjectives as well. The adjectives are often used to form
time-when phrases by combining with units of time to form NPs as in (20).
These NPs may themselves serve as time-when phrases or may be used as
objects of the prepositions in Chart 1, as in (21).

(20)   the previous hour
        the preceding year
        the very same day
        the next month
        the following morning

(21)   (a)   We arrived [(on) the very same day].
        (b)   He arrived [(on) the following morning].
        (c)   Terrible things were to happen [(in) the next few days].
        (d)   You'll find a job [in the next month or two].

CHART 4. TIME-WHEN EXPRESSIONS
(Indexed to TR)

PRIOR TO	SIMULTANEOUS WITH	FOLLOWING
Adverbs		
earlier	at the same time	later
before	at one and the same time	afterward(s)
beforehand	at that time	next
once		later on (infml)
at one time		after (infml)
		after a while (infml)
previously	simultaneously	subsequently
formerly	concurrently	thereupon
hitherto	co-temporaneously	thereafter
		from that point on
		from that time on
Prepositions		
earlier than	during	in
before	while (+ clause)	after
prior to		following
Adjectives		
previous	(very) same	next
preceding		following

5. COMPLEX TIME-WHEN PHRASES

Some of the adverbs in Chart 4 are used in complex time-when phrases. For example, the word *earlier* indicates that the action happened at a time prior to TR. *Earlier* can combine with an NP indicating a time interval, which answers the question, "How much earlier?" as in (22).

(22) How much earlier did he arrive?
      three weeks earlier   =   earlier by three weeks
      two days earlier   earlier by two days
      several years earlier   earlier by several years

The adverbs *earlier* and *later* can be part of a different kind of complex time-when expression, illustrated in (23).

(23)   (a)   earlier this week
       (b)   earlier in the morning
       (c)   later tonight

Expressions of this type contain an adverb from Chart 4 followed by a time-when phrase. The time-when phrase has its usual force and specifies the time interval during which the *earlier* is operative.

Exercise 5

Look over the adverbs in Chart 4. Which ones can take NP modifiers in the way that *earlier* does? Give relevant examples.

Exercise 6

Choose a text of at least several paragraphs. Read it and underline each time-when expression. Then classify each expression according to syntactic category (PP, Adv, or NP) and, if applicable, classify it according to one or more of the semantic categories discussed above (present, past, future, prior to, simultaneous with, following, point of time, interval of time).

7

TALKING ABOUT TIME
PART 2
DURATION AND
FREQUENCY PHRASES

IN THE LAST CHAPTER we discussed temporal phrases used to express the *time when* a situation takes place. In this chapter we discuss TPs used to express duration and frequency. At the conclusion of this chapter, there is a brief discussion of the external syntax of all TPs.

1. DURATION

Durational TPs measure an interval of time and answer the question, "How long?" They can be PPs, NPs, or adverbs, as in (1).

(1) (a) How long did it last?
     (b) It lasted [for an hour].
     (c)   [all day].
     (d)   [momentarily].

1.1 Prepositional Phrases as TPs of General Duration

TPs of *general* duration do not have an orientation forward or backward. They are most often expressed with a PP headed by *for* in combination with a NP that names an interval of time, as in (2).

(2) (a) They stayed with us   [for three hours].
     (b)   [for six weeks].
     (c)   [for the morning/afternoon/night].
     (d)   [for the summer].

Durational expressions can also be constructed with *time* as the head noun (*(for) a long time, (for) the whole time,* etc.). Note that in durational phrases the word *for* is frequently omitted. (See 1.2.)

(3)   (a)   My parents stayed [for three days] / [three days].
       (b)   The baby cried [for a long time] / [a long time].

Exercise 1

Name at least four other nouns which name a period of time, using a thesaursus if necessary. Can they all be used in durational expressions? Give relevant examples.

Although *for* is the preposition most frequently used to express duration, others include *over, (all) through,* and *throughout.* The paired prepositions *from ... to/until/till/up to ...* also express duration by specifically mentioning the beginning and end points of an interval of time.

(4)   (a)   They are staying [over the weekend].
       (b)   Attitudes toward TV have changed [over the past ten years].
       (c)   The baby cried [all through the performance].
       (d)   Those people were talking [throughout the concert].
       (e)   She stayed with us [from April to June].
       (f)   The baby cried [from morning till night].

The preposition *during* seems to suggest duration, but it is most often used to indicate time-when. For instance, (5)(a) could be used to answer the question, "When did she fall asleep?" but not the question, "How long did she sleep?"

(5)   (a)   She fell asleep [during the speech].   (= at some time
                                                              during the speech)

       (b)   They talked [during the meeting].

When other words which indicate duration are added, a PP with *during* may indicate duration, as in (6).

(6) (a) The baby slept [during the whole speech].
     (b) They were talking [during the entire meeting].

1.2 Noun Phrases as TPs of General Duration

Although the most common way to express duration is with a *for* phrase, sometimes the word *for* is omitted, resulting in a TP that is a NP. This is especially common with verbs that express states (see Chapter 16).

(7) (a) PP   We waited [for three hours].
     (b) NP   We waited [three hours].
     (c) PP   I lived there [for several months].
     (d) NP   I lived there [several months].

Other NPs that express duration begin with *all* followed by a noun that names a period of time (a part of the day, a unit of time larger than an hour, a season, etc.). Note the lack of article in most of the NPs in (8). Some NPs with *all* can be followed by the word *long,* which emphasizes the duration.

(8) (a) The fight lasted [all morning (long)].
     (b)   [all day (long)].
     (c)   [all week].
     (d)   [all summer].
     (e)   [all the time I was in college].

1.3 Adverbs as TPs of General Duration

A few adverbs in English express duration, usually extremely long duration or something of permanence, as shown in Chart 1. Some NPs often used in durational phrases are given in Chart 2. Common nouns which name intervals and which are used for expressing duration are presented in Chart 3.

CHART 1. DURATIONAL ADVERBS

Nearly Instantaneously ⟷	Briefly ⟵⟶	Of Long Duration ⟵—⟶	Forever (Without End) ⟵—⟶
fleetingly	briefly	protractedly	forever
flittingly	transiently		always
	temporarily	permanently	
momentarily			perpetually
			everlastingly
			eternally
			indefinitely
			endlessly
			unendingly
			interminably
			ceaselessly
			incessantly
			ad infinitum

CHART 2. DURATIONAL NOUN PHRASES

Nearly Instantaneous ⟷	Short ⟵⟶	Long ⟵—⟶	Very Long ⟵—⟶
an instant	a short time	a long time	a lifetime
a moment	a brief time	a long while	an eternity
a second	a little while		generations
a split second	no time at all		centuries
a minute	a time		years on end
	a while		ages
			an age

CHART 3. NOUNS WHICH NAME INTERVALS

Units of time:	second, minute, hour, day, week, month, year, decade, century, millennium
Parts of the day:	morning, afternoon, evening, night
Seasons:	spring, summer, fall/autumn, winter
Other nouns:	time, while, period, term, interval, season, times, days, generation, age, era, epoch interim, interlude, hiatus, break, pause, recess, intermission (and many others)

1.4 Duration Forward or Backward

Some TPs of duration refer to an interval of time which looks *forward* from a TR.

(9)   (a) How long will you wait?
       (b) I'll wait [until noon].

(10)   (a) How long did you wait?
       (b) I waited [until noon].

In (9)(b) the phrase *until noon* covers the interval of time from TU (now) to noon. In (10)(b) it covers the interval from some past point in time (assumed by the speaker but not mentioned) forward to noon. Although the expression *until noon* "looks forward," its reference time can be set in the past, the present, or the future.

   The main way to express duration forward is with the prepositions *until* and *till*, but others with this meaning include *up to, for, before, by,* and *by the time (that)*.

(11)   (a) We have to finish this [before noon].
       (b) They are supposed to call us [by 4:00].
       (c) [By the time that the ambulance had arrived], the victim had recovered.

Some TPs of duration look backward from a TR, as with the prepositions *since* and *for*.

(12) (a) I have waited for you [since noon].
     (b) Anne had waited for him [since graduation from high school], but at age 26 she finally married someone else.
     (c) It has been snowing [for the past three days].

In (12)(a) the phrase *since noon* covers an interval beginning with TU (the present), going backward, and ending with noon. Note that the present perfect is required here because the state begins in the past and continues into the present (see Chapter 18).

(13)

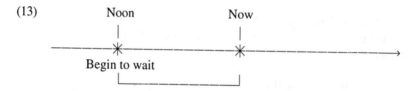

In (12)(b) the phrase *since ... high school* covers an interval beginning with the end of Anne's waiting period and marriage, looking backward and ending with graduation from high school. Because the state began at one point in the past and continued to another point in the past, the past perfect is used.

1.5 Restrictions Between Verb and Durational Phrases

Though there are many observations one could make about the compatibility of the lexical verb, verb form, and durational TP, we confine ourselves to two. The first involves momentary event verbs (see Chapter 17), which do not "take time" and so do not, under ordinary interpretations, co-occur with durational phrases. The sentences of (14) are ungrammatical if the durational phrases are included.

(14) (a) *We recognized him [for two minutes].
     (b) *Flight 710 landed [for two hours].
     (c) *Columbus discovered America [for several months].

Some momentary event verbs, when used in combination with a durational phrase, convey repeated events, as in (15).

(15) (a) She blinked.   (= one time, a single event)
        (b) She blinked [for a few minutes].   (= repeated blinking)

A second observation involves time span and tense. A durational phrase may refer to an interval of time completely in the past (relative to the time of the utterance), as in (16), or completely in the future, as in (17). If the time interval is in the past, the past tense form of the verb is used, while if it is in the future, one of the many ways of expressing the future in English is used (see Chapter 19).

(16) (a) King George ruled [for 40 years].
       (b) I lived in Chicago [for 8 years].
       (c) Susie waited for her mother [for ten minutes] yesterday.

(17) (a) My daughter will be away at college [for four years].
       (b) Our trip across the U.S. is going to last [all summer].

If the time span begins in the past and includes the present, however, the present perfect must be used.

(18) (a) I have lived here [for ten years].
       (b) They have waited [all day].

Exercise 2
Draw a time line for sentences (12)(b) and (c).

Exercise 3
Read the following passage and underline all the durational phrases. Then plot the events on a time line. Mark TU with an "X." Mark the time intervals with brackets and the transition points (events) with crosses.

Carlos is from Colombia. He has been in the United States for four years and has been a student at GMU since 1992. He studied English in Colombia for six months and at NOVA for one year. At that time he got a 590 on the TOEFL and enrolled at a private school. He studied there until his money ran out and transfered here a few months later. For one year he studied mathematics, but switched to English. He has been an English major since last fall. He will graduate in two years and hopes to remain in the U.S. until he finishes a masters degree in economics.

Exercise 4

Construct a narrative like the one in Exercise 3 that could be given to intermediate-level ESL students. It should contain at least four durational phrases.

Exercise 5

Think of at least four different situations in which information about the length of time something lasts is important. Construct several questions which would elicit answers using durational phrases from ESL students.

Example: Situation   studying (English)
          Questions   How long did you study English in your country?
                       How long will you study English in this school?
                       How long is your English class?
                       How long should I study for this test?

Exercise 6   For Discussion

Do you understand the semantics of durational phrases more clearly when you plot them on a time line? Do you think the concept of a time line would help language learners gain a better understanding of what they mean and how they are used?

---

2. FREQUENCY

Some temporal phrases express the frequency with which something happens. Some frequency expressions answer the question "How often?" or "How many times?"

(19) (a) How often do you brush your teeth?
    (b) I brush my teeth [daily].
                          [every day].
                          [twice a day].
                          [frequently].

In terms of syntactic category, frequency expressions are most often adverbs or NPs. Occasionally frequency is expressed by a PP, often an idiomatic one, fixed or invariant in form. In terms of semantics, they divide into definite and indefinite frequency expressions.

2.1 Noun Phrases as Definite Frequency Expressions

Some *definite* frequency phrases name the number of occasions on which something happens, a meaning expressed most often by NPs with the noun *time(s)*, as in (20). A few adverbs and PPs can also express definite frequency, as in (21).

(20) (a) How often did you steal from your grandmother?
    (b) I stole   [one time].
                 [four times].
                 [several times].
    (c) How many times did you lie to me?
    (d) I lied   [two times].
                 [many times].

(21) (a) once   (= one time)
    (b) twice   (= two times)
    (c) on five occasions

Other definite frequency phrases name the repeating period of time in which something happens. This meaning is most often expressed by an NP composed of the quantifier *each* or *every* plus a noun that names a unit of time.

(22) (a) How often do you call home?
    (b) I call home [every day].
    (c)   [every week].
    (d)   [each Christmas].

Another type of noun phrase which expresses definite frequency is simply
the plural form of a day of the week used without a determiner. Less often,
the singular is used.

(23)   (a) How often do you go to the movies?
        (b) We go [Tuesdays].   (= every Tuesday)
        (c) We do the washing [Tuesday]. (= every Tuesday)

   Finally, some definite frequency expressions are adverbs formed from
units of time: *hourly, daily, weekly, quarterly.* Most adverbs, however,
express indefinite frequency, discussed in 2.3.

2.2 Prepositional Phrases as Definite Frequency Expressions

PPs are quite rare as expressions of frequency. Most common is the
preposition *on*, used with days of the week in the plural (less often in the
singular). (They can also occur without the preposition as in (23).)

(24)   (a) How often do you ride?
        (b) We ride [on Saturdays].   (= every Saturday)
                      [Saturdays].
                      [on Saturday] / [Saturday].

Other prepositions used to express frequency are listed in (25).

(25)   *with*   + adjective   + frequency   with regular frequency
        at   + adjective   + intervals   at irregular intervals
        on   + adjective   + occasions   on important occasions
        at   + all   + plural   at all hours
        at   + each   + singular   at each visit

2.3 Adverbs as Indefinite Frequency Expressions

Many adverbs express indefinite frequency as shown in Chart 4, which also
includes idiomatic PPs.

CHART 4. EXPRESSIONS OF INDEFINITE FREQUENCY

LOW FREQUENCY		
NEVER	RARELY	OCCASIONALLY
never	rarely	occasionally
not ever	seldom	sometimes
at no time	infrequently	at times
	hardly ever	
not under any	almost never	
condition	(very) little	(every) now and then
	every so often	
	once in a blue	from time to time
	moon	on occasion
		irregularly
		sporadically

HIGH FREQUENCY		
USUAL OCCURRENCE	FREQUENTLY	ALWAYS
usually	frequently	always
commonly	often	constantly
ordinarily	repeatedly	continually
normally	recurrently	continuously
routinely		incessantly
customarily	regularly	permanently
generally	again and again	
in general	over and over	consistently
as a rule		
as a matter of course	more often than not	all the time
	many times	at all times
habitually	a lot (infml)	night and day

Exercise 7

Negative frequency adverbs cannot occur in a negative sentence. (cf. *They don't hardly ever call us.) Make a list of negative frequency adverbs, using adverbs in Columns 1 and 2 of Chart 4 and any others you think of.

Exercise 8

Choose a passage of at least three paragraphs. Identify all the frequency expressions and classify them using the groupings discussed above.

Exercise 9

Think of at least three different situations in which information about the frequency of an event is important. Then construct several questions which would elicit answers using frequency expressions from ESL students.

Example: Situation: taking medicine / seeing doctors
            Questions: How often should I take this medicine?
                          When should I take this pill?
                          How often does a well person visit the doctor?
                          A very sick person?

---

3. THE EXTERNAL SYNTAX OF TEMPORAL PHRASES

3.1 *TPs as Modifiers (Adjuncts)*

TPs of all three types occur most commonly as modifiers of VPs.

(26)

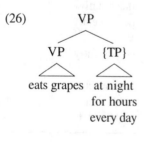

VP {TP}	(PP, NP, Adv)
eats grapes at night	(time-when)
for hours	(duration)
every day	(frequency)

There are obvious restrictions on combinations of TPs and VPs. Whether a TP can occur as the modifier of a particular VP depends on the meaning of the verb, the tense of the verb (present versus past), the aspect of the verb phrase (simple versus progressive, perfect), the presence of modals, and so on. For example, the TP and VP can co-occur in (27) but not in (28).

(27) (a) I saw her yesterday.
　　 (b) We will leave tomorrow.
　　 (c) For exercise, we run every day.
　　 (d) We have lived here all our lives.

(28) (a) *I saw her tomorrow.
　　 (b) *We are leaving yesterday.
　　 (c) *For exercise we are running every day.
　　 (d) *We live here all our lives.

TPs may also modify nouns, as in (29). (For details, see Chapter 28.)

(29) (a) the party [on Friday]
　　 (b) a scandal [last summer]

Exercise 10

Most TPs occur at the end of the VP they modify, but certain frequency expressions form an exception to this generalization. They appear preverbally, as in (1).

(1) (a) I *often* sleep late.
　　 (b) Bill has *always* been faithful to his principles.
　　 (c) My sister is *frequently* helpful.

Look over the expressions in Chart 4 and determine which frequency expressions occur preverbally. Taking the main verb, auxiliary verbs, and the negative *not* into consideration, give a rule that accounts for their placement.

3.2 TPs as Complements of Verbs

TPs occurs as complements of a small number of verbs (discussed in Chapter 10). The verbs in (30) take complements which are durational phrases of any syntactic category, while those in (31) take durational NPs.

(30) (a) *last*   The concert lasted [(for) 4 hours].
      (b) *go on*   The speech went on [all day].
      (c) *continue*   He continued [(for) another 10 minutes].
      (d) *run on*   The speaker ran on [for 2 hours].

(31) (a) *spend*   He spent [all day] on the problem.
      (b) *waste*   We wasted [several hours] playing around.
      (c) *take*   You took [five weeks] to do this project.

The verb *live* in the sense "be alive" takes a time-when phrase as complement, as do the verbs *dwell* and *reside*.

(32) He lived [in the 15th century].

TPs which are complements combine with the verb (and not the VP) to form a VP.

(33)   (a)   VP   (b)   VP

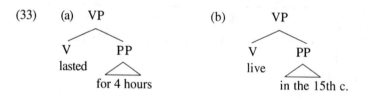

Finally, some verbs take a durational NP as subject. These include *elapse, pass, pass by, go by, slide by,* and a few others.

(34) (a) [Three hours] elapsed.
      (b) [Four years] passed.
      (c) [Several days] slid by, and I forgot to call.

UNIT III

UNPACKING THE VERB PHRASE

THE VERB is the central element of the clause. Important properties of verbs and verb phrases are explored in the seven chapters of Unit III.

Chapter 8 is an introduction to verbs and verb forms. Different forms express important verbal categories such as tense and aspect (discussed in Unit IV), which are relevant to the external syntax of the VP. Chapter 9 focuses on auxiliary verbs, which are involved in important grammatical phenomena such as inversion and negation.

The verb itself determines the internal syntax of the verb phrase, in particular what other elements may or must appear in the phrase and the form they take. The structures that must accompany a verb in order for the VP in which it appears to be grammatical (e.g. some verbs must be followed by a direct object NP or by a time-when phrase) are known as its complements, and verbs with the same complements form different subclasses. For instance, verbs which occur with a direct object form the subclass of transitive verbs. Verbs and their complements are discussed in Chapters 10—12.

A description of the complements of a verb is known as its subcategorization. Many verbs have more than one subcategorization, a topic taken up in Chapter 13.

The special properties of passive verb phrases are discussed in Chapter 14, the final chapter of the unit.

8
VERBS AND THEIR FORMS

1. A DEFINITION FOR VERBS

VERBS, like all word classes, are defined by their morphological and syntactic properties.

1.1 Syntax
Verbs are the heads of verb phrases (VPs), and, as we saw in Chapter 2, VPs combine with NPs to form clauses. The VPs in (1) contain only a head.

(1)   NP   VP
- (a) babies   *cry*
- (b) many children *died*
- (c) the people   *protested*
- (d) the women   *fainted*

1.2 Derivational Morphology
There are numerous word formation rules which apply only to verbs, as in (2) or which create new verbs, as in (3).

(2) (a) Suffixation of *-able*   Verb   → Adjective
                                read   readable
                                wash   washable
                                break   breakable

    (b) Suffixation of *-er*   Verb   → Noun
                                  write   writer
                                  read   reader
                                teach   teacher

(c) Prefixation of *re-*   Verb   →   Verb
                               read   reread
                               write   rewrite
                               decorate   redecorate

(3)   (a) Suffixation of *-ize*   Noun   →   Verb
                               colony   colonize
                               magnet   magnetize
                               priority   prioritize

   (b) Conversion of noun to verb (zero affixation)
                               Noun   →   Verb
                               bottle   (to) bottle
                               can   can
                               bag   bag
                               box   box

1.3 Inflectional Morphology

Of all the word classes in English, verbs have the largest number of inflected forms. The forms of regular verbs are constructed by adding a suffix to the base form (the citation form, the form we find in dictionaries). The past tense of *regular* verbs is expressed by the suffix /d/ (spelled <d> and <ed>. (Phonetic forms of the suffix are explored in Exercise 2.) The past tense of *irregular* verbs is expressed in different ways, often by vowel changes.

(4) Base form	*walk*	*snow*	*swim*	*ride*
Past tense form regular	*walk-ed*	*snow-ed*		
irregular			*swam*	*rode*

In the present tense, verbs show special agreement with a subject in the third person singular by means of the suffix /s/, spelled <s> and <es>. (The three phonetic forms of this suffix are explored in Exercise 3.) For other subjects, the general present form is used.

(5)   Present tense
      3rd Singular Form   *walk-s*   *kiss-es*
      General Present Form   *walk*   *kiss*

VERBS & THEIR FORMS

Most members of the class of verbs also have a present participle, formed by adding /ing/ to the base, and a past participle, formed for regular verbs by adding /d/ to the base. For irregular verbs, the past participle is formed in a number of different ways, often involving vowel changes and/or suffixation of /en/.

(6)	Present participle		*walk-ing*	*kiss-ing*
	Past participle	regular	*walk-ed*	*kiss-ed*
		irregular	*swum*	*ridden*

2. A CLOSER LOOK AT VERB FORMS

When we take into account all the forms of both regular and irregular verbs, as well as the different ways that verb forms are used, we must posit for English a system with six different forms, three finite, and three nonfinite, as shown in the chart on the following page.

The distinction between finite and nonfinite verb forms is an important one. A finite verb form is the head of a finite VP and only finite VPs function as the predicates of basic clauses (see Chapter 3). That is, finite VPs combine with NPs to form basic clauses.

(7) (a) VPs with finite verb forms → Basic Clause
          walks to school   He walks to school.
          swam two miles   Sally swam two miles.
          rode on an elephant   She rode on an elephant.

     (b) VPs with nonfinite verb forms → Not a Basic Clause
          walking to school   *he walking to school
          swum two miles   *Sally swum two miles
          ridden on an elephant   *she ridden on an
                                           elephant
          be quiet   *the baby be quiet

Nonfinite VPs have a variety of uses discussed below.

forms 1, 3, 4, and 6.

The verbs in Row D (*can, may*) are modal auxiliaries, which show syncretism between forms 2 and 3. We don't want to say that modals don't have a third singular present form, because modals are used in contexts which call for it, i.e. in the present tense with a subject in the third person singular (*he can, she must*). We say that they have an irregular third singular present form, one that lacks the suffix -*(e)s*. Modals also have irregular past tense forms.

Moreover, modal auxiliaries are defective in that they lack the three non-finite forms. Because they lack the forms, they cannot be used in contexts which require them. For example, since modals do not have a present participle form, they cannot occur in progressive verb phrases, which require one (**I am maying go home*).

Finally, the verb *be* shown in Row E is extremely irregular in English. Unlike other verbs, this verb has a base form (*be*) which is differentiated from present tense forms, and in the present tense, it has not two, but *three* forms: *am* for first person singular subject, *are* for second person or plural subject, and *is*, for third person singular subject.

(8) Present Tense Forms of the verb *be*

	Singular	Plural
1st	*am*	*are*
2nd	*are*	*are*
3rd	*is*	*are*

Thus, in spite of the fact that the overall system of verb forms and functions requires us to establish six verb forms as shown in the table above, these forms will not be differentiated by all verbs. The forms for *regular* English verbs are summarized in (9). Irregular verbs have between two and eight different forms.

(9)   Forms of Regular Verbs

1 + 6	3 + 4	2	5
Past Tense AND Past Participle	General Present AND Base	3Sg-form	Present Participle
walked	*walk*	*walks*	*walking*
laughed	*laugh*	*laughs*	*laughing*
cried	*cry*	*cries*	*crying*

3. USES OF THE SIX VERB FORMS

One justification for setting up a system of six verb forms is that it enables us to give a clear statement of the use of each of the forms.

3.1 Base Form

The base form is, first of all, the citation form, the form given in dictionaries. It is also the form used in imperatives. (See Chapter 25.)

(10)　(a)　*Write* him at once.
　　　(b)　*Swim* two more laps.
　　　(c)　*Be* quiet and *finish* your work.

Second, the base form is used in one type of subordinate clause (CP), a use often called a subjunctive in traditional grammars (see Chapter 20). Some verbs (*insist, require, demand*, among others) require a subordinate clause with base form, as in (11). (The CP with the base form is in square brackets.)

(11)　(a)　I insist [that he *write* him at once].
　　　(b)　The coach required [that the Olympic hopeful *swim* 100 laps].
　　　(c)　The judge demanded [that the prisoner *be* confined for 30 days].

Third, the base form is used in infinitive VPs, the VP of infinitive clauses. Infinitive VPs can be identified by the marker *to*, as seen in the examples of (12), where the infinitive clauses are in square brackets. (See Chapter 21.)

(12)　(a)　I prefer [for you to *win* the race tomorrow].
　　　(b)　[For Suzie to *swim* the English Channel] would be quite a feat.
　　　(c)　It would be nice [for the children to *be* a little more quiet in the library].

Finally, VPs whose head is a base form combine with other verbs, notably modal auxiliaries. (This is discussed below in 4.2 and in Chapter 9.) In (13) the VPs with heads that are base forms are in square brackets.

(13) (a) We may [*write* you a letter soon].
      (b) Suzie will [*swim* across Lake Superior tomorrow].
      (c) The children must [*be* quiet at this concert].

3.2 Present Participle

VPs whose head is a present participle combine with a form of the auxiliary verb *be* to form progressives (discussed in Chapter 17). In (14) the VPs with present participle heads are in square brackets.

(14) (a) My son is [*writing* a novel].
      (b) Suzie was [*swimming* across Lake Superior].
      (c) The baby is [*crying* again].

VPs whose head is a present participle also occur in gerundives (see Chapter 22). The gerundives in the sentences of (15) are in square brackets.

(15) (a) [Your *writing* that letter to the Post] amazed me.
      (b) [Suzie's *swimming* the Channel] surprised everyone.
      (c) I can't stand [the baby's *crying* so loudly all night].

3.3 Past Participle

The past participle form has two main uses. VPs whose head is a past participle combine with a form of the auxiliary *have* to form perfect verb phrases (discussed in Chapter 18).

(16) (a) I have [*written* many letters today].
      (b) Suzie had [*swum* the Channel many times before].
      (c) The baby has [*been* crying all night].

The past participle is also the form found in passive VPs (see Chapter 14).

(17) (a) The letters were [*written* this morning].
      (b) Those dangerous waters have never been [*swum* in].
      (c) We were [*invited* to a gala reception].

3.4 Past Tense Form

The only use of the past tense form is to express the past tense, which is discussed in Chapter 15.

(18)   (a)   I *wrote* the letter yesterday.
       (b)   The baby *cried* all night last night.
       (c)   Last month Suzie *swam* a mile every day.

3.5 Third Singular Present Tense Form

The third singular present tense form is used to express the present tense when the subject is in the third person singular. (On the present tense, see Chapter 16.)

(19)   (a)   He *writes* letters often.
       (b)   Suzie *swims* very well.
       (c)   The baby *loves* her mother.

3.6 General Present Form

Finally, the general present form is used to express the present tense when the subject is not third person singular.

(20)   (a)   I/you/we/they *write* letters often.
       (b)   I/you/we/they *cry* at sad movies.
       (c)   I/you/we/they *swim* very well.

Exercise 1

Name the form of each italicized verb in the following sentences, giving a reason for your answer.

1.   The children *played* in the park all afternoon and then *came* home to eat dinner and *watch* TV.
2.   Don't *cry* over spilt milk.
3.   I *remember* Mama and the way she always *counted* money on Friday night.
4.   The boy's face *was* badly *cut* and his arm *was* broken. He was *crying*, "The other kids made me *do* it."
5.   It *must be raining*. (Name each of the three verb forms.) Everyone *seems* wet. They all *come* in and *wipe* their feet.
6.   You *should let* children *make* their own mistakes.

7.   My mother always *let* me stay up late.
8.   Don't *hit* others even if they *hit* you.

Exercise 2

For regular verbs, the past tense form and the past participle form are constructed by adding a suffix to the base form of the verb. This suffix has three different phonetic forms. Read the following verbs out loud and figure out the three different forms of this suffix and their distribution. (Remember that phonetics has to do with sound and not spelling.)

> *walked, talked, frowned, laughed, sweated, smiled, batted played, judged, watched, nodded, grinned, buzzed, grounded, flitted, mopped, roamed, lifted, kissed, sanded, timed*

Exercise 3

For regular verbs, the third singular present form is made by adding a suffix to the base form of the verb. This suffix has several written forms (*-s, -es*) and three phonetic forms. Read the following verbs out loud and figure out the three different phonetic forms of this suffix and their distribution. (Remember that phonetics has to do with sound and not spelling.)

> *walks, talks, frowns, laughs, kisses, smiles, gushes, bags, plays, licks, judges, bites, grins, buzzes, roams, watches, mops, reaches, bids, chooses*

Exercise 4

As discussed above, the modal auxiliaries have irregular third singular present forms. In what way are these forms irregular? There are four other very common verbs in English that have phonetically irregular third singular forms. Name them and explain the irregularity.

Exercise 5

Consult a good reference grammar of English for a list of verbs that have irregular past tense and past participle forms. How many irregular verbs are there? How are they presented?

4. VERB PHRASES

Verbs function as the heads of VPs, which combine with NPs to form clauses. In the remainder of this chapter we will consider briefly some aspects of the internal and external syntax of verb phrases.

4.1 Internal Syntax

In addition to the verb, a VP can contain complements and modifiers. As noted in Chapter 2, it is the verb itself, as head of the phrase, that determines what complements can or should be present. Consider, for example, the following sentences.

(21) (a) *The enemy destroyed.
      (b)   The enemy destroyed the city.

As seen in the ungrammatical (21)(a), when we use the verb *destroy*, we must mention the thing that gets destroyed. This implied or required constituent is its complement. A description of the complements of a verb is known as its subcategorization—the verb *destroy* is subcategorized for a NP. The subcategorization of a verb is something a speaker must know in order to use it grammatically; it has to be learned when one learns the verb.

There is a formalism to represent subcategorization, known as a subcategorization frame. The frame consists of square brackets (indicating the boundaries of the VP), a line to indicate the position of the verb itself, and a listing of the complements of the verb in the order in which they occur in the VP. For example, the subcategorization frame for *destroy* is given in (22).

(22) *destroy* [_____ NP]

This frame says that a verb phrase in which *destroy* is used has two constituents. The first is the verb (represented by the blank line), and the second is a NP, its direct object. No other constituents are required.

A subcategorization frame can be translated directly into a tree diagram. The upper level of the diagram is the VP node; the lower level consists of each of the constituents mentioned in the frame. The two levels are connected by straight lines, as shown in (23), a diagram for (21)(b).

(23)   VP

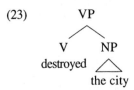

Verbs with the same subcategorization (the same array of complements) belong to the same verb type. Because of the very large number of possibilities for subcategorizations, there are a very large number of verb types, as discussed in Chapter 10.

4.2 External Syntax

In addition to understanding how verb phrases are constructed, we want to know how they are used, i.e. how they fit into larger constructions. How a VP is used depends crucially on the form of the head verb. For convenience, we name the VP by the form of its head, so that a finite VP is one whose head is a finite verb form, a present participle VP is one whose head is a present participle, and so on. A *finite* VP has only one function: it combines with a NP to form a basic clause.

On the contrary, a *nonfinite* VP does not combine directly with a NP to form a clause, as shown in the ungrammatical strings in (24) (repeated from (7)).

(24)   NP + Nonfinite VP
     (a) *he walking to school
     (b) *Sally swum two miles
     (c) *she ridden on an elephant
     (d) *the baby be quiet

Rather, nonfinite VPs commonly combine with auxiliary verbs, as shown in (25). Present participle VPs combine with a form of *be* to form a progressive, past participle VPs combine with a form of *have* to form a perfect, and so on.

(25)   Auxiliary   Nonfinite VP
     (a)   is   [walking to school]
     (b)   has   [swum two miles]
     (c)   should   [be quiet]

The auxiliary and nonfinite VP form a yet larger VP, as shown in (26). (Triangles abbreviate the internal structure of the nonfinite VP, since it is not relevant to the point under discussion.) Auxiliaries are discussed in detail in the next chapter.

(26) (a)   VP   (b)   VP

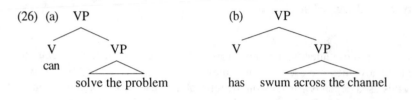

Exercise 6
What does the internal syntax of a verb phrase depend on? What does the external syntax of a verb phrase depend on?

Exercise 7
For each VP draw a tree diagram and give examples of three more verbs that have the subcategorization indicated, using the verbs in sentences.

1.   love my children   *love*   [_____ NP]
2.   give the children a present   *give*   [_____ NP NP]
3.   report the accident to the police   *report* [_____ NP PP*]
     *The preposition in this PP must be *to*.
4.   seem rather silly   *seem*   [_____ AdjP]
5.   should love my children   *should* [_____ VP_{Base}*]
     *"VP_{Base}" stands for "a VP whose head is the base form."

9

AUXILIARIES, INVERSION, AND NEGATION

IN THIS CHAPTER we explore some important aspects of the syntax of verb phrases in English. In the first section we discuss the syntactic and semantic properties of auxiliary verbs. In the second, we explore the rule of Inversion, a rule involved in forming yes-no questions, and in the third, the expression of negation.

1. AUXILIARY VERBS

Auxiliary verbs, sometimes known as helping verbs, are opposed to lexical verbs. Unlike lexical verbs, auxiliaries do not contribute lexical meaning to the sentence, but express aspectual or modal meanings. The subclass of auxiliary verbs is a closed class whose members are listed in (1).

(1)   (a) *have*
      (b) *be*
      (c) modals: *can, may, will, shall, must*
                      could, might, would, should
      (d) *do*

Each of the auxiliaries in (1) combines with a nonfinite VP, as shown schematically in (2). The auxiliary determines the *form* of the head of the VP.

(2)   VP

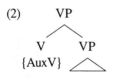

    V   VP
 {AuxV}

It is important to distinguish the auxiliary verbs *have* and *do* from lexical verbs with identical phonetic form. The lexical verbs are not subcategorized for VPs; they have the subcategorizations given in (3).

(3)   Lexical Verbs
    (a) *have* "possession"   [____ NP]
    (b) *do* "make, fix"   [____ NP]

(4)   (a) I *have* a house on Maple Street.
    (b) You should *do* the dishes now.
    (c) They don't *do* windows.

We will have nothing further to say about the lexical verbs, since this chapter is concerned only with auxiliaries.

The syntax and semantics of auxiliary verbs are discussed below. Syntactically, they differ in terms of the kinds of VPs they combine with. Semantically, they differ in the modifications to meaning they make.

1.1 The Auxiliary Verb have

The syntax of the auxiliary *have* is this: It combines with a VP whose head is a past participle, as in (5). Its subcategorization frame is given in (6) and a tree diagram in (7).

(5)   (a) We   *have*   [seen that movie].
    (b) You   *have*   [been students for a long time].
    (c) The lawyer   *has*   [given the car away].

(6)   *have*   [____ VP$_{\text{Past Participle}}$]

(7)

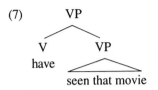

A finite VP headed by the auxiliary *have* forms a verbal construction known as a perfect. If *have* is in the present tense, it is a present perfect; if *have* is in the past tense, it is a past perfect. (See Chapter 18.) VPs headed by the auxiliary *have* are also used to indicate past time in nonfinite VPs (see Chapter 15, Section 6).

1.2 The Auxiliary Verb be

The auxiliary verb *be* combines with a VP whose head is a present participle. VPs formed in this way express progressive aspect (see Chapter 17). Examples are given in (8), the subcategorization frame in (9), and a tree diagram in (10).

(8) (a) Mary   *was*   [drinking tea].
     (b) John   *was*   [being obnoxious].
     (c) Their son   *is*   [walking the dog].
     (d) They   *were* [studying all day].

(9) *be*   [_____ VP$_{\text{Present Part}}$]

(10)   VP
      /   \
     V   VP
    was   /‾‾‾‾‾\
        drinking tea

The auxiliary verb *be* is also subcategorized for a predicate NP or an AP. This use of an auxiliary verb is unusual in that there is no lexical verb at all. The auxiliary is the *only* verb in the clause.

(11) (a) Pat   *is*   [a lawyer].
      (b) Mike   *is*   [a good student].
      (c) You   *were*   [very obnoxious].

(12) *be*   [_____ NP$_{Pred}$]
                  [_____ AP]

(13) (a)   VP   (b)   VP

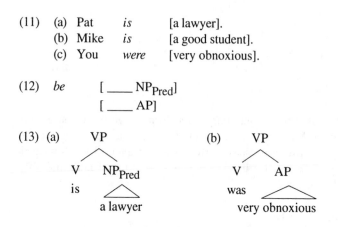

1.3 *The Modal Auxiliaries*

Modal auxiliaries express a variety of modal meanings such as possibility, probability, necessity, obligation, habituality, and volition. The modals of (14) are italicized. What kind of VP do they combine with? State it in the form of a subcategorization frame and draw a tree diagram.

(14) (a) She   *may*   [be sleeping].
      (b) They   *might*   [have walked the dog].
      (c) I   *will*   [have finished studying].
      (d) He   *should*   [give the car away].
      (e) The children *must*   [be quiet while I'm talking].

Modals combine with a VP whose head is _____.

The subcategorization frame for modals is _____.

Tree diagram:

1.4 The Auxiliary Verb do

The auxiliary *do* combines with a VP whose head is a base form. Examples are given in (15), the subcategorization frame in (16), and a corresponding tree diagram in (17).

(15) (a) That guy certainly   *does*   [talk quickly].
     (b) You   *do*   [drink tea], don't you?
     (c) He   *doesn't*   [eat meat].

(16) *do*   [_____ VP$_{Base}$]

(17)   VP
        /   \
       V   VP
       do   /   \
          drink tea

Unlike the others, this auxiliary makes no contribution at all to the semantics of the clause; i.e. it does not modify the meaning of the lexical verb. It is a "dummy auxiliary" used when a phonological or syntactic operation requires an auxiliary, but the sentence does not otherwise contain one.

1.5 More than One Auxiliary

Finally, note that it is possible to have more than one auxiliary verb in the same clause. As the examples in (18) show, a modal auxiliary may combine with a VP whose head is the auxiliary *have* (as in (18)(a) and (b)), the auxiliary *have* may combine with a VP whose head is the auxiliary *be* ((18)(c) and (d)), and so on.

(18) (a) They   *may*   *have*   gone by now.
     (b) You   *must*   *have*   checked the doors.
     (c) He   *has*   *been*   playing cards all night.
     (d) You   *have*   *been*   staring at me for some time.
     (e) She   *will*   *be*   starting work next week.
     (f) They   *should* *be*   arriving in New York now.

These VPs have several levels, each consisting of an auxiliary verb and a verb phrase, built up following the patterns discussed above. As we saw, a modal auxiliary combines with a verb phrase whose head is a base form, so the highest VP level for (18)(a), for example, consists of the modal auxiliary *may* as its head and the VP [*have gone by now*] as its second constituent, as shown in (19)(a).

(19) (a)

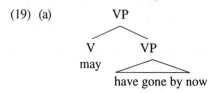

The internal structure of the VP [*have gone by now*] consists of the auxiliary verb *have* as its head and the VP [*gone by now*] as its second constituent, as in (19)(b).

(19) (b)

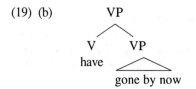

The combination of the two trees gives three levels of structure shown in (19)(c).

(19) (c)

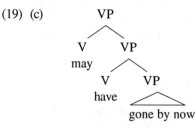

Though it is possible to have more than one auxiliary verb in the same clause, not every combination is allowed. For instance, the examples in (20) are all ungrammatical.

(20) (a) *They   *have*   *may(ed)*   go.
      (b) *You   *have*   *must(ed)*   check the doors.
      (c) *He   *is*   *having*   played cards all night.
      (d) *You   *are*   *having*   stared at me.
      (e) *She   *is*   *will(ing)* start work.
      (f) *They   *are*   *should(ing)* arrive in New York City.

We can explain why some of these combinations are bad. The ungrammaticality of (20)(a) and (b) is due to the fact that the auxiliary *have* combines with a VP whose head is a past participle form, but modals lack that form (as discussed in Chapter 8). Similarly, the ungrammaticality in (20)(e) and (f) is due to the fact that the auxiliary *be* combines with a VP whose head is a present participle, but modals do not have that form either.

The auxiliary *do* combines only with a lexical verb; it does not combine with VPs headed by other auxiliaries. This is due to the fact, noted above, that the auxiliary *do* is used only when there are no other auxiliaries in the sentence.

(21) (a) *I   *may*   *do*   go shopping tomorrow.
      (b) *We   *have*   *done*   go shopping.
      (c) *We   *do*   *have*   go shopping.

Exercise 1
When there is more than one auxiliary verb in a single clause, the auxiliaries must appear in a particular order. Using the sentences of (18), (20), and (21), and any others you wish to consider, figure out what that order is. (Do not use passives in doing this exercise.)

Exercise 2
Draw tree diagrams for each of the following verb phrases. Don't draw the internal structure of the VP headed by the lexical verb; use a triangle as in the example.

Example: can visit you tomorrow

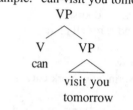

1.   may stay overnight
2.   were singing in the rain
3.   have seen a ghost
4.   might have broken her arm
5.   could be starting college next year
6.   should have been sleeping by now
7.   will buy the food and cook dinner
8.   must stay in bed and take medicine every four hours
9.   should do your math homework and must finish your history test

---

2. INVERSION

2.1 The Rule of Inversion

Clauses are composed of an NP and a VP. In basic clauses the subject NP precedes the VP, as in the declarative sentences of (22).

(22)   NP   VP
      (a)   Wanita   can swim.
      (b)   The baby   is crying.
      (c)   They   have written the letter.

In yes-no questions, however, there is a different order, as in (23).

(23) (a)   Can   Wanita swim?
      (b)   Is   the baby crying?
      (c)   Have   they written the letter?

The process involved in the formation of questions is called inversion; it reverses the order of the subject NP and an auxiliary verb. A preliminary version of the rule of inversion is given in (24).

(24)   Inversion #1:   Invert the subject and the auxiliary verb.

What happens in sentences without an auxiliary, like those in (25)?

(25)   (a) Sally likes fish.
       (b) Peter golfs.
       (c) They have a house in Centreville.

Lexical verbs cannot invert with the subject. When there is no auxiliary, the dummy auxiliary *do* is used, as in (26).

(26)   (a) Does Sally like fish?
       (b) Does Peter golf?
       (c) Do they have a house in Centreville?

In sentences that contain more than one auxilary verb, only the *first* auxiliary is inverted, as in (27) and (28).

(27)   (a) She should have left already.
       (b) You have been cheating again.
       (c) They will be studying all day.

(28)   (a) Should she have left already?
       (b) Have you been cheating again?
       (c) Will they be studying all day?

A revision of the rule of inversion which takes these facts into account is given in (29).

(29) Inversion #2:   Invert the subject and the *first* auxiliary verb.
                     If there is no auxiliary, add the auxiliary *do*.

2.2 *The Syntax of Inversion*

The statement of inversion in (29) correctly describes the switch in word order that we find in yes-no questions, but does not indicate the syntactic structure that results. We adopt an analysis in which the rule of inversion moves the auxiliary out of its clause to form a new constituent with it, as in (30). The new constituent is labeled S_2 in (30); the original position of the auxiliary is marked with a blank line.

(30) (a)   Declarative   (b)   Interrogative

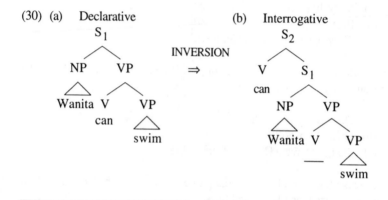

Exercise 3

Inversion has other uses in English. For example, it applies when certain adverbials occur in sentence initial position, as in (1).

(1)   (a)   Never have I seen such a mess!
      (b)   *Never I have seen such a mess!

There are other adverbials in English that "cause" inversion when they appear in sentence initial position. Find at least four and use them in sentences. Is inversion in these cases optional or obligatory?

Exercise 4

Has the rule of inversion applied in the following sentence? Give a reason for your answer.

(1)   Here comes the bride!

Exercise 5

When speakers of English want to disagree with a negative statement, they can use contrastive stress in a corresponding positive sentence. (Contrastive stress is indicated with small capitals.)

Speaker A: You won't like it.   Speaker B: I WILL like it.
                   Kim can't do that.   Kim CAN do it.
                   They wouldn't know.   They WOULD know.

What element in the clause receives contrastive stress? Figure this out not just for the three sentences above, but for English in general, by examining other sentences as well.

Exercise 6

Draw tree diagrams for the following sentences. (Use triangles to abbreviate the internal structure of phrases headed by lexical verbs.)

1.   You should help us.
2.   Should you help us?
3.   The baby was drinking milk.
4.   Was the baby drinking milk?
5.   Are you crazy?
6.   Must he be so obnoxious?

Exercise 7

When *not* is used to negate an entire clause, it must appear in a particular position in the clause. Examine the following sentences, and any others you wish to consider, and state a general rule for the placement of *not*.

Grammatical
(1)   She will not help us.
(2)   They must not win the game.
(3)   She is not very tall.
(4)   I am not going to give in.
(5)   They have not finished their assignment.
(6)   We are not doctors; we are teachers.

Not Grammatical
(1)   *She not will help us.
(2)   *She will help not us.
(3)   *They not must win the game.
(4)   *They must win not the game.
(5)   *She not is very tall.
(6)   *They not have finished.
(7)   *They have finished not.
(8)   *Not they have finished their assignment.

---

3. NEGATION

In English the negation of a constituent is often expressed syntactically with the word *not,* which combines with members of nearly every syntactic category, as shown in (31). It forms a constituent of the same syntactic category as the one it combines with, as in (32).

(31)   (a)   I tried [not to laugh].
        (b)   I prefer [not going].
        (c)   Who do you like?   [Not John.]
        (d)   [Not everyone] was pleased with the outcome.
        (e)   When should we meet?   [Not in the morning.]
        (f)   She was wearing [not white], but red.

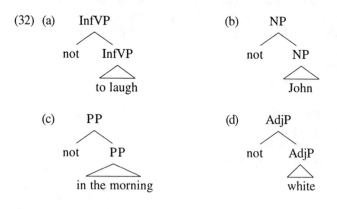

Not occurs in a different position when it expresses the negation of a finite clause. It comes after the (first) auxiliary verb, as in (33). Structurally, it combines with the verb to form a "compound" verb, as in (34).

(33)   (a)   We may not arrive on time.
      (b)   You cannot watch TV tonight.
      (c)   I'm not a doctor.

(34)   (a)   (b)

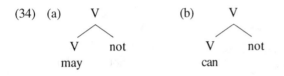

Post-auxiliary *not* is ordinarily unstressed and most often contracted: It loses its vowel and is pronounced (and written) like a suffix on the verb, as shown in (35).

(35)   (a)   I wasn't ready.
      (b)   We haven't eaten yet.
      (c)   You can't watch TV.
      (d)   They aren't coming to my party.

(36)   (a)   V   (b)   V
            | |
        wasn't   can't

Not all auxiliaries allow the contraction of *not*, but if an auxiliary and negative *can* contract, they *must* contract. In sentences where an unstressed negative has not contracted, it does not negate the clause as a whole, but only the VP that follows it. Note the subtle, but real, difference between (37) (a) and (b).

(37)   (a)   I couldn't go to the party.
      (b)   I could not go to the party.

The word *not* in (37)(a) negates the clause as a whole and can be paraphrased, "It was not the case that I could go to the party." The negation in (37)(b), on the other hand, negates the VP *go to the party*. It can be paraphrased, "One of my options is to not go to the party." This semantic difference is reflected in the corresponding tree diagrams.

(38)   (a)   Clause Negation   (b)   Verb Phrase Negation

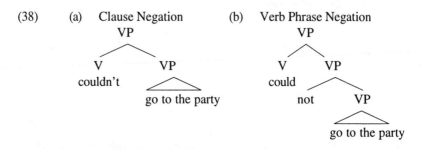

The word *not* does not contract when it receives special emphasis or is in contrast, in which case it is pronounced with primary stress. In (39) stress is indicated with small capitals.

(39)   (a)   You are happy.   I am NOT happy.
       (b)   They were ready.   They were NOT ready.
       (c)   You could go to the party.
             I could NOT go to the party.

Exercise 8
Which auxiliaries allow contraction of *not* and which ones do not? Consider the all inflected forms of each of the auxiliary verbs given in (1). Is the phonetic form of the contraction always predictable? (Pay attention to the number of syllables.) Be prepared to explain your answer.

Exercise 9
Can negative auxiliaries (*can't, don't, shouldn't*, etc.) undergo inversion? Can an auxiliary verb plus uncontracted *not* undergo inversion? Give examples to support your answers.

Exercise 10

Examine the following sentences and state a rule to account for the distribution of the words *too* and *either*.

(1)   (a)   I'm going to the movies, and Mary is going to the movies.
      (b)   I'm going to the movies, and Mary is, too.
      (c)   *I'm going to the movies, and Mary is, neither.

(2)   (a)   Sheep doesn't like fish, and Charlie doesn't like fish.
      (b)   Sheep doesn't like fish, and Charlie doesn't, either.
      (c)   *Sheep doesn't like fish, and Charlie doesn't, too.

(3)   (a)   I don't eat meat. My sister is a vegetarian, too.
      (b)   My sister is a vegetarian. I don't eat meat, either.

Exercise 11

Draw tree diagrams for the following sentences. Use triangles to abbreviate the internal structure of NPs and VPs headed by lexical verbs.

1.   The children were not prepared for the play.
2.   The adults struggled not to laugh at them.
3.   They didn't want to hurt their feelings.
4.   The main characters couldn't remember their lines.
5.   Weren't you embarrassed?

Exercise 12

In this chapter a number of different properties of modal auxiliary verbs were given. Make a list of these properties and, using the list, decide whether the word *need* is a modal auxiliary. It may help to consider the sentences below. (The question mark in (1)(f) indicates an uncertain grammaticality judgement.)

(1)   (a)   You need to go.
      (b)   *You need go.
      (c)   You don't need to go.
      (d)   You needn't go.
      (e)   Do you need to go?
      (f)   ?Need you really go?
      (g)   One need only reflect for a moment ...
      (h)   He needs to be more patient.
      (i)   *She need to save some money for college.

Using data similar to that in (1), decide whether the verbs *dare* and *ought* are modal auxiliaries.

10
VERBS AND THEIR COMPLEMENTS

CONSIDER THE UNGRAMMATICAL SENTENCES in (1). Can you say why they are ungrammatical?

(1) (a) *The enemy captured the town and destroyed completely.
     (b) Here is your chair. *Where should I put?
     (c) *Why did he say me those things?

The ungrammaticality of these sentences is due to the verbs *destroy*, *put*, and *say*. Like all verbs, they impose certain requirements on the verb phrases they occur in, and if those requirements are not met, the resulting sentence is ungrammatical. The requirements of a verb are known as its complements. The verb not only dictates the presence of complements, it dictates their form. For example, the verb *destroy* implies the existence of something which is destroyed, which must be expressed as an NP, and not, for example, as a PP.

The description of the complements of a verb is known as its subcategorization, expressed formally with a subcategorization frame. The frame for *destroy* is shown in (2).

(2) *destroy* [_____ NP]

Verbs that have the same subcategorization (the same array of complements) form subcategories, or subclasses. In this chapter 11 major subclasses of English verbs are presented. They divide into two groups: Transitive verbs, which are subcategorized for an argument NP, and intransitive verbs, which are not.

1. MAJOR TYPES OF INTRANSITIVE VERBS

1.1 Pure Intransitive Verbs

Some verbs don't take any complements at all. They don't imply the existence of any other person or thing besides the subject. These verbs, which appear alone in the most minimal VP, are pure intransitive verbs. Examples from this rather small subclass are given in (3).

(3) Subcategorization frame for pure intransitives: [_____]
   (a) God   *exists.*
   (b) The problems *disappeared.*
   (c) Mary was   *standing.*
   (d) The baby   *slept.*
   (e) My brother   *cried.*

1.2 Linking Verbs

Verbs that take a predicate noun phrase or an adjective phrase as complement are called linking verbs, since the verb serves as a link between the subject and the predicate NP or AP which describes it. A sample of verbs in this rather small subclass is given in (4). The verb is in italics and the complement in square brackets.

(4) Subcategorization frames for linking verbs:
   [_____ NP$_{Pred}$]
   [_____ AP]
   (a) She   *is* [a doctor].
   (b) They   *are* [rather nice].
   (c) My daughter *became* [a doctor].
   (d) They   *became* [quite considerate].

1.3 Intransitive Verbs Subcategorized for an Adverbial Complement

Some intransitive verbs are subcategorized for an adverbial complement. Although adverbials are usually optional constituents of the sentence (see Chapter 4), an adverbial complement is usually obligatory. Without it, the sentence either has a different meaning or is ungrammatical.

Most verbs in this subclass require a place adverbial, as in (5). A very small number of verbs are subcategorized for a time adverbial as in (6). (The verb is in italics and the the adverbial complement in square brackets.)

(5)   Subcategorization frame: [____ PlP]
        ↳ where; express the place

      (a)   She   *is* [at home].
      (b)   They   *live* [in Cleveland].
      (c)   I   *snuck* [into the museum].

(6)   Subcategorization frame: [____ TP]
        ↳ when; duration of time

      (a)   They   *lived* [in the 18th century].
      (b)   The war   *lasted* [two weeks].
      (c)   The test   *took* [an hour].

1.4 Intransitive Verbs Subcategorized for a Preposition

Some verbs require a complement with a specific preposition. For example, the verb *rely* always occurs with the preposition *on* , as in (7).

(7)   (a)   I relied on his help.
      (b)   *I relied.

Moreover, with this verb no other preposition is possible. Because we don't say: *rely for her*, *rely to her*, *rely at her*, etc., the subcategorization frame for this verb must list as complement a prepositional phrase whose head is *on*.

Subcategorization frame for *rely*:   [____ PP*]   *P = *on*

Examples of the many verbs subcategorized for a particular preposition are given in (8), followed by their subcategorizations in (9).

(8)   (a)   The professor   *referred* [to a very expensive grammar book].
      (b)   We might   *indulge* [in a little entertainment].
      (c)   You should   *call* [on your neighbors more often].

(9)   (a)   *refer*   [____ PP*]   *P = *to*
      (b)   *indulge*   [____ PP*]   *P = *in*
      (c)   *call*   [____ PP*]   *P = *on*

1.5 Intransitive Verbs Subcategorized for a Particle

Some intransitive verbs require a specific particle as complement. (As discussed in Chapter 5, a particle is a preposition without a complement.) For example, *pass* when it means "faint" always occurs with the particle *out*, as in (10).

(10)   She passed out.

Since the particle *out* is a complement of the verb *pass* (in the meaning "faint"), it must be listed in its subcategorization frame. When *pass* occurs without this particle it has a different meaning and is, therefore, a different verb. (Particle is abbreviated "Par".) Other examples are given in (11), followed by their subcategorizations in (12).

Subcategorization frame for *pass* ("faint"): [____ Par*]   *Par = *out*

(11)   (a)   I couldn't listen any longer, but Peter *went* [on], anyway.
         (b)   Suzie became very faint and then *passed* [out].
         (c)   Later she *came* [to].
         (d)   Things are finally *looking* [up].

(12)   Verb   Meaning   Subcategorization
         (a)   *go*   "continue"   [____ Par*]   *Par = *on*
         (b)   *come*   "regain consciousness"   [____ Par*]   *Par = *to*
         (c)   *look*   "improve"   [____ Par*]   *Par = *up*

Verbs which are subcategorized for a specific preposition or particle are known as multi-word verbs. These idiomatic combinations are the topic of Chapter 11. In addition to the five types of intransitive verbs given above, there are intransitives subcategorized for VPs (the auxiliary verbs of Chapter 9) and intransitives subcategorized for clauses (that-clauses, infinitive clauses, etc., the topic of Unit V).

No direct object in these
5 kinds of intransitive verbs

2. MAJOR TYPES OF TRANSITIVE VERBS → *have an object.*

2.1 Monotransitive Verbs

Verbs which are subcategorized for a single argument NP (a direct object) are monotransitive verbs, a very large class of verbs in English.

(13) Subcategorization frame for monotransitive verbs: [____ NP]
    (a) She   *kissed* [her Dad].   *↳object*
    (b) The girl   *touched* [his hand].
    (c) Let's   *wash* [the car].
    (d) They   *killed* [the goldfish].
    (e) The coach *demonstrated* [a new technique].

→ this is last #6 so that the others stay in comparative order w/ the intransitive verbs.

2.2 Ditransitive Verbs

Verbs whose complements include two argument noun phrases are called ditransitives verbs. The first object is an indirect object, the second one a direct object. *It can also be [___ NP PP] see next pg*

(14) Subcategorization frame for ditransitive verbs: [____ NP NP]

	Verb	IndObj	DirObj
(a) They	*gave*	Sally	the present.
(b) Let's	*show*	the teacher	the classroom.
(c) Sam	*threw*	his father	the ball.
(d) They	*told*	me	the bad news.

2.3 Complex Transitive Verbs *as w/ intransitive linking, verbs just add an extra NP preceding other phrases.*

Complex transitive verbs take a direct object and a predicate NP or adjective phrase as their complements. Some examples of this subclass, which is not very large, are given in (15).

(15) Subcategorization frames for complex transitives:
    [____ NP NP$_{Pred}$]
    [____ NP AP]

		DirObj	NP$_{Pred}$
(a) The people	*elected*	Smith	president.
(b) The action	*made*	him	a hero.

(15)   DirObj   AP
  (c) Let's   *paint*   our room   blue.
  (d) We should   *keep*   the salad   cold.

2.4 Transitive Verbs Subcategorized for an Adverbial Complement

Some verbs are subcategorized for a direct object and an adverbial complement, most often a place phrase.

(handwritten: again just add NP)

(16) Subcategorization frame: [___ NP PlP]
  (a) We   *put*   the car   in the garage.
  (b) She   *took*   the child   to the doctor.
  (c) They   *keep*   the car   in the garage.

2.5 Transitive Verbs Subcategorized for a Preposition

Some transitive verbs require a complement with a specific preposition. For example, the verb *blame* takes a direct object and a prepositional phrase with *on*.

(17) (a) She blamed the accident on me.
  (b) *She blamed the accident.

Note that the only possible preposition is *on*. Since we don't say: *blame the accident to me*, *blame the accident for me*, etc., the subcategorization frame for the verb *blame* must list a NP and a PP whose head is *on*. The word *on* itself must be mentioned. Other examples are given in (18).

(handwritten: add)

Subcategorization for *blame*:   [___ NP PP*]   *P = *on*

(handwritten: the same as intransitive)

(18) (a) We   *congratulated*   him   on his manners.
  (b) They   *dedicated*   this article   to us.
  (c) They   *deprived*   the prisoner   of access to a lawyer.

(19) (a) *congratulate* [___ NP PP*] *P = *on*
  (b) *dedicate*   [___ NP PP*] *P = *to*
  (c) *deprive*   [___ NP PP*] *P = *of*

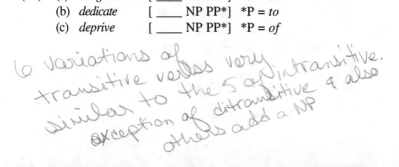

2.6 Transitive Verbs Subcategorized for a Particle

Some verbs take an argument noun phrase and a particle as complements. For example, the verb *turn*, when it means 'illuminate,' requires a noun phrase and the particle *on* (*turn the light on*). Since we don't say **turn the light* (to express the meaning 'illuminate'), the particle *on* must be mentioned in the subcategorization frame of the verb *turn*. Other examples are given in (20).

Subcategorization for *turn* "illuminate"   [___ NP Par*]   *Par = on

(20) (a) We   *looked*   the answer   up.
      (b) She   *pointed* the problem   out.
      (c) Harvard   *turns*   most applicants   down.

(21) (a) *look*   "refer to"   [___ NP Par*] *Par = up
      (b) *point*   "call attention to" [___ NP Par*] *Par = out
      (c) *turn*   "reject"   [___ NP Par*] *Par = down

In addition to the six types of transitive verbs listed here, there are transitives that are subcategorized for an NP and a VP (see Chapter 14) and others subcategorized for a NP and a clause (see Unit V).

3. VERBS WITH MORE THAN ONE SUBCATEGORIZATION

Some verbs take more than one array of complements. For example, in (22)(a) *demonstrate* is used as a transitive verb, but in (22)(b) it is used as an intransitive.

(22) (a) Julia Child demonstrated a new technique for boiling water.
      (b) The protesters demonstrated in front of the White House.

The change in subcategorization is accompanied by a change in meaning. The transitive *demonstrate* means to show or describe something (a way of doing something, a technique), while the intransitive *demonstrate* means to take part in a public show of feeling or opposition. This is a case of homophony, where two different verbs, with different meanings and different subcategorizations, happen to have the same phonetic form.

In other cases, however, the same verb in the same meaning may appear with a different array of complements, as in (23) - (25). Because the change in complement structure doesn't correlate with a change in meaning, we don't consider these to be homophony.

(23)   (a)   Gena was knitting a sweater.
       (b)   Gena was knitting.

(24)   (a)   They gave Irma the present.
       (b)   They gave the present to Irma.

(25)   (a)   Let's show the teacher the classroom.
       (b)   Let's show the classroom to the teacher.

There are many verbs in English that appear with more than one array of complements. This phenomenon, known as dual subcategorization, is explored further in Chapter 13.

Exercise 1

In this chapter, 11 subclasses of verbs were presented. Make a list of these subclasses and their subcategorization frames and add five more examples to each subclass. Use the verbs in sentences to demonstrate that they have the subcategorization you think they do. Your sentences should not be passives or questions.

Exercise 2

Give the subcategorization frame for each italicized verb in the following sentences. (Though the verb may have more than one subcategorization, give only the one shown in the sentence.) Be careful to distinguish verbs which require particular prepositions or particles from those which require place phrases. *Place phrase - be able to replace it with the word, "there."*

Example: We *keep* our cat in the basement.
           Subcat frame for *keep*:   [_____ NP PlP]

1. The Flick Co. is *marketing* a new squirt gun.
2. I wondered why my daughter *sounded* so surprised.
3. The Queen has *christened* the new battleship The Good Ship Lollipop.
4. The player *stepped* out of bounds and was declared ineligible.
5. Who *knows* the answer to this question?
6. The sheriff *pointed* to problems in the security system as the cause of the break-in.
7. That sweet old lady *sent* all her neighbors a box of candy.
8. She *leaned* the umbrella against the couch.
9. My uncle *made* me a new bed and bedside table.
10. On her birthday, the children *made* their mother Queen-for-the-Day.

Exercise 3 For Discussion

Do students of English need to know the subcategorizations for the verbs they are learning? If so, how can this information best be presented to them?

Exercise 4 For Discussion

Many textbooks for ESL students recognize the difficulty that students have with verbs subcategorized for particular prepositions and often give lists of such verbs. Different lists can contain different kinds of information, however. Look over the two lists of verb-preposition combinations below. What information is present in List B but absent in List A? Is this information important? Try to imagine that you don't know what these words mean or how to use them. Which list would you find more helpful and why?

(List A is adapted from Azar 1989:A24-A25 and List B from Robinson 1989:301-4. In both, verbs have been added and deleted to make them more comparable.)

LIST A	LIST B
accuse of	accuse (someone) of (something)
agree with	agree with (someone) about (something)
apologize for	apologize to (someone) for (something)
apply to, for	apply to (an institution or organization)
	apply for (a job, admission, membership)
approve of	approve of (someone or something)
argue with, about	argue with (someone) about (something)
arrive in, at	arrive in (a city, state, country)
	arrive at (a building, activity, general location)
believe in	believe in (something / someone)
blame for	blame (someone) for (something)
borrow from	borrow (something) from (someone)
break up	break up (with someone)
care about, for	care about (someone / something)
	care for (someone / something)
complain about	complain to (someone) about (something)
count (up)on	count on (someone / something) for (something)
cover with	cover (someone / something) with (something)
decide (up)on	decide on (something)
distinguish from	distinguish (something) from (something)
disagree with	disagree with (someone) about (something)
dream of, about	dream about / of (someone / something)
escape from	escape from (something / someplace)
excel in	excel in (something)
excuse for	excuse (someone) for (something)
fight for	fight with (someone) about (something)
forgive for	forgive (someone) for (something)
hide from	hide (something) from (someone)
insist (up)on	insist on (something)
prevent from	prevent (someone) from (something)
protect from	protect (someone) from (something)
provide with	provide (someone) with (something)
recover from	recover from (an illness)
rely (up)on	rely on (someone / something) for (something)
rescue from	rescue (someone) from (something)

4. INTERNAL SYNTAX OF VERB PHRASES

As noted at the end of Chapter 8, a subcategorization frame can be translated directly into a tree diagram. The upper level of the diagram is the VP node; the lower level contains the verb and its complements, each connected to the VP node by a straight line. Diagrams for three intransitive verb phrases are given in (26) and for transitive ones, in (27).

(26)   (a)   Pure intransitive verb: [_____]

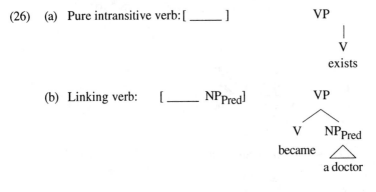

       (b)   Linking verb: [_____ NP_Pred]

       (c)   Intransitive verb subcategorized for a particular preposition:
             rely [_____ PP*]   *P = on*

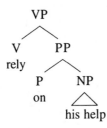

(27)   (a)   Ditransitive verb: *give* [_____ NP NP]

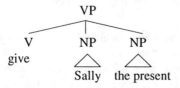

(b) Complex transitive verb: *paint* [_____ NP AP]

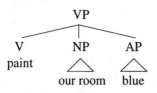

(c) Transitive verb with particle: *turn* [_____ NP Par*]

*Par = *on*

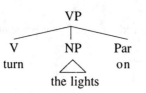

Exercise 5

Draw tree diagrams for the following sentences. Use triangles as abbreviations for the internal structure of the noun phrases.

1. The expert witness disappeared.
2. Sam threw his father the ball.
3. We stared at the clown.
4. Those naughty children snuck into the museum.
5. The composer dedicated the new quartet to her beloved mother.
6. I considered you a reliable witness.
7. The lights should go out.
8. The artist will paint the back wall of this room a new shade of blue.
9. The car shuddered and died.
10. You are a liar and a thief.

Exercise 6

As noted briefly above, some verbs have more than one subcategorization. Considering the pairs of sentences below, give the two subcategorization frames for the verbs *open* and *boil*. Then, in a sentence or two characterize the difference between the sentences in (a) and (b).

(1) (a) The door opened.
(b) Someone opened the door.

(2) (a) The water boiled.
(b) The assistant boiled the water.

Exercise 7

Give a reason for the ungrammaticality of each of the sentences in (1).

DITRANSITIVES AND INDIRECT OBJECT MOVEMENT

1. TWO SUBCATEGORIZATIONS

AS DISCUSSED ABOVE, ditransitive verbs are subcategorized for two argument noun phrases. The first, the indirect object, is often a person, the recipient or benefactive of the verbal action. The second, the direct object, is often an inanimate entity, the thing that moves or changes possession as a result of the action.

(1)

			IndObj	DirObj
(a)	Santa	may bring	the children	a sack of toys.
(b)	John	gave	Mary	a book.
(c)	The mother	sang	her baby	a sweet song.
(d)	The farmer	showed	Peter	his corn field.

Add five more ditransitive verbs to this list and use them in sentences.

Many ditransitives have a second subcategorization, in which they occur with a noun phrase and a prepositional phrase, as in (2) - (4).

(2)   (a)   Santa may bring the children a sack of toys.
         (b)   Santa may bring a sack of toys to the children.

(3)   (a)   John gave Mary a book.
         (b)   John gave a book to Mary.

(4)   (a)   The mother sang her baby a sweet song.
         (b)   The mother sang a sweet song to her baby.

Put your sentences in this alternative form, if possible. Then write out the two different subcategorization frames for these verbs.

Subcategorization 1: _____

Subcategorization 2: _____

Consider the meaning of the sentences (2) - (4). Is there any difference in meaning between the sentences in (a) and those in (b)?

2. INDIRECT OBJECT MOVEMENT - A RULE?

Some linguists have proposed that these pairs of sentences are related by a rule, sometimes called indirect object movement. (It is also known as dative movement, because in languages which have overt case marking such as German or Russian, the indirect object is in the dative case.) Assume *for the moment* that there is such a rule in English. The proposed rule would apply to a ditransitive like the (a) sentences above and change it to the structures shown in the (b) sentences. State in words of English what this rule would do. Your statement should be as clear as possible, making use of the syntactic terminology you have learned.

The proposed rule of indirect object movement would run into complications, however. First, compare the following sentences with those in (2) - (4). Why are the starred sentences ungrammatical?

(5) (a) *Santa may bring the children it.
     (b)   Santa may bring it to the children.

(6) (a) *John gave Mary it.
     (b)   John gave it to Mary.

(7) (a) *The mother sang the baby it.
     (b)   The mother sang it to the baby.

We could prevent the ungrammatical sentences from occurring if we added a specific condition to the rule of indirect object movement. What would it be?

The sentences in (8) and (9) present a second complication for the proposed rule. How do these differ from the sentences in (2) - (4)?

(8)   (a)   The children baked their mother a cake.
        (b)   The children baked a cake for their mother.

(9)   (a)   Margaret played her boyfriend a song.
        (b)   Margaret played a song for her boyfriend.

There are still further complications for the proposed rule. What do the sentences of (10) and (11) show?

(10)   (a)   That book cost the professor a fortune.
        (b)   *That book cost a fortune to the professor.

(11)   (a)   Regretfully, we must refuse John his request.
        (b)   *Regretfully, we must refuse his request to John.
        (c)   *Regretfully, we must refuse John's request to him.

The three complications show that (1) the rule of indirect object movement would have to be *obligatory* if the direct object is a pronoun; (2) some verbs require the preposition *to*, while others require *for*; (3) there are ditransitive verbs that do *not* undergo indirect object movement. A speaker must know for each verb whether it undergoes the rule or not and which preposition is added.

Since syntactic rules operate on structure and should be blind to particular words in the structure, we conclude that the proposed rule does not describe a general syntactic process of English. For these reasons, we reject the rule of indirect object movement. We treat the phenomenon discussed in this worksheet as an instance of dual subcategorization, discussed further in Chapter 13.

11

MULTI-WORD VERBS: PHRASAL VERBS AND PREPOSITIONAL VERBS

SOMETIMES STUDENTS OF English produce sentences like those in (1).

(1)   (a) *We need to pick out some milk for dinner.
       (b) *He will call up me this evening.
       (c) *I looked up it in the dictionary.

These errors involve multi-word verbs, verbs which consist of more than one word. Multi-word verbs are extremely common in English, but are nearly always a source of confusion for ESL learners. A major reason for the confusion comes from their idiomaticity. Because there is often no way to predict the meaning from the pieces, one must learn each combination separately.

In this chapter we develop a typology of multi-word verbs, introducing different types of multi-word verbs and exploring their properties. At the end of the chapter is an appendix containing further examples of each type.

1. PREPOSITIONS AND PARTICLES

Multi-word verbs consist of a verb and a preposition as in (2) and (3). The multi-word verbs are in italics and the PPs in square brackets.

(2)   (a) She *called* [*on* her sick neighbor].
       (b) We *cared* [*for* our sick parents].
       (c) They *deprived* the prisoners [*of* their rights].

149

(3)   (a) The missing girl mysteriously *turned* [*up*].
       (b) She suddenly *passed* [*out*].
       (c) They *called* [*up*] the pizza parlor.
       (d) We *turned* [*down*] the students.

The multi-word verbs in (2) contain a preposition that takes a complement, while those in (3) contain a preposition that does not. As noted in Chapter 5, prepositions without complements are called particles. Accordingly, in this chapter (as elsewhere) we use the term preposition to stand *only* for prepositions with complements. Since the same phonetic and orthographic forms function both as prepositions and as particles, however, we need to be able to tell them apart.

1.1 Variable Position

One characteristic of particles but not prepositions is that they have variable position. If a particle is part of a transitive multi-word verb, it may appear to the left or the right of the direct object. If the direct object is a pronoun, the particle *must* be to the right of the object. This pattern is shown in (4), where the direct object is in brackets and the particle in italics.

(4)   Particle (a) They called *up* [the pizza parlor].
                  (b) They called [the pizza parlor] *up*.
                  (c) *They called *up* [it].
                  (d) They called [it] *up*.

Prepositions, on the contrary, always appear before their complements, as in the intransitive multi-word verb in (5), where the complement of the preposition is in square brackets.

(5)   Preposition (a) She called *on* [her neighbor].
                    (b) *She called [her neighbor] *on*.
                    (c) She called *on* [her].
                    (d) *She called [her] *on*.

If a preposition is part of a transitive multi-word verb, the phrase it is head of will always follow the direct object, as in (6). (The direct object and the prepositional phrase are in square brackets.)

(6)   Preposition   (a) They deprived [the prisoner] [*of* sleep].
                      (b) *They deprived [*of* sleep] [the prisoner].

1.2 Stress

Prepositions are not usually stressed. When they are emphasized or put in contrast, they may receive stress, but in the absence of such focus, they are unstressed. Particles, on the other hand, are stressed. This is particularly clear when they are in final position. (Stress is indicated with small capitals.)

(7)   (a) Preposition   She CALLED on her.
                          She CARED for him.

        (b) Particle   They called her UP.
                          She turned them DOWN.

1.3 Manner Adverb Placement

A manner adverb can be inserted between a verb and preposition, but *not* between a verb and a particle. (Manner adverbs are in square brackets.)

(8)   Preposition   She called [unexpectedly] *on* her neighbor.
                      They cared [lovingly] *for* their mother.

(9)   Particle   *They called [unexpectedly] *up* the police.
                      *She turned [graciously] *down* their offer.

This criterion is really an indication of constituency, discussed in more detail below.

Exercise 1

Underline all the multi-word verbs in the following passage. Within each one, put a square around a preposition and a circle around a particle.

Will was heading for the library on campus. He ran into Bill who he hadn't heard from for a few weeks. But Bill didn't have much time to talk to Will. He had to check out some information for a paper he was working on. He had been looking it over and came across a few contradictions. Now he needed to look for a new source of information. He had to turn the paper in in an hour and if he couldn't come up with a way to fix up the errors quickly, he would have to think up a good excuse to get an extension from the teacher.

Will, egoist that he is, cut Bill off and brought up his own problems. His teacher had asked them to hand their papers in that morning, but he hadn't checked his paper over. He didn't even have time to look up the spelling of *preceeded* or to check on the punctuation he always messed up. And his teacher always picked on him because of his poor editing. She pointed out all his minor flaws in front of the whole class. Well, he hadn't let her down this time. His paper would really set her off, and she would likely run him down in class once again.

(Adapted from Hook 1981:5)

2. PHRASAL VERBS AND PREPOSITIONAL VERBS

Both prepositions and particles combine with verbs to form multi-word verbs. Multi-word verbs are idioms in that they are frozen, fixed expressions that are listed in the dictionary and have to be learned as a unit. The idiomatic combination of a verb and a preposition is called a prepositional verb; the idiomatic combination of a verb and a particle is called a phrasal verb.

(10) Idiomatic Combination = Resulting Construction
      verb + particle   phrasal verb
      verb + preposition   prepositional verb

The verb in these constructions may be either transitive or intransitive, giving the four possibilities shown in (11) and (12). The blank line after the prepositions *at, for, with,* and *of* indicates that they *must* be followed by a complement; the line thus emphasizes the syntactic difference between prepositions and particles.

(11) Intransitive Multi-word Verbs
      (a) Prepositional verb   *look at* ___
                                 care for ___
      (b) Phrasal verb   *turn up* "appear"
                                 pass out "faint"

(12) Transitive Multi-word Verbs
      (a) Prepositional verb   *ply* (him) *with* ___
                                 deprive (her) *of* ___
      (b) Phrasal verb   *turn* (them) *off*
                                 put (him) *down*

The difference between prepositional verbs and phrasal verbs appears clearly in their constituent structure. Tree diagrams for prepositional verbs (like those in (11)(a) and (12)(a)) are given in (13).

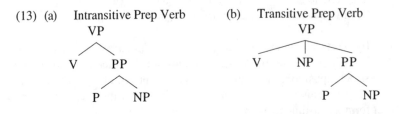

(13) (a)   Intransitive Prep Verb   (b)   Transitive Prep Verb

Tree diagrams for phrasal verbs (like those in (11)(b) and (12)(b)) are given in (14). Note that the particle is not part of a PP, but a sister of the verb.

(14) (a)   Intransitive Phrasal Verb   (b)   Transitive Phrasal Verb

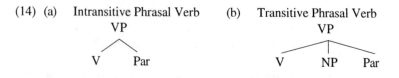

The facts about adverb placement discussed in 1.3 follow from the constituent structure posited here. Because the preposition and its object form a constituent, it is possible to insert material between this constituent and the preceding one. Since there is no major constituent break between a particle and a verb, however, no insertion is possible. The relevant examples are repeated in (15) and (16).

(15)   Prepositional Verb
        (a) She *called* unexpectedly [*on* her neighbor].
        (b) They *cared* lovingly [*for* their mother].

(16)   Phrasal Verb
        (a) *They *called* unexpectedly *up* [the police].
        (b) *She *turned* graciously *down* [their offer].

Consistent with these facts are also facts about pauses. It is often possible to pause briefly before a preposition, where there is a constituent break, but not before a particle.

(17)   (a)   Preposition   She *cared* (pause) [*for* her aunt].
        (b)   Particle   ??They *turned* (pause) *on* [the lights].
        (c)   More natural   They *turned on* (pause) [the lights].

Finally, facts about movement are also explained by the constituent structure. When the rule of WH-movement (see Chapter 23) moves the *object* of a preposition, the preposition may be moved along with it, as in (18) and (19). This is a consequence of the fact that the preposition and object form a constituent, as shown in the trees in (13).

(18) WH-Movement in Questions
      (a) [Which picture] was he *looking at*?
           [*At* which picture] was he *looking*?
      (b) [Which neighbor] did you *call on*?
           [*On* which neighbor] did you *call*?

(19) WH-Movement in Relative Clauses
      (a) the picture [which] he was *looking at*
           the picture [*at* which] he was *looking*
      (b) the sick neighbor [who(m)] we *called on*
           the sick neighbor [*on* whom] we *called*

Because of the idiomatic nature of the verb + prepositional combinations, movement of the preposition is not *always* possible. Idioms are often resistant to being broken up by movement rules, as in the examples of prepositional verbs in (20) and (21).

(20) Question
      (a) [Which brother] do you *take after*?
           ?[*After* which brother] do you *take*?
      (b) [Which old friend] did you *run into*?
           ?[*Into* which old friend] did you *run*?

(21) Relative Clause
      (a) the brother [which] I *take after*
           ?the brother [*after* which] I *take*
      (b) the friend [which] I *ran into*
           ?the friend [*into* which] I *ran*

Unlike prepositions, particles are *never* moved by WH-movement, as shown in (22). This is a consequence of the fact that they do not form a constituent with the NP (see the tree in (14)(b)).

(22) Question
      (a) [Which lights] should I *turn on*?
           On [which lights] should I *turn*?
      (b) [Who(m)] did you *call up*?
           Up [who(m)] did you *call*?

(23)   Relative Clause
    (a)   the lights [which] I *turned on*
          *the lights *on* [which] I *turned*
    (b)   the guy [who] I *called up*
          *the guy *up* [who] I *called*

3. PHRASAL PREPOSITIONAL VERBS

In addition to the verbs discussed above, there are multi-word verbs that consist of a verb, a preposition, *and* a particle, which are known as phrasal prepositional verbs. The phrasal prepositional verbs in (24) are intransitive, those in (25), transitive.

(24)   (a)   Winston would not *put up with* it.
    (b)   He could not *go through with* it.
    (c)   I wanted to *hold on to* the string, but I couldn't.
    (d)   We need to *check up on* it.
    (e)   Mary will *fill in for* her mother.
    (f)   Did you see how she *played up to* her boss?
    (g)   I don't *feel up to* it.
    (h)   You won't *get away with* it.

(25)   (a)   Don't *take* your frustrations *out on* me.
    (b)   They *put* our success *down to* hard work.
    (c)   Please *let* me *in on* your secret.
    (d)   They *fixed* me *up with* her brother.

Tree diagrams for the VPs in (24)(a) and (25)(a) are given in (26).

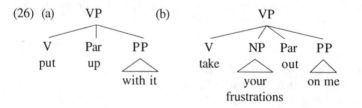

(26) (a)

A summary of the types of multi-word verbs introduc
given in the chart below (based on Quirk 1985:1161).

CLASSIFICATION OF MULTI-WORD VERBS

	Verb	Direct Object	Par	Prep	Prep Object
PHRASAL VERB					
Intransitive	turn	—	up	—	—
Transitive	turn	someone	down	—	—
PREPOSITIONAL VERB					
Intransitive	care	—	—	for	someone
Transitive	ply	someone	—	with	something
PHRASAL-PREPOSITIONAL VERB					
Intransitive	put	—	up	with	someone
Transitive	fix	someone	up	with	someone

Exercise 2

Identify each multi-word verb and figure out whether it is a phrasal verb or a prepositional verb, a transitive verb or an intransitive verb, and draw a tree diagram for the sentence. (Use triangles for NPs.)

1. We should write up the results of our investigation.
2. Susan really gets around.
3. Fortunately, this parka will protect you from the snow.
4. The accountant looked over the receipts from his client's trip.
5. A surly elderly man waited on us last night.

Exercise 3
Use each of the following multi-word verbs in a sentence. Then classify it using the table above.

1. strip (someone) of (something)
2. look forward to (something)
3. show up (= "appear")
4. put (someone) up to (something)
5. hold (someone) off
6. get over (an illness) (= "recover from")

Exercise 4
Draw tree diagrams for the following sentences. Use triangles to abbreviate the NPs and PPs, but draw out the other constituents.

1. The label is wearing off.
2. The student put the teacher down.
3. My sister will care for our aging mother.
4. The girls blamed the problem on the boys.
5. The car thieves let the police in on their little secret.
6. She played up to her boss.
7. We congratulated them on their good fortune and thanked them for their cooperation.
8. They gave up, but we are going through with it.
9. Jacob doesn't get along with anyone.

Exercise 5
Look over the examples of phrasal prepositional verbs given in (24) and (25). Which word is the preposition and which one the particle? Give reasons for your answer.

Exercise 6   For Discussion
We have identified six different types of multi-word verbs. These types are not equal in size. Which category do you think has the largest number of verbs? Which category do you think has the smallest? Why should this matter to an ESL teacher?

Exercise 7

How does the analysis of multi-word verbs presented in this chapter compare to the treatment in books for ESL students? Pick one or two grammar books for ESL students and analyze the presentation. Write a one-page comparison.

---

4. POSTSCRIPT

In addition to the six types of multi-word verbs given above, there is one further type, a hybrid that shows some characteristics of prepositional verbs and some characteristics of phrasal verbs. The examples in (27) show that these verbs are prepositional, because the object must follow the preposition, even when it is a pronoun.

(27) (a) I hadn't seen Joan for months, but yesterday I *ran into* her.
     (b) My son had the flu, and it took weeks to *get over* it.
     (c) The bus stopped, and the old man *got on* it.

However, these verbs have the stress pattern of phrasal verbs. If you pronounce the examples of (27), you will notice that the preposition receives the main stress. We say: *I ran* INTO *her* and not *I* RAN *into her*.

Hybrid multi-word verbs are extremely common. A list of them is given in the appendix to this chapter.

Transitive

    fix ___ up with ___ , let ___ in on ___ , put ___ up for ___ ,

    put ___ down to ___ ("attribute"), take __ out on ___

HYBRID MULTI-WORD VERBS — *examples of languages in process of modernization/ globalization*

break into	He broke INTO it.	(a conversation)
come across	I came ACROSS it in an old book store.	("find accidentally")
do/go without	They did WITHOUT it.	
get around	They got AROUND it.	("evade")
get in	She got IN it.	(car)
get on / off	We got ON it.	(train)
get over	She got OVER it.	("recover")
go over	They went OVER it.	("review")
get through	They got THROUGH it.	(a test)
hang around	He hangs AROUND us.	("remain idly")
keep at	They keep AT it.	("persevere")
look after	She looks AFTER him.	("take care of")
look into	They looked INTO it.	("investigate")
run across	We ran ACROSS it ...	("find accidentally")
run against	Clinton ran AGAINST him. Who did he RUN against? ??Who did he run AGAINST?	("compete")
run into	We ran INTO her.	("meet accidentally")
see through	They saw THROUGH it.	(the trick)
take after	?My son takes AFTER him. ?My son TAKES after him	("resemble")
turn into	She turned INTO it.	("become")

12
FOUR VERB SUBCLASSES

IN CHAPTER 10 we introduced 11 subclasses of verbs and their complements. In this chapter we examine four of these subclasses in greater detail, focusing on their semantics and major subgroups. The verb classes discussed in this chapter are not necessarily the most important ones, but they sometimes cause difficulty.

1. LINKING VERBS

A verb which takes as complements a predicate NP or AP is a linking verb. The word linking refers to the fact that the verb functions as a link between the subject and the predicate NP or AP while supplying tense to the sentence. In some descriptions these verbs are called copulas.

(1)		Subject NP	Linking Verb	Predicate NP / AP
	(a)	My son	*is*	a teacher.
	(b)	They	*became*	best friends.
	(c)	This town	*seems*	friendly.
	(d)	You	*look*	quite perplexed.

The most common linking verb is the colorless verb *be*, used to express either an essential, permanent property of the subject or an incidental, temporary one, as illustrated in (2) and (3).

(2)   Essential Property
    (a)   My child *is* a female.
    (b)   Sugar *is* sweet.
    (c)   New York *is* a large city.

(3) Incidental Property
   (a) Yuri *is* angry today.
   (b) This sugar *is* lumpy.

It is not always clear whether a permanent or a temporary characteristic of the subject is being described, as in (4).

(4) That child *is* obnoxious.

Other linking verbs have more meaning than *be*. Some link the subject to some property which it *currently* has, while others link the subject to some property which it *comes to have* as a result of the change described by the verb. The most common linking verbs of English are listed below.

Current Linking Verbs   Resulting Linking Verbs

Current Linking Verbs		Resulting Linking Verbs	
be		become	(older)
act	(silly, stupid)	come	(true)
appear	(happy)	get	(ready)
feel	(annoyed)	go	(sour)
keep	(cool)	grow	(tired)
lie	(scattered)	fall	(sick)
look	(dejected)	run	(wild)
remain	(uncertain)	turn	(sour)
rest	(assured)	wax	(calm)
ring	(true)		
seem	(restless)		
smell	(sweet)		
sound	(surprised)		
stand	(corrected)		
stay	(young)		
taste	(bitter)		

Exercise 1

As noted, linking verbs are subcategorized for either NPs or APs, but many are restricted to only one of these two syntactic categories. Determine the subcategorization for six verbs from the lists above. Does the verb occur with both NPs and APs or does it allow only one? Give grammatical and ungrammatical sentences as evidence for your answers.

Example:	What is the subcategorization of *appear*?
Evidence:	She appeared scared. (AP)
	*She appeared a smart person. (NP)
Conclusion:	The verb appear occurs only with APs.
	Subcat frame: [_____ AP]

Which group is larger: Linking verbs which occur only with adjective phrases or those which occur only with noun phrases?

Exercise 2

Some linking verbs correspond to transitive verbs that are causative in meaning. For each of the following sentences, determine whether the italicized verb is a linking verb, a transitive verb, or neither.

1.   Keiko *tasted* the soup.
2.   The soup *tasted* good.
3.   His explanation *was* a bit fishy. It didn't quite *ring* true.
4.   They *rang* bells at the conclusion of the concert.
5.   My sister *remained* a delightful companion throughout her illness.
6.   We *turned* the plant so it could face the sun.
7.   My stomach *turned* at the thought of such violence.
8.   Her face *turned* green at the thought of eating frogs.
9.   We *remained* good friends our whole lives.
10.   I *got* my children new shoes for school.
11.   We *got* the flu in Florida.
12.   Those flowers *smell* strange.
13.   Go *smell* those flowers for yourself.
14.   *Get* real!

2. COMPLEX TRANSITIVE VERBS

A complex transitive verb has two complements, an argument NP direct object and either a predicate NP or an AP.

			Direct Object	Predicate NP or AP
(5)	(a)	We *considered*	Sam	our best friend.
	(b)	They *elected*	Mrs. Jones	president of the PTA.
	(c)	They *pronounced*	the prisoner	guilty.
	(d)	She *painted*	the barn	bright red.

There is a special relationship between the two complements of a complex transitive verb. The predicate NP or AP says something about or describes the direct object, just as the predicate NP that is a complement of a linking verb describes the subject. The predicate NP or AP is either *currently* true of the direct object or *comes to be* true of the direct object as a result of the action of the verb. Part of the meaning conveyed by (5)(a), for example, is that Sam *is* our best friend. Part of the meaning conveyed by (5)(b), for example, is that Mrs. Jones *comes to be* president as a result of the action named by the verb. Thus, complex transitive verbs, like linking verbs, are either current or resulting verbs.

(6)   Current Complex Transitives
    (a) *consider* Sue a good friend
    (b) *keep* her a friend for life
    (c) *find* his behavior very obnoxious
    (d) *deem* Sally worthy of this honor

(7)   Resulting Complex Transitives
    (a) *appoint* her head of the commission
    (b) *declare* the suspect innocent
    (c) *rip* the letter open

Three subgroups of complex transitive verbs are given below. The first group contains verbs subcategorized for a predicate NP and the second group, those subcategorized for an AP. The third group contains complex transitives subcategorized for APs in which the range of adjectives that appear with a particular verb is very restricted. These combinations are semi-idiomatic. They probably have to be learned as units and not as individual words.

As you can see by looking over these lists, complex transitive verbs belong to many different semantic classes. We can, however, point out a few common subclasses. Some complex transitives express the speaker's judgements, evaluations, or opinions about the direct object: *assess, certify, consider, find, imagine, judge, rank, suspect, think.* Some complex transitives report more or less official acts which determine the status of the direct object: *appoint, christen, crown, ordain, proclaim.* Many of these verbs can be used as performative verbs. With performative verbs, under the right circumstances, "saying it makes it so." For example, if the speaker of (8) is someone with the requisite authority, the uttering of the sentence itself under the appropriate circumstances is sufficient to make you the ambassador to France.

(8)   I appoint you ambassador to France.

Finally, most of the verbs in Group 3 are verbs of contact. The verb names a particular kind of contact between the subject and direct object (e.g. *hitting, kicking, pushing*), and the predicate adjective names the state the direct object NP comes to be in as a result of this contact (*hammer it flat → it is flat, kick it open → it is open*).

These lists of complex transitive verbs were adapted from lists of verbs assembled by researchers at Indiana University (Alexander and Kunz 1964). Not everyone would agree with all the judgements represented here, however, and particularly controversial judgements are indicated with a "?."

Group 1. Subcategorization Frame: [_____ NP NP$_{Pred}$]

acknowledge	deem	make	?read
?advertise	?depict	?mark	reckon
annoint	designate	name	?record
appoint	determine	nickname	?register
brand	dub	nominate	report
call	elect	ordain	rule
certify	establish	paint	?select
christen	fancy	perceive	stamp
color	find	?prefer	suppose
commission	guarantee	presume	suspect
consider	imagine	proclaim	vote
count	judge	profess	want
crown	keep	pronounce	wish
declare	leave	rank	

Group 2. Subcategorization Frame: [_____ NP AP]

acknowledge	depict	leave	remember
admit	?determine	make	render
affirm	?discover	mark	report
announce	fancy	need	?require
assume	fear	observe	rule
believe	feel	?order	rumor
build	figure	paint	see
call	find	perceive	sense
certify	get	prefer	show
claim	guarantee	presume	specify
color	guess	presuppose	stamp
compute	have	proclaim	suppose
conclude	hold	pronounce	suspect
consider	imagine	prove	think
content	?indicate	rank	turn
count	judge	realize	vote
declare	keep	reckon	?want
deem	label	recognize	?will

Group 3.   Subcategorization Frame: [_____ NP AP]**

**The range of adjectives which appear with the verbs on this list is quite
restricted. Some common ones are given in parentheses after the verb.

bang	(shut)	shoot	(dead)
bend	(crooked, straight)	slam	(shut)
clip	(close, short)	slash	(open)
crop	(close, short)	slice	(open)
cut	(short, free)	slit	(open)
drain	(dry)	snap	(open, shut)
file	(smooth)	squash	(flat)
fling	(open)	squeeze	(open, dry)
force	(open, shut)	stain	(red, blue, ...)
hammer	(flat, shut)	stretch	(wide, open,
hold	(open, closed)		tight)
kick	(open)	suck	(dry)
knock	(flat, free, open, silly)	sweep	(clean)
lay	(flat, open)	swing	(open, free)
lick	(clean)	tear	(open, free)
nail	(shut)	throw	(open, shut)
pick	(clean)	tint	(red, blue, ...)
plane	(smooth, flush)	wash	(clean)
pry	(open, loose)	wear	(thin, threadbare)
pull	(open, loose, shut, free)	wipe	(clean)
push	(open, shut)	work	(open, free, loose)
put	(straight)	wrench	(free, loose)
rake	(clean, smooth)		
rip	(open, free)		
roll	(flat)		
scrape	(smooth, clean)		
scrub	(clean)		
set	(free)		
shake	(open, dry, free, loose)		

Exercise 3

Not all native speakers of English would agree that every verb listed above has the subcategorization of a complex transitive. Identify at least five verbs which you *would* include on the list and three verbs which you *would not*. Give evidence for your judgements in the form of grammatical and ungrammatical sentences.

Exercise 4

Some of the predicate adjectives on Group 3 are similar to particles (discussed in Chapters 10-11) in that they can appear on either side of the direct object NP. Compare the particle *out* in (1) with the adjective *open* in (2).

(1) (a) She knocked the thief out.
     (b) She knocked out the thief.

(2) (a) They kicked the door open.
     (b) They kicked open the door.

Using the verbs in Group 3, find five which allow the adjective to appear on either side of the direct object. Give evidence for your answer.

---

3. VERBS SUBCATEGORIZED FOR ADVERBIAL COMPLEMENTS

Some verbs of English are subcategorized for an adverbial complement. As noted in Chapter 4, adverbials are a complex and diverse category, not defined by their internal syntax, but by their function in a clause. They express semantic categories such as direction, location, time, manner, instrument, condition, purpose, etc. Most verbs that take an adverbial complement take a *place* phrase; a few require a time phrase.

Some verbs in this subclass are ungrammatical without the complement, as in (9) - (10).

(9)   (a)   The prowler was *lurking* in the bushes.
       (b)   *The prowler was *lurking*.

(10)   (a)   They *placed* the letter on the table.
       (b)   *They *placed* the letter.

The meanings of other verbs imply a place adverbial, though it is not required. For example, the verb *stay* ("to remain in a location") implies a location that may be mentioned explicitly in (11)(a), or only implied, as in (11)(b).

(11)   (a)   She *stayed* at home.
       (b)   She *stayed*.

Like *stay*, the verb *lead* also implies a location ("to guide or conduct someone from one location to another"), whether stated as in (12)(a), or not, as in (12)(b).

(12)   (a)   The dog *led* us up the stairs.
       (b)   The dog *led* us.

   Verbs subcategorized for adverbials are given below in sentences so that the intended sense will be clear. (The adverbial is in square brackets.)

Group 1:   Intransitive Verbs Subcategorized for a Place Adverbial
            [___ PlP]

Verb denotes the location of someone or something:
dwell	She *dwells/resides/lives*	in Kentucky.
live		
reside		
stay	She *stayed*	[home].
settle	They *settled*	[in Ohio / down].
lean	The boys were *leaning*	[against the car].
lie	Mother was *lying*	[down].
lurk	The prowler was *lurking*	[in the bushes].

Verb denotes a change of location:

burst	He *burst*	[into the room].
creep	The girl *crept*	[up the stairs].
go	They *went*	[to Boston].
jump	They *jumped*	[into the pool].
ran	She *ran*	[down the stairs].
rush	They *rushed*	[out the door].
sneak	He *snuck*	[into the museum].
step	The child *stepped*	[off the curb].
steal	The thief *stole*	[away].

Group 2: Intransitive Verbs Subcategorized for Temporal Adverbials
[_____ TP]

last	The movie *lasted*	[three hours].
take	The cruise *took*	[ten days].

Group 3: Transitive verbs Subcategorized for Place Adverbials
[___ NP PlP]

Verb denotes leading/moving/taking something to a new location:

bring	The boys *brought* the ball	[to school].
carry	My father *carried* dinner	[into the dining room].
direct	The usher *directed* me	[to the bathroom].
lead	The dog *led* us	[up the stairs].
show	The steward *showed* me	[out].
took	The doctor *took* the patient	[away].

Verb denotes putting, placing, or fastening something to a particular location:

drape	They *draped* the cloth	[over the bench].
hang	We *hung* their coats	[up].
lay	They *laid* the sweater	[on the bed].
lean	She *leaned* the pole	[against the lamp].
place	They *placed* the letter	[on the table].
put	We *put* the beer	[in the fridge].
sew	He *sewed* the button	[onto the shirt].

slide	*Slide* this letter	[under the door].
slip	He *slipped* the ring	[on (her finger)].
spread	They *spread* the tablecloth	[on the table].
toss	She *tossed* the shirt	[into the hamper].

Verb denotes maintaining something in a specific location:

lock	They *locked* the car	[in the garage].
keep	They *kept* us	[upstairs].
store	We *store* our wine	[in the cellar].
stow	*Stow* your gear	[over here].

4. DITRANSITIVE VERBS

Ditransitive verbs are subcategorized for two argument noun phrases, an indirect object and a direct object. Semantically, ditransitives can be divided into two main groups and a third minor one.

4.1 Verbs of Transfer

The largest group of ditransitives denote the transfer of something to someone. The direct object denotes the thing which is transferred, the indirect object denotes the recipient, the person who receives the direct object or comes to possess it as a result of the action denoted by the verb. For example, in (13)(a) John comes to possess the book; in (13)(c), Peter, the new car.

(13)			IndObj	DirObj
	(a)	Sue	*gave*	John	the book.
	(b)	Mary	*brought* the teacher	an apple.
	(c)	The dealer	*sold*	Peter	a new car.

With some ditransitive verbs, the transfer is not literal, but metaphoric. The direct object, the thing transferred, is something abstract, such as knowledge, permission, etc., as in (14).

(14)	(a)	My mother	*taught*	me	everything I know.
	(b)	Kim	*showed*	John	her ring.
	(c)	The judge	*granted*	the prisoner	his last request.

When the ditransitive denotes a kind of communication, the verbs may perhaps be thought of as representing a transfer of information.

(15) (a) They *told* the children a story.
      (b) Mother *wrote* her brother a letter.

Verb denotes transfer of possession (signify acts of giving):
bring, feed, give, hand, lease, loan, lend, pass, pay, refund, render, rent, repay, sell, serve, take, trade

Verb denotes future having (commitments that a person will have something at a later point in time):
advance, allocate, allow, assign, bequeath, cede, concede, extend, grant, guarantee, issue, leave, offer, own, promise, vote, will, yield

Verb denotes sending:
forward, mail, send, ship

Verb causes a change of position (used as verbs of transfer):
bounce, drop, float, roll, slide, slip

Verb causes motion in a specific manner:
carry, drag, drive, haul, hoist, pull, puch, schlep, shove, wheel

Verb denotes the transfer of an idea:
cite, preach, quote, read, relay, show, teach, tell, write

Verb denotes communication by means of an instrument:
cable, e-mail, fax, phone, radio, telephone, telegraph, wire

4.2 Benefactives
Another large group of ditransitives represent actions performed for the benefit of the indirect object, a benefactive (see also Chapter 5).

(16)   IndObj   DirObj
    (a) They *baked* Mother   a cake.
    (b) She *reserved* her dog   a place at the table.
    (c) Dad *found*   my sister   a cute apartment.

Verb denotes building:
arrange, assemble, bake, blow (bubbles), *build, carve, chisel, churn, compile, cook, cut, fashion, fold, grind, grow, hammer, knit, make, mold, sew, weave*

Verb denotes creating:
design, draw, paint, write

Verb denotes preparing:
bake, boil, brew, clean, fix, fry, iron, mend, pour, prepare, sharpen, wash

Verb denotes performance:
dance, hum, perform, play, read, recite, sing, whistle

Verbs of obtaining:
buy, call, cash, catch, charter, earn, fetch, find, gain, gather, get, keep, lease, order, pick (fruit), *procure, rent, reserve, save, snatch, steal, win*

4.3 Residual Group
A small number of ditransitives are neither transfer verbs nor benefactives.

(17)   IndObj   DirObj
    (a) They   *owe*   the government $5.00.
    (b) Mary   *paid*   her neighbor   a visit.

Residual ditransitives:
accord, ask, assign, bear, begrudge, bet, charge, cost, do, envy, excuse, fine, forbid, forgive, offer, overcharge, owe, refuse, save, spare, wish

13

DUAL SUBCATEGORIZATION

IT IS NOT UNUSUAL for a single verb to have two subcategorizations, a phenomenon known as dual subcategorization. In this chapter we will look at some common patterns of dual subcategorization. We will see that to a certain extent, verbs which share subcategorization frames express similar meanings as well.

1. TRANSITIVITY ALTERNATION - 1

Many verbs subcategorized for an NP may also appear without it, without any significant change in meaning. Such verbs are both transitive and intransitive. There are two types of transitivity alternations. In one type, the subject of the intransitive verb is expressed as the direct object of the transitive, as in (1) - (4).

(1)   (a) Intransitive: The door *opened.*
       (b) Transitive: They *opened* the door.

(2)   (a) The glass *broke.*
       (b) The children *broke* the glass.

(3)   (a) The lemonade *froze.*
       (b) We *froze* the lemonade.

(4)   (a) The ball *rolled* under the couch.
       (b) We *rolled* the ball under the couch.

A very large number of verbs work like these. When used as intransitives they depict a change of state, but when used as transitives, they depict an event which causes, or brings about, the change of state. The subject of the transitive is understood as the agent (or causer) of the change. This dual subcategorization is schematized in (5). The NP *outside* the square brackets stands for the subject.

(5)   Transitivity Alternation - 1
        Subject of Intransitive = Direct Object of Transitive
        NP-1   [_____]   and   NP-2   [_____ NP-1]

Some of the many verbs with these two subcategorization patterns:

Verbs of change of position: *bounce, drop, float, glide, move, roll, slide*
Verbs of breaking: *break, crack, crash, crush, fracture, shatter, smash, snap,*
        splinter, split, rip, tear
Verbs of bending: *bend, crease, crinkle, crumble, crumple, flake, fold,*
        rumple, rupture, stretch, twist, wrinkle
Verbs of cooking: *bake, boil, broil, brown, burn,* (cook,) *roast, simmer*
Verbs depicting a change of color: *blacken, redden, whiten*
Verbs that depict other changes of state: *alter, blast, burn, burst, capsize,*
        change, close, condense, deflate, defrost, dissolve, double, ease,
        expand, explode, fade, freeze, grow, harden, heat, light, melt, open,
        shrink, shut, sink, slam, soften, sprout, stretch, tilt, wake up

Other verbs that exhibit transitivity alternation-1 are middles, a special intransitive use of a basically transitive verb. The intransitive usually occurs with a manner adverbial, as in (6) - (8) and often implies that anybody could perform the action on the subject in the manner specified by the adverb.

(6)   (a)   Transitive: This store *sells* her books.
        (b)   Intransitive: Her books *sell* like hotcakes.

(7)   (a)   Transitive: I can *extend* this tripod.
        (b)   Intransitive: This tripod *extends* easily.
               Implication: Anyone can extend this tripod.

(8)   (a) Transitive: They can *handle* German cars.
       (b) Intransitive: German cars *handle* well.
            Implication: Anyone can handle German cars well.

Middles are especially pervasive in the language of commercials, where
the advertiser wishes to assert that the product possesses certain desirable
qualities that anyone can reproduce. Some "Madison Avenue" examples are
given in (9).

(9)   (a) Your new oven will clean in minutes!
       (b) This new material washes like a dream.

Exercise 1
In the following sentences can the intransitive verbs in italics also be used
as transitive verbs? For each verb, construct a sentence or two to support
your answer. If the verb has a dual subcategorization, does it work like
open, like a middle, or neither?

1.   After the engine *exploded*, the steamboat *floated* down the river.
2.   The meat *browned* too quickly, and then it *burned.*
3.   Because the lecture *began* so late, many people *left* before it started.
4.   It was dark. Something *moved* in the bushes and an owl *screeched.*
5.   This meat is very tender. It *cuts* so easily.
6.   The dog *barked* and then *trotted* over to us and licked our hands.
7.   We got this house for a song. Because of the peeling paint and dark
      interior, it didn't *show* very well.
8.   Even though I like to *eat,* I never *cook.*

---

2. TRANSITIVITY ALTERNATION - 2

In a second kind of transitivity alternation, the direct object of the transitive
is unexpressed in the intransitive, as in (10).

(10)   (a) Transitive: Mother was *cooking* dinner.
       (b) Intransitive: Mother was *cooking*.

This alternation is schematized in (11). The NP outside square brackets stands for the subject.

(11)   Transitivity Alternation - 2
       Direct Object of Transitive Suppressed in Intransitive
       NP-1   [_____ NP-2]   and   NP-1   [_____]

We can identify a number of subgroups that differ in the way the missing direct object is understood.

3.1 Reflexive Object

One group of transitive verbs may be used as intransitives when the direct object of the transitive is understood as a reflexive, i.e. as co-referential with the subject, as in (12) - (14). (The direct objects are in square brackets.)

(12)   (a) The girl *dressed* [her little brother] quickly.
       (b) The girl *dressed* [___] quickly.
            (unexpressed object = herself, i.e. the girl)

(13)   (a) Cary *shaves* [Brian] two times a day.
       (b) Cary *shaves* [___] two times a day.
            (unexpressed object = himself, i.e. Cary)

(14)   (a) We *packed* [the children] onto the bus.
       (b) We *packed* [___] onto the bus.
            (unexpressed object = ourselves)

Though the verbs of (12) - (14) can be used as both transitives and intransitives, the intransitives are always understood reflexively. (13)(b), for example, conveys that the person who will be shaved will be Cary and not some other, unnamed person. It cannot be understood as conveying any of the meanings of (15).

(15)   Cary shaves Brian / someone / people two times a day.

A small number of English verbs work like *shave*, including some verbs of grooming and bodily care (*bathe, bundle up, change, disrobe, dress, dry off, prepare, primp, shave, undress, wash*), some verbs depicting loading (*jam, cram, load, pack, shove*), and a few others (*hide, identify with, prove* (to be)).

3.2 *Indefinite Object*
A second group of transitive verbs may be used as intransitive verbs when the direct object is understood to be indefinite, as in (16)(b) and (17)(b). An indefinite NP is one which has not been established in the prior discourse, one which the speaker does not assume that the addressee can identify (see Chapter 29).

(16)   (a)   Grandma was *mending* [the socks].
         (b)   Grandma was *mending* [___].

(17)   (a)   My husband was *baking* [bread] yesterday.
         (b)   My husband was *baking* [___] yesterday.

(16)(a) gives the object of mending as something specific and definite. (16)(b) gives no object of mending, but from the sentence we understand that Grandma was mending something one typically mends; she was mending "something or other," but we don't know what it was. That is, it is indefinite. If, in the previous context for the utterance, a definite object of mending has been established, the direct object cannot be omitted (i.e. the verb cannot be used intransitively), as in the ungrammatical exchange in (18).

(18)   (a)   Where are my socks?
         (b)   I don't have them. *Grandma is mending.

(18)(b) is ungrammatical in the meaning "Grandma is mending your socks." The object of *mend* can be omitted *only* when it is indefinite.

    One other fact about these verbs worth mentioning is that the intransitives name activities. For this reason, they are odd in the simple present tense and most natural in the progressive (see Chapters 16 and 17).

Some of the many verbs that participate in this transitivity alternation
are: *bake, carve, chop, clean, cook, crochet, draw, drink, dust, eat,
embroider, hum, hunt, fish, iron, knead, knit, mend, mow, nurse, pack,
paint, play, plow, polish, read, recite, sew, sculpt, sing, sketch, sow,
study, sweep, teach, type, sketch, vacuum, wash, weave, whittle, write.*

3.3 Generic Object
A third group of transitive verbs may be used as intransitives when the
direct object is understood as generic.

(19) (a) That child *hit* [his little brother].
      (b) We don't want Sam to play with our child. He *hits* [___].

(20) (a) I *wrote* [this novel].
      (b) I *write* [___].

(21) (a) I *pinched* [my little sister].
      (b) These shoes *pinch* [___].

In the intransitive sentences, the unexpressed object, understood as generic,
doesn't name a specific person or thing, but a class of things in general. For
instance, by (19)(b) we understand that Sam hits kids in general and by
(20)(b) we understand that the speaker writes things in general.

Of the verbs which exhibit this alternation, the transitives depict actions
or events, while the intransitives express a characteristic property of the
subject. The intransitives are stative (they name states); they do not occur in
the progressive.

(22) (a) We don't want him to play with our child. *He is hitting.
      (b) I am writing.

Though (22)(b) is grammatical, it does not have the same sense as (20)(b),
the generic object sense. Unlike (20)(b), it cannot be paraphrased, "I am a
writer."

Verbs which participate in this transitivity alternation include: *bite, hit,
kick, pinch, prick, scratch, sting, clip, cook, cut, record, slice, write.*

Exercise 2
Do the italicized verbs in the following sentences follow the pattern of *shave*? Give sentences as evidence for your answer.

1. They *showered* quickly and then *got ready*.
2. There's only one bathroom. You *wash* first and I'll go later.
3. Why can't you children *behave*?
4. The guard heard a noise and *turned* suddenly.

Exercise 3
In the following sentences, a transitive verb is used as an intransitive, i.e. it occurs without a direct object. For each italicized intransitive verb, say whether the unexpressed object is understood as a reflexive noun phrase, an indefinite noun phrase, a generic noun phrase, or something else.

1. When I came home, it was midnight, and mother was *reading* in bed.
2. We couldn't find little Polly. She was *hiding* in the garden.
3. This medicine *stings* a little bit, but it will only last a minute.
4. Oh, no! The old man's *drinking* again.
5. We all *loaded* into the station wagon and set off for Alaska.
6. This child *draws* beautifully, but lately she's been *painting*, too.
7. Speed *kills*.
8. Don't bother my mother. She's *packing*.
9. I'll help with the dishes. You *wash*, and I'll *dry*.

Exercise 4
The following conversation is odd if the assistant's response is intended to be cooperative. Can you explain why?

Boss: Where's that report? I need it immediately.
Assistant: Please be patient, sir. The secretary is typing now.

3. DITRANSITIVE ALTERNATIONS

As explored in the worksheet in Chapter 10, many ditransitive verbs occur as monotransitives with a prepositional phrase. When the PP has the preposition *to,* it is a complement of the verb, as in (23).

(23) (a) Ditransitive: He *gave* his mother the book.
       (b) Monotransitive: He *gave* the book to his mother.

In the terms of this chapter, these ditransitive verbs have the dual subcategorization shown in (24).

(24) (a) Ditransitive: [_____ NP-2 NP-1]
       (b) Monotransitive: [_____ NP-1 PP*]   *P = *to*

NP-2 stands for the indirect object, the recipient, NP-1 for the direct object. In the monotransitive frame given in (24)(b) there is no indirect object; the recipient is expressed as the object of a preposition.

We might expect all ditransitives to exhibit this alternation, but, as shown in the worksheet, not all of them do. Some ditransitives correspond to a monotransitive verb with an optional benefactive adverbial modifier, as in (25). In terms of this chapter, these verbs have the dual subcategorization shown in (26). Since the adverbial is a modifier and not a complement, it does not appear in the subcategorization frame.

(25) (a) Ditransitive: She *played* her baby a song.
       (b) Monotransitive: She *played* a song for her baby.

(26) (a) Ditransitive: [_____ NP-2 NP-1]
       (b) Monotransitive: [_____ NP-1]

Other ditransitives do not have a second subcategorization at all. For example, the verb *cost* occurs only as a ditransitive, as shown in (27).

(27) (a) Ditransitive: It *cost* John a fortune.
       (b) Monotransitive: *It *cost* a fortune to John.

Further, not all verbs with the subcategorization frame in (25)(b) are ditransitives. The verb *report* is restricted in this way.

(28) (a) Ditransitive: *We *reported* the police the robbery.
      (b) Monotransitive: We *reported* the robbery to the police.

Finally, not all verbs which occur with a benefactive modifier can also occur as ditransitives. In fact, only a few have this second subcategorization.

(29) (a) Ditransitive: *I did mother the dishes.
      (b) Monotransitive: I did the dishes for mother.

It is an unfortunate fact of English that one can't know in advance which verbs will occur in which subcategorization frame. Some verbs occur in one, some in the other, and some in both, so that the subcategorization facts must be learned separately for each verb. Some verbs which do not have the expected patterns are given below.

•Some verbs are only ditransitive.

[___ NP NP]	[___ NP PP*]
	*P = to
allow your sister a look	**allow* a look to your sister
begrudge someone his good luck	**begrudge* good luck to someone
bet Dad five dollars	**bet* five dollars to Dad
cost John a fortune	**cost* a fortune to John
fine the defendant $30	**fine* $30 to the defendant
forgive Pete the offense	**forgive* the offense to Pete
permit the prisoner a last request	**permit* a last request to the prisoner
refuse you your request	**refuse* your request to you
wish the contestants luck	**wish* luck to the contestants
give her father a pain in the neck	**give* a pain in the neck to her father
give Mom a scare	**give* a scare to Mom

•Some verbs have a dual subcategorization, but the preposition is not *to*.

[____ NP NP]	[____ NP PP*] *P does not = *to*
play Sasha a game of chess	**play* a game of chess to Sasha *play* a game of chess *with* Sasha
ask Kim a favor	**ask* a favor to Kim *ask* a favor *of* Kim

•Some verbs are only monotransitives.
(These verbs are mentioned because of their semantic similarity to *give* and other ditransitive verbs with a dual subcategorization. One might expect them to occur as ditransitives, but they don't.)

[____ NP NP]	[____ NP PP*] *P = *to*
**administer* the children punishment	*administer* punishment to the children
**admit* you my faults	*admit* my faults to you
**deliver* Peter paper	*deliver* paper to Peter
**describe* Sue the scene	*describe* the scene to Sue
**explain* me the problem	*explain* the problem to me
**mention* them the incident	*mention* the incident to them
**report* the police the robbery	*report* the robbery to the police
**say* her nasty things	*say* nasty things to her
**suggest* them the idea	*suggest* the idea to them
**transfer* him stock	*transfer* stock to him
**donate* UNICEF $10	*donate* $10 to UNICEF
**return* Mom books	*return* books to Mom

[____ NP NP]	[____ NP] + benefactive modifier
**choose* us wine	*choose* wine for us
**clarify* me this	*clarify* this for me
**do* mother the dishes	*do* the dishes for mother
**open* us the door	*open* the door for us
**select* him wine	*select* wine for him
**set* Mom the table	*set* the table for Mom
**solve* me this problem	*solve* this problem for me

4. ADVERBIALS AS SUBJECT

Semantic categories like place, time, and instrument usually appear in clauses as optional adverbials, as in (30).

(30) (a) Place: Bees were swarming [in the garden].
      (b) Time: The world saw the beginning of a new era
                        [in August 1991].
      (c) Instrument: I broke the window [with a hammer].

Some verbs also have a subcategorization in which an NP with adverbial meaning can appear as subject.

(31) (a) Place: [The garden] was swarming with bees.
      (b) Time: [August 1991] saw the beginning of a new era
                        in the world.
      (c) Instrument: [The hammer] broke the window.

A number of English verbs show an alternation like this. In this section we present four groups, which differ in terms of the semantics of the adverbial.

5.1 Place
A number of verbs are like *swarm* in that they allow a place adverbial to occur as a subject.

(32) (a) Their voices *echoed* [in the halls].
      (b) [The halls] *echoed* with their voices.

(33) (a) Blood was *oozing* [out of the infected wound].
      (b) [The infected wound] was *oozing* with blood.

Verbs subcategorized for a place adverbial as subject include: *abound, blaze, bustle, buzz, crawl, creep, dance, drip, echo, explode, foam, flame, flash, flow, flutter, froth, gleam, glisten, glitter, glow, gush, hop, hum, ooze, pour, ring, reel, resound, reverberate, run, shimmer, shine, sparkle, spurt, sputter, squeak, stir, stream, swarm, teem, throng.*

5.2 Time

A much smaller number of verbs allow a time adverbial to appear as subject. They include *catch, find, mark, realize,* and *see.*

(34) (a) We *found* ourselves waiting at the station [at noon].
      (b) [Noon] *found* us waiting at the station.

5.3 Instrument

Like the verb *broke*, a small number of verbs allow an adverbial that expresses an instrument to occur as subject. Instruments are tools which are used to bring about the physical change depicted by the verb. Most often they are expressed as prepositional phrases with *with.*

(35) (a) I *opened* the door [with the red key].
      (b) [The red key] *opens* this door.

(36) (a) We *cut* the wood [with a chain saw].
      (b) [The chain saw] *cut* the wood.

Verbs which allow an adverbial expressing instrument as subject: *bar, fasten, open, lock, mark, remove break, cut, splinter, pierce, poke.*

   If the notion of instrument is extended to apply to abstract actions and ideas, we see that a fairly large number of verbs with abstract meaning allow an adverbial expressing an instrument to appear as the subject.

(37) (a) He *established* his innocence [with the letter].
      (b) [The letter] *established* his innocence.

(38) (a) She *revealed* her stupidity [with that remark].
      (b) [That remark] *revealed* her stupidity.

The *with*-phrases do not name concrete objects which are used as instruments in physical actions, but depict instruments in verbal or mental actions. One could paraphrase both adverbials in the same way.

(39) (a) I used [the red key] to open the door.
      (b) He used [the letter] to establish his innocence.

Abstract verbs with instrument as subject: *assert, confirm, create, demonstrate, establish, explain, imply, indicate, justify, nullify, obscure, proclaim, predict, prove, refute, reveal, show, suggest.*

5.4 *Instrument of Emotional Change*

Many verbs occur with an optional adverbial which expresses an additional kind of abstract instrument. Like the instruments discussed above, these adverbial instruments can also appear as the subject.

(40) (a) Sally *comforted* me [with her kind words].
      (b) [Her kind words] *comforted* me.

(41) (a) He *frightened* me [with his evil look].
      (b) [His evil look] *frightened* me.

Verbs with this pattern convey that an agent causes an experiencer to have some emotion or feeling. The adverbial expresses the instrument by which the agent brings about the emotional change. In (40)(a) and (41)(a) the agent is subject, the experiencer is direct object, and the instrument is an optional adverbial modifier, expressed as a prepositional phrase with *with*. In (40)(b) and (41)(b) the instrumental adverbial appears as the subject, and the agent is not expressed as an argument of the verb. It may be expressed as a genitive within the subject NP, as in (40)(b) and (41)(b).

A very large number of verbs in English show this alternation including: *alarm, amuse, anger, annoy, astonish, bore, charm, cheer, chill, comfort, concern, confuse, crush, delight, depress, disappoint, discourage, displease, distract, distress, disturb, encourage, enlighten, entertain, excite, exhaust, fascinate, flatter, frighten, frustrate, humiliate, hurt, impress, infuriate, interest, intimidate, irritate, mortify, offend, outrage, please, provoke, revolt, scare, shock, startle, stimulate, sting, strike, surprise, tantalize, tease, tempt, terrify, threaten, thrill, throw, trouble, unnerve, upset, worry.*

5. SUMMARY

One of our goals is to make explicit what speakers of English know about their language. To know a verb means to know the complements it takes and the form they are in, the information represented in its subcategorization frame. In addition, native speakers know whether a verb has more than one subcategorization. In this chapter we have explored the systematic nature of dual subcategorization.

We have examined a number of types of verbs which have more than one subcategorization, considering verbs which occur as both transitives and intransitives, verbs which are ditransitive and monotransitive, and verbs which allow an optional adverbial to appear as subject. These are the most common patterns of dual subcategorization.

Exercise 5

Not everyone will agree with the judgements about dual subcategorization presented in this chapter. Explore your own intuitions by choosing three of the verbs listed in 5.1 that allow a place adverbial to occur as subject. For each verb, make up pairs of examples like those in (32) and (33) to determine whether it has a dual subcategorization in your dialect.

Exercise 6

Choose five of the verbs listed in section 5.4 and make up pairs of examples like those in (40) and (41). Does each of the verbs allow the alternation discussed in 5.4?

Exercise 7

Learning the subcategorization patterns for verbs is one of the most difficult aspects of learning English. The following sentences were produced by non-native speakers of English. Identify the source of the ungrammaticality, using the concepts discussed in this and previous chapters.

1.   *Why you say me those bad things?
2.   *Please give me some ice cream. I like very much!
3.   *I gave it for the teacher.
4.   *I try to talk him, but he doesn't listen.
5.   *We went shopping today and picked some real bargains.
6.   [When offered a second piece of cake]
      *No, thank you, I don't want.

14

PASSIVE VERB PHRASES

TRADITIONAL GRAMMARS OF ENGLISH distinguish active voice from passive voice. For example, in (1) - (4), sentence (a) is in the active voice and (b), in the passive voice.

(1)   (a) The farmer killed the duckling.
       (b) The duckling was killed by the farmer.

(2)   (a) A famous linguist wrote this book.
       (b) This book was written by a famous linguist.

(3)   (a) Mary has finished the project.
       (b) The project has been finished.

(4)   (a) John was hitting Peter when Mother came home.
       (b) Peter was being hit (by John) when Mother came home.

Generally speaking, the two sentences express the same situation, but from two different perspectives. The active tells us what an agent does to a patient. For instance, (1)(a) conveys that the farmer, the agent, did the killing to the duckling, the theme. (The theme is sometimes called the patient.)

The passive sentence, on the other hand, tells us what happened to the theme. (1)(b) conveys that the theme, the duckling, was killed. A sentence in the passive voice puts the theme in the foreground and the agent in the background. In many passive sentences, the agent is not expressed at all.

Exercise 1

Examine (1) - (4) and describe the structure of the passive sentence by comparing it to the active one.

In this chapter, we are not going to focus on passive sentences per se, but on passive verb phrases, the special kind of nonfinite verb phrases they contain. As you will see, passive sentences are only one of a number of constructions in which passive VPs are used. We look at the syntactic properties of passive verb phrases in the same way we looked at other English phrases. In Section 1 we examine their internal syntax and in Section 2, their external syntax. In Section 3 we consider the use of passive sentences and in Section 4, restrictions on verbs that occur in passive VPs.

1. THE INTERNAL SYNTAX OF PASSIVE VERB PHRASES

There are three syntactic properties that differentiate passive VPs from other VPs. The first involves the *form* of the head verb, which must be a past participle, as in (5). (The passive verb phrases are in square brackets and the head verb in italics.)

(5)　(a)　The duckling was [*killed* by the farmer].
　　　(b)　This book was [*written* by a famous linguist].
　　　(c)　Peter was being [*hit* by John].
　　　(d)　The project was [*finished*].

The second property of passive VPs involves the complements of the head verb. What complements are required by the italicized verbs in (5)? To answer this question, don't consider the passive VPs of (5), but look at the active VPs in (6) (in square brackets). Subcategorizations of these verbs are given in (7).

(6)　(a)　The farmer [*killed* the duckling].
　　　(b)　A famous linguist [*wrote* this book].
　　　(c)　John was [*hitting* Peter].
　　　(d)　Mary [*finished* the project].

(7) Subcategorization frame:

kill	[_____ NP]
write	[_____ NP]
hit	[_____ NP]
finish	[_____ NP]

Comparing the subcategorizations in (7) with the passive VPs in (5), we see that the passives are missing the direct object NP.

A third property of passive VPs is that the agent of the action is expressed as the object of the preposition *by*. It is optional and frequently not expressed.

In a tree diagram, passives are indicated with the special label "PassVP" to differentiate them from other VPs. We draw in the missing NP, but leave a blank line under the NP node. This represents the fact that a NP is required by the verb, but not actually present in the VP. The agent phrase with *by* is a VP modifier and combines with the VP, as shown in (8).

(8)

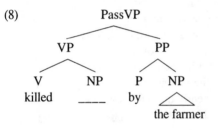

Exercise 2
Give the subcategorization frame for each verb in the following passive VPs. (The subcategorization frame should indicate how it is to be used in an *active* verb phrase, not a passive one.) Then draw a tree diagram for each passive VP. In your diagram be sure to include a node for the missing NP.

1. destroyed by the enemy
2. painted red by the farmer
3. brought to the party by my neighbor
4. ¯shown to a prospective buyer
5. insulted

Exercise 3

For each of the sentences below, write out the passive VP, showing with a dash where the missing NP should be. State the function the missing NP would have if the sentence were active and not passive. In the examples of PassVPs thus far, the missing NP has been a direct object, but it could also be an indirect object or the object of a preposition. It may help to construct the active counterpart.

Example:	A rabies shot was given to the dog.
Passive VP:	[given _____ to the dog]
Active VP:	[give *a rabies shot* to the dog]
Missing NP:	*a rabies shot* = direct object of the verb *give*

1.   The dog was given a rabies shot.
2.   A bill was sent to all our customers.
3.   All our customers were sent a bill.
4.   This bed was slept in by George Washington.
5.   Coins were thrown into the fountain by all the tourists.
6.   *The fountain was thrown coins into by everyone.
7.   These children will be cared for by their grandmother.
8.   A lovely meal was served to the volunteers.
9.   The newspapers were inadvertently thrown out with the trash.
10. *The trash was inadvertently thrown the newspapers out with.

Look over your answers and state a condition on the NP which is missing in the passive. Your condition should account for all the grammatical sentences and rule out the two ungrammatical ones.

Exercise 4

Not all NPs following a verb are eligible to be the missing NP in a passive verb phrase. Look over the following sentences and state a restriction on the missing NP in a passive VP.

(1)   (a)   My sister became a doctor.
       (b)   *A doctor was become by my sister.

(2)   (a)   My neighbors were famous artists.
      (b)   *Famous artists were been by my neighbors.

(3)   (a)   Sally was the teacher of the year.
      (b)   *The teacher of the year was been by Sally.

The properties of passive VPs are summarized in (9), where the statement of the missing NP has been clarified in light of the answers to Exercises 3 and 4. (For further discussion of the missing NP see the end of Section 2.)

(9)   (a)   Verb Form: Passive VPs are headed by a verb which is a
                         past participle.
      (b)   Missing NP: Passive VPs are missing an NP which is the
                         first argument NP following the verb in the
                         corresponding active VP.
      (c)   Agent: Passive VPs may contain a by-phrase that
                         expresses the agent of the action.

2. THE EXTERNAL SYNTAX OF PASSIVE VERB PHRASES

We have thus far identified the internal syntax of a new constituent, a passive VP. The next step is to see how this constituent fits into larger syntactic structures. Most often, a passive VP combines with the auxiliary verb *be*, as in (10). In traditional grammars, these sentences are said to be in the passive voice.

(10) (a)   The duckling *was* [killed by the farmer].
      (b)   This book *was* [written by a famous linguist].
      (c)   The project has *been* [finished].

This fact requires us to recognize two different auxiliaries *be*: The first combines with VPs whose head is a present participle to form progressive VPs (see Chapter 17), and the second combines with passive VPs. The subcategorization for "passive *be*" is in (11) and a tree diagram, in (12).

(11) *be*   [_____ PassVP]

(12)   VP

                 be   PassVP

A passive VP can be a complement of other verbs as well, as in (13).

(13)   (a)   My car *got* [stolen].
       (b)   We *had* the secretary [transferred to another job].
       (c)   They *got* the lights [fixed].
       (d)   The boss *wants* this report [finished by morning].

The verbs that take passive VPs as complements and their subcategorization frames are listed in (14). Note that the first two are intransitive, while the others are transitive. Tree diagrams for causative *have* and *want*, are given in (15).

(14)   (a)   *be*   [_____ PassVP]
       (b)   *get-1*   [_____ PassVP]
       (c)   *get-2*   ("cause")   [_____ NP PassVP]
       (d)   *have*   ("cause")   [_____ NP PassVP]
       (e)   *want*   [_____ NP PassVP]
       (f)   *see*   [_____ NP PassVP]
       (g)   *hear*   [_____ NP PassVP]

(15) (a)

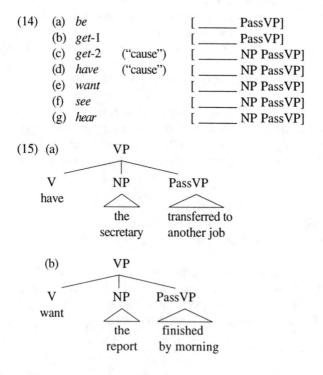

PASSIVE VERB PHRASES

The sentences of (16) show that passive VPs can be modifiers of nouns (the nouns are in italics). For instance, the phrase *examined by the new doctor* modifies the noun *baby*.

(16) (a) The *baby* [examined by the new doctor] was sent home.
 (b) The *horse* [killed in the storm] was buried yesterday.
 (c) The *necklace* [stolen by Tony from the museum] was returned in excellent condition.

A passive VP combines with a noun to form a new type of constituent, one larger than a noun, but smaller than a NP. This new constituent, labeled mnemonically N+, combines with a determiner to form a NP, as in (17).

(17)

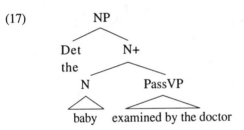

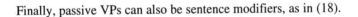

Finally, passive VPs can also be sentence modifiers, as in (18).

(18) (a) [Beaten again], the team headed for the clubhouse.
 (b) [Frightened by the noise], the children hid in the closet.

In summary, passive VPs occur in more contexts than the passive voice sentences of traditional grammars. They function as complements of certain verbs and are used as modifiers of nouns and sentences. In Unit VI, we introduce existential constructions, an additional context for passive VPs.

Before we leave the external syntax, let us return to the issue of missing NPs. We saw in Section 1 that a passive VP is missing the first argument NP following the verb. In tree diagrams missing NPs are indicated with a blank line, as in (19). Although an NP is missing from the VP, it is not missing from the sentence as a whole. It can always be "filled in" with an NP elsewhere in the sentence. In the passive VP of (19)(a), for example, the missing NP is understood as the NP in subject position (*this book*).

onding active sentence: *a famous linguist wrote this*
ink between the missing NP and the subject NP is
N.

(19) (a)

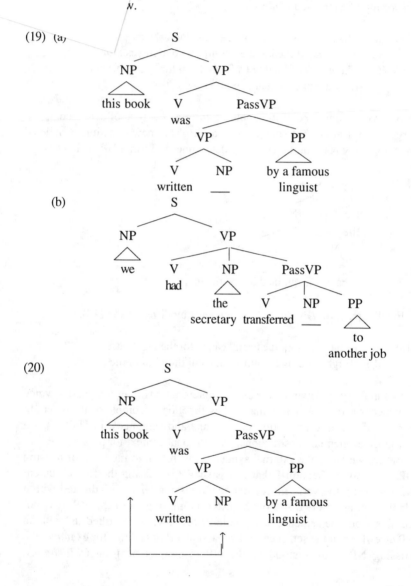

(b)

(20)

Because the missing NP of a passive VP is always linked to another NP in the sentence, it is not literally "missing," but only displaced. If the passive VP is a complement of an *intransitive* verb, like the verb *be* in (19)(a), the NP with which it is linked is the subject. If the passive VP is a complement of a *transitive* verb, like *transferred* in (19)(b), the NP is the direct object. (Compare the corresponding active VP: *transfer the secretary to another job.*) This linking is shown with an arrow in (21).

(21)

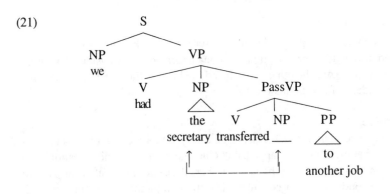

Exercise 5

In the following sentences, state whether the VPs in square brackets are passive or not. For each VP, give at least one piece of evidence from its internal or its external syntax.

Example: The boss had the secretary [type the report].
Evidence: The VP is not missing an NP.
               A by-phrase cannot be added.
Conclusion: The VP is not passive.

1.   The boss will have the report [typed by his personal secretary].
2.   I have already [typed the report].
3.   A painting by Picasso was [hung on this wall].
4.   Picasso [hung the painting on this wall].
5.   I had my curtains [hung by a specialist].
6.   Do you remember the photo that [hung on this wall]?
7.   The teacher [assigned those children to the same group].
8.   The children [assigned to my group] were very rowdy.

9.   I want these children [assigned to a different group].
10.   Do you think that this teacher has [given too much homework]?
11.   Mary told me that her son had [finished the project].
12.   I wondered if the project had been [finished on time].
13.   The painting [stolen from our museum] was found in the trashcan.
14.   The store [opened at 9:00].
15.   The boss wants the store [opened at 9:00].

Exercise 6
Review the special properties of auxiliary verbs, then give one piece of evidence that the verb *be* that is subcategorized for a passive VP is an auxiliary verb. Are the other verbs listed in (14) auxiliary verbs or not? Give some evidence for your answer.

Exercise 7
If a sentence contains the passive auxiliary *be* as well as other auxiliary verbs, what order do they appear in? One way to answer this question is to examine sentences which have a number of auxiliaries, including passive *be*. A second way is to consider only the complement structure of each auxiliary, i.e. by examining their subcategorization frames.

Exercise 8
Give tree diagrams for the following sentences, using a triangle to abbreviate the internal structure of PPs and NPs that do not contain passive VPs, but drawing out all VPs. For passive VPs, indicate the position of the missing NP and draw an arrow to link it with the NP which "fills it in."

1.   My sister got arrested.
2.   We were insulted by that fool.
3.   You should have your car washed by the Boy Scouts.
4.   The teacher wants the first drafts of our papers turned in.
5.   The children assigned to my group will be very rowdy.
6.   The animals must be given their vitamins.
7.   The project was started by Team A and finished by Team B.
8.   We want those boys arrested for indecent exposure.
9.   When I was in New York, my purse got stolen and my car got towed.

10. The jewels stolen from the Princess and hidden in the vase were found by some boys.

Exercise 9
The intransitive verbs *be* and *get-1* are both subcategorized for a passive VP, but sentences with these two verbs are not semantically equivalent. Consider (1) - (3) and try to characterize the difference.

(1)   (a) My car was stolen last week.
       (b) My car got stolen last week.

(2)   (a) My neighbor was invited to the White House.
       (b) My neighbor got invited to the White House.

(3)   (a) Peter was hurt in the explosion.
       (b) Peter got hurt in the accident.

Exercise 10
Pick a text of several pages, identify all the passive VPs, and calculate how many lack a by-phrase. Compare your figure with the results of one study that reports it to be omitted over 75% of the time (Huddleston 1984:441). Why might it be so common to omit the by-phrase?

---

3. USES OF PASSIVE SENTENCES

In this section we shift our focus from passive VPs to passive sentences, those with the passive auxiliary *be* and a passive VP. As noted, an active sentence and a corresponding passive express the same event. (In sentences involving negatives or quantifiers this is not always true, but we will ignore them here.) For example, both the active and passive in (1), repeated here as (22), can be used to express the same event of killing.

(22) (a) The farmer killed the duckling.
       (b) The duckling was killed by the farmer.

An active sentence is the neutral, or unmarked, way to express an event; the passive is a marked variant. Whether a speaker chooses to use a passive depends on a number of factors explored in this section. First, we consider the main reason for using passive sentences in general, and then look at some motivations for using passives *with* agent by-phrases and *without* by-phrases.

3.1 Passives in General

In a discourse about a particular person (or thing), there is a general tendency to structure each sentence so that the NPs referring to that person (or thing) appear in subject position, the favored syntactic position for a sentence topic. If the person is an agent, the resulting sentence will be active; if the person is a theme, the sentence will be passive. That is, the speaker uses the passive construction when the theme, and not the agent, is the focus of attention. For example, the sentences in (23) are "about" Sally Johnson. The switch from active to passive in (23)(c) keeps an NP which refers to her in subject position. The active counterpart would shift the focus from Sally Johnson to the Orchestra Board.

(23)   (a)   Sally Johnson completed her musical studies in 1974.
        (b)   She joined the Cleveland Orchestra ten years ago.
        (c)   In 1996 she was chosen Musician of the Year by the
              Orchestra Board.

3.2 Agented Passives

Agented passives are passives with a by-phrase that expresses the agent of the action. Given that a passive is used when the speaker wishes to focus on the theme, why might the agent be mentioned at all? One reason is that it has some transitory interest for the discourse. It is of fleeting relevance, but not irrelevant, and is clearly secondary in salience to the theme, as in (23)(c). The agent in (23)(c) is mentioned because (the speaker believes) it is of transitory interest to the discourse. As discussed below, if the agent is irrelevant (i.e. if the speaker considers it irrelevant) it would be omitted, as in (24).

(24)   In 1971 Sally Johnson was accepted as a scholarship student
        at the Peabody Institute.

Additional examples of agented passives are given in (25) and (26), with the passives in square brackets. Extended contexts are given to show clearly that the conditions for use of the agented passive are met: the agent is of secondary importance relative to the theme, but of fleeting relevance. The agents in (25) and (26), Becky D'Angelo and Sargent, introduce new information in the discourse, but this information is only of transitory relevance.

(25)   Gerald Arpino began choreographing in 1961, and he is currently The Joffrey's resident choreographer. He is the first choreographer commissioned to create a ballet to honor the American Presidency. [His 1986 Birthday Variations was commissioned by Becky D'Angelo as a birthday gift to her husband, Dino D'Angelo.] Mr. Arpino's ballets, sought after worldwide, are in the repertoires of many of the world's great ballet companies.

(26)   He saw ... that there were pictures on the walls. One of these struck a familiar note. He went close to it and recognised a portrait of Alice Wetherall ... [It was painted by Sargent in his happiest mood,] and the lovely wild-flower face seemed to lean down to him .... (Sayers 1969:41). (This painting is referred to several pages later as "the Sargent portrait.")

A second reason for including an agent by-phrase in a passive is when the agent signals a new sentence topic. That is, a passive sentence with an agent by-phrase can be used to shift topics, as in (27) (cited in van Oosten 1984:266).

(27)   I was never home as a kid.... I was always roaming around. I was born out of wedlock so [I was raised by my grandfather,] who was very hard with me at times. But he was a strong influence because he was very politically oriented .... My grandfather was a crew leader ...

3.3 Agentless Passives
In addition to using a passive to focus on the theme, a speaker might use a passive sentence to avoid mentioning the agent at all. A speaker might do this, first of all, because there *is* no agent, as in (28). Because these events

do not involve agents, the passives (in square brackets) do not have semantically equivalent actives, which readers can demonstrate for themselves.

(28) (a) The boat capsized and three children were [drowned].
      (b) It was [rumored] that the president would resign.
      (c) This rumor was [widely believed].

A speaker might also avoid mentioning the agent if "the identity of the agent is irrelevant to the progress of the discourse" (van Oosten 1984:205). The agent may be irrelevant because it is unknown, as in (29), or very general, as in (29). Stating the agents in (29) (something like farmers in (a) and weavers in (b)) would add no information beyond that which can be deduced from the context.

(29) (a) I don't know what happened. There was a terrible crash, the jar of soy sauce fell over, and my new dress was ruined.
      (b) I left my purse here for just a moment and all my money was stolen.
      (c) The injured child was taken to the hospital where she was treated for smoke inhalation.

(30) (a) Three main crops are grown in this part of the country; they are planted in the spring and harvested in the fall.
      (b) This cloth was made in India. Isn't it lovely?

Sometimes, it is *expedient* not to name the agent of an action. Perhaps it would reveal a source of information or place the blame in a way that would be impolite, tactless, or indiscrete, as in (31).

(31) (a) We have been informed that the president will resign soon.
      (b) I'm sorry if you have been inconvenienced, but you were given some very bad advice.
      (c) [Tax preparer to client:]
           A serious error was made in calculating your taxes.

This is a special case of the irrelevant-agent passive because by pretending that the agent is irrelevant, the speaker accomplishes the aim of hiding his identity. Van Oosten suggests (1984:240-41) that the frequent overuse of passives in scholarly writing also represents a kind of expediency passive. By not mentioning the agent, the speaker or writer implies that the results being reported are more important than their agent.

The uses of passive sentences are summarized in (32).

(32)　(a)　Passives are used when the theme is the topic.
　　　(b)　Agented passives are used when
　　　　　(i)　 the agent is of transitory relevance or
　　　　　(ii)　the agent is to be the new topic.
　　　(c)　Agentless passives are used when
　　　　　(i)　 there is no agent or
　　　　　(ii)　the agent is unknown or otherwise irrelevant to the progress
　　　　　　　 of the discourse.

Exercise 11
Put square brackets around the passive VPs and for each, give a reason why the passive has been used.

1.　The police are anxious to get in touch with a man who is known to have visited the museum before the robbery. The man is 35, has fair hair and a small moustache. He is thought to be travelling with a small child with bright red braids.

2.　One February night in 1987, ... Ernil Bernal tunneled into a pyramid where the body of a Peruvian monarch had lain undisturbed for more than a thousand years. Bernal thrust an iron rod upward, and was almost smothered by an avalanche of sand, gold and silver ornaments. ... Several hours later Bernal and his associates carried out 11 rice sacks filled with treasure. The looters then began to quarrel, one was murdered, and another fled through the surrounding sugar cane fields to notify police.

3.   (Continuation of 2.) Dr. Walter Alva, director of the Bruning
      Museum, was asked by police to examine some items confiscated at
      the Bernal farmhouse ... He expected to see a few gold beads and
      decorated pots, nothing unusual. Instead, the police chief showed him
      a beautifully crafted mask of hammered sheet gold with silver eyes ...
      Alva learned that it had been taken from a pyramid complex near the
      village of Sipan. (Connell 1992)

4.   A young Basque named Pedro Altube ... made enough to buy a herd
      of cattle. He trailed the herd over the Sierra and across the deserts of
      Nevada until he chanced on Independence Valley. He was so struck by
      its beauty and the opportunity it offered that ... he founded the
      historic Spanish Ranch. (Laxalt 1966.881)

Exercise 12   For Discussion
In many grammar books for ESL students, the uses of passive sentences are
taught by giving a few principles, followed by example sentences. For
instance, one principle given in Azar (1989:123): "The 'by phrase' is
included only if it is important to know who performs an action." The
example: "*Life on the Mississippi* was written by Mark Twain." The
student is then given a list of passive sentences and asked to discuss why the
use of the passive is appropriate. What is wrong with this approach?

---

4. RESTRICTIONS ON VERBS IN PASSIVE VPs

In Section 2, which dealt with the internal syntax, we saw that passive VPs
are missing a NP and that both transitive and intransitive verbs can be head
of a passive. In this section we will explore some transitive verbs that
cannot be head of a passive VP.

4.1 Symmetric Verbs
Symmetric verbs express logically symmetric relationships, those in which
the subject and direct object are interchangeable, such as *resemble*, *date*, or
marry (when it means that the subject and object are married to each other).

(33) (a) Mary resembles Susan.
      (b) Susan resembles Mary.

(34) (a) My brother married my best friend.
      (b) My best friend married my brother.

Symmetric verbs do not occur in passive VPs.

(35) (a) *Mary is resembled by Susan.
      (b) *Susan is resembled by Mary.

This restriction can be explained by recalling that the passive foregrounds
the theme by putting it into subject position. With symmetic verbs this
effect can be achieved by merely switching the NPs, obviating the need for a
passive.

4.2 Measure Verbs
Some verbs express a measure of the subject NP with the direct object
denoting a quantity or an amount, as in (36).

(36) (a) This room holds 300 people.
      (b) You weigh 150 pounds.

Examples of container and measure verbs include: *carry, contain, fit, hold,
house, include, measure, seat, sleep, stand, total, weigh.* These verbs do
not occur in passive verb phrases.

(37) (a) This room sleeps six.
      (b) *Six are slept by this room.

(38) (a) My sister weighs 150 pounds.
      (b) *150 pounds are weighed by my sister.

If measure words are analyzed as transitive verbs, they are exceptional in
not occurring in passive VPs. However, they can be analyzed as a type of
linking verb, one that links an NP with a measure phrase. In this view
measure verbs are not exceptional. Because they are not followed by an
argument noun phrase, they do not meet the conditions for a passive VP.

4.3 Other Verbs

Some other transitive verbs that do not occur in passive VPs are listed in
(39). Verify for yourself that the corresponding passives are ill-formed.

(39)   (a) *have, possess, lack*   Mary has a cat.
                                       She lacks tact.
        (b) *fit, suit, become*   That dress fits you.
        (c) *mean, intend*   This means war.
        (d) *bear, take*   She bore his insults with grace.
        (e) *approach*   We slowly approached the throne.
        (f) *touch*   Her dress touched the ground.

In general, for a passive to be acceptable, the theme must be affected in
some way by the action. This "makes sense" in that one function of the
passive is to focus attention on the theme, and it would be odd to choose as
the focus of attention an entity entirely unaffected by the action. The fact
that the verbs of (39) are not used in the passive is believed to be due to this
principle.

Finally, this principle can also be invoked in cases where the object of a
preposition is unacceptable as the subject of a passive, as in (40)(b) and
(41)(b). A bed is more likely to be affected by a visit from George
Washington than from some unknown person. And, while a toe is affected
by someone stepping on it, a bench is generally *not* affected by someone
sitting on it.

(40)   (a) This bed was slept in ____ by George Washington.
        (b) ?This bed was slept in ____ by someone.

(41)   (a) My toe was stepped on ____ .
        (b) ?That bench was sat on ____ by three people.

UNIT IV
VERBAL CATEGORIES: TENSE AND ASPECT

IN UNIT IV we explore some important grammatical categories expressed in the verb phrase in English. We begin in Chapter 15 with a discussion of the distinction between the universal notion of time and the linguistic category of tense, with a special focus on the meaning of the past tense.

As part of the discussion of the present tense in Chapter 16, we introduce a classification of verbs into events, activities, and states. This enables us to characterize the different meanings conveyed by the present tense with different lexical verbs.

The category of aspect and the progressive aspect are discussed in Chapter 17. The English perfect, a quasi-tense that relates the time of one state or event to an earlier one, is the topic of Chapter 18.

Finally, in Chapter 19 we present the different devices used in English for talking about future situations, which are known as futuritives.

15
TIME AND TENSE:
FOCUS ON THE PAST TENSE

"DOLPHIN?" the clerk repeated. "Dolphin. Well, yerse. We hold the keys. Were you wanting to view?"

"If I might, I was," Peregrine Jay mumbled, wondering why such conversations should always be conducted in the past tense. "I mean," he added boldly, "I did and I still do. I want to view, if you please."

As these lines from the beginning of the novel *Killer Dolphin* (Marsh 1966: 213) indicate, even ordinary speakers wonder on occasion about tense use in English. In this chapter we explore the circumstances in which the past tense is used, but begin by looking at tense in general and how it relates to a non-linguistic notion, time.

1. INTRODUCTION TO VERBAL SEMANTICS

There are two kinds of meaning expressed by a verb phrase. The first is lexical meaning, the meaning conveyed by the lexical verb (as opposed to the auxiliary verbs) and its complements. The lexical verb *wash*, for example, conveys a different meaning from the verbs *wipe, sweep, kiss,* and so on. The second kind of meaning involves modifications to lexical meaning, which we make by means of alteration or addition. We alter the form of the verb (i.e. inflect it) or add another verb (often an auxiliary), as in (1).

An overall picture of verbal modification involves three major categories: tense, aspect, and mood. In the next section of this chapter we explore the category of tense. Aspect is discussed in Chapter 17.

(1)   MODIFICATIONS OF MEANING   EXAMPLE
       (a)   the situation   She spoke quietly.
             occurred in the past
       (b)   the situation occurs exactly   He shoots and misses!
             at the moment of speaking
       (c)   the situation will take place   We will miss you.
             sometime after the moment
             of speaking
       (d)   the situation is ongoing   The kids are playing
                                                outside.

       (e)   the situation is complete   I wrote that book.
       (f)   the situation is habitual   Sue used to play tennis.
       (g)   the situation might happen   It may rain.
       (h)   the situation is supposed   You should do your
             to happen   homework.

2. TIME AND TENSE

Time is universal. It is common to all peoples and exists independently of
language. It is conceived of as having one dimension, like the straight line
in (2).

(2)   Time Line: ───────────────────────────────→

We can put an X on this line to represent the here and now, the time at
which we are speaking or writing. The X divides the line into 3 parts. The
current moment is referred to as present time, or the present. The time
before now is past time, or the past, while the time after now is future time,
or simply, the future.

(3)   ───────────────────── X ─────────────────────→

          < BEFORE NOW >< NOW >< AFTER NOW >

To describe the tenses of English we need to make reference to three other
times. The first is the time of speaking, or, the time of the utterance,

abbreviated "TU." The second is the time of the situation described by the lexical verb and its complements, abbreviated "TS." The third is reference time ("TR"), particularly important in the discussion of the perfect in Chapter 18. We can plot the time of the situation on a time line to show the relationship between it and the time of the utterance, using an "X" to indicate a moment of time and a bracket to indicate an interval. For instance, in (4), the time of the situation ("Sam's arrival") is before the time of the utterance (TS before TU), as shown on the time line in (4)(b).

(4)   (a)   Sam came home last night at 8:00.

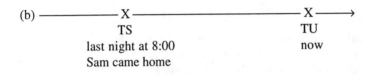

(b) ─────────── X ─────────────────── X ──⟶
                TS   TU
            last night at 8:00   now
            Sam came home

In (5) the time of the situation ("our eating dinner") is also before the time of the utterance. Since this situation is presented as an interval of time, it is indicated with a bracket, as in (5).

(5)   (a)   We were eating dinner during the Redskins game yesterday.

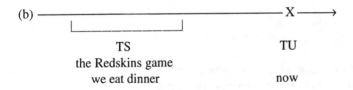

(b) ──────────────────────────── X ──⟶
        └_____┘
                TS   TU
        the Redskins game
          we eat dinner   now

When talking about time, notions like the present, the past, and the future are extra-linguistic notions having nothing to do with language or grammar. Tense, on the other hand, is a linguistic category indicated in verb forms. We alter the form of the verb, or inflect it, to show tense. The expression of tense varies from language to language because different languages have different numbers of tenses and different morphological means for expressing them. We define a tense as in (6).

(6)   A tense is a set of verb forms whose distribution
       is defined in terms of the relationship between TS and TU.

That is, a verb form is considered a tense when its definition makes reference to the relationship between the time of the situation (TS) and the time of the utterance (TU). This way of defining tense results in only two tenses in English, a present tense and a past tense. The other constructions called tenses (such as the progressive, the perfect, and the use of the modal *will* often called the future tense) are not expressed by altering the form of the verb; most of them are not defined primarily in terms of TS and TU, either.

Turning to the English tenses, note that the past tense in English is expressed by the form we call the past tense form (see Chapter 8). It shows no variation for person or number of the subject, as shown in (7). (The verb *be* is an exception; see below.)

(7)   (a)   I / we / you / she / they *ate* supper at 8:00.
        (b)   I / we / you / she / they *lived* in Chicago.
        (c)   I / we / you / she / they *took* a walk in the park.

The present tense in English is expressed by two forms, the 3rd person singular present tense form and the general present form, as shown in (8).

(8)   (a)   3rd singular present: She   *eats* at 8:00.
        (b)   General present: I / we / you / they   *eat* at 8:00.

In summary, in the discussion of tense and time it is important to distinguish the following four things.

1.   the verb form (3rd person singular form, general present form, past tense form, present participle form, etc.)
2.   the verb tense (present tense or past tense), where a tense is a set of forms
3.   the use of the tense (where each tense has one primary use and several secondary uses)
4.   the time of the situation expressed by the lexical verb and its complements

The remainder of this chapter is concerned with the form and the use of the past tense.

3. THE FORM OF THE PAST TENSE

As noted, the past tense is expressed by the past tense form of the verb. Regular past tense forms are constructed by adding the suffix /-d/ to the base form (phonetic variants [-əd], [-t], [-d]); irregular past tense forms show a variety of patterns, usually involving a change in the vowel of the verb. The verb *be* is even more irregular in that it has two past tense forms: *was* is used if the subject is first or third person singular and *were*, if the subject is second person or plural. Some past tense verb forms are given in (9).

(9) Regular forms: *waited, walked, laughed, lived, died*
     Irregular forms: *ate, came, wrote, sang, left, put, was*
     The verb *be*:   *was, were*

The past tense is a tense because it is expressed by changes in the form of the verb and because its primary meaning has to do with the relation between TS and TU. In Section 4 we discuss this primary use in more detail. In Section 5 we introduce some secondary uses of the past tense, uses which do not involve reference to time.

Exercise 1
What is the relationship between TS and TU in each of the following sentences? Plot them on a time line using X's and brackets, assuming that TU is now.

1. Peter the Great died in 1721.
2. Mary is going to New York next week.
3. (Watch carefully as) I pour the oil into the vinegar.
4. Sally is a famous physics professor.
5. Steven left for New Zealand last week.
6. We leave for Paris on the 15th.
7. Mother always laughs at my jokes.
8. Student to teacher: "Did you want to see me?"

Exercise 2
Give the name of the tense of the head verb in each finite verb phrase below
and state whether the time of the situation is in the present, the past, or the
future. Where possible, state the relationship between TS and TU.

1.   Marina is very tall.
2.   The Wizards play the Celtics this weekend.
3.   Last week this strange man called me up. First he asked me my name
      and then he starts telling me all sorts of strange things.
4.   Peter is coming this afternoon.
5.   I was wondering if you could help me.
6.   Jay Wilson may leave tomorrow.
7.   If I won the lottery, I would take all my friends to Paris.
8.   Don't worry, when you come, I'll be ready.
9.   Bears hibernate during the winter.
10.   The thief may have stolen the money yesterday.

---

4. THE PRIMARY USE OF THE PAST TENSE: TS IS BEFORE TU

The primary use of the past tense is to indicate that the situation is true in
the past, before the time of the utterance, as in (10).

(10)   (a)   They *studied* in Chicago for five years.
       (b)   Shakespeare *lived* in Stratford on Avon.
       (c)   I *was* born in 1928.
       (d)   Someone *ate* all the chocolate cake.

We can identify three subtypes of this primary use.

4.1 The Situation is Over
In some cases the situation expressed with a verb in the past tense has
ended. The situations depicted in the sentences of (11) took place in the past,
but are not going on at the time of the utterance. They are over and done
with.

(11) (a) They *studied* in Chicago for five years.
      (b) Shakespeare *lived* in Stratford on Avon.
      (c) Someone *ate* all the chocolate cake.

4.2 The Situation Persists 344

It is possible, however, for the situation described by a verb in the past tense to still be going on or still be true in the present, at the time of the utterance, as in (12).

(12) (a) I had a wonderful time on my vacation. This place *was* just gorgeous. (The place still is gorgeous.)
      (b) Your ex-husband *was* such a creep! (Presumably he still is.)
      (c) That stranger who helped you yesterday *was* really tall. (He still is tall.)

Since the situations expressed with the past tense in (12) are true in the present, one could have used a present tense instead (e.g. *the place is just gorgeous, your ex-husband is such a creep*). Using the past tense conveys the nuance that the situation, though still true at the time of the utterance, is no longer relevant or important to the speaker. For example, we can assume that there is no ongoing relationship between the speaker and the stranger mentioned in (12)(c). This lack of relationship is underlined verbally by the use of the past tense. It conveys that the reference point for the relationship is in the past.

4.3 Attitudinal Pasts 544

An additional context in which we use the past tense involves wishes or desires that existed in the past, but still hold in the present. In such contexts we can use either the present or the past tense, as in (13).

(13) (a) Excuse me, I *want* to ask you a question.
      (b) Excuse me, I *wanted* to ask you a question.

A speaker who utters (13)(b), using the past tense, might very well still want to ask a question. The past tense conveys that the wanting began prior to the time of speaking. Further examples are given in (14) and (15).

(14)   (a) Here I am, sir. *Do* you want to see me?
      (b) Here I am, sir. *Did* you want to see me?

(15)   (a) Customer: I'll have a T-bone steak.
           Waitress: How *do* you want that cooked?
      (b)   How *did* you want that cooked?

The situations described by (13) - (15) are true in the past and continue to be true in the present so that either tense could be used. Presenting them as taking place in the past, however, distances them from the here and now. The effect achieved by distancing is politeness. A past tense in sentences like these is more deferential and less brusque than a present tense would be. This is the use which momentarily irritated Peregrine Jay in the opening passage of this chapter.

5. SECONDARY USES OF THE PAST TENSE

Secondary uses of the past tense are *not* defined in terms of the relationship between TS and TU. We examine two of them here.

5.1 Secondary Use—1
One secondary use of the past tense occurs in backshifting, a phenomenon probably most familiar from direct and indirect speech, as in (16) and (17).

(16)   (a) Direct: I'*m* tired.
      (b) Indirect: You said that you *were* tired so go home.

(17)   (a) Direct: The race *starts* here at this tree tomorrow at 4:30.
      (b) Indirect: (Uttered later the same day)
                 Sally repeated that the race *started* there at that tree tomorrow at 4:30.

Direct speech reports the exact words uttered. Indirect speech, sometimes called reported speech, reports the meaning of the utterance and typically involves adjustments to the exact words, including shift in pronouns (e.g. from *I* to *you*), adverbials (from *here* to *there*), and tense (e.g. from present to past). In the examples of direct speech in (16)(a) and (17)(a), we have the present tense, while in the reports of these utterances in (16)(b) and (17)(b), the verb in the main clause is in the past tense (*said* and *repeated*) and the verb in the reported clause has been shifted to the past tense. The use of the past tense in the reported clause conveys nothing about the time of the situation ("the start of the race"), which is future, as shown by the adverbial *tomorrow*. More examples are given in (18).

(18)   Direct   Indirect
    (a) I *hate* sports.   Billy said that he *hated* sports.
    (b) You *are* lying to me.   I told her she *was* lying to me.
    (c) Where *can* we eat?   They asked us where they *could* eat.

Backshifting occurs not only with indirect speech, but also with reported feelings and thoughts expressed frequently with verbs such as *know, think, realize,* and *forget.*

(19)   (a) She knows that we *are* meeting tomorrow.
       (b) She knew that we *were* meeting tomorrow.

In (19)(a) the reporting verb (*knows*) is in the present tense, as is the verb in the reported clause (*are*). In (19)(b), when the reporting verb is past tense (*knew*), the verb in the reported clause is backshifted to past tense (*were*). Note that the time of the situation ("we are meeting") has not changed; it remains in the future. More examples are given in (20).

(20)   (a) They thought, correctly, that the trial *was* scheduled for July.
       (b) Suddenly we realized that we *would* miss the first day of school.
       (c) We forgot that the papers *were* due next Monday.

In summary, the use of the past tense in these clauses has nothing to do with the time of the situation, but follows from the tense of the main clause. If the main clause verb is past tense, a present tense in direct speech may be backshifted to past tense in reported speech.

We can also backshift when the verb of direct speech is in the past tense. The past tense is backshifted to the past perfect (see Chapter 18).

(21)   (a) Direct: *Did* the murdered man leave a will?
       (b) Indirect: We wondered whether the murdered man *had* left a will.

(22)   (a) Direct: *Were* you happy with him?
       (b) Indirect: They asked me if I *had* been happy with him.

There is a related circumstance in which we use the past tense, a phenomenon known as free indirect speech. It is a report of someone's words or thoughts indirectly by backshifting, but with omission of the reporting clause, as shown in the examples of (23), adapted from Leech (1987:110).

(23)   (a) Indirect speech: Agnes wondered why they always *picked* on her.
       (b) Free indirect speech: Why *did* they always pick on her?

The use of free indirect speech has become a standard practice in twentieth century fiction, allowing a writer "to retell someone's words or thoughts indirectly and at length without having to keep inserting expressions like *He said* or *She exclaimed*" (Leech 1987:110). In (24) is a longer example of an interior monologue from "The Boarding House" by James Joyce, a master of this technique (Joyce 1962:64).

(24)   Mrs. Mooney glanced instinctively at the little gilt clock on the mantelpiece ... She would have plenty of time to have the matter out with Mr. Dorian ... She was sure she would win. To begin with she had all the weight of social opinion on her side: she was an outraged mother. She had allowed him to live beneath her roof, assuming he was a man of honor, and he had simply abused her hospitality.... He had simply taken advantage of Polly's youth and inexperience: that was evident. The question was: what reparation would he make?

5.2 Secondary Use—2
The second secondary use of the past tense is to indicate hypothetical meaning. When a construction conveys hypothetical meaning, there is an assumption on the part of the speaker that the situation did not, does not, or will not take place, as in unreal conditional clauses. Consider the contrasts

in (25) and (26). The speaker of (25)(a) uses a present tense and specifies a real (or open) condition to dying. He or she makes no assumption about whether leaving will take place. The speaker of (25)(b), on the other hand, expresses an unreal condition; he or she assumes that the leaving will *not* take place. The if-clause expresses something hypothetical, and the verb is in the past tense.

(25) (a) Real condition: If you *leave* me, I'll die.
     (b) Unreal condition: If you *left* me, I'd die.

Similarly, the speaker of (26)(a) expresses a real condition using the present tense; it conveys no assumptions about the happiness of the addressee. The speaker of (26)(b), on the other hand, expresses an unreal condition with the past tense; it conveys the assumption that the addressee is not happy.

(26) (a) Real: If you *are* happy, you should try to help others
                  be happy.
     (b) Unreal: If you *were* happy, you could make others happy, too.

The difference between the present and past tenses in the if-clauses does not involve time, since they all express conditions whose time reference is future. Rather, using the past tense presents the situation in the if-clause as less likely to take place. The past tense conveys that the condition is more tentative or remote.

Unreal conditions are only one construction in which we use the past tense to express hypothetical meaning. We also find it in other subordinate clauses introduced by expressions such as *as if, as though, suppose, supposing, imagine,* and *would rather.* With these expressions, like with the conditions discussed above, both the present and the past tense may be used, with the past tense conveying hypothetical meaning.

(27) (a) She acts as if she *owned* the place, but she doesn't.
     (b) It's not as though we *were* dumb. After all, we have
         degrees in linguistics.
     (c) Suppose you and I *were* married ... Thank God, we're not.
     (d) I'd rather you *treated* your teachers with respect, but alas, I
         know you won't.

We also use the past tense to convey hypothetical meaning with modal auxiliaries. This occurs in independent clauses as well as subordinate ones. Consider (28) and (29), in which the modals express possibility. The past tense conveys that the possibility is more "tentative and guarded" (Leech 1987:127) and could be paraphrased, "it is possible, though unlikely."

(28)   (a) You *may* be right.
        (b) You *might* be right.

(29)   (a) I *can* help you tomorrow.
        (b) I *could* help you tomorrow.

(29)(a) expresses that it is possible for the speaker to help, whereas (29)(b) with the past tense casts that possibility as less likely or more remote.

We find a slightly different take on hypothetical meaning with modals when they have a sense of permission. In (30) the use of the past tense, strictly speaking, should convey that the speaker thinks that permission is unlikely to be granted.

(30)   (a) *Could* I borrow a cup of sugar?
        (b) *Might* I trouble you for a match?

Such examples point to a weakening of hypothetical meaning because people choose *could* and *might* out of politeness, even when they *expect* their requests to be complied with. The sentences seem to imply a "suppressed unreal condition," such as "...if I were bold enough to ask you." We find a similar expression of politeness in the use of the past tense *would* in place of the present tense *will*, to express volition.

(31)   (a) *Would* you pass me the sugar?
        (b) I wonder if someone *would* help me with these packages.

In many descriptions of English the use of the past tense to express hypothetical meaning is treated as a special inflectional form, called the past subjunctive. The analysis presented here does not recognize a special subjunctive form of the verb but, on the contrary, says that the primary difference between the forms *come/came* or *may/might* is one of tense.

One secondary use of the past tense is to convey hypothetical meaning.

There is one problem with this analysis concerning the verb *be*, which, as noted at the beginning of the chapter, has two past tense forms: *was* (used with a first or third person singular subject) and *were* (used with a second person or plural subject). In those contexts where the past tense form expresses hypothetical meaning, prescriptive grammatical tradition requires the form *were*, regardless of the subject.

(32) (a) If he *were* (*was) to move to Chicago, we could live together.
           (Such a move is presented as very unlikely.)
      (b) I wish I *were* (*was) a man.   (Uttered by a woman.)
      (c) She acts as though she *were* the star of the play, but she's only
           an understudy.

In less formal styles of speaking, invariant *were* is frequently replaced by *was* (when the subject is first or third person singular). According to Quirk (1985:158), this special form of *were* may be regarded as a "fossilized inflection: It is nowadays a less usual alternative to the hypothetical past indicative" (i.e. to the use of the past tense to express hypothetical meaning). The fact that prescriptive tradition continues to insist on the use of invariant *were* in such contexts has led to speaker confusion on this issue and occasionally, to hypercorrection of appropriate *was* to an incorrect *were*. In (33) (from Hemingway 1961:6), one would expect the form *was* (a backshifted third person singular *is* (cf. the direct question, "it is snow?" and the indirect question, "he asked if it was snow"), but invariant *were*, which "should" express hypothetical meaning, has been used instead.

(33)   That was one of the things he had saved to write, with, in the morning at breakfast, looking out the window and seeing snow on the mountains in Bulgaria and Nansen's Secretary asking the old man if it *were* snow...

6. EXPRESSING PAST TIME IN NONFINITE VPs

Past time cannot be expressed with the past tense in *nonfinite* VPs, since the past tense is a *finite* verb form. Consider the sentences of (34), which have the modal *may*, which expresses possibility.

(34) (a) It may rain.
      (b) Molly may behave at the concert.

The situations ("it rains" and "Molly behaves") may be understood as taking place in the present or the future, as can be demonstrated by adding time adverbials.

(35) Present Time
      (a) It may be raining now.
      (b) Molly may be behaving at the concert this afternoon.

(36) Future Time
      (a) It may rain tomorrow.
      (b) Molly may behave at the concert tomorrow night.

How do we express a situation whose possibility took place in the past, though? The sentences of (37) show that the combination of base form and past time adverbial is ungrammatical. The base form cannot be used to convey that the situation took place in the past.

(37) (a) *It may rain yesterday.
      (b) *Molly may behave at the concert yesterday.

On the other hand, we cannot use a past tense form of the verb, either, as in (38), since modal auxiliaries must combine with VPs whose head is a base form.

(38) (a) *It may rained yesterday.
      (b) *Molly may behaved at the concert yesterday.

Nor is it possible to use the past tense of the modal *may* itself to convey that the situation ("it rains" or "Molly behaves") took place in the past since, as discussed above, the past tense of modals conveys hypothetical meaning. The sentences of (39) do not convey that the situations took place in the past; they convey that the possibility of them happening is remote. Note that one cannot add a past time adverbial to these sentences, either.

(39) (a) *It might rain yesterday.
    (b) *Molly might behave at the concert yesterday.

To convey the meaning we are looking for, we must use the auxiliary verb *have*, which is a substitute for a past tense in nonfinite VPs.

(40) (a) It may *have* rained yesterday.
    (b) Molly may *have* behaved at the concert yesterday.

Additional examples are given in (41), where *have* conveys that the situations 'take shirts to the cleaners' and 'lose the notebook' took place in the past.

(41) (a) John must *have* taken the shirts to the cleaners last week.
    (b) He appears to *have* lost his notebook.

Exercise 3
Pick a short, narrative passage, such as a children's story, and identify all instances of the past tense. Of the primary uses note whether the situation is over or persists, and of secondary uses, whether the use is due to backshifting or hypothetical meaning.

Exercise 4
Pick a front page news article and number each situation in the simple past tense (ignoring progressives and perfects). Plot the situations on a time line and note the difference between the order in which events are narrated and the order in which they actually occurred.

Exercise 5
The verb *used*, subcategorized for an infinitive phrase ([____ InfVP]), is used to talk about past situations, as in (1).

(1) (a) Magic used to play basketball.
    (b) We used to see a lot of Cathy.
    (c) Sarah used to like grammar.

Make up three more sentences using this verb and characterize its meaning. Consider ungrammatical sentences, as in (2), as well as grammatical ones.

(2)　　(a)　*I used to borrow this book from the library last week.
　　　　(b)　*The busdriver used to kill a deer on the highway.
　　　　(c)　*The children used to eat pizza for lunch on January 20.

Does the verb *used* have a present tense form? Is the verb *used* an auxiliary verb?

Exercise 6

"Translate" the following passages. Since the focus of this exercise is the phenomenon of backshifting in nonfinite clauses, use as many backshifted forms as you can. Make a list of the adjustments you have to make.

1. Susan calls in to work one morning and says, "I am not feeling very good today. My head hurts and I can't think clearly. I would come to work, but I am also sick to my stomach. I think I will stay home." How would you report her remarks to her supervisor that afternoon?

2. In July your mother writes you a letter. "I don't know what we will do on our vacation next month. We may go to Bermuda and we may go to Hawaii. We can't decide because travel packages to both locations are so attractive this time of year." In August your brother calls. He wants to know where your parents are. What do you tell him?

3. One afternoon the following events occur. Later you tell someone else about them. You are in the grocery store and meet your elderly neighbor, Mrs. Crumpet. She seems awfully confused. She is looking for her purse and can't find it. She asks everyone who walks by, "Have you seen my purse?" You think it is possible that she left it at home and politely suggest that she look there. You drive her home and she finds her purse on the kitchen table. She did forget it at home. You think she will be grateful and believe that she has a social obligation to reciprocate in some way, like by inviting you to stay for tea. But she doesn't.

16

THE PRESENT TENSE
AND VERBAL MEANING

LEARNERS OF ENGLISH have difficulty knowing when to use the simple present tense and when to use the present progressive. Consider, for instance, the sentences in (1), which illustrate typical non-native speaker errors.

(1) (a) *I write the letter now.
     (b) *They are having a new car.

In (1)(a) the present progressive should have been used instead of the simple present, while in (1)(b), the simple present should have been used instead of the progressive.

Understanding these errors requires knowledge of two important grammatical categories expressed in the verb phrase, tense and aspect. As we saw in the preceding chapter, tenses are defined in terms of the relation between the time of the situation and the time of the utterance. In English there are just two tenses, present and past. Aspect involves the way in which we view the passage of time involved in a situation. English has only one aspect, the progressive aspect, which views the situation as in progress.

In this chapter we focus on the present tense and in the next, on progressive aspect. In order to understand the different nuances they convey and to be able to state constraints on their use, we must also look at how these categories interact with the meaning conveyed by the lexical verb. For this reason we also introduce a well-known semantic classification of lexical verbs into events, activities, and states.

1. THE FORM OF THE PRESENT TENSE

The present tense is expressed by two of the three finite verb forms (see Chapter 8). The third singular form is used with third person singular subjects, and the general present form with all other subjects. The general present is identical to the base of the verb (for all verbs but the verb *be*), while the third person singular form of regular verbs is constructed by adding the suffix /-s/ (phonetic variants [-əz], [-s], [-z]) to the base.

(2)   (a)   Third person singular:
              She/he   *watch-es, write-s, know-s*
        (b)   General present:
              We/you/they   *watch, write, know*

Modal auxiliaries are irregular in that they have no suffix in the third person singular, as in (3). Other verbs with irregular third person singular forms are listed in (4).

(3)   (a)   She *can* write very well.
        (b)   He *must* be on time for this meeting.
        (c)   It *will* be difficult to finish this on time.

(4)   (a)   *have*   has   [hæz]
        (b)   *do*   does   [dʌz]
        (c)   *say*   says   [sɛz]

The verb *be* is even more irregular in that it has not two, but three different forms in present tense (*am* with first person singular subjects, *is* with third person singular subjects, and *are* with second person and plural subjects).

2. INTRODUCTION TO THE USES OF THE PRESENT TENSE

Consider the sentences of (5), in which the present tense is used to convey the fact that the situation is simultaneous with the utterance. It is presented as instantaneous, as lasting only an instant.

(5)   (a) Jordan *races* down the court and *dunks* it for two points!
      (b) Watch carefully: I *break* the egg into the bowl and *add* a
           teaspoon of sugar.

Next, consider the sentences of (6), which also contain verbs in the present tense. These situations are not instantaneous, but are understood to extend indefinitely back into the past and forward into the future. The present tense conveys that the time of the situation is unrestricted.

(6)   (a) My parents live in Cleveland.
      (b) The green lamp stands in that corner.
      (c) My sister knows French very well.

The sentences in (7) and (8) also involve unrestricted time, but they convey additional nuances as well. The sentences in (7) convey that the situation is repeated over and over, i.e. is habitual. The sentences in (8), on the other hand, convey the fact that the situation is characteristic for the subject. They name attributes of the subject, rather than specific actions at specific times.

(7)   (a) Mrs. Jones *answers* the phone in our office.
      (b) We *walk* to work every day.
      (c) They always *shop* at Safeway.

(8)   (a) Suzie *laughs* a lot.
      (b) What do you do for exercise? I *run*.
      (c) My brother *writes* for a living.

In summary, the present tense is used to convey four main senses.

(9)   (a) The time of situation is simultaneous with the time of the
           utterance.
      (b) The time of the situation is unrestricted.
      (c) The situation is a present habit of the subject.
      (d) The situation is a present characteristic of the subject.

The present tense does not convey these four senses in every sentence, however. A sentence like (6)(a) cannot be used to convey meaning (9)(a) or (9)(c). Sentence (5)(b) cannot convey meaning (9)(b) or (c) or (d). The meaning conveyed by the tense depends partly on the tense and partly on the meaning of the lexical verb (more accurately, on the meaning of the situation conveyed by the verb and its complements). That is, to understand what the present tense conveys, we need to know not only what the present tense itself means, but also how that meaning interacts with the meaning of the verb.

Following a proposal made by the philosopher Zeno Vendler, many linguists accept a classification of verbs into three semantic groups: event verbs, activity verbs, and state verbs. These three categories will be discussed in the next section. Once we have introduced these categories, we will then look at how each interacts with the present tense.

In addition to the meaning of the tense and of the verb, two other factors influence how a tense is interpreted. First, temporal adverbials are used to block or reinforce particular meanings. For instance, if a habitual sense is intended, it might be reinforced by using an adverbial such as *regularly, as a matter of course, every day,* etc. (Temporal adverbials are discussed in Chapters 6 and 7.)

Second, the extra-linguistic context in which a sentence is uttered is also important, particularly for conveying the instantaneous meaning of the present tense. For instance, during a sports broadcast, (10) would be understood as an instantaneous present, but in a different context, say a retrospective of Jordan's career, it could be understood as habitual, particularly if adverbials which bring out that meaning are added (e.g. *always* or *whenever he gets the ball*).

(10)   Jordan *dunks* it for two points.

3. EVENTS, ACTIVITIES, STATES

The different nuances of the present tense derive in part from differences in the situation depicted by the lexical verb. There are essentially three kinds of situations: events, activities, and states. Although these terms describe situations and not verbs, we will talk about event verbs, activity verbs, and state verbs. An event verb is a verb which depicts an event, an activity verb, one which depicts an activity, and so on.

3.1 Events

Events take place. During an event, something happens; something is changing or developing. The change or development is directed toward a goal or built-in end point. When it has been reached, the change is accomplished, and the event is over. For this reason, events have more or less well-defined boundaries. Events which take some time to happen have beginnings, middles, and ends. Can you describe what is changing or developing in the examples of events in (11)? Can you describe when the end point of the event has been reached?

(11)   (a)   We ate dinner.
         (b)   They wrote a very good novel.
         (c)   My sister showed me her new house.
         (d)   She became a doctor.

Since events describe actions that lead to an end point, it is often possible to ask how long it takes for the end to be reached. The question, "How long did it take to...?" or the frame, "it took [durational phrase] to..." can be used as a test for events, as in (12).

(12)   (a)   How long did it take to eat dinner?
         (b)   It took an hour to eat dinner.
         (c)   How long will it take her to show you the house?
         (d)   It took her 10 years to become a doctor.

Not all events take time, however. Events such as *jump, sneeze, knock,* and *wink* last only a moment. Momentary event verbs cannot be used in the test frames given of (12), but they do answer the question, "What happened?" Examples of momentary event verbs are given in (13).

(13)   (a)   The cat jumped.
         (b)   Kim sneezed.
         (c)   They knocked on the door.
         (d)   He punched me.

Transitional event verbs depict a transition from one state to another and constitute a subtype of momentary event verbs. Although the point of transition is usually viewed as instantaneous, the event verb can sometimes be used to depict the "approach to the transition, rather than the transition itself" (Leech 1987:23).

(14) (a) The plane landed.
      (b) My dog died.
      (c) They lost their keys.

The different kinds of events are summarized in (15).

(15)   Events

        Not Momentary   Momentary
              |
        eat dinner   Not Transitional   Transitional
        write a novel | |
        become a doctor   jump   land
                                   sneeze   die
                                   knock   lose

3.2 Activities

Like events, activities take place. Unlike events, they don't involve changes or developments, and they are not directed towards a goal or end point, such that when the end is reached, the activity is over. Activities simply start and stop. Some examples are given in (16).

(16) (a) Suzie is laughing.
      (b) Peter is drawing.
      (c) The children are playing outside.
      (d) She studied grammar for ten years.

Activities cannot be used in the test frames for events. Questions like those in (17) are odd or ungrammatical.

(17) (a) *How long did it take Suzie to laugh?
      (b) *How long did take Peter to draw?
      (c) *It took the children an hour to play outside.

Exercise 1

Think about the situations in the following sentences and classify each one as an event, an activity, or a state.

1. It was cold last night.
2. Please finish your homework and get ready for bed.
3. We were strolling in the park.
4. In high school I studied French nearly every day for three years. I must have learned it well, because I placed out of French in college. I'm glad that I know French.
5. That meat smells bad.
6. The baby cried all night.
7. The two armies fought all afternoon and at dusk the Union troops won the battle and headed north to Virginia. They reached Virginia by midnight and remained there for several weeks.

4. THE USES OF THE PRESENT TENSE

We can identify a number of uses of the present tense. The two primary uses are those in which the time of the situation includes the time of the utterance (TS includes TU), while the secondary uses are those in which it does not.

4.1 Primary Uses of the Present Tense: TS includes TU

Unrestricted Use. Most frequently, the present tense conveys the idea that the time of the situation is unrestricted. There is no inherent limitation on the time of the situation, and in the absence of any restriction, it seems to extend from the present, back into the past, and forward into the future. This can be shown on a time line as in (24).

(24)

$$\text{———————————— X ————————→}$$
$$\text{TU}$$
$$\vert\text{————————————————————}\vert$$
$$\Leftarrow \quad \text{TS} \quad \Rightarrow$$

This meaning is completely compatible with the meaning of a state, which is unbounded and also extends naturally in time. A state verb in the simple present tense conveys that the state is true at the present time and that it extends back into the past and forward into the future, as in (25).

(25)   (a) She *is* kind.
        (b) They *are* students.
        (c) We *own* a house in Florida.
        (d) That child *loves* her mother.
        (e) He *lives* in Chicago.

There is a potential clash, however, between the unrestricted use of the present tense and event verbs, since event verbs depict situations which do not extend naturally in time. Because events have end points, the unrestricted use of the present cannot convey that a single event extends indefinitely back into the past and forward into the future. For instance, (26) does not mean that I am constantly and without stopping eating breakfast.

(26)   I *eat* breakfast.

When the meaning of an event and the meaning of the unrestricted present tense are combined as in (26), the resulting sentence is interpreted as a series of events. A usual interpretation of (26) is that I eat breakfast generally, every day. It is the repetition of the event that is understood to be unrestricted (to extend back into the past and forward into the future), as shown in (27), where repeated events are indicated with X's.

(27)   --------------- X --- X --- X --- X ---X --- X --- X———————→
                             TU
                         ⇐ TS ⇒

Additional examples in (28) refer to repeated acts of answering the phone, shopping at Safeway, scanning *The Post*, and so on. If the subject of a repeated event is a human being, the event is often interpreted as a habit, a use of the present tense called the habitual present.

(28) (a) Mrs. Jones *answers* the phone in our office.
      (b) They always *shop* at Safeway.
      (c) I *scan The Post* and *read The Times*.

An activity verb in the simple present does not convey that the activity itself extends back into the past and forward into the future. For instance, (29) does not mean that Sally is in a constant state of laughing.

(29) Sally *laughs*.

(29) conveys that Sally engages in repeated episodes of laughing. This is similar to the meaning of an event in the simple present. In the present tense, activities, which lack end points, shade into habitual events.

Activity verbs in the simple present tense can also convey the nuance that the activity is characteristic of the subject. Sentence (29) implies that it is characteristic of Sally to laugh; it is one of her attributes. The attribute reading of an activity verb is similar in meaning to a state verb as well, as shown in the paraphrases of (30).

(30) (a) What does she do?   She *writes*.
                                She's a writer.
      (b) What does he do?   He *sews*.
                                He's a tailor.

Other activities in simple present with attribute readings are given in (31).

(31) (a) This doll *drinks* and *wets*.
      (b) For relaxation, I *paint*.
      (c) For exercise, Maggie *runs*.

Finally, any type of verb in the simple present tense can be used to express an eternal truth. An eternal truth is a generic statement taken to be true for all time, such as statements about mathematical relationships or scientific facts. Proverbs are also meant to be eternal truths.

(32) (a) One and one *are* two.
      (b) Water *floats* on oil.

(32) (c) Birds *sing*; dogs *bark*.
      (d) A stitch in time *saves* nine.
      (e) Birds of a feather *flock* together.

Instantaneous use. Occasionally the present tense conveys the idea that the situation is instantaneous and simultaneous with the time of the utterance.

(33) ———————————— X ————————————→
                           TU
                           TS

The instantaneous use of the present tense is most frequent with event verbs and serves as a commentary on the action. The description is presented as though it is completely simultaneous with the action, though in reality, of course, it is likely to be slightly later. Such uses of the simple present tense are found in sports commentaries, demonstrations, performances by magicians, etc. as in the examples of (34).

(34) (a) He *puts* it up! It *goes* in! The buzzer *rings*. The Bullets *win* another one!!
      (b) I carefully *drop* the vanilla into the batter, *stir* it once, and *set* the bowl aside.
      (c) I *put* the marble under the middle cup and *touch* it twice with my wand. Voila! It's gone.

The instantaneous use of the present tense is also found with performative verbs. Uttering a sentence with a performative verb, under the right circumstances, makes it at that instant true. That is, saying it makes it so (Austin 1965).

(35) (a) Uttered by the proper official:
           I now *pronounce* you man and wife.
      (b) Uttered by a judge on the bench:
           I hereby *sentence* you to life imprisonment.
      (c) I *bet* you $5.00 you won't finish on time.

The instantaneous present is impossible with states, whose meanings are incompatible with the idea of lasting only an instant. Attempts to force verbs which ordinarily depict states into instantaneous readings of the present tense result in the state verb expressing a change of state. In (36) *know* is not a state; it is an event, a synonym of *come to know* or *realize*.

(36)   Aha! Now I *know* why she was lying.

The instantaneous present is also odd with activities. Making an unbounded activity into something which takes place instantaneously results in an activity of very abbreviated form. It is possible, but rather odd, to imagine the sentences of (37) as instantaneous. They could, for example, occur as a running commentary of action on a movie screen.

(37)   (a) She *laughs*.
        (b) He *cries*.
        (c) They *kiss*.

In short, the instantaneous use of the present is generally restricted to events.

4.2 Secondary Use—1: Future Time (TS follows TU)
We can identify a number of secondary uses of the present tense. They are secondary because the time of the situation does not include the time of the utterance. The differences between events, activities, and states are less relevant to these uses, so the meaning of the lexical verb will not be taken into account here.

The first two secondary uses involve situations which are in the future, after the time of the utterance, as shown schematically in (38).

(38)   ——————— X ——————— X ———————→
                 TU   TS

We sometimes use a present tense to indicate future time in independent clauses, as in the sentences of (39).

(39) (a) Tomorrow *is* Saturday, January 2.
      (b) Halloween *falls* on Friday the 13th this year.
      (c) The Bullets *play* the Celtics next Tuesday in Boston.
      (d) Our plane *leaves* at 6:30.

The situations in (39) are presented as facts already at TU. By using the present tense, they are given a degree of certainty that we normally reserve for present or past events. The future use of the present tense is often found with situations which are either unable or unlikely to be changed, such as statements about the calendar or events that are firmly scheduled for some future date. For instance, (39)(d) conveys that the departure is as fixed and unalterable as the calendar. The sentences in (40) are odd because they involve events which humans cannot predict with absolute certainty.

(40) (a) ??You *die* tomorrow.
      (b) ??It *rains* next Tuesday.
      (c) ??(To a college freshman) You *graduate* in four years.

A second circumstance in which the present tense is used of situations in the future is in subordinate clauses, as in (41). (The present tense verb under discussion is in italics.)

(41) (a) When he *calls*, tell him I've left.
      (b) As soon as you *leave*, we'll do the dishes.
      (c) I will do it myself, unless you *have* time before next week.

In subordinate clauses with future time reference, the simple present tense is required; other devices for expressing the future (the modal *will*, the progressive, etc.) are odd or ungrammatical, as in (42).

(42) (a) *When he *will call*, tell him I've left.
      (b) *As soon as you *are leaving*, we'll do the dishes.

This use of the present tense does not have the special meaning ("high degree of certainty") that accompanies the use of the present tense with future time reference in independent clauses. (Expression of future time is discussed in detail in Chapter 19.)

4.3 Secondary Use—2: Past Time (TS before TU)

In another secondary use, the present tense expresses situations that took place in the past, prior to the time of the utterance, as shown in (43). In (44), the present tense verbs with past time reference are in italics.

(43)

(44) (a) I was walking along the street and suddenly, out of nowhere, this car *races* by and the driver *slams* on the brakes.
      (b) At that point, I got really scared. The guy *gets* up and *comes* over to me and *starts* waving his fists in my face.

When we talk about a past situation using the present tense, we present it as though it is happening in the present. In (44), the use of the present tense gives the situation a sense of immediacy, a very common device in historical narratives, especially less formal, oral ones.

The present tense is commonly used for past situations that involve verbs of communication. For instance, the sentences in (45) report acts of telling that took place in the past. The use of the present tense seems to highlight the present relevance of the past telling or hearing.

(45) (a) Your mother *tells* me you'll graduate this year.
      (b) I *hear* you've dropped out of school.

Finally, we also find the present tense used in discussions of artists and their work, as in (46).

(46) (a) Monet *exhibits* an unusual sense of light.
      (b) Alex Haley *writes* with clarity of purpose.
      (c) In this painting Mary Cassat *uses* texture and color to give a feeling of dreamlike contentment.

Because the artists are no longer alive, situations in which they are agents, strictly speaking, do not include the present. The use of the present tense seems justified, however, because the work of an artist exists in the present and, through the work, the artist as well.

Exercise 2

In this chapter a number of different uses of the present tense were discussed. Make a list of the primary and secondary uses and for each give two more examples.

Exercise 3

Circle each present tense verb in the following passage (Taylor 1993) and identify its use as primary or secondary. State whether primary uses are unrestricted or instantaneous and discuss the effect of the author's tense choice.

"The world knows South Africa as a caldron of political violence—which it is—but the people who live here fear it most as a place where the common criminal is king. One recent morning's crop of crime stories in the local newspaper helps make the point:

A policeman escorts the driver of a bread truck into the township of Alexandra, where commercial deliveries are always risky. At their first stop, a man approaches laughing, and shoots the policeman in the face. He then steals the policeman's gun and rushes off. The policeman dies.

A taxi driver drops off passengers in the township of Wattville. Four men surround his vehicle and demand he give it up. He refuses. They shoot him dead."

Exercise 4

In a passage of one page or so, identify all instances of the present tense and classify each as primary (unrestricted or instantaneous) or secondary. Though the present tense is infrequent in many kinds of writing, it is common in introductions (to books or articles) and reviews (of books, movies, or performances).

Exercise 5

Compare the uses of the present tense in English with those of another language you know well. Are there circumstances where a present tense in English corresponds to a different tense in that language? Give clear examples in your answer.

17

PROGRESSIVE ASPECT

WHY IS THE PROGRESSIVE POSSIBLE with some verbs and not others? Why are sentences (1)(a), (2)(a), and (3)(a) grammatical, while (1)(b), (2)(b), and (3)(b) are not?

(1) (a) Joan is writing a novel.
     (b) *Joan is liking her children.

(2) (a) I am studying grammar this semester.
     (b) *I am knowing grammar.

(3) (a) Susan is looking at the stranger.
     (b) *Susan is recognizing the stranger.

To explain these patterns, we need to understand both the meaning of the progressive and how it interacts with the different classes of lexical verbs discussed in Chapter 16. Before doing that, however, we need to introduce the category of aspect, since the English progressive is a kind of aspect.

---

1. ASPECT

Consider the following objects.

●   _____

They seem to be a dot and a line, but imagine that they are both a pencil, the same pencil viewed from two different perspectives. Holding the pencil perpendicular to your body, looking at the eraser or tip, you see more or less a dot. Holding it parallel to your body, you see a line. The dot suddenly has length. The object hasn't changed. You are simply viewing it from a different perspective.

Within the verbal system, aspect categories provide special perspectives on the situation much like the orientation of the pencil. If we take the situation "writing a novel," for example, it can be viewed as being in progress, as having length and taking time. The sentences in (4) emphasize the duration.

(4)   (a)   He was writing the novel for ten years.
        (b)   He wrote on and on on the novel.
        (c)   He worked on this novel for a long time.
        (d)   He has been writing the novel for ages.

Writing a novel can also be viewed as though it consists of only a moment, as in (5).

(5)   (a)   He wrote the novel in 1985.
        (b)   Next year he will write his third novel.

The sentences in (4) and (5) can be used about the very same situation of writing a novel. The situation does not change, only the perspective from which the speaker views it.

The main distinctions of aspect involve viewing situations in these two ways: as a point, or punctually, and as a line, or duratively. The category of aspect is thus quite different from the category of tense. Tenses code something about the time of the situation in relation to the time of the utterance, while aspects provide different perspectives on how the situation spreads out in time. The English progressive is an aspect category, a special type of verb phrase which views the action duratively.

2. THE SYNTAX OF THE PROGRESSIVE

A progressive VP consists of the auxiliary verb *be* in combination with a VP whose head is a present participle, as in (6). The subcategorization frame for progressive *be* is given in (7) and a tree diagram in (8).

(6) (a) They are playing outside now.
     (b) We were writing letters to soldiers in the Gulf War.
     (c) Mother is talking on the telephone.

(7) *be*:   [___ VP_{Present Part}]

(8)

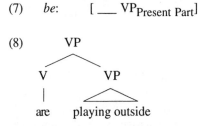

3. THE MEANINGS OF THE PROGRESSIVE

The progressive aspect in English indicates a situation in progress. Contrast the progressives in (9) and (10) with the corresponding simple tenses.

(9)   (a) Sally paints.
      (b) Sally is painting.

(10) (a) Sally painted a portrait.
      (b) Sally was painting a portrait.

Though both sentences in (9) are in the present tense, they have different aspects. The non-progressive aspect in (9)(a) describes what Sally does in general, her profession or perhaps her avocation. It is an instance of the unrestricted use of the present tense. The progressive aspect in (9)(b) describes her activity at the present time. It tells what she is doing at the time of the utterance.

The sentences in (10) also have the same tense but different aspects. The non-progressive past in (10)(a) presents the situation as a whole, rather like looking at the end of a pencil. It conveys that the action was completed, i.e. the end point of the event was reached. The past progressive in (10)(b) depicts the situation as an activity in progress, like looking at the length of a pencil. From the point of view of the past progressive, we can't tell whether the event was completed or not.

The meaning of the progressive can be separated into three components: duration, limited duration, and not necessarily completed. Not all of these components are present in all occurrences of the progressive, but when the first two are present, they give a temporary meaning to the situation. Thus (9)(b) conveys a temporary activity in contrast to (9)(a), which conveys an enduring quality or habit.

3.1 Progressive as Duration

The progressive is often used to emphasize the duration of a situation, the fact that an ongoing situation is taking time. This use of the progressive is in contrast to a corresponding non-progressive (a simple present or simple past tense), which emphasizes the instantaneous nature of a situation, as illustrated in (11) and (12).

(11)   (a)   He is running up the court.
       (b)   He runs up the court, he shoots, he makes it.

(12)   (a)   She is mixing the eggs and cream.
       (b)   She mixes the eggs and cream.

The progressive in this meaning occurs with single events and all activities. States do not occur in this sense of the progressive because they do not involve change and cannot be viewed as in progress.

(13)   (a)   *It is being cold today.
       (b)   *We are owning our house.
       (c)   *She is loving her children.

3.2 Progressive as Limited Duration

In addition to expressing duration, the progressive frequently emphasizes the limited nature of the duration. Using the progressive instead of the simple present or past tense imposes a time restriction on the situation. In (14) and (15), for example, the progressive contrasts with the unrestricted use of the simple present tense.

(14)   (a)   Restricted: My son is walking to work.
       (b)   Unrestricted: My son walks to work.

(15) (a) Restricted: Sally is painting portraits this month.
      (b) Unrestricted: Sally paints portraits.

Sentence (14)(a) could be used to express the fact that at the time of the
utterance my son is in the process of walking to work. It could also express
the idea that the habitual event of walking to work is for only a limited
time. For example, if my son usually drives to work but has his car in the
shop this week, I could utter (14)(a) to convey the limited duration of his
habit. This nuance is often brought out by adverbials such as *these days* or
for the time being. This is in clear contrast to (14)(b), which expresses the
idea that walking to work is unrestricted.

This component of progressive meaning is most salient with habitual
events and activities. It is possible with states, as well, if the state can be a
temporary one, like *sit, stand, lie,* or *live*.

(16) (a) Susan is standing by the statue.   (temporary)
      (b) The new statue stands in the park. (permanent)

(17) (a) She is living with her mother for the next few weeks
           until her apartment is ready.   (temporary)
      (b) She lives with her mother.   (permanent)

Many states cannot (in an ordinary world) be temporary, and they do not
occur in this meaning of the progressive.

(18) (a) *She is being tall.
      (b) *They are knowing Russian.
      (c) ?Harry is loving his kids.

3.3 Progressive as Not Necessarily Completed

The progressive is also used to indicate events which are not necessarily
completed or finished. The end point of the event is not necessarily reached.
In this respect, progressives are in contrast with non-progressives, which
view the event as completed.

(19) (a) Helen was reading that new book.
      (b) Helen read that new book.

(20)   (a)   Kim was fixing his car.
         (b)   Kim fixed his car.

(19)(a) does not indicate whether Helen finished the book or not, and could be continued, "but she never finished it." (19)(b) conveys that she read and finished it.

This sense of the progressive is possible with events since they have built-in end points. It is not possible with activities or states, since they do not, and therefore, it does not make sense to talk about them being completed.

4. SPECIAL NUANCES OF THE PROGRESSIVE

In addition to these meanings, the progressive conveys special nuances when used in combination with certain subclasses of verbs.

4.1 Momentary Events in the Progressive

Momentary event verbs name situations that take but an instant to occur, as for example *jump, cough,* or *twitch.* In (21) momentary situations are combined with the durational meaning expressed by the progressive.

(21)   (a)   I am jumping.
         (b)   He was coughing.
         (c)   They were blinking.

(21)(a) does not describe a single jump, probably because a single jump does not take enough time to have duration. A sentence like (21)(a) is used, rather, to convey several jumps. Momentary event verbs in the progressive express multiple events, known as iteratives, shown schematically in (22).

(22)   ----------- X --- X ---X --- X --- X ————⟶
                              TU

4.2 Transitional Events in the Progressive

As discussed in Chapter 16, transitional event verbs describe a transition into a state. Since the transition is usually viewed as instantaneous, there

should be no room for progressive meaning, which focuses on an action in
its duration. In (23), though, are transitional event verbs in the progressive.

(23) (a) The plane is landing.
      (b) My mother was leaving when the phone rang.
      (c) She was dying.

In these sentences, the progressive indicates the approach to the transition,
the period of time leading up to transition, rather than the transition itself.
(23)(a) conveys preparation for landing, rather than the actual moment of
landing. (23)(b) conveys that mother is getting ready to leave and not
necessarily that she was (literally) crossing the threshold. She might have
been combing her hair, getting her coat, putting on her boots, etc. The time
period covered by the transitional event verbs in the progressive can be
indicated with a bracket as in (24).

(24) ─────────────────── X ───────────→
      └──────────────────┘

        preparation for   moment of
        landing/leaving   landing/leaving

4.3 States in the Progressive ≠ ⁊
As frequently noted, states do not normally occur in the progressive, thus
the ungrammatical sentences of (25).

(25) (a) *John is being tall.
      (b) *Susan is being a professor
      (c) *They are loving their families.
      (b) *I'm liking my new job.

Occasionally, such sentences do occur, however, as in (26). In such cases,
the verb is no longer referring to a situation which is a state, but has been
reinterpreted as dynamic, changing, or in progress.

(26) A: How's your new job?
      B: I'm liking it more every day.

In (26) the verb *like* does not depict an enduring, unchanging state. It describes an ongoing change of state.

When a state describes a more or less permanent quality, progressive aspect can be used to convey a nuance of temporary behavior, as in (27) and (28).

(27) (a) Peter is obnoxious.   (a permanent quality)
      (b) Peter is being obnoxious.   (a temporary behavior)

(28) (a) Pam is very friendly.   (permanent)
      (b) Pam is being very friendly.   (temporary)

An additional nuance which can be conveyed by (28)(b) is that Pam is working at being friendly, and so is perhaps insincere.

4.4 *Emotions in the Progressive*

The progressive conveys a sense of temporariness with stative verbs that depict emotions or attitutes, such as *intend, wish, want,* or *hope.*

(29) (a) I hope you can help me.
      (b) I am hoping you can help me.
      (c) I was hoping you can/could help me.

The progressive conveys that the speaker is more tentative, which is also more polite. This use of the progressive often appears in combination with the past tense, as in (29)(c). (The use of the past tense to convey distance and, by implication, politeness, is discussed in Chapter 15.)

4.5 *Bodily Sensations in the Progressive*

With verbs that depict bodily sensations, progressive and non-progressive VPs are virtually interchangable. Contrary to what we might expect, the progressive does not indicate a more temporary state than the non-progressive. Some verbs in this group are *hurt, ache, tickle, itch,* and *feel* [AdjP].

(30) (a) My back hurts.
      (b) My back is hurting.

(31) (a) This scratch itches.
   (b) This scratch is itching.

5. OTHER USES OF PROGRESSIVE VERB PHRASES

In addition to the primary use of the progressive to express a situation in progress, progressive VPs can be used to express future situations, as in (32).

(32) (a) We are leaving in 5 minutes.
   (b) She is having a baby in March.

The past progressive is used to express a future in the past. (33) conveys that from some point in the past, their leaving for Paris was in the future, i.e. the next day.

(33) They were leaving for Paris the following day.

The progressive may combine with the modal auxiliary *will* or the expression *be going to* to form a futuritive with the special meaning, "the situation described is a matter of course." In (34) the progressive VPs are in square brackets.

(34) (a) The train will [be leaving in 30 minutes].
   (b) We will [be flying at an altitude of 10,000 feet].
   (c) I am going to [be giving a lecture on grammar in May].

Expressions that are used to encode future states and events are known as futuritives, the topic of Chapter 19.

To recapitulate, there is not a difference in the situation itself that leads to the choice between progressive and non-progressive VPs. The difference has to do with the way in which the speaker views the situation and what aspect of it he or she wishes to highlight. To express single (i.e. non-habitual) events and activities in the present, the progressive is the usual form. The non-progressive present tense is used only in special circumstances, specifically if a habitual reading or an instantaneous reading is desired, as in demonstrations or play-by-play commentaries. States do not occur in the progressive without a special context involving reinterpretation, unless the state is a temporary one, in which case the progressive can be used.

Because the progressive looks at a situation in its duration, it often forms a temporal frame in which other actions can be situated, as in (35).

(35) (a) As he was singing, the bell rang.
      (b) I was writing the letter when he came in.

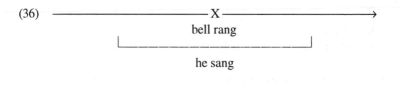

(36)

bell rang

he sang

Exercise 1
List the meanings that can be conveyed by the progressive and find at least two additional examples of each one.

Exercise 2
Explain why the following sentences are ungrammatical.

1.   *Joan is liking her children.
2.   *I am knowing grammar.
3.   *Susan is recognizing the stranger.

Exercise 3
Discuss the differences among the following sets of sentences.

(1) (a) The Seine runs through Paris.
     (b) *The Seine is running through Paris.
     (c) The athletes are running through Paris.

(2) (a) Children throw coins into the fountain.
     (b) Children are throwing coins into the fountain.

(3) (a) Sally sits on the bench by the entrance.
   (b) Sally is sitting on the bench by the entrance.

(4) (a) The new statue stands at the entrance to the park.
   (b) The new statue is standing at the entrance to the park.

Exercise 4
Identify each progressive VP in the following passages and state the meaning it conveys. Could a simple present or past tense have been used in place of the progressive?

1. The police are looking for the person who robbed the First National Bank. He is 25 to 30, and when last seen, was wearing a blue jogging suit and yellow tennis shoes. He was riding an aqua bicycle and heading toward the ocean.

2. Mr. Egg took a drop of the liquid on his tongue. "Oh, dear," he said. "Tastes to me as though the old gentleman had been dropping his cigar-ends into it." The inspector smiled, "They are doing an analysis now, but the doctor says it looks like nicotine poisoning." (Adapted from Sayers 1969:94.)

3. From the description of a murder victim: He seems to have been smoking a cigar, and I'm told he was suffering from a slight cold, so that his taste and smell may not have been in full working order. (Adapted from Sayers 1969:95.)

4. We usually read the morning paper while we are having breakfast. We subscribe to *The Washington Post*, but are contemplating switching to *The New York Times*. Our friends are trying to convince us that *The Times* has better international news coverage.

Exercise 5

The progressive is often used in sentences like the following. Describe the special nuance it conveys.

(1)   He's always calling me names.
(2)   Sally is always interrupting the teacher.
(3)   Why are you always pushing me around?
(4)   That student is always coming in late.

Exercise 6

Give tree diagrams for the following sentence. Use triangles to abbreviate the internal syntax of noun phrases.

1.   He was calling me names.
2.   My son is walking to work these days.
3.   The farmer was painting his barn red.
4.   The children should be doing their homework or getting ready for bed.
5.   The police may have been watching us, but should have been following the real culprits.

Exercise 7   For Discussion

In Azar 1984, the present progressive is introduced in Chapter 3, while the simple present tense is introduced in Chapter 4. Why might they be presented in this order? In Chapter 4, Azar also introduces adverbs of frequency (such as *always, often, rarely*). Do you see any advantages to teaching these lexical items along with the simple present tense?

18
THE PERFECT

TO TALK ABOUT A SITUATION THAT TOOK PLACE IN THE PAST, a speaker often has a choice between a simple past tense and a present perfect as in (1) and (2).

(1)   (a) Simple Past: Sam read *War and Peace.*
      (b) Present Perfect: Sam has read *War and Peace.*

(2)   (a) Simple Past: I broke my leg.
      (b) Present Perfect: I have broken my leg.

These choices differ in rather subtle ways. In this chapter we discuss the syntax and the meaning of the perfect construction and learn what is conveyed by the choice between the past tense and the present perfect. The perfect is not a tense because it is not coded by changes in the form of the verb and is not defined in terms of the relationship between TS and TU. Syntactically, it is a special VP; semantically, it indicates relative time.

1. THE SYNTAX OF THE PERFECT

The syntax of the perfect is very straightforward. It is signaled by the auxiliary verb *have* in combination with a VP headed by a verb in the past participle form. The subcategorization frame for perfect *have* is given in (3) and a tree diagram in (4), with further examples in (5).

(3)   *have*   [_____ VP$_{\text{Past Part}}$]

(4)   VP

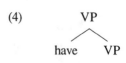

         have   VP

(5)   (a) We have lived in Chicago for 20 years.
       (b) I can't go to work. I've broken my leg.
       (c) Sam has read *War and Peace.* So ask him about it.
       (d) The Prime Minister has just been assassinated!

2. THE MEANING OF THE PERFECT

Though the syntax of the perfect is straightforward, its meaning is subtle. Generally speaking, it indicates anterior time: A situation expressed with a perfect takes place at a time prior to some other time, which is called the reference time (TR). The perfect expresses that the anterior situation has continuing relevance for the TR. The TR may be a *present* moment (hence, a present perfect), a *past* moment (past perfect) or a *future* moment (future perfect), as in (6).

(6)   (a) Sam [has already written his paper].
       (b) Susan arrived quite late, after we [had finished dinner].
       (c) By Saturday, we [will have prepared the case for trial].

In (6)(a), since no specific reference time is mentioned, we take it to be the present (TU). The situation expressed by the perfect construction ("write a paper") took place before TR (=TU), but has continuing relevance for it, as shown in (7).

(7)   ─────── X ─────── X ───────→
              TS   TR = TU
          Sam writes   S has continuing
          the paper   relevance at TR

In (6)(b), the reference time for the situation ("finish dinner") is the time of Susan's arrival. Because the reference time is in the past (TR before TU), the past perfect is used. It is schematized in (8).

(8)   ———————— X ———————— X ———————— X ——→
            TS   TR   TU
        we finish   Susan arrives   now
          dinner   S has continuing
                          relevance at TR

In (6)(c) the reference time for the situation ("prepare the case") is Saturday, a future time. Both TR and TS are in the future with respect to TU. The situation expressed by the perfect occurs before the TR, but has continuing relevance for it, as in (9).

(9)   ———X ————— X ————— X ——→
            TU   TS   TR
          now   we prepare   Saturday
                         the case   S has continuing
                                            relevance

One other property of the perfect should be noted: The time of the situation must be indefinite. If a specific, definite time is mentioned or even understood from the context, the perfect is ungrammatical, as in (10). (The definite time adverbials are in italics.)

(10)   (a) *Sam has read War and Peace *last week.*
       (b) *I have been to Wales *the first week of July.*
       (c) *Have you spoken to Jeffrey *yesterday?*
       (d) *They have graduated *in 1965.*
       (e) A: Did you read this book *yesterday?*
           B: ?I have read it. (Answer is not responsive, since
           it assumes an indefinite time, whereas a definite time was
           mentioned in the question.)

Note the contrast in pairs like (11).

(11)   (a) Have you read *War and Peace?*
       (b) Did you read *War and Peace?*

(11)(a), with a perfect, asks about reading *War and Peace* at some unspecified, but indefinite time in the past, a meaning often emphasized by the word *ever*. (11)(b), on the other hand, with a past tense, asks about reading the novel at some unspecified, but definite past time. One could add a definite time adverbial, like *in 1984, during high school,* or *last summer*. Whether a definite time adverbial is stated explicitly or not, a definite time is assumed by the use of the simple past tense and is not allowed by a perfect.

   In the next section we focus on the present perfect and explore the ways in which a situation can have continuing relevance.

3. THE PRESENT PERFECT

To clarify the idea of continuing relevance, we can identify four ways that a past situation can have relevance to the present.

3.1 The Perfect of Persistent Situation

A past situation can be relevant to the present if it persists or continues into the present. This is perhaps the most familiar use of the perfect: It is used to describe a situation that begins in the past, but extends into the present and is true at the time of the utterance.

   Not all situations (events, activities, and states) can extend indefinitely in time, and, thus, not all situations can be used in this sense of the perfect. Extending in time is typical of states, which are often found in the perfect, as in (12).

(12)   (a)   We have lived in Chicago for 20 years.
       (b)   They have always loved the weather in New Zealand.
       (c)   I've known Max since 1958.
       (d)   She's been a professor since 1940.

(12)(a) conveys that the situation ("live in Chicago") began at a point in the past and continues to be true at the time of the utterance, as schematized in (13) with a bracket representing the 20-year interval.

(13)
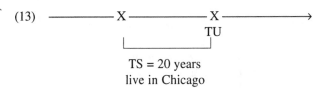

TS = 20 years
live in Chicago

Although it is not possible for single events to extend indefinitely in time, because they have end points, a series of events can. When an event is used in the present perfect, it depicts repeated events which began at some time in the past and persist into the present, as in (14).

(14) (a) She has walked to work every day since May.
      (b) Billie Jean has delivered the newspaper in this neighborhood
           for five years.
      (c) My brother has taken a vacation in Key West every January
           for the past ten years.
      (d) I have eaten an orange for breakfast as long as I can remember.

For the perfect to convey persistence into the present, there must also be an adverbial of duration (e.g. *every day since May* or *for 5 years;* see Chapter 7). The sentences of (14) without duration adverbials do not indicate that a past habit continues into the present, but are consistent with interpretations in which the situation is not true at the time of the utterance, as demonstrated in (15). Without the durational adverbial a different sense of the perfect, the experiential perfect, is conveyed (see below).

(15) (a) She has walked to work. But she gave it up years ago.
      (b) Billie Jean has delivered the newspaper in this neighborhood. She
           did it once last week.
      (c) He has taken a vacation in Key West. He'd like to go back.

3.2 The Perfect of Result 344

A past situation can have continuing relevance for the present if it has a result which persists into the present. The result is a state that is a direct effect of the past event. By choosing the perfect, the speaker highlights the result and its present relevance. In (16)(a) the result of breaking one's leg is that one has a broken leg. The perfect focuses on the present relevance of this result, and the broken leg serves, therefore, as an excuse for not attending a party (i.e. I can't come because I have a broken leg).

(16)   (a)   I can't come to your party. I've broken my leg.
        (b)   Mr. Smith has gone to London.
        (c)   There, we've finished the project!

This use of the perfect is only possible with events that express a change of state. States and activities do not express a change of state and cannot convey this sense of the perfect.

594

3.3 The Experiential Perfect

The experiential perfect is somewhat more complicated than the other senses. It is used for a situation that took place at an indefinite time in the past that must still be possible in the present, at TU. The experiential perfect conveys that the experience of the past situation has relevance to the present. Some experiential perfects are given in (17).

(17)   (a)   I've been to Wales.
        (b)   Sam has read *War and Peace.*
        (c)   This class has already gone to the O'Keefe exhibit.

Sentence (17)(a) might be used to highlight one's past experience with Wales, perhaps as a preface to suggesting places to visit there. Larger contexts which help bring out the experiential sense are given in (18).

(18)   (a)   I've been to Wales. Let me recommend some nice restaurants in
              Aberystwyth.
        (b)   I've been to Wales. I advise you not to go there this time of
              year.
        (c)   I've been to Wales and can tell you that they do speak
              Welsh in the streets.

An important feature of the experiential perfect is that events of the type expressed by the perfect must still be possible at time of the utterance. This is, in fact, one way that the past situation has continuing relevance. The perfect highlights the present possibility of the situation in a way that the simple past does not. Consider the sentences in (19).

(19) (a) I've seen the new exhibit at the National Gallery. Have you?
     (b) I saw the O'Keefe exhibit. Did you?

(19)(a) is appropriate if the exhibit in question is still running, and, therefore, it is still possible to view it. It is in contrast to the simple past (in (19)(b)), which is consistent with the knowledge that the exhibit has closed.

This component of the meaning of the experiential perfect ("events of this type are still possible") may be brought out by considering situations which are no longer possible, situations which are ruled out by knowledge of the real world. They are odd in the experiential perfect.

(20) (a) ?I've dated Marilyn Monroe. Have you?
     (b) ?I've spoken to Harry Truman. Have you?
     (c) ?Have you seen the Barnes exhibit at the National Gallery?
        (Odd if uttered with the knowledge that this temporary
        exhibit closed in July 1993.)

These sentences are odd because the events named in them are no longer possible. This fact clashes with the requirement of the experiential perfect that events of this type still be possible at the time of the utterance.

The experiential perfect is often used with event verbs, as can be seen in all the examples in this section. It is also possible with some states, as shown in (21) and, only rarely, with activities, as in (22).

(21) (a) We've lived in California and plan to return when we retire.
     (b) I've known some pretty obnoxious people in my life.
     (c) I've liked every cat I've ever met.

(22) (a) He's worked as a bricklayer, so he could always find a job doing that again.
     (b) I've laughed before, and I'm sure I'll laugh again.

It is often difficult to distinguish the experiential perfect from the perfect of result. This is because the experience resulting from a past situation can be viewed as one possible result of it. For example, if someone worked as a bricklayer in the past, one result is that he has experience as a bricklayer.

748

3.4 The Hot News Perfect

A fourth use of the perfect is to convey very recent past events. We call it the hot news perfect, as it is often used in news reporting, as in (23).

(23)   (a)   We are grieved to report that the Prime Minister has just been assassinated.
       (b)   Ross Perot has been named Ambassador to Azerbaijan.

We use a hot news perfect when a past event is known and past for the speaker, though new and, therefore, present for the hearer. It is in the sense that the past event is new information for the hearer that it has continuing relevance for the present.

4. THE PAST PERFECT

The past perfect is expressed with the past tense of *have*. It can be used to convey each of the meanings of the present perfect discussed above, the difference between them being the reference time, the time for which the past situation has continuing relevance. In the present perfect, TR = TU, while in the past perfect, TR is prior to TU, as in (24).

(24)   (a)   Persistent situation:
             We sold our house last year. We had lived in it for 30 years.
       (b)   Result:
             I wanted to play in the tournament, but I had broken my leg.
       (c)   Experiential:
             They asked for advice, and since we had been to Wales, we were able to recommend some nice restaurants.
       (d)   Hot News:
             We were eating dinner when we heard that the Princess of Wales had died in a car crash.

In (24)(a) the TR for the perfect VP is *last year*, a time that is prior to TU. The time of the situation expressed by the perfect (live in the house) began prior to the past TR and continues to it. The relation between TS, TR, and TU for (24)(a) and (b) are shown in (25).

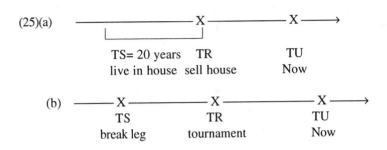

(25)(a)

TS= 20 years   TR   TU
live in house sell house Now

(b)

TS   TR   TU
break leg tournament   Now

In addition to expressing perfect meaning, the past tense of the auxiliary
have (in combination with a VP headed by a past participle) is also used to
express an event that is past time with respect to a past time of reference (a
"past in a past"), as the bracketed VPs in (26). The auxiliary *have* in these
sentences does not express perfect meaning, which can be seen in that it co-
occurs with definite time adverbials (*in 1984, at 4:30,* etc.). If these were
perfect, the adverbials would not be possible.

(26) (a) My daughter, Susan, just got her degree from VMI. She [had
           graduated from high school in 1984], but spent several years in
           Europe and didn't start college until 1989.
      (b) Monday was a busy day. Mr. Smith cleaned house, did the
           laundry, and at 5:00, set the table. Then he sat down to wait for
           dinner, a pizza that he [had ordered at 4:30].
      (c) The government admitted today that [last night soldiers had
           killed 11 citizens who had been protesting].

5. CONCLUDING NOTES

Many languages have a verb form or construction with perfect meaning,
though forms which are called "perfect" in other languages do not
necessarily express the meaning described here ("a prior situation has
continuing relevance"). The perfect of persistent situation, in particular, is
characteristic of English. It represents a compromise between conflicting
demands that the present tense be used to convey a situation true in the
present and that past time be marked with a past tense. English resolves this
demand with the present perfect. Many other languages, even languages with

a perfect construction, use a present tense.

Throughout this chapter we have contrasted the perfect with the simple past tense. It is also instructive to contrast it with the unrestricted use of the present tense, as in (27).

(27) (a) Perfect: I've known my boss for years.
      (b) Present: I know my boss.

In (27)(a) the situation is viewed as beginning in the past and continuing into the present, the interval being marked with the adverbial *for years*. In (27)(b), the situation is viewed from the present and is seen as extending back into the past and forward into the future.

Finally, note that the auxiliary *have* is also used idiomatically in combination with a VP headed by *got* to express the same meaning as the lexical verb *have* alone. This informal construction does not convey perfect meaning and can usually be replaced by the lexical verb *have*, as in (28).

(28) (a) He's got an office on Baker Street. = he has an office
      (b) I've got a cold.   = I have a cold
      (c) They've got six children.   = they have six children

The "have got" construction is frequently preferred over stative *have*. It is particularly common in negative and interrogative clauses.

(29) (a) Do you have any money?   I don't have any money.
      (b) Have you got any money?   I haven't got any money.

(30) (a) Does she have AIDS?   She doesn't have AIDS.
      (b) Has she got AIDS?   She hasn't got AIDS.

Exercise 1

Plot the events of the sentences below on a time line, noting the TR for each perfect VP.

1.   I smiled when I thought about all the wonderful teachers I have known in my 20-year teaching career.

2. Sandy and Paul had lived together for two years before they got married.
3. We are working on the project full time now, and by the time you get this, we will have completed Phase I.
4. "How well she remembered the first time she had seen him; he was lodging in a house on the main road where she used to visit." (Joyce 1962:38)
5. The office is in chaos. The office manager's taken early retirement and the receptionist has quit. We have arranged for temporaries to fill in, but they won't start until Monday.

In a similar way, plot the events involved in the sentences of (26) on a time line, noting the TR for each perfect VP.

Exercise 2
For each of the meanings of the present perfect, find at least two additional examples. Provide enough context for your examples to make it clear which meaning of the present perfect is involved.

Exercise 3
The sentences in (1) and (2) are intended as apologies or confessions. What difference(s) do you see between them?

(1) (a) I made a mistake.
     (b) I stole some money.
     (c) I sinned.

(2) (a) I've made a mistake.
     (b) I've stolen some money.
     (c) I have sinned.

Exercise 4

In the following paragraphs, excerpted from a concert program, underline each past tense and circle each perfect VP, identifying which of the four perfect meanings it expresses. For each VP you marked, consider why the writer made the choice he/she did.

   James Galway was born in Belfast, and ... began serious musical training on the flute. He continued his studies and held a series of orchestral positions ... and was appointed as Principal Flute of the Berlin Philharmonic in 1969. After six years, Mr. Galway decided to establish a solo career, and within a year, had recorded his first four RCA LPs, played more than 120 concerts, and appeared as a soloist with London's four major orchestras.

   James Galway has won numerous awards for his recordings. His newest recording is a collection of ballads .... Mr. Galway has circled the globe many times, keeping his artistry fresh with a mixture of recitals, concert appearances, ... and master classes. Mr. Galway has dazzled television viewers with his virtuosity and engaging personality as host of his own holiday specials and as a regular guest on a variety of programs ....

Exercise 5

In a passage of three paragraphs, for each finite verb phrase, identify (1) the form of the verb, (2) the tense (present or past), (3) the aspect (progressive or nonprogressive), and (4) whether it is perfect or not.

Exercise 6

Find a passage of at least three paragraphs that is set in the past, such as a biography or other history. Underline each past tense and circle each perfect. Write a brief description explaining what is conveyed by each of them, drawing on the discussion of the past tense in Chapter 15 and the perfect in this chapter.

19

TALKING ABOUT THE FUTURE

THERE IS NO FUTURE TENSE IN ENGLISH because there are no verb forms whose primary meaning is to express situations in the future (TS after TU). Though there is no future tense, this doesn't mean that one can't talk about the future. In the absence of a tense, English draws on a number of different constructions, called futuritives, including the simple present tense, the present progressive, modal auxiliaries, and combinations of these.

One important dimension in the discussion of futuritives is the degree of certainty the speaker has about the future situation. In this chapter we present eight English futuritives in order from least certain to most certain. The more likely a speaker thinks a future situation is to take place, the farther down on this list she would go to choose a futuritive. The last few futuritives are used to express situations that the speaker thinks are very likely to take place. They are close to certain or are imminent.

The only modal auxiliaries on this list are *will* and *shall*. The other modals, though not included here, often express futurity in addition to modality. The modals that indicate possiblity and probability (*may, might, could*) express an even greater degree of uncertainty about future events than the futuritives presented here. The degree of certainty is not the only factor that differentiates futuritives from each other, for each conveys other nuances as well, as discussed below.

1. EIGHT FUTURITIVES

1.1 be going [_____ InfVP]
The first futuritive consists of the verb *be*, combined with a VP headed by *going*, subcategorized for an infinitive VP (the verb *going* and *to* are often pronounced as [gʌnə]). Examples are in (1), a tree diagram in (2).

(1)   (a) We're going to go to France next year.
        (b) What are you going to do tonight?
        (c) We're going to watch TV.

(2)

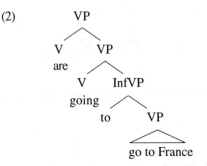

This futuritive is a very common way to express future time, especially in informal spoken English. It is rather neutral semantically and has two sub-meanings. First, it often expresses an intention or plan for the future, as in (1). The question in (1)(b), for instance, seems to be asking about intention. The subject in such sentences is usually human, since we do not attribute intention to non-human things. Second, this futuritive expresses a future culmination of a present cause, as in (3).

(3)   (a) (Hearing shouting from a classroom)
             There's going to be trouble when the teacher comes back.
        (b) She's going to have a baby.

This futuritive is used when the factors which cause the future situation are already present. "The train of events leading to the future happening is already underway" (Leech 1971:60). If we consider intention to be one of the factors, these two points actually describe a single nuance. This is the preferred futuritive in result clauses referring to the future, as in (4), where the result is a future culmination of a present cause.

(4)   (a) He has worked overtime for six months now, so soon
             he's going to have enough money to buy a new car.

(b) I plan to work out every day on my new exercise bike and
     by summer I'm going to be in much better shape.

This futuritive is somewhat odd in contexts where the future outcome is
viewed as settled, as in (5).

(5) (a) ?Later in this book I'm going to deal with this issue.
     (b) ?The plane is going to take off at 4:00.

The clash arises from the fact that the context tells us that the future
situation is settled and therefore very certain, but the futuritive itself (*be
going* InfVP) does not convey the same degree of certainty. Settled
situations are better expressed with a futuritive that expresses a greater
degree of certainty.

1.2 Present Progressive: be [_____ VP$_{PresPart}$]
The second futuritive consists of present tense progressive aspect, a
construction which is used to express future situations that are planned
events. "The future event is anticipated by virtue of a present plan, program,
or arrangement" (Leech 1971:62). Some examples are given in (6) and a tree
diagram in (7).

(6) (a) We've just set the program, and they're playing Mozart at next
          week's concert.
     (b) OK, guys, the practice is starting at five. Don't be late.
     (c) I've planned the meals and done the shopping:
          We're having fish on Friday and beef on Saturday.

(7)   VP
                    ⌒⎯⎯⎯⎯⎯⌒
               V   VP
              are   ⌒⎯⎯⎯⌒
                    playing Mozart

This futuritive is odd with situations that one can't plan or pre-arrange,
including most states, which explains the ungrammaticality of (8)(c).

(8)   (a)   ??It's raining tomorrow.
       (b)   ??Next semester I'm getting an A in all my classes.
       (c)   *Next year I am knowing a lot of interesting people.

1.3 will / 'll [___ VP$_{Base}$]

The third futuritive consists of the modal *will*, unstressed and most often contracted to *'ll*. Like all modals, it is subcategorized for a verb phrase whose head is the base form of a verb. Examples are given in (9) and a tree diagram in (10).

(9)   (a)   It will rain tomorrow.
       (b)   You'll feel better after you drink this medicine.
       (c)   Conclusion of discussion:
             It's settled, then. We'll have fish tomorrrow.
       (d)   Later in this book we will discuss relative clauses.
       (e)   If you drink this medicine, you'll feel better soon.

(10)   VP
               ╱   ╲
             V   VP
            will   ╱‾‾‾‾‾╲
                 rain tomorrow

This futuritive is used in a wide range of contexts to express future states and events. It is used to make predictions, as in (9)(a) and (b), and for settled notions, as in (9)(c). It is often found in the main clause of conditional sentences, as in (9)(e).

If the speaker wishes to be neutral about the likelihood of something happening or to be noncommittal about whether it will take place, she would probably use this futuritive, the most neutral way to express a future situation. It has no strong or overriding modal meaning. Note that in other contexts, *will* can convey modal meanings of willingness, as in (11)(a), or intention, as in (11)(b), and the futuritive meaning seems secondary or backgrounded.

(11) (a) Teacher: I need some volunteers.
           Student: I'll help.   (= I am willing to help.)
      (b) I'll call you as soon as we land.   (= I intend to call you.)

1.4 will / 'll be [____ VP_{PresPart}]

1.4 will / 'll be [____ VP_PresPart]

The fourth futuritive consists of the modal auxiliary *will* in combination
with a progressive VP, as in (12).

(12) (a) The train will be arriving at 4:00.
      (b) Kim will be starting her new job next week.
      (c) Will you be offering this course again next semester?

(13)

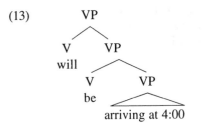

This construction is not only a syntactic combination of futuritives 2 and 3,
it is a semantic one as well. It combines the semantics of arrangement
(futuritive 2) with prediction or settled notion (futuritive 3). Leech (1971:
68) characterizes the meaning as the "future as a matter of course." It is used
to describe a predicted event which will happen quite independently of the
will or intention of any particular person, as in the examples of (12).
Sometimes the future event can be deduced from other knowledge.

(14) (a) (Observing a young couple in love)
           They'll be getting married soon.
      (b) That child lies to his friends and cheats in school.
           Before long, he'll be beating up little kids.

Note that this use of the verb *be* in combination with a VP whose head
is a present participle is not an instance of the present progressive. This
futuritive can be used with stative verbs that would not be used in the

progressive, as in (15).

(15)   (a)   They will be wanting your answer by next week.
       (b)   That deadbeat has really surprised me. He has a job and
             a girlfriend. Next thing you know, he'll be owning his
             own house.

   Similar in structure and meaning to this futuritive, a combination of
futuritives 2 and 3, is the combination of futuritives 1 and 3, shown in (16),
with the tree diagram in (17).

(16)   *be going to be* [___ VP$_{PresPart}$]
       (a)   We're going to be interviewing all day tomorrow.
       (b)   We're going to be landing in just a few minutes.
       (c)   I'm going to be giving a lecture tonight.

(17)

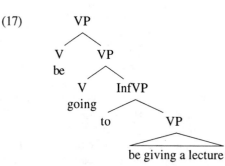

1.5 (Simple) Present Tense

The simple present tense is also a futuritive, as noted in Chapter 16. When
a speaker uses a present tense to discuss a future situation, the situation is
being presented as a present fact. This futuritive is commonly used for
situations which are fixed and unalterable, such as the rising and setting of
the sun, the days of the week, and so on, as in (18).

(18)   (a)   Tomorrow the sun sets at 6:54.
       (b)   This year Halloween falls on a Saturday.
       (c)   High tide is at 4:20 this afternoon.

By extension, this futuritive is used about situations which have a fairly high degree of certainty, such as scheduled events or very fixed (and unlikely to be changed) plans.

(19) (a) The Mets game starts at 8:00.
      (b) The Redskins play the Cowboys in the Super Bowl this Sunday.
      (c) We leave for Paris on the 16th.

1.6 be [___ InfVP]
The sixth futuritive consists of the verb *be* subcategorized for an InfVP.

(20) (a) The game's to start at eight.
      (b) We are to be married soon.
      (c) I'm to handle arrangements for the meeting. (= am expected to)

(21)

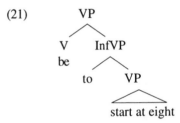

This futuritive expresses fairly strong expectation, conveying a sense of arrangement or predetermination. In some contexts it conveys a command.

(22) Mother to child: You are to be back by 10:00.

In the past tense, this futuritive acquires even stronger connotations, conveying not just expectation, but obligation. In negative sentences, it sounds more like a prohibition than mere lack of expectation.

(23) (a) My sister was to fix the dinner.
           (Not just "was expected to" but "was supposed to.")
      (b) Our organization was to provide the necessary funds.
      (c) She's not to do that!

1.7 be about [___ InfVP]
The seventh futuritive consists of a form of the verb *be* subcategorized for
about and an InfVP. There is a question mark instead of a label in (25)
since it is not clear what word class *about* belongs to. Recall that
prepositions do not otherwise combine with InfVPs.

(24)   (a) Shh! The play's about to start.
        (b) We're about to serve dinner. Please come to the table.

(25)

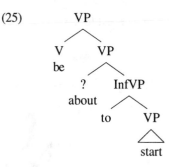

This futuritive expresses a situation which is not just strongly expected to
take place. It is imminent.

1.8 shall [____ VP$_{Base}$]
In British English, the modal auxiliary *shall* is used as a futuritive that
expresses determination against opposition. Many American English
speakers do not use this modal.

(26)   (a) The game shall start at 8:00 and nothing will stop it!
        (b) We shall have fish tomorrow, if I have to catch it myself.

  By way of summary, we can take a single situation and show how the
different futuritives convey an increasing sense of certainty, as in (27).

(27) (a) I'm going to leave in a few minutes.   intention
                                                        (human subject)

         The train's going to leave in a few minutes. culmination of
                                                        present cause

   (b) The train is leaving in a few minutes.   a present
                                                        plan / arrangement

   (c) The train will leave in a few minutes.   neutral or a
                                                        prediction

   (d) The train will be leaving in a few minutes. matter of course,
                                                         out of our hands

   (e) The train leaves in a few minutes.   present fact

   (f) The train is to leave in a few minutes.   strong expectation

   (g) The train is about to leave.   imminent

2. CONCLUDING NOTES ON FUTURITIVES

Futuritives have been presented along a scale of certainty, going from less certain to more certain. This scale works as described only in positive declarative sentences. In nondeclaratives, the degree of certainty and relation between the futuritives change. In questions, for example, the scale of strength gets reversed to some extent. In a question, *shall* is a suggestion, sometimes solicitous and polite, but it never expresses determination.

(28) (a) Shall we go now, ma'm?
    (b) Shall we join you for dinner?

Special things happen in subordinate clauses as well. The neutral way to express future time in subordinate clauses is to use the present tense, as noted in Chapter 16. In such clauses the present tense does not have the nuance "future as present fact" described above; it is neutral. Subordinate clauses with future time reference include clauses introduced with temporal conjunctions (e.g. *when*) and conditional clauses (with *if* or *unless*).

(29) (a) When he arrives, tell him I've been delayed.
      (b) If you come on time, we will be very grateful.

When a futuritive other than the present tense is used in subordinate clauses, the sentence either conveys something very unusual or is ungrammatical.

(30) (a) ?When you're going to be in bed already, they'll start calling.
      (b) ?Plant them next week, when it's to rain.
      (c) ?If they'll be left out, perhaps we should change the plan.
      (d) ?It'll ring when they'll be asleep.
      (e) ?He'll be calling about the time when you're going to be arriving.

Note that when the word *will* is stressed, it is no longer a neutral way to express a future situation. Stressing the word signals something special, such as emphasis, impatience, insistence, or determination.

(31) (a) Mother: You can't go out tonight.
      (b) Child: I WILL go and you can't stop me.

This chapter presented eight different ways to express a situation that will take place in the future. In all the examples, future time was marked from a reference point in the present (TS follows TR; TR = TU) and the head of the futuritive was in the present tense. Future time can also be marked from a reference point in the past (TS follows TR; TR before TU). A future in the past is marked with a futuritive whose head is in the past tense, as in (32) and (33). A time line is shown in (34).

(32) (a) Future: I will be home by six.
      (b) Future in the past: She said she would be home by six.

(33) (a) Future: They're playing Mozart next week.
      (b) Future in the past: I bought tickets because they were playing Mozart.

(34)   ———————— X ——————— X ——————— X ———→
               TR   TS   TU
           she says   6:00   Now
                              she is home

Exercise 1

Below are some excerpts from a newspaper article (Grove 1992) in which the author talks to some presidential candidates who hadn't been nominated to ask them what they would be doing on Election Day. Identify the futuritives.

[He calls Jerry Brown.] What, Brown was asked, will he be doing today?
"I couldn't tell you," chirped the former governor of California.... "I'll be voting, but I don't have any specific plans ...."
And for whom will Brown be casting his ballot?
"Oh, come on!" the governor chirped....
Tsongas ... said that today he'll be going for his usual swim, having lunch with his former campaign manager..., and spending tonight doing television commentary.
Virginia Gov. Doug Wilder, meanwhile, sounded similarly upbeat, saying he hopes to fly to Little Rock, Ark., tonight to be part of a huge celebration.
"This is Pat Buchanan," said a familiar voice leaving a message for an inquiring reporter. "I'm afraid you're not going to be able to get back to me, because I'm going on a bus trip through Alabama that's starting in a few minutes. I was just returning your call...."

Exercise 2

1.   I'm expecting a call from my brother tomorrow. Why can I use the present tense to talk about this future situation in (1)(a), but not (1)(b)?

(1)   (a)   When he calls, tell him to come over.
      (b)   ??Tomorrow he calls.

2.   If a speaker wanted to make a threat, which of the following would be most effective and why?

(2)   (a) I'm going to get you.
       (b) I'm getting you.
       (c) I will get you.
       (d) ??I get you.

Exercise 3

1.   What different nuances are conveyed by the following sentences? Are there contexts in which you might use one but not the other?

(1)   (a) They're going to Paris next month.
       (b) They go to Paris next month.
       (c) They're to go to Paris next month.

2.   Why are (2)(b) and (c) odd? What is the difference between (2)(a) and (2)(d)?

(2)   (a) I'm going to study harder next semester.
       (b) ?I'm studying harder next semester.
       (c) ?I study harder next semester.
       (d) I'm to study harder next semester.

Exercise 4   Future in the Past

Identify each future in the past, construct a time line showing the situation and its reference time, and note which futuritive has been used.

1.   Mable Crawford was born into a poor family, the second of eight children. Though she went only occasionally to the local one-room schoolhouse and worked evenings and weekends to support her family, she would grow up to become one of the wealthiest women in the world.

2.   Last Thursday was a beautiful day. My sister called and wanted to see me. I met her at a nearby coffee shop. We sat and chatted for a few minutes, and then she said she was going to tell me a strange story. It was indeed very strange.

3.   "Two days after the outbreak of war, ... [Reilly] received a very attractive proposition from the brothers Jivatovsky.... [they] invited him to go first to Japan and then to the U.S.A. as the bank's representative. Acting on the behalf of the Russian Government, he was to buy raw materials ... and other war supplies.... He accepted without hesitation. Two weeks later ... he caught the Trans-Siberian Express. It was to be nearly four years before he was to see Russia again." (Lockhart 1967:67)

4.   My grandfather had cancer. He was dying. The doctors informed him that they had done all they could and that he would not live much longer.

5.   When I met him in 1984, Roger S. had been working in Washington for two years. I didn't know it then, but he was going to be an important influence on my development. By 1989 we had co-authored several papers and begun to plan a new research center.

6.   When I was 17, I joined the Marines. Our instructor was a veteran of the Korean War, and he said he was going to teach us to live in the darkness. "We're all afraid of what we don't know, but I'm going to teach you to know the darkness." He could tell us those words because he had experienced the darkness. He had experienced that terror in a war.

7.   "She looked round the room, reviewing all its familiar objects which she had dusted once a week for so many years ... Perhaps she would never see again those familiar objects from which she had never dreamed of being divided.... She had consented to go away, to leave her home....What would they say of her in the Stores when they found out that she had run away with a fellow? Say she was a fool, perhaps; and her place would be filled up by advertisement. Miss Gavan would be glad." (Joyce 1962:37)

8.   "Even now, though she was over nineteen, she sometimes felt herself in danger of her father's violence....She had hard work to keep the house together and to see that the two young children who had been left to her charge went to school regularly and got their meals regularly. It was hard work -- a hard life -- but now that she was about to leave it she did not find it a wholly undesirable life. She was about to explore another life with Frank. Frank was very kind, manly, open-hearted. She was to go away with

him by the night-boat to be his wife ..." (Joyce 1962:37-38)

Exercise 5

In this chapter eight ways of talking about a future situation are presented in terms of the degree of certainty they express. This is not necessarily the best way to teach these expressions to a student of English. Examine an ESL text or text series and determine which futuritives are taught and the order in which they are presented. Why are the futuritives introduced in the order they are? Can you suggest a better order?

UNIT V

CLAUSES

IN THIS UNIT we explore the syntactic properties of clauses. In the first four chapters, we introduce the major forms of subordinate clauses and focus on their functions as nominal clauses, clauses that function within other clauses as subjects or complements.

We begin in Chapter 20 with that-clauses. We look at their syntactic properties, consider classes of verbs subcategorized for that-clauses, and explore the special positioning of some clauses within the predicate known as extraposition. In Chapter 21 we examine in a similar way the properties of infinitive clauses and in Chapter 22, gerundives. Gerundives are a peculiar construction because they have the internal structure of a clause, but the external syntax of a noun phrase.

In Chapter 23 we introduce the rule of WH-movement and look specifically at its role in the formation WH-clauses. At the end of the chapter, we turn to the first of several functions of WH-clauses, their use in indirect questions. In Chapter 24 we examine relative clauses, a second function of WH-clauses. Relative clauses are not nominal clauses; they function as modifiers of nouns.

In the final chapter of this unit, we discuss the special forms of independent clauses—declarative, interrogative, imperative, and exclamative. Some interrogative clauses and all exclamatives are WH-clauses.

20
THAT-CLAUSES

IN THIS CHAPTER we introduce that-clauses, which function in other clauses as subjects and complements, as in (1). (That-clauses are in square brackets.)

(1)   (a) [That we might actually lose the game] had not occurred to anyone.
        (b) [That Sam arrived late again] was not surprising, given his past record.
        (c) Everyone knows [that your cat eats broccoli].

In the first section we examine the internal syntax of that-clauses, and then in the second turn to their external syntax. We consider verbs, adjectives, and nouns that are subcategorized for that-clauses and discuss a special type of nonfinite that-clause. The chapter concludes with a worksheet on extraposition.

1. THE INTERNAL SYNTAX OF THAT-CLAUSES

Like all subordinate clauses, a that-clause consists of a complementizer (C), in this case *that*, and a clause (S), as in the examples of (2) (the S is in square brackets), and the tree diagram in (3). Though these are CPs (see Chapter 3), we give them the more specific label "that-S."

(2)   (a) that [we might actually lose the game]
        (b) that [Sam arrived late again]
        (c) that [your cat eats broccoli]

(3)   That-S

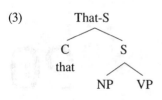

There is nothing unusual about the S part of a that-S. It is an ordinary finite clause that could stand on its own as a complete sentence, as in (4).

(4)   (a) We might actually lose the game.
       (b) Sam arrived late again.
       (c) Your cat eats broccoli.

Often, the complementizer *that* is omitted, as in (5) and (6). The null symbol Ø shows the place of the missing complementizer.

(5)   (a) Everyone knows [that your cat eats broccoli].
       (b) Everyone knows [Ø your cat eats broccoli].

(6)   (a) We believe [that you are telling the truth].
       (b) We believe [Ø you are telling the truth].

Omission of *that* is to a large extent a matter of style. It is more common when the that-S itself is short and is increasingly less common the longer and more complex the that-S. Omission of *that* is rather rare when the that-S is preceded by an adverbial or parenthetical remark and is usually impossible if the preceding constituent is long or complex, as in (7) and (8).

(7)   Preceding constituent—omission of *that* is rare
       (a) We believe, unfortunately, [that / Ø you are telling the truth].
       (b) They know, alas, [that / Ø he's an agent].
       (c) The guests insisted, wisely, [that / ?Ø he leave].

(8)   Preceding constituent is long—omission is impossible
       (a) I believe, and everyone agrees with me, [that you are lying].
       (b) The guests insisted, after being ignored for much of the evening, [that they had been mistreated].

In a tree diagram, complementizer position is always indicated, even when the complementizer itself is omitted, as in (9).

(9) (a)   That-S

```
              That-S
              /    \
            C        S
            Ø      /   \
               NP      VP
              /  \     /   \
          your cat  eats broccoli
```

Before turning to the external syntax of that-clauses, note that the word *that* has many other functions. It can be a demonstrative, a word which functions as a determiner in the noun phrases, as in (10), or a pronoun, as in (11).

(10) (a) *that* clever woman
      (b) *that* idea of yours

(11) (a) *That* was a fine thing to say.
      (b) I don't believe *that*.

That can be a complementizer in clauses other than that-Ss, for instance in relative clauses (see Chapter 24). One difference between that-clauses and relative clauses is that the S part of a that-clause can stand on its own (as in (4) above), while the S part of a relative clause (often) cannot. The relative clauses of (12) (in square brackets) are ungrammatical when used alone. The strings of words in (13) are not complete sentences: (13)(a) is missing the direct object of *bought*, while (13)(b) is missing the subject.

(12) (a) The house [*that* you bought] has a leaky basement.
      (b) I like children [*that* are respectful and honest].

(13) (a) you bought
      (b) are respectful and honest

Another way to distinguish the two uses of the complementizer *that:* in a relative clause the complementizer may be replaced with a relative pronoun (*who* or *which*) (cf. *the house* which *you bought*). Such a substitution is impossible with the complementizer in a that-S.

That along with some other word(s) can also be a complementizer in adverbial clauses. Three such combinations are *so that* and *in order that*, used in clauses that express the purpose of an action (as in (14)(a) and (b)), and *except that*, used in clauses that express an exception (as in (14)(c)).

(14) (a) The judge dismissed the jury temporarily [*in order that* the lawyers could give their arguments in private].

(b) I started dinner early [*so that* we could eat before the game].

(c) I would have come on time [*except that* my car wouldn't start and I missed the bus].

In short, *that* occurs as a complementizer in three kinds of clauses, but the name "that-S" is reserved for those with nominal functions, which are explored in the next section.

Exercise 1

Circle the word *that* if it is a complementizer and put square brackets around each that-S.

1. I believe that you are lying to me.
2. I know some students that are very hard working.
3. That you got an "A" in math proves that you have some ability after all, if you only apply yourself.
4. That teacher tries to encourage her children so that they will have a positive self-image.
5. Mother warned me that I shouldn't go out with men like you, and that's where she was wrong.
6. The girl that I sit next to in chemistry is from that city on the Eastern Shore near Rehobeth.
7. Everyone thought that I was afraid that the Redskins would lose, but I wasn't afraid of that.
8. It is amazing that the thief that stole my purse sent it back.

9.   The judge ordered that the prisoner that had tried to escape be held without bail.
10.   And that's that!

Exercise 2
Determine whether the complementizer *that* can be omitted from the that-clauses below and make a generalization about what you find. Test your generalization on at least two other sentences *that have the same structure.*

1.   That we might lose the game had not occurred to anyone.
2.   That Sam arrived late again was not surprising.
3.   That you got an "A" in math proves my point.

Exercise 3
Draw tree diagrams for the that-Ss in the following sentences. Remember to include a position for the complementizer, whether it is present or not.

1.   That Sam arrived late was not surprising.
2.   Everyone knows that your cat eats broccoli.
3.   I think Sam is sick.
4.   Some students told me that they like grammar.
5.   The police assume the thief is hiding in that building.
6.   Kim is worried that Kip likes Carlie and that Ryan will find out.

---

2. THE EXTERNAL SYNTAX OF THAT-CLAUSES

In this section we examine the ways in which that-Ss fit into other clauses. First of all, they can be the subject of a clause, as in (1)(a) and (b). This fact requires us to revise a statement made in Chapter 3 about basic clauses, repeated here as (15)(a). The revision is given in (15)(b) and tree diagrams in (16).

(15)   (a) Original Statement: A clause consists of a NP and a VP.
       (b) Revision: A clause consists of a NP or a That-S and a VP.

(16) (a)   S   (b)   S

            NP   VP   That-S   VP

Whether a that-S can be the subject of a clause depends on a constituent in the predicate. The sentences of (17) show that some verbs allow that-S subjects, while those of (18) show that others do not.

(17) (a) [That you arrived on time] *surprised* everyone.
      (b) [That you are reliable] *pleases* your boss.
      (c) You hate me. [That you're deserting me] *proves* it.

(18) (a) *[That you arrived on time] *knows* the answer.
      (b) *[That you are reliable] *promoted* you.
      (c) *[That you're deserting me] *leaves* me alone.

If a verb allows a that-S subject, this information is included in its subcategorization frame. Subcategorizations for the verbs *surprise* and *please* are given in (19) and (20), where the subject is stated to the left of the square brackets that indicate the verb phrase.

(19) *surprise*   NP   [_____ NP]
                     That-S [_____ NP]

(20) *please*   NP   [_____ NP]
                     That-S [_____ NP]

That-S subjects are also sanctioned by some adjectives, as in (21). Other adjectives do not allow them, as in (22).

(21) (a) [That you arrived on time] was very *pleasing*.
      (b) [That Max loves Fannie] is *obvious*.
      (c) [That the cat died] was *regrettable*, but *unavoidable*.

(22) (a) *[That you arrived on time] was *big / tall / red*.
      (b) *[That Max loves Fannie] is *cold / hungry*.
      (c) *[That the cat died] was *necessary*.

In addition to functioning as subjects, that-Ss function as complements of both verbs and adjectives, as shown in (23) and (24).

(23)   Verbs with that-S complements
    (a)   My children *believe* [that there is a Santa Clause].
    (b)   The student *denied* [that she had cheated on the test].
    (c)   The officer *told* me [that I was about to be arrested].
    (d)   My mother *warned* me [that I shouldn't talk to strangers].

(24)   Adjectives with that-S complements
    (a)   You seem *disappointed* [that your opponent lost the election].
    (b)   They are *afraid* [that you might cheat them].
    (c)   I am *confident* [that you will pass this course].

Not all verbs and adjectives are subcategorized for that-S complements, as shown in the ungrammatical sentences of (25).

(25)   (a)   *I *eat* [that it is good].
    (b)   *The children *talked* [that they were afraid].
    (c)   *Mary is *intelligent* [that she gets good grades].
    (d)   *Your daughter is *insecure* [that you don't love her].

Once again, whether a verb or adjective occurs with a that-S complement must be listed in its subcategorization frame, as in (26). Some verbs combine with a that-S alone, while others take both a NP and a that-S.

(26)   (a)   Verbs: *believe, deny*   [_____ that-S]
    (b)   Verbs: *tell, warn*   [_____ NP that-S]
    (c)   Adjectives: *disappointed, afraid, confident*   [_____ that-S]

The number of verbs subcategorized for that-Ss is quite large; the number of adjectives is comparatively small, and many of them are derived from verbs (e.g. *alarmed, amused, disappointed, frightened*). In the tree diagrams given below, the internal structure of the clause part of the that-S is abbreviated with a triangle.

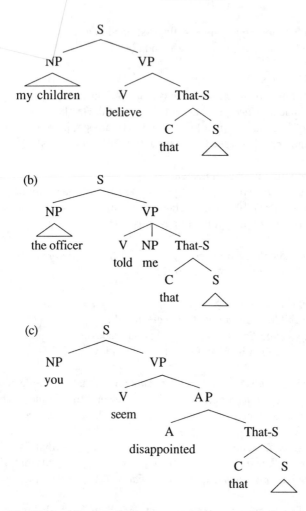

Finally, besides functioning as complements of verbs and adjectives, that-Ss function as complements of nouns as well, as in (28).

(28)   (a) The *fact* [that he's lying] is obvious.
       (b) The *belief* [that the world was flat] was held by many people.
       (c) Some people are of the *opinion* [that grammar is boring].

The that-S combines with a noun and forms a N+. As discussed in Chapter 14, a N+ is larger than a noun, but smaller than a NP. It combines with a determiner to form a NP, as shown in the diagrams of (29).

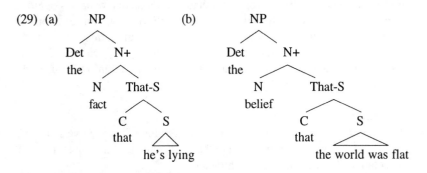

Subcategorizations for three of the hundred or so nouns subcategorized for that-Ss are given in (30).

(30) (a) *fact*   [_____ that-S]
      (b) *belief*   [_____ that-S]
      (c) *opinion*   [_____ that-S]

Exercise 4

Draw tree diagrams for these sentences. Use a triangle to abbreviate the internal structure of the S of the that-clause, as was done in (27) and (29), in all sentences but 9 and 10.

1.   I believe that you are lying to me.
2.   They promised the client that the report would be ready.
3.   You give us the impression that you are bored.
4.   They were sad we didn't call.
5.   I must protest the accusation that we are lying.
6.   The hypothesis that grammar can be learned by anyone is unproven.
7.   That you can't come to our party is unfortunate.
8.   That you like grammar proves you can have good grammar and good taste.
9.   My doctor insisted that I tell my husband that I am sick.

10. No one can believe you denied the rumor that you are pregnant.

Exercise 5

Many verbs subcategorized for a that-clause complement express cognitive or verbal processes, such as *know, think, believe, say*, and *tell*. Find at least eight other verbs that take that-S complements, give their subcategorization frames (either [_____ that-S] or [_____ NP that-S]), and use each in a sentence that illustrates its subcategorization. Do your verbs express cognitive or verbal processes?

Exercise 6

Which of the following nouns is subcategorized for a that-S? Give sentences as evidence for your answer. (Be sure that your sentences contain that-Ss and not relative clauses that begin with *that*.)

1.	promise	9.	illusion
2.	hope	10.	sincerity
3.	book	11.	program
4.	transportation	12.	declaration
5.	denial	13.	disappointment
6.	wisdom	14.	happiness
7.	discovery	15.	committee
8.	toy	16.	reply

Exercise 7

In what way are the that-clauses below different from the that-clauses discussed in Section 1?

(1) The judge ordered [that the prisoner be held without bail].
(2) The League of Women Voters demanded [that the Senator resign].
(3) The committee urges [that the witness come forward and tell her story].

3. NONFINITE THAT-CLAUSES

There is a second kind of that-S, illustrated in (31) and (32).

(31) (a) The judge ordered [that the prisoner be held without bail].
      (b) The League of Women Voters demanded [that the Senator
           resign].
      (c) The committee urges [that the witness come forward and
           tell her story].

(32) (a) [That he resign] is absolutely necessary.
      (b) [That she perform well tomorrow] is vital to the success
           of this project.

The that-Ss in (31) and (32) are nonfinite clauses. The verb is the base form
and thus does not show agreement with a third singular subject and does not
distinguish present or past tense. Note that the verbs in the that-Ss of
(31)(a) and (b) are not in the past tense, as might be expected if they were
finite. We will refer to this special type of that-S as a nonfinite that-S.

   In many traditional approaches to English grammar this use of the base
form is called a subjunctive and is considered a special form of the verb,
similar to subjunctives in Romance and other languages. Since the so-called
subjunctive is never different in form from the base form of the verb,
however, we consider it a special use of the base form, rather than a separate
form or tense.

   A small number of verbs and a few adjectives and nouns are
subcategorized for nonfinite that-S complements, while a small number of
adjectives are subcategorized for nonfinite that-S subjects. Further examples
are given in (33) - (35).

(33) Adjective subcategorized for a nonfinite that-S complement
      The teacher was *insistent* [that the student be allowed
      to repeat the course].

(34) Nouns subcategorized for a nonfinite that-S complement
      (a) The *decree* [that the Princess give up the children]
           was nullified by a higher authority.

..e board of directors issued an *order* [that all employees be
..rced to take a pay cut or resign].

(35) Adjectives subcategorized for nonfinite that-S subjects
    (a) [That the Princess resign] is both *fitting* and *proper*.
    (b) [That the patient be given more attention immediately] is
       absolutely *imperative*.

Sample subcategorization frames are given in (36) and tree diagrams in (37).

(36) (a) Verbs: *order, demand, urge*   [_____ that-S$_{Base}$]
    (b) Adjectives: *insistent*   [_____ that-S$_{Base}$]
    (c) Nouns: *degree, order*   [_____ that-S$_{Base}$]

(37) (a)

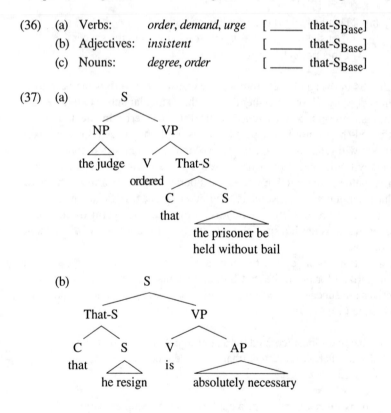

Exercise 8

From the following list of verbs that are subcategorized for that-clause complements, choose five and use each of them in a sentence. Is the that-clause finite, nonfinite, or are both possible? Except for the verb *be*, the difference between a base form and a general present form of a verb is only visible if the subject is in the third person singular, so be sure to test your verbs with third person singular subjects in the present tense,

1.	acknowledge	10.	fear	19.	recommend
2.	advise	11.	guarantee	20.	regret
3.	advocate	12.	hope	21.	require
4.	agree	13.	insist	22.	rule
5.	decide	14.	learn	23.	say
6.	decree	15.	petition	24.	specify
7.	demand	16.	prefer	25.	stipulate
8.	ensure	17.	propose	26.	suggest
9.	forbid	18.	realize	27.	urge

Exercise 9

Look over the words that are subcategorized for nonfinite that-Ss in this chapter and in your answer to Exercise 8. In what styles or topics of discourse would you expect to find such words? In what styles would they be less likely to occur? What implications does this have for teaching the construction?

Exercise 10

Further evidence that nonfinite that-Ss are indeed not finite comes from how they are negated. Make the negative for at least five nonfinite that-Ss in Section 3 and five finite that-Ss in Sections 1 and 2. How do they differ?

EXTRAPOSITION

IT CAN BE AWKWARD to have a clause in subject position, and we often encounter sentences in which a clausal "subject" appears in the VP, as in (1) - (3). (That-Ss are in square brackets.)

(1)　(a)　[That the world is round] is obvious.
　　　(b)　It is obvious [that the world is round].

(2)　(a)　[That Sam snores] bothers me.
　　　(b)　It bothers me [that Sam snores].

(3)　(a)　[That we have to clean the house on Saturday] is a drag.
　　　(b)　It is a drag [that we have to clean the house on Saturday].

Make up at least four more pairs of sentences like those above. In the first there should be a that-S in subject position, while in the second the that-S should occur in the VP and be replaced by the pronoun *it*. Compare the sentences in (a) with those in (b). Is there any difference in meaning?

We assume that the sentences in (b) are derived from those in (a) by means of a syntactic rule called extraposition. In this worksheet we examine the special properties of sentences with extraposition, looking particularly at the syntactic function of *it* and at the position of the that-S in the VP.

1. THE SYNTACTIC FUNCTION OF *IT*

The sentences in (4) - (6) provide evidence for the syntactic function of the pronoun *it*. What is it?

(4)　(a)　It is obvious that the world is round.
　　　(b)　Is it obvious that the world is round?

294

(5) (a) It bothers me that Sam snores.
     (b) Does it bother me that Sam snores?

(6) (a) It is noteworthy that she won the contest.
     (b) Is it noteworthy that she won the contest?

In sentences (4)(b), (5)(b), and (6)(b) the rule of inversion has applied, inverting the pronoun *it* with the first auxiliary. Since *it* inverts, it must be the subject. Not only is *it* in the position we expect of the subject, it is also treated as the subject by the rule of inversion.

2. THE POSITION OF THE THAT-CLAUSE

Second, consider the that-S. Though it is a subject in (1)(a), (2)(a), and (3)(a), in the corresponding (b) sentences, it has been shifted into the verb phrase. More specifically, it forms a VP with the VP with which it combined to form a clause. This is shown in the tree diagrams in (7), where the VPs have subscripts to help distinguish them. The that-S forms a clause with VP_1 in ((7)(a)). When shifted into the predicate, it combines with VP_1 to form a new VP, labelled VP_2 in (7)(b).

(7) (a)   (b)

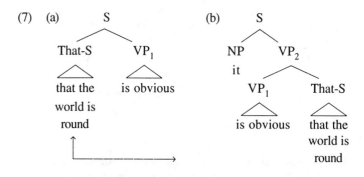

If the VP with which the that-S combines contains an auxiliary, there will be more than one VP node in the sentence. The that-S forms a constituent with the auxiliary and its VP, the VP with which it combined to form a clause, as shown in (8).

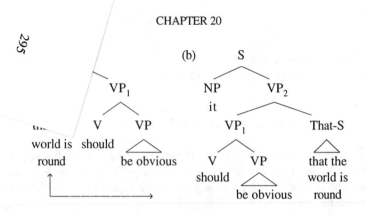

We cannot simply say that the that-S shifts to the end of the sentence. In sentences like (9), which contain an adverbial clause that modifies the entire sentence, the that-S shifts to the end of the VP, the position described above. This is shown in (10).

(9)　(a)　[That Sam snores] bothers me because I'm a light sleeper.
　　　(b)　It bothers me [that Sam snores] because I'm a light sleeper.

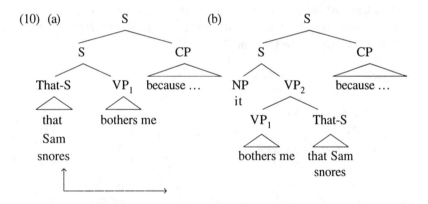

It is important to stress that the shifted that-S is not a complement, even though it is within the VP, a syntactic position in which we expect to find complements. The verbs and adjectives in these sentences are subcategorized for that-S subjects, and not for complements. We call the shifted that-S a "pseudocomplement."

In conclusion, the rule of extraposition shifts a that-S subject into the predicate, where it forms a VP with the VP it combined with to form a clause, and puts the pronoun *it* in the vacated subject position. It is usually an optional rule, which creates a stylistic variant of the original sentence. With a few verbs such as *seem* and *appear*, however, extraposition is obligatory, as shown in (11) and (12), where the sentences in which extraposition has not applied are ungrammatical. These verbs, a subset of the linking verbs (see Chapter 12), are discussed in the appendix to Chapter 21, Section 3.

(11)   (a)   *That Mary is guilty seems.
       (b)   It seems that Mary is guilty.

(12)   (a)   *That John is innocent appears.
       (b)   It appears that John is innocent.

Exercise 1
The that-Ss in this worksheet are all finite. Can nonfinite that-Ss undergo extraposition? Provide at least three pairs of sentences as evidence for your answer.

Exercise 2
Extraposition has applied in the following sentences. Give tree diagrams that show their structure before and after its application. (Abbreviate the internal structure of the that-Ss and NPs with triangles.)

1.   It is amazing that you like grammar.
2.   It annoys me that you like grammar.
3.   It must frighten you that you have no insurance coverage.
4.   It was surprising to me that Helen won.
5.   It should be a warning to you that your brother was caught.

Exercise 3

Give tree diagrams for the following sentences. Draw out the internal structure of all constituents but the NPs.

1.   It seems that those children were calling the teacher names.
2.   I am sorry that it was necessary that the offer be withdrawn.
3.   It confused the students that it was unclear that class was cancelled.
4.   That it frightens you that a stranger is lurking outside your window shows that you are normal.

Exercise 4

Can the complementizer be omitted in pseudocomplements created by the rule of extraposition? Give evidence for your answer.

21
INFINITIVE CLAUSES

IN THIS CHAPTER we explore the internal syntax of infinitive clauses and learn about their nominal functions. Many verbs are subcategorized for reduced forms of infinitive clauses, which are discussed in Section 3.

1. THE INTERNAL SYNTAX OF INFINITIVE CLAUSES

Some examples of infinitive clauses (Inf-Ss) are given in square brackets in (1).

(1)   (a)   We all prefer [for Peter to do the honors].
        (b)   My mother would like [for you to leave now].
        (c)   [For you to swim the English Channel] would be ridiculous.

Like all clauses, infinitive clauses are composed of a complementizer and a clause. In this case the complementizer is *for* and the clause, in addition to a subject NP, contains a VP marked with the word *to*, which combines with a VP whose head is a base form. VPs with these properties are infinitive VPs (InfVPs). In the tree diagram in (2), there is no label for the word *to* since it seems to be in a word class by itself. Though infinitive clauses are CPs, we give them the more specific label Inf-S.

(2)

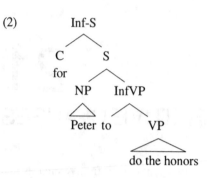

Often, the complementizer *for* is omitted, as in (3) and (4), where the symbol Ø shows the place of the missing complementizer.

(3)   (a)   We all prefer [for Peter to do the honors].
       (b)   We all prefer [Ø Peter to do the honors].

(4)   (a)   My mother would like [for you to leave now].
       (b)   My mother would like [Ø you to leave now].

As with the omission of the complementizer *that*, omission of *for* is generally not possible when the Inf-S is preceded by an adverbial or parenthetical remark, as in (5).

(5)   (a)   We all prefer, quite strongly, [for / ?Ø Peter to do the honors].
       (b)   They would like very much [for / ?Ø you to chair this meeting].

Omission of the complementizer *for* depends to a certain extent on properties of the head, the verb or adjective that is subcategorized for the Inf-S. Adjectives do not generally allow omission, while verbs vary. Some verbs require or strongly favor omission, some allow it, while others seem not to allow it, as shown in (6) - (9). There is a great deal of individual variation here, and not all readers will agree with these grammaticality judgements.

(6)   Adjectives -- Omission of complementizer *for* not possible
       (a)   We are *anxious* [for you to leave].
       (b)   *We are *anxious* [Ø you to leave].
       (c)   The children were *eager* [for Santa to arrive].
       (d)   *The children were *eager* [Ø Santa to arrive].

(7)   Verbs strongly favoring omission of complementizer *for*
       (a)   The parents *wanted* [?for / Ø their daughter to win].
       (b)   We all *expect* [?for / Ø you to do your best].

(8)   Verbs allowing omission of complementizer *for*
       (a)   Mommie *needs* [for / Ø you to behave today].
       (b)   Children *prefer* [for / Ø their own parents to pick them up].

(9)   Verbs not allowing omission of *for*
       (a)   They *long* [for / *Ø you to visit].
       (b)   The guide will *arrange* [for /*Ø us to arrive late].

As with the complementizer *that*, omission of the complementizer *for* is
generally not possible when the Inf-S does not directly follow the head, even
when the verb is one that otherwise favors it, as do *want* and *expect*.

(10)   (a)   The parents *wanted* desperately [for / ?Ø their daughter to win
              first prize.
       (b)   We all *expect*, and I hope we are not mistaken, [for / ?Ø you to
              do your best].

In a tree diagram, the position of an omitted complementizer is indicated
with Ø, as in (11), the diagram for the Inf-S of (7)(a).

(11)   Inf-S

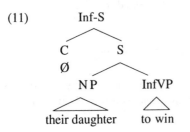

Exercise 1
Give a tree diagram for the internal structure of each infinitive clause.

1   for us to visit them
2.   (Mrs. Smith prefers) her children to remain at home.
3.   for the committee to elect me chairman.
4.   (Suzie wants) the cushions to be green.
5.   (The guide will arrange) for us to arrive late.

Exercise 2
The infinitive clauses in square brackets below are not complete clauses. Which constituent(s) are missing? Give an alternative way of expressing each sentence which contains a complete infinitive clause that is roughly synonymous with the original sentence.

1.   [To cross this desert in mid-day] is equivalent to suicide.
2.   [To play the piano well] takes practice, dedication, and talent.
3.   It is pure pleasure [to watch a sunrise in the Keys].

Exercise 3
Above it was claimed that the head verb in an infinitive clause must be the base form of the verb. Provide some evidence for this claim.

2. THE EXTERNAL SYNTAX OF NOMINAL INFINITIVE CLAUSES

Inf-Ss occur in the same syntactic positions in a clause that that-Ss do. For one thing, they can function as subjects, as illustrated in (12).

(12)   Inf-S as Subject
        (a) [For me to remain silent on this matter] is clearly
            undesirable and impossible.
        (b) [For you to leave now] would be really embarrassing.
        (c) [For the press to hound them like that] is positively immoral.

This possibility requires us to revise again the statement about the internal structure of a basic clause, made in Chapter 3 and revised in Chapter 20. The revision is given in (13) and tree diagrams in (14).

(13)   A clause consists of a NP or a that-S or an Inf-S and a VP.

(14) (a)   S   (b)   S   (c)   S

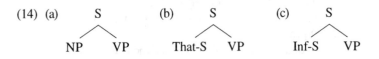

    NP   VP   That-S VP   Inf-S   VP

An Inf-S cannot be the subject of any verb, however. Often they occur as the subject of the verb *be* in combination with an adjective that makes a comment on the content of the clause, as in the examples of (12). A large number of adjectives are subcategorized for an Inf-S subject, but only a small number of verbs. They occur most naturally with a modal such as *would*, which highlights the hypothetical nature of the situation expressed in the Inf-S, as shown in (15). Corresponding subcategorizations are given in (16).

(15)   Inf-S as Subject of Verb
    (a)   [For Sally to insult Margaret in public] would *shock* her parents.
    (b)   [For Mable to win a role in the new play] would *take* a lot of lobbying on the part of her agent.
    (c)   [For you to get an 'A' on this test] will *require* that you study much harder than usual.

(16)   (a)   Adjectives:
        ridiculous, impossible, embarrassing   Inf-S   [_____]
    (b)   Verbs:
        shock, take   Inf-S   [_____   NP]
        require   Inf-S   [_____   That-S]

Inf-Ss also occur as *complements* of verbs and adjectives, as in (17) and (18).

(17)   Infinitive Clause as Complement of Verb
        (a) They are *longing* [for us to visit].
        (b) I would *hate* [for the committee to elect me chairman].
        (c) Suzie *wants* [Ø the cushions to be green].

(18)   Infinitive Clause as Complement of Adjective
        (a) We are *eager* [for them to show us the solution to this
            difficult problem].
        (b) On Christmas Eve little children everywhere are *anxious*
            [for Santa to come and fill their stockings].

Subcategorization frames for these verbs and adjectives are given in (19) and
tree diagrams in (20).

(19)   (a) *long, hate, want*   [_____ Inf-S]
        (b) *eager, anxious*   [_____ Inf-S]

(20) (a)

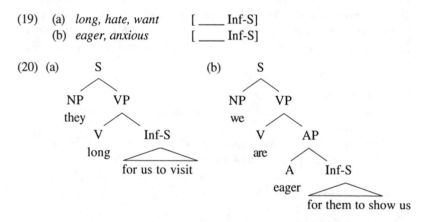

There are actually several different ways that a verb or adjective can be
subcategorized for an Inf-S. Some verbs and adjectives are subcategorized for
a full infinitive clause, while others are subcategorized for a reduced one, the
topic of the next section.
    Before turning to reduced infinitive clauses, note that Inf-Ss can be
adverbials as well, modifying sentences (in (21)) or VPs (in (22) - (23)). As
VP modifiers, they frequently express the purpose of an action and can be
replaced by a clause with the complementizer *so that*. Trees are given in
(24).

(21) (a) [To tell you the truth], syntax is fun.
      (b) [To be honest for a change], I think that is an awful idea.

(22) (a) We stopped [for the children to use the bathroom].
      (b) We stopped [so that the children could use the bathroom].

(23) (a) The students handed their papers in early
                  ...[for the teacher to give them some comments].
      (b)   ...[so that the teacher could give them some comments].

(24) (a)   S   (b)   VP

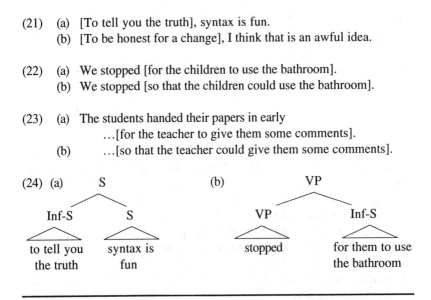

        Inf-S   S   VP   Inf-S

        to tell you   syntax is   stopped   for them to use
        the truth   fun   the bathroom

Exercise 4
Find five adjectives not used above that can occur with an Inf-S subject and five adjectives which cannot. Use all of them in sentences that show their occurrence or non-occurrence with Inf-S subjects.

Exercise 5
Give tree diagrams for the following sentences using triangles to abbreviate the internal structure of NPs.

1. They are longing for us to visit them.
2. I would hate for the committee to elect me chairman.
3. For us to help you is impossible.
4. The people can't stand for politicans to vote themselves pay raises.
5. The lawyers will arrange for the clients to be released.
6. For them to name their baby Elvis was in bad taste.

Exercise 6
Can infinitive clause subjects undergo extraposition? Give three examples as
evidence for your answer.

---

3. REDUCED INFINITIVE CLAUSES

A reduced Inf-S consists of only an InfVP. It is missing the complementizer
for and the subject, as in (25), where the reduced Inf-Ss are in square
brackets.

(25) (a) Suzie wants [to leave now].
      (b) Mother is longing [to visit Paris].
      (c) Phil would hate [to embarrass you in public].

The missing subject can be understood in different ways. When the Inf-S is
in subject position, it is often understood generically, as in (26).

(26) (a) [To cross the desert in mid-day] is equivalent to suicide.
      (b) [To play the piano well] takes practice, dedication, and talent.
      (c) It is pure pleasure [to watch a sunrise at the beach].

(26)(a) is understood to mean that to cross the desert in mid-day is suicide
for anyone, i.e. for people in general. Similarly, (26)(b) is understood to say
that, for people in general, to play the piano well requires practice, etc.
    The missing subject of a reduced infinitive clause in other cases is
understood to be co-referential with another NP in the sentence, often the
subject. For example, the missing subject in (25)(a) is understood to be
Suzie (i.e. Suzie is to leave), while the missing subject in (25)(b) is
Mother (i.e. Mother is understood as the one to visit Paris).
    In terms of occurrence with full and reduced Inf-Ss, we need to recognize
three subclasses of verbs. Some verbs, like *want*, occur with both full and
reduced clauses. They are subcategorized for full Inf-Ss, which are reduced
when the subject of the Inf-S is co-referential to the subject of the main
clause, as can be seen in in (27) and (28). We name this first subclass the
want class.

(27) (a) Suzie wants [(for) you to leave now].
      (b) Suzie wants [to leave now].

(28) (a) Mother is longing [for us to visit Paris].
      (b) Mother is longing [to visit Paris].

Tree diagrams for (27) are given in (29), where the unexpressed complementizer is shown with Ø and the missing subject with a blank line.

(29) (a) Full Inf-S   (b) Reduced Inf-S

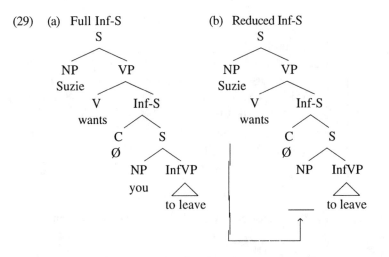

A second subclass, known as the *try* class, consists of verbs that are subcategorized for only a reduced infinitive, like the verb *try* in (30). As above, the missing subject of the Inf-S is understood to be co-referential with the subject of the verb, but in this case, understood co-reference is required.

(30) (a) Reduced Inf-S   We tried [to escape].
      (b) Full Inf-S   *We tried [for Bill to escape].

Other verbs with this subcategorization are given in (31) and (32), and a tree diagram in (33).

(31)   (a)   Reduced Inf-S   They began [to panic].
       (b)   Full Inf-S   *They began [for us to panic].

(32)   (a)   Reduced Inf-S   She promised [to help us].
       (b)   Full Inf-S   *She promised [for them to help us].

(33)

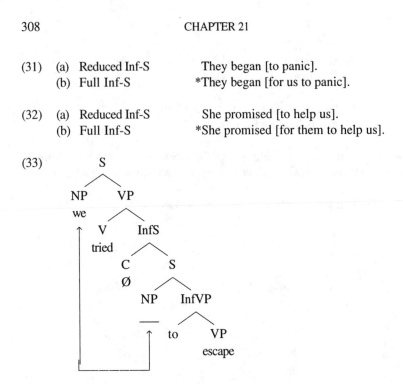

The verbs in (34) demonstrate the need to recognize a third subclass of verbs.

(34)   (a)   They *forced* me [to give them the money].
       (b)   They *challenged* me [to do better on the next test].
       (c)   They *invited* us [to stay for the weekend].

Verbs in this subclass, which we will call the *force* class, are subcategorized for a direct object and a reduced infinitive clause. The missing subject of the infinitive clause is understood to be co-referential to the direct object of the verb, as shown in (35).

9.   Netty will get her sister to pay her friend to help her.
10.   Jim should persuade his mother to allow him to learn to drive.

Exercise 9

For each of the verbs listed below, determine whether it is subcategorized for
a full or a reduced infinitive clause. On the basis of the kind of complements
they allow, divide them into three classes: the *want* class, the *try* class,
the *force* class. Give sentences to support your classification.

begin	(can't) stand	decide	demand	expect	eat
fail	finish	need	offer	prefer	promise
regret	shout	tease	threaten	want	worry

Exercise 10

Review the discussion in Section 1 about omission of the complementizer
for. Then classify at least six verbs in the *want*-subclass according to the
groups established in (7) - (9) (favors omission, allows omission, does not
allow omission).

Exercise 11

Why are the following sentences ungrammatical?

1.   *They abandoned to learn any grammar.
2.   The enemy destroyed everything. *The general even ordered to cut
      down forests and vineyards.
3.   *Shawn Brown recommended me to get in touch with you.
4.   *On January 9, 1905, the Tsar commanded to shoot down a peaceful
      demonstration.

APPENDIX

The appendix provides more detailed treatments of five classes of verbs that
are subcategorized for Inf-Ss, including lists of verbs in each subclass
adapted from Alexander and Kunz (1964).

The following abbreviations are used in the lists below:
P   Inf-S is most natural if the VP is progressive.
I   restricted to informal discourse
F   restricted to formal discourse

1.   The *want* class   [_____ Inf-S]

The verbs in the *want* class are subcategorized for an Inf-S, the pattern shown in (1)(a). They can also occur with a reduced Inf-S, as in (1)(c). In the reduced clause, the missing subject of the infinitive is understood to be co-referential with the subject of the verb in the main clause. As for the complementizer *for*, with some verbs in this subclass it may be omitted when the Inf-S directly follows the verb, as in (1)(b). With a few verbs (e.g. *want*, *expect*) this deletion is nearly obligatory. When an adverbial or parenthetical expression is inserted between the verb and the infinitive clause, however, the complementizer *for* cannot be omitted, as in (1)(a).

(1)   (a)   Full Inf-S
              They want desperately [for us to spend the holidays in France].
        (b)   Full Inf-S with Omitted Complementizer
              They want [us to spend the holidays in France].
        (c)   Reduced Inf-S
              (subject of Inf-S = subject of main verb)
              They want [to spend the holidays in France].

ache, P	elect ("choose")	plan
(can't) afford	expect	plead, P
aim, I	hate	prefer
arrange	intend	prepare
ask	itch, P, I	propose
(can't) bear	like	request
beg, P	long	see fit
(not) care, F	(would) love	(can't) stand
choose ("desire")	mean ("intend")	want
demand	need	wish, F
desire	opt	yearn, F

2.   The *try* class   [_____   Inf-S*]
                                *Must be reduced.

The *try* class includes verbs which occur only with a reduced Inf-S, as
shown in (2)(b). (One might be able to fashion a sentence with a full Inf-S
for some verbs in this list, but it would be both rare and awkward.) The
missing subject of the Inf-S is always understood as the subject of the main
verb. That is, in (2)(b), the person who might *get A's* is understood as *the
children.*

(2)   (a)   Full Inf-S
              *They tried (desperately) [for the children to get A's in math].
        (b)   Reduced Inf-S
              The children tried [to get A's in math].

   Note that these verbs describe the relationship of the subject to an action
named in the reduced Inf-S, including:

        •an attempt to do something (cf. *attempt, endeavor, fight, labor,*
              manage, struggle, try, undertake)
        •a verbal commitment to do something (*agree, consent, offer,*
              pledge, promise, threaten, volunteer)
        •an intention to do something (*decide, figure, fix, hope, resolve,*
              vow)
        •a beginning or ending of doing something (*begin, commence,*
              start; cease)
        •a failure to do something (*decline, fail, (not) bother, forget,*
              neglect, refuse)

Such actions (attempting, making a verbal commitment, having an
intention, etc.) are the kinds of actions that one can only perform for
oneself. It is odd to imagine attempting, agreeing to, or beginning someone
else's activities. There is, thus, a semantic motivation for the restriction
that the main verb and the reduced Inf-S must have the "same subject."

agree	decline, F	labor, F	regret
apply	deign	learn	remember
attempt	deserve	manage	resolve
begin	endeavor, F	neglect	start
(not) bother	fail	offer	strive, F
cease	fight	pledge	struggle
commence	figure, I	presume	tend
condescend	fix, P, I	pretend	threaten
consent	forget	proceed	try
continue	get	profess, F	undertake
dare*	hasten, F	promise	volunteer
decide	hope	refuse	vow, F

*In the sense "have the audacity to."

3.   The *seem* class   [_____Inf-S*]
                                *Must be reduced.

These verbs have the same surface syntactic pattern as the verbs in List 2, but express a different meaning. They do not describe a relationship between a person and an action, but rather the occurrence of some state of affairs. The verbs in this short list all occur with that-S subjects as well, as in (3)(b) and (4)(b) (though they favor or require extraposition).

(3)   (a)   Mary appears [to have won the race].
       (b)   It appears that Mary won the race.

(4)   (a)   Clinton seems [to have been elected].
       (b)   It seems that Clinton was elected.

appear, happen, seem, turn out

4. The *force* class [_____NP Inf-S*]
                     *Must be reduced.

The verbs in the *force* class are subcategorized for a direct object and a reduced infintive clause, as in (5)(a). It is important to stress that the noun phrase that follows these verbs is the direct object of the verb and not the subject of the Inf-S. We do not consider it part of the Inf-S because, as noted in the chapter, the complementizer *for* may not, under any circumstances, occur before it (see the ungrammatical (5)(b) and (5)(c)).

The verbs in the *force* class never occur without the direct object (as shown in the ungrammatical (5)(f)) (except when the direct object is missing in a passive verb phrase). In this also they show a different pattern than the verbs in the *want* class, which occur without a following noun phrase (when it is co-referential to the subject, as in (1)(c)).

The missing subject of the reduced Inf-S is always understood to be co-referential with the direct object of the verb. Thus, in (5)(a) the person that is to do the giving is *me* and not *they*.

(5)   (a)   They forced me [to give them the money].
      (b)   *They forced [for me to give them the money].
      (c)   *They forced, after some time, [for me to give them the money].
      (d)   *They forced, after some time, [me to give them the money].
      (e)   They forced me, after some time, [to give them the money].
      (f)   *They forced [to give them the money].

The verbs in this list describe advocating that some person or persons (rarely, a thing) undertake a course of action. This advocating may involve, among other things:

• asking for a course of action: *ask, request*
• granting permission for a course of action: *allow, permit*
• insisting verbally on a course of action: *beg, challenge, dare, hound, invite, nag, persuade, plead with, urge*
• providing inspiration for a course of action: *bribe, incite, inspire, provoke, spur on, tempt*
• ordering or coercing into a course of action: *command, direct, force, order, require*
• prohibiting in some way a course of action: *forbid*

allow	get ("cause")	prevail upon	warn
ask	hire	provoke	wire
authorize	hound	radio	write
beg	incite	request	
bribe	inspire	require	
cause	instruct	remind	
challenge	invite	retain	
choose ("select")	nag	select	
command	name	solicit	
convince	order	spur on	
dare*	pay	teach	
direct	permit	tell	
drive	persuade	tempt	
employ	pester	train	
forbid	pick	trust	
force	plead with	urge	

*In the sense "issue a dare."

5.   The *believe* class   [_____ NP Inf-S*]
                                    *Must be reduced.

The remarks made above about the syntax of the verbs in the *force* class apply to this class as well. The noun phrase which follows the verb (*John* in (6)(a)) is the direct object of the verb and not the subject of the reduced Inf-S. As with the verbs in the *force*-class, we never find the complementizer *for* (see the ungrammatical (6)(b) and (c)). It is very awkward to insert an adverbial or parenthetical expression between the verb and the direct object (as in (6)(c)).

Also like the verbs in the *force* class, the verbs in the *believe* class never occur without the direct object (the ungrammatical (6)(f)) (except when the direct object is missing in a passive VP). The missing subject of the Inf-S is interpreted as the direct object of the verb. Thus, for example, in (6)(a) the person who is innocent (the missing subject) is *John*.

(6)   (a)   We believe John [to be innocent].
       (b)   *We believe [for John to be innocent].
       (c)   *We believe, after much consideration, [(for) John to be
              innocent].
       (d)   We believe John, after much consideration, [to be innocent].
       (e)   *We believe [to be innocent].
       (f)   We believe [that John is innocent].

The reason for separating the *force* class and the *believe* class is that the
verbs are very different semantically. The verbs in the *believe* class express
a relationship between the subject of the verb and a proposition (i.e. a state
of affairs, a fact, a hypothesis, a statement, etc.). As can be seen from the
examples below, the state of affairs is expressed with a reduced infinitive
clause whose verb is nearly always *be, have,* or some other state verb,
never an event or an activity verb. This is in sharp contrast to the verbs in
the Inf-S occurring with verbs in the *force* class. They always express
actions.

The semantic relationship between the subject and the state of affairs can
cover a range of possibilities:

•one *believes, considers, imagines, thinks, understands,* etc.
    a certain state of affairs to hold
•one *assumes, presumes, supposes, suspects* a certain state of affairs
    to hold
•one *announces, declares, guarantees, professes, states* that a certain
    state of affairs holds
•one *discovers, finds, proves* that a certain state of affairs holds

Finally, the state of affairs expressed by the reduced Inf-S can also be
expressed with a that-S; i.e. every verb in this subclass is also
subcategorized for a that-S. In many cases, the Inf-S is somewhat formal or
stilted, whereas the that-S is less formal and more natural. More examples
are given in (7).

(7)   (a) *assume* the police [to be honest in this matter]
       (b) *believe* him [to be trustworthy]
       (c) *consider* my sister [to be a very lucky person]
       (d) *guarantee* it [to last for five years]
       (e) *hold* these truths [to be self-evident]
       (f) *judge* them [to have good taste]
       (g) *presuppose* it [to be true]
       (h) *prove* the theory [to be true]

acknowledge	figure	presuppose	state
announce	find	proclaim	suppose, F
assume	guarantee	?profess, F	suspect
believe	hold	?pronounce	?think
consider	imagine	prove	understand
declare	judge	?realize	
?demonstrate	know	recall	
discover	make out	report	
estimate	perceive	reveal	
feel	presume	show	

Exercise 3

List the functions of a nominal that-clause. Can gerundives be used in the same functions? Give examples to support your answer.

Exercise 4

The sentences below contain reduced gerundives, gerundives missing a subject. Give an alternative way of expressing each sentence which contains a full gerundive. The alternative should be roughly synonymous with the original, but may be somewhat awkward or unnatural.

1. [Eating low-salt, low-fat foods] is important to [maintaining good health].
2. [Getting a Ph.D these days] takes money and perseverance.
3. I am always annoyed by [humming in class].

---

2. THE EXTERNAL SYNTAX OF GERUNDIVES

Like that-Ss and Inf-Ss, gerundives can function as subjects, as in (6). The verbs or adjectives subcategorized for gerundives subject are in italics.

(6) (a) [Peter's singing in the shower] *disturbs* us.
     (b) [Mary's tripping off to Spain with a complete stranger] *surprised* and *shocked* everyone.
     (c) [Your complaining about everything] is quite *unnecessary*.
     (d) [The children's showing up unexpectedly for dinner] is unfortunately very *awkward* and *inconvenient*.

This seems to require, once again, a revision of the statement made in Chapter 3 about the internal structure of basic clauses. This temporary revision is shown in (7) and will be revisited at the end of this section. A tree diagram for a gerundive subject is given in (8).

(7) A clause consists of an NP, a that-S, an Inf-S, or a gerundive and a VP.

(8)   S

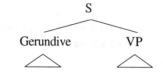

Like that-Ss and Inf-Ss, gerundives function as the complements of some verbs, as in (9). The subcategorization of these verbs and a tree diagram are given in (10).

(9)   (a) We *hate* [Suzie's whining about everything].
       (b) They *regret* [our missing the birthday party].
       (c) Do you *recall* [my putting the keys down here]?

(10)   (a) *hate, regret, recall*   [_____ Gerundive]

       (b)

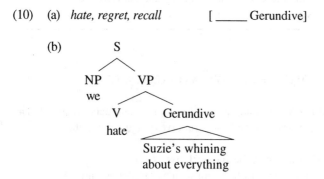

Gerundives, unlike that-Ss and Inf-Ss, do not occur directly as complements of adjectives. In combination with an adjective, there must be an intervening preposition, shown in bold in (11) - (12). In terms of structure, gerundives are the complement of the preposition, as shown in (13).

(11)   (a) *We are *afraid* [Sam's losing the keys].
       (b)   We are *afraid of* [Sam's losing the keys].

(12)   (a) *They were *pleased* [the children's remembering to do their homework].
       (b)   They were *pleased about* [the children's remembering to do their homework].

(13)

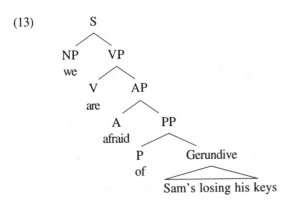

The pattern in (11) - (12) is more typical of NPs than of clauses, as in (14) and (15), which show the contrast in patterns for NPs, gerundives, and that-Ss.

(14) (a) We are *afraid of* [the dark].
  (b) We are *afraid of* [his losing the keys].
  (c) We are *afraid* [that he may lose the keys].

(15) (a) They were *anxious **about*** [the exam].
  (b) They were *anxious **about*** [the children's forgetting their lines].
  (c) They were *anxious* [that the childen might forget their lines].

This is consistent with a more general fact about gerundives. They occur in all the functions that NPs do. Both can be subjects and complements of verbs and prepositions, but neither serves as a complement of adjectives. That-Ss and Inf-Ss, on the other hand, function as subjects and complements of verbs and adjectives, but not of prepositions. In (16) are examples of the four constituents as complements of prepositions.

(16) Complement of a Preposition
  (a) NP   *After* [the play], we all wanted to go home.
  (b) Gerundive *After* [the children's forgetting their lines and bursting into gales of laughter] ...
  (c) That-S **After* [that the children forgot their lines] ...

(d) Inf-S   *After [for the children to forget their lines] ...

Another difference is that NPs and gerundives can function as direct objects of complex transitive verbs like *consider*, but clauses cannot, as in (17).

(17) Direct Object of a Complex Transitive Verb
 (a) NP   Some parents *consider* [this option] completely unacceptable.
 (b) Gerundive   Some parents *consider* [the children's drinking at the party] completely unacceptable.
 (c) That-S   *Some parents *consider* [that the children were drinking at the party] completely unacceptable.
 (d) Inf-S   *Some parents *consider* [for them to drink at the party] completely unacceptable.

Finally, note that NPs and gerundives can function as appositives, as in (18) and (19), where the appositives are in square brackets. (Appositive gerundives are often reduced (see Section 3).)

(18) (a) My sister, [Sally], is coming to visit next week.
 (b) Mrs. Brown, [my English teacher], doesn't like grammar.
 (c) The verb [*destroy*] is a monotransitive verb.

(19) (a) After the fire, I had to give up my favorite activity, [watching television in the afternoon].
 (b) His current research, [investigating the life and times of John Wayne], has not been going well.

In these sentences there is a relationship of apposition between a noun phrase and the following appositive (in square brackets). The noun phrase (e.g. *my sister, my favorite activity, his current research*) provides a characterization or description of the appositive and either one could be left out without affecting the acceptability of the sentence. Appositives, like parenthetical remarks, are often set off by pauses and a drop in pitch in speaking and commas in writing, unless they are particularly brief, as in (18)(c). The constituent structure of noun phrases with appositives is shown in (20).

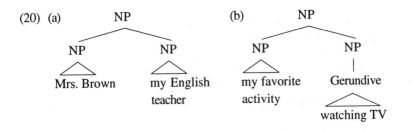

(20) (a) NP / NP (Mrs. Brown) NP (my English teacher) (b) NP / NP (my favorite activity) NP — Gerundive (watching TV)

In conclusion, in terms of their external syntax, gerundives behave exactly like NPs and not like clauses. We therefore consider them to be a special type of NP and assign them the external structure in (21). Looking inward they are clauses, but looking outward they are NPs. This treatment of the external syntax of gerundives means that the revision of the statement about basic clauses given in (7) is redundant, and we therefore withdraw it. (A final revision will be made in Chapter 23.)

(21)

NP
|
Gerundive
NP$_{Gen}$ VP$_{PresPart}$
NP   Gen   V   NP
Sam   's   losing   the keys

Exercise 5

Can gerundives undergo extraposition? Provide evidence for your answer. With respect to the rule of extraposition, do gerundives behave more like clauses or like NPs?

Exercise 6

Provide tree diagrams for the following sentences, writing out all constituents, except for appositive gerundives and NPs that are not gerundives.

1.   They complained about their son's flunking chemistry.
2.   Those girls' talking in class disturbs me.
3.   We can't bear your putting us down.
4.   You should try to ignore the children's humming in class.
5.   I dislike the new craze, racing skateboards in the library.
6.   The judge wouldn't tolerate the lawyer's trying to intimidate the witness.
7.   Mary's fighting with Bill was quite disruptive.
8.   Roger told me about his latest scheme, buying gold futures and selling the index of precious metal stocks.

Exercise 7

The sentences below contain reduced gerundives. Put square brackets around the gerundive and specify how the missing subject is understood.

1.   The baby finally stopped waking up at 3:00 am.
2.   We regret being the bearers of bad news.
3.   The men denied stealing money from the open drawer.
4.   Only a few Senators favor giving more money to Russia.

---

3. REDUCED GERUNDIVES

Reduced gerundives lack a subject NP. As was the case with reduced Inf-Ss, the missing subject may sometimes be interpreted as generic, as in (22).

(22)   (a)   [Eating low-salt, low-fat foods] is important to [maintaining good health].
        (b)   [Getting a Ph.D. these days] takes money and perseverance.
        (c)   I am always annoyed by [humming in class].

(22)(a) states that eating low-salt, low-fat foods is important for anyone, i.e. for people in general. Similarly, (22)(c) asserts that humming in class by anyone, by people in general, is annoying to me.

The missing subject of a reduced gerundive in other cases is interpreted as co-referential with the subject of the main clause, as in (23) and shown in the tree diagram in (24).

(23) (a) We *hate* [whining about everything].
      (b) They *regret* [missing the birthday party].
      (c) Jim *imagined* [sitting by a warm fire, surrounded by friends].

In (23)(a), for example, we are doing the whining; in (23)(c) it is *Jim* who is to sit by the fire.

(24)

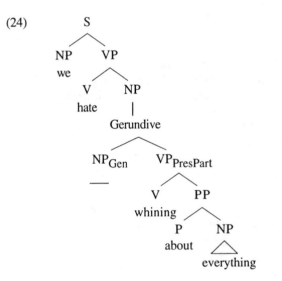

In terms of occurrence with full and reduced gerundives, we need to recognize two subclasses of verbs. Some verbs are subcategorized for a full gerundive, but occur with a reduced gerundive if the subject of the main clause and the (unexpressed) subject of the gerundive are co-referential.

(25) Full Gerundive
      (a) We *hate* [your whining about everything].
      (b) They *regret* [our missing the birthday party].
      (c) John *contemplated* [Mary's loosing her job].

(26)   Reduced Gerundive
    (a)   We *hate* [whining about everything].   (= our whining)
    (b)   They *regret* [missing the birthday party].   (= their missing)
    (c)   John *contemplated* [losing his job].   (= John's losing)

Other verbs are subcategorized specifically for reduced gerundives and never occur with full gerundives, as shown in (27) and (28).

(27)   Reduced Gerundive
    (a)   They *began* [putting the money in the bag].
    (b)   The baby *kept* [drooling on the rug].
    (c)   You should *try* [singing on key for a change].

(28)   Full Gerundive
    (a)   *They *began* [Sally's putting the money in the bag].
    (b)   *The mother *kept* [the baby's drooling on the rug].
    (c)   *You should *try* [Mary's singing on key for a change].

Subcategorizations for these two subclasses are given in (29) and a tree diagram for a reduced gerundive in (30).

(29)   (a)   Full Gerundive   [_____ Gerundive]
          hate, regret, recall, contemplate
    (b)   Reduced Gerundive   [_____ Gerundive*]
          stop, begin, keep, try, deny   *Must be reduced.

(b) The sauce was too bland. We tried to improve it, but
unfortunately weren't very successful.

Try plus a gerundive, as in (35)(a), indicates testing a new approach. When
in the past tense, it indicates that the event expressed by the gerundive really
took place; i.e. we did indeed add pepper. *Try* plus an Inf-S indicates an
attempt to do something; the event expressed by the infinitive may or may
not be realized. In (35)(b) it is not; the improvement does not take place.
  The verb *regret* also occurs with gerundives and infinitives.

(36) (a) We regretted adding pepper to the sauce.
      (b) We regret to inform you that dinner is ruined.

Regret plus a gerundive indicates sorrow for some past action, for an event
that took place, as in (36)(a). *Regret* plus an Inf-S is quite different,
indicating sorrow for an event which is about to take place. The event
expressed by the Inf-S is restricted to one of informing, saying, or telling.
Such sentences also function as performatives; uttering (36)(b) constitutes
an act of informing.
  Many other verbs are subcategorized for both gerundives and Inf-Ss, but
the difference between them is more subtle and more difficult to describe.
Consider, for instance, the sentences of (37).

(37) (a) I like driving this car.
      (b) I like to drive this car.

It seems that (37)(a) would be the preferred sentence if the speaker is driving
the car under discussion at the time of the utterance. The event of driving the
car is fulfilled and one is expressing pleasure at it. (37)(b), on the other
hand, seems to express pleasure about a potential event, but possibly one
which has not yet taken place at the time of the utterance. Inf-Ss are
frequently used with the modal *would*, which underscores their hypothetical
or conditional nature.

(38) (a) I would like to drive this car.
      (b) She would prefer to be left alone.

With yet other verbs, however, there seems to be little difference in meaning between gerundives and Inf-Ss.

(39) (a) The baby began crying.
     (b) The baby began to cry.

(40) (a) It continued raining all afternoon.
     (b) It continued to rain all afternoon.

Exercise 10
Discuss the difference in meaning, if any, between these pairs of sentences.

(1) (a) We prefer growing our own vegetables.
    (b) We prefer to grow our own vegetables.

(2) (a) I can't stand being pushed around.
    (b) I can't stand to be pushed around.

(3) (a) He stopped to smell the flowers.
    (b) He stopped smelling the flowers and went back to the path.

Exercise 11
Compare the verbs in the appendix to Chapter 21 with those in the appendix to this chapter. Find at least five which occur with both infinitives and gerundives and construct pairs of sentences. Discuss any differences in meaning.

Exercise 12
The verb *go* can be followed by a reduced gerundive with certain verbs, as in (1), but not with others, as in (2). Make up at least four more good examples and four more ungrammatical ones and characterize the meaning of the verbs that can occur with *go*. What is this construction used to express?

(1) *go*   [_____ Gerundive*]   *Must be reduced.
    (a) Every fall Dad goes [hunting].
    (b) The kids went [swimming in the lake today].

(2)   (a)   *The students go studying every evening.
       (b)   *My mother went buying food.

APPENDIX

This appendix contains verbs with the subcategorization [___ Gerundive], a
list adapted from Alexander and Kunz (1964).

(can't) abide	delay	can't help	refrain from
accept	deliberate	ignore	register
acknowledge	deny	imagine	regret
adore	deserve	insist on	relate
admit	detest	keep	relish
advise	discontinue	keep from	remember
anticipate	dislike	loathe	report
appreciate	doubt	love	require
attempt	dread	mention	resent
avoid	dream of	mind	resist
(can't) bear	enjoy	miss	reveal
begin	envisage	omit	risk
(can't) help	escape	plan on	scorn
(can't) stand	evade	practice	start
cease	explain	prefer	stop
commence	fancy	postpone	suggest
complete	fear	propose	tolerate
consider	finish	question	try
contemplate	forget	quit	understand
continue	give up	recall	
count on	go on	recollect	
debate	hate	recommend	

23

WH-CLAUSES AND THE RULE
OF WH-MOVEMENT

IN THIS CHAPTER we discuss a fourth type of clause, WH-clauses. They have a more complex internal structure than other clauses, and in Section 1 we propose a syntactic rule, WH-movement, to account for their properties. In Section 2 we look more closely at the complementizer of WH-clauses, a WH-constituent, and in Section 3, at their external syntax. WH-clauses have many different functions in English, but in this chapter we focus on their use as nominal clauses. Such WH-Ss are known as indirect questions. Other functions of WH-clauses are explored in Chapters 24 and 25.

1. THE INTERNAL SYNTAX OF WH-CLAUSES

Consider the WH-clauses (WH-Ss) in (1), given in square brackets.

(1)   (a)   They asked [who you kissed ___].
        (b)   He wondered [what we bought ___].
        (c)   We know [what they put ___ on the table].

Like other subordinate clauses, WH-Ss consist of two parts, a complementizer and a clause. The complementizer is a WH-constituent; that is, a constituent from one of the familiar syntactic categories (NP, PP, AP, etc.) which consists of or contains a WH-expression (*who, what,* etc.). The clause of a WH-S is incomplete. It is missing a constituent of the same syntactic category as the WH-constituent.

In the WH-S of (1)(a), the WH-constituent is an NP (*who*) and the clause (*you kissed*) is missing an NP, the direct object of *kiss* (cf. *you kissed Jim*). A tree diagram for (1)(a) is given in (2). In a tree diagram the position of the missing constituent is indicated with a blank line. WH-constituents are labelled with a subscript WH (e.g. NP$_{WH}$, PP$_{WH}$, etc.).

(2)

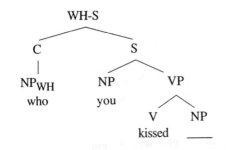

Although it contains a clause that is incomplete, the sentence itself doesn't seem incomplete because we understand the missing NP to be "filled in" by the WH-constituent (*who* in (2)), as shown in (3).

(3)

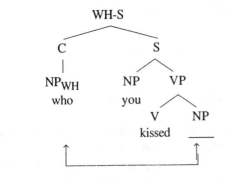

Linguists account for the syntactic properties of WH-Ss by proposing that they are formed in two stages by a rule called WH-movement. At the first stage there is a basic clause that contains a WH-constituent. The C position is empty and the clause is complete. The rule of WH-movement applies to this structure, moving the WH-constituent out of the clause and into complementizer position, leaving behind a gap. The two stages in the formation of (1)(a) are shown in (4), with the operation of WH-movement indicated by an arrow. The rule of WH-movement is stated in (5).

(4)   (a) First Stage: Before WH-Movement

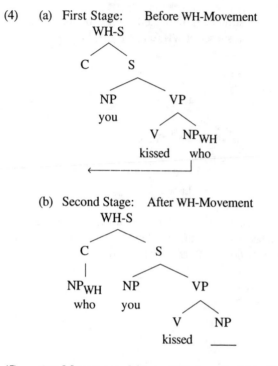

(5)   WH-Movement: Move a WH-constituent to C.

This treatment of WH-Ss accounts for the fact that the first constituent of a WH-S (the complementizer) is always of the same syntactic category as the one that is missing in the second. Saying that the WH-constituent starts within the clause itself and is moved into complementizer position ensures that this will always be the case.

In (1)(a), WH-movement moves a NP_{WH} into complementizer position; in (6), it moves an AP_{WH}.

(6)   (a) No one could tell [how tired we were ___].
       (b) We asked [how smart they were ____].

The derivation of (6)(a) is shown in (7). The arrow indicates the effects of the application of WH-movement.

(7)   (a) First Stage: Before WH-Movement

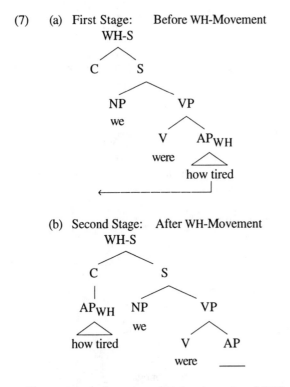

       (b) Second Stage: After WH-Movement

The WH-constituent moved by the rule of WH-movement can be an adverbial of place, time, or reason, as in (8). The two levels of structure for the WH-clause of (8)(a), which contains a PIP, are shown in (9).

(8)   (a) I know [where [the thieves put the money _____]].
       (b) We asked [where [you are going ___ on vacation]].
       (c) They know [when [the children get out of school ___]].
       (d) We wondered [why [he stole the money ___]].

(9)   (a) First Stage: Before WH-Movement

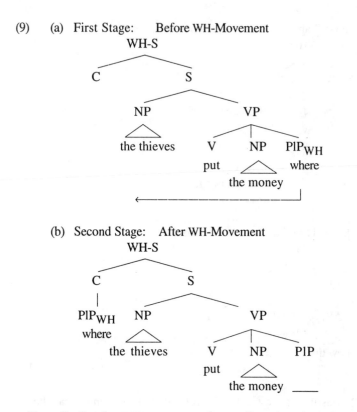

       (b) Second Stage: After WH-Movement

Note, finally, that WH-movement also applies when the WH-constituent is
a NP in subject position, as in (10). Although WH-movement changes the
internal syntax of such WH-clauses, the surface word order remains the same.
A derivation for (10)(a) is shown in (11).

(10)   (a) The police learned [who [___ stole the money]].
       (b) We finally guessed [who [___ wrote the poison pen letter]].
       (c) The children asked [what [___ was missing]].

(11) (a) First Stage: Before WH-Movement

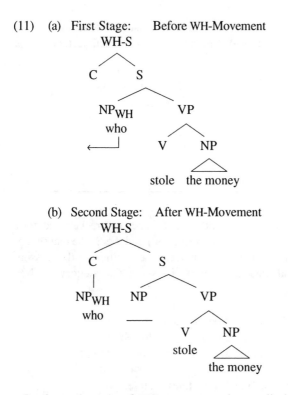

(b) Second Stage: After WH-Movement

In short, the rule of WH-movement is not limited to any particular syntactic category or function, but moves *any* WH-constituent into complementizer position, resulting in WH-Ss shown schematically in (12).

(12)

WH-S

C   S

NP$_{WH}$
AdjP$_{WH}$
PP$_{WH}$
PlP$_{WH}$
TP$_{WH}$

We therefore generalize the description of WH-clauses by labelling the first constituent "XP" (which stands for "a phrase of any syntactic category") as shown in (13).

(13)   WH-S

                  C   S

                  | △
                XP_WH

Exercise 1

In each of the following sentences put the WH-S in square brackets and draw a vertical line between the C (the WH-constituent) and the S (the clause that is missing a constituent). In the latter, indicate the position of the missing constituent with a blank line and identify its syntactic category (as NP, AdjP, PP, TP, or PlP).

Example: We know what they put on the table.
           WH-clause: [what | they put ___ on the table]
           Missing constituent is a NP, the direct object of *put*.

1.   The judge misunderstood what the thieves stole.
2.   He asked who they gave the money to.
3.   The reporters wonder what the money will be used for.
4.   I know where the thieves hid the money.
5.   I can't imagine how upset the rightful owners are.
6.   The police learned who had stolen the money.
7.   The lawyers asked which account the money was placed in.
8.   Do you know when the money was stolen?
9.   They didn't know how ruthless the thieves could be.
10. We finally guessed what was missing.
11. The police figured out where the thieves were staying.
12. Everyone was asking when the drama would be over.

Exercise 2

For sentences 1 - 8 of Exercise 1, give two tree diagrams for each WH-S, showing the stages before and after the application of WH-movement.

---

2. FURTHER NOTES ON WH-CONSTITUENTS

In this section we look in more detail at the makeup of WH-constituents. We consider different WH-expressions (words and phrases) and the position they have within the WH-constituent.

2.1   WH-*Expressions*

WH-expressions are a subclass of proforms, and, like all proforms, they stand for constituents of different syntactic categories. For example, the familiar WH-words *what* and *who* (with its morphological variants *whom* and *whose*) stand for noun phrases, and we find them in NP positions—as subjects, direct objects, prepositional objects, etc., as shown in (14) and (15), where WH-words are in italics and WH-clauses are paired with finite clauses for ease of comparison.

(14)   (a)   WH-S   They know [*what* [we ate ___]].
       (b)   WH-S before WH-movement   [we ate *what*]
             what stands for an NP (direct object of the verb *eat*) as in
       (c)   Finite S   [we ate *a piece of chocolate cake*]

(15)   (a)   WH-S   They asked [*who* [you gave the money to ___]].
       (b)   WH-S before WH-movement   [you gave the money to *who*]
             who stands for an NP (object of the preposition *to*) as in
       (c)   Finite S   [you gave the money to *the Salvation Army*]

One WH-word, *how*, stands for an intensifier in an AP, as in (16) - (17).

(16)   (a)   WH-S   No one could tell [*how* tired [we were ____]].
       (b)   WH-S before WH-movement   [we were *how* tired]
             how stands for an intensifier as in
       (c)   Finite S   [we were *extremely* tired]

(17)   (a) WH-S   We asked [*how* smart [they were ____]].
       (b) WH-S before WH-movement   [they were *how* smart]
            how stands for an intensifier as in
       (c) Finite S   [they were *rather* smart]

The WH-word *which* and the WH-phrase *what kind of* stand for either determiners or modifiers, as shown in (18) - (20).

(18)   (a) WH-S   I know [*which* book [you read ___]].
       (b) WH-S before WH-movement   [you read *which* book]
            which stands for a determiner as in
       (c) Finite S   [you read *that* book]
       (d) Finite S   [you read *Macy's* book]

(19)   (a) WH-S   We wondered [*which* child [they adopted ___]].
       (b) WH-S before WH-movement   [they adopted *which* child]
            which stands for a modifier (an A) as in
       (c) Finite S   [they adopted the *very sick* child]

(20)   (a) WH-S   You know [*what kind of* room [I want ___]].
       (b) WH-S before WH-movement   [I want *what kind of* room]
            what kind of stands for a modifier (a PP) as in
       (c) Finite S   [I want a room *with a view*]

The WH-words *where, when, why,* and *how* stand for adverbials of place, time, reason, and manner, as shown in (21) - (24).

(21)   WH-word as an adverbial expressing place (PlP)
       (a) WH-S   They know [*where* [we hid the money ___]].
       (b) Finite S   [we hid the money *in the bathroom*]

(22)   WH-word as an adverbial expressing time (TP)
       (a) WH-S   The police knew in advance [*when* [the bank
                              would be robbed ___]].
       (b) Finite S   [the bank will be robbed *tomorrow at midnight*]

(23)   WH-word as a reason adverbial
        (a) WH-S   Mom knows [*why* [they stole the money __]].
        (b) Finite S   [they stole it *so they could live in luxury*]

(24)   WH-word as a manner adverbial
        (a) WH-S   We know very well [*how* [they left ___]].
        (b) Finite S   [they left *very noisily*]

Finally, two WH-phrases stand for quantity expressions in NPs, *how much* and *how many*, as shown in (25).

(25)   (a) WH-S   I know [*how many* paintings [they sold ___]].
       (b) Finite S   [they sold *three* paintings]

The WH-expressions of English are summarized in (26). Except for *how*, they all begin with the letters <wh> pronounced [w] in some words and [h] in others (some dialects have [ʍ]).

(26)   WH-Expression   Stands For
       who (whom), what   Noun Phrase
       what, which   Determiner in an NP
       whose   Genitive NP (a determiner in an NP)
       which, what kind of   Modifier in an NP
       how   Intensifier of an A or Adv
       how much, how many   Quantity expression in an NP
                                     Adverbial of
       where   Place   (PlP)
       when   Time   (TP)
       why   Reason
       how   Manner
       *wheth*er   Other

2.2   WH-Constituents
Sometimes the WH-constituent consists of the WH-expression alone. This occurs when a WH-word stands for an NP or adverbial, as in (1) - (4) or (21) - (24) and schematized in (27).

(27)   (a)   WH-word stands for NP   (b)   WH-word stands for an adverbial

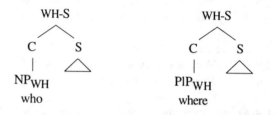

Sometimes the WH-constituent consists of more than the WH-expression. This happens when a WH-word stands for a subconstituent *within* an NP, AP or PP. It is not the WH-word alone that is moved by WH-movement, but the larger constituent of which it is a part, as in (28) - (29).

(28)   WH-word stands for a feterminer in an NP
       The WH-constituent is the NP

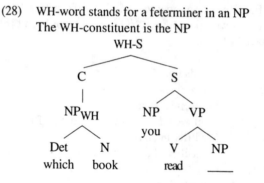

(29)   WH-word stands for an intensifier in an A or AP
       The WH-constituent is the A or AP

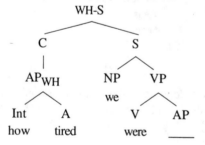

3. THE EXTERNAL SYNTAX OF WH-CLAUSES

WH-clauses have many functions in English. Three major ones are noted briefly below and will be examined more closely in later chapters. In the remainder of this section we focus on nominal WH-clauses known as indirect questions.

One type of WH-S functions as a modifier of an NP, as in (30). Clauses with this function are known as relative clauses, the topic of Chapter 24.

(30) Relative Clauses
    (a) I saw the man [who you kissed].
    (b) She knows the person [who left].
    (c) He likes the car [which we bought].

Some WH-Ss function as independent NPs or adverbials in structures known as free relative clauses, illustrated in (31). These are discussed briefly at the end of Chapter 24.

(31) (a) I read [what you wrote].
    (b) Take that back [where you found it].
    (c) We'll talk to [whomever we choose].
    (d) They will leave [whenever they please].

WH-clauses are used to ask questions, a sentence type known as a content question, illustrated in (32) and discussed in Chapter 25.

(32) Content Questions
    (a) Who left?
    (b) Who did you kiss?
    (c) Which room did you sleep in?
    (d) Where did he go?

WH-clauses are also used in exclamatives, another special sentence type illustrated in (33) and also discussed in Chapter 25.

(33)   Exclamatives
       (a)   How pretty she is!
       (b)   What nice teeth you have!

Note that there are restrictions between the WH-expressions listed in (26) and WH-clause functions. Only a small subset of WH-words are used in relative clauses (see Chapter 24) while all the WH-expressions are used in indirect questions and all but *whether,* in content questions. Only two WH-words (*how* and *what*) are used in exclamatives.

We turn now to the use of WH-Ss as nominal clauses. Because of their similarity to content questions, as shown in (34) - (35), these WH-clauses have come to be known as indirect questions (IQs), a practice we use here.

(34)   (a)   Content (Direct) Question
             They asked, "Who ate the cookie?"
       (b)   Indirect Question
             They asked us [who ate the cookie].

(35)   (a)   Content (Direct) Question
             Where are the cookies?
       (b)   Indirect Question
             We wonder [where the cookies are].

IQs resemble questions semantically in that the WH-constituent represents unknown or unexpressed information. Contrast the questions and WH-Ss below with that-Ss, in which the information is given.

(36)   (a)   Who is guilty?
       (b)   The commission will determine [who is guilty].
             Question and IQ: The guilty party is unknown or not stated.
       (c)   The commission will determine [that Harry is guilty].
             That-S: The guilty party is stated (*Harry*).

(37)   (a)   Where did you put the cookies?
       (b)   We discovered [where you put the cookies].
             Question and IQ: The location is unknown or not stated.

(37) (c) We discovered [that you put the cookies in the refrigerator].
That-S: Location is stated (*in the refrigerator*).

As illustrated in the many examples in this chapter, IQs occur as complements of verbs. The examples in (38) show some verbs that are subcategorized for an IQ and others, for an NP and an IQ. The examples in (39) show IQs as complements of adjectives. Subcategorization frames for these verbs and adjectives are given in (40) and tree diagrams in (41).

(38) (a) He *wondered* [what we bought].
(b) They *asked* us [what we bought].
(c) We *showed* them [where you hid the money].

(39) (a) I wasn't *sure* [which picture she wanted].
(b) We were *uncertain* [where they hid the money].

(40) (a) *wonder, know, learn*   [_____ IQ]
(b) *ask, inform, show, tell*   [_____ NP IQ]
(c) *sure, uncertain*   [_____ IQ]

(41)

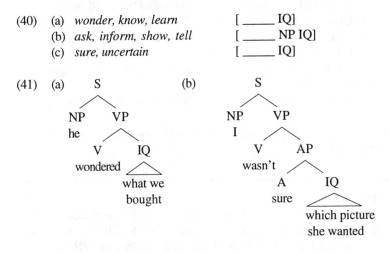

Like that-Ss and Inf-Ss, IQs can also function as subjects of certain verbs and predicate adjectives, as in (42), with a tree shown in (43).

(42) (a) [Which solution is best] *depends* on the outcome we want.
(b) [Who is at fault] is *unclear* at this time.

(43)   S

        IQ   VP

That is, subjects can be NPs or any of the fully clausal constructions discussed in this unit, leading to the final revision of the rule in (44).

(44)   A clause consists of a NP or a clause (That-S, Inf-S, or IQ) and a VP.

While the verbs and adjectives subcategorized for IQ subjects and complements seem to be very disparate semantically, they can be connected by a "chain of resemblance" posited in (45) (from Quirk 1985:1051).

(45)   (a)   A direct question   *Who will help?*
       (b)   A reported question   *She asked [who will help].*
       (c)   Uncertainty about the answer *She wondered [who will help].*
       (d)   Certainty about the answer   *She knows [who will help].*
       (e)   Other mental states/processes
             involving the answer   *We debated [who will help].*
       (f)   Informing someone
             of the answer   *We told you [who will help].*

In all instances, a question focused on the WH-constituent is implicitly or explicitly raised.

Exercise 3
Which of the verbs below is subcategorized for an IQ complement? Give examples to support your answer. (Hint: Avoid WH-Ss with the WH-words *what*, *where*, and *when*, which also occur in free relatives, WH-Ss which are easily confused with IQs.)

1. prove   5. suggest   9. remember
2. guess   6. maintain   10. believe
3. decide   7. recommend   11. announce
4. insist   8. stipulate   12. learn

Exercise 4

Can IQs occur as objects of prepositions? Give examples to support your
answer. (In constructing test sentences, note the hint in Exercise 3.)

Exercise 5

Can sentences with IQs as subject undergo extraposition? Give evidence for
your answer.

Exercise 6

Give a tree diagram for each of the following sentences, abbreviating NPs
with triangles.

1.   The children wondered what Santa would bring them.
2.   The teacher didn't realize how hard the test was.
3.   The police have asked us who pulled the alarm.
4.   We explained which car we liked.
5.   Which car we buy depends on how much money we can earn.
6.   Where the money was hidden remained unclear.
7.   They aren't certain where they should go.

Exercise 7

Why are the following sentences ungrammatical?

(1)   *I don't know what does she want.
(2)   *My children realize now what does it mean to be poor.

Exercise 8

Consider the clauses in square brackets. Do they have the internal syntax of
a WH-clause? Why or why not? Do they have the external syntax of an IQ?
Give reasons for your answers.

(1)   I wonder [whether that man stole the money].
(2)   I am not sure [whether that man stole the money].
(3)   Tomorrow they will tell me [whether that man stole the money].
(4)   [Whether that man stole the money] remains unclear.

24
RELATIVE CLAUSES

IN THIS CHAPTER we investigate relative clauses, which serve as modifiers of nouns. A relative clause has the structure of a WH-clause, formed with a subset of WH-words known as relative pronouns, or of a clause with the complementizer *that*, as in (1). (Relative pronouns are in italics.)

(1)   (a) The girl [*who* you kissed] is my sister.
      (b) I bought the book [*which* you recommended].
      (c) The policeman [that gave you a ticket] went home.
      (d) I lost the book [that you lent me].

In Section 1 we discuss the internal syntax of relative clauses that are WH-Ss, paying special attention to relative pronouns. In Section 2 we introduce relative clauses with the complementizer *that*, which have no relative pronoun and are not formed by WH-movement. In Section 3 we turn to the external syntax of all relative clauses and in Section 4, offer a brief treatment of structures similar to relative clauses known as free relatives.

1. THE INTERNAL SYNTAX OF RELATIVE CLAUSES

Like other clauses, relative clauses consist of a complementizer and a clause. The complementizer is a WH-constituent, while the clause is missing a constituent of the same syntactic category, as in (2) and shown schematically in (3).

(2)   (a) The girl [*who* [you kissed ___]] is my sister.
      (b) I bought the book [*which* [you recommended ___]].
      (c) We question the data [on *which* [this theory is based ___]].
      (d) We will meet at the place [*where* [you want to meet ___]].

(3)

Rel-S
- C
  - XP_{WH}
- S

The label "Rel-S" marks the clause as a relative clause, while "XP$_{WH}$" stands for a WH-constituent from one of the three syntactic categories possible in complementizer position in a relative clause—NP, PP, or adverbial (of time, place, or reason).

The WH-constituent in complementizer position and the clause missing a constituent, taken together, form a complete clause. We assume that the syntactic rule of WH-movement, introduced in Chapter 23 to account for the internal syntax of WH-clauses, operates in the formation of relative clauses too, as shown in (4).

(4)   (a)   Before WH-Movement

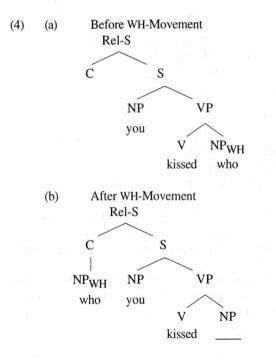

(b)   After WH-Movement

1.1   The Relative Pronouns who *and* which
Turning to WH-words, only a small number of those presented in Chapter 23 occur in Rel-Ss, a subclass known as relative pronouns.

(5)   Relative Pronouns
       (a) NPs   *who/whom, which*
       (b) Genitive NPs   *whose*
       (c) Adverbials   *when, where, why*

The relative pronouns *who* and *which* function as NPs, as shown in (2), (6), and (7). (As noted in Chapter 23, in other WH-Ss *which* functions as a determiner or modifier in a NP.) The choice between *who* and *which* depends on the antecedent: The pronoun *who* is used when the antecedent is human, while *which* is used when it is non-human, as in (6) and (7) (the antecedent and relative pronoun are in italics).

(6)   Human Antecedent
       (a) The *women* [*who* [___ work here]] are very talented.
       (b) The *boy* [*who* [I like ___]] is named Peter.
       (c) She is a *friend* [*who* [I can rely on ___]].
       (d) *I bought a *house* [*who* [___ overlooks the water]].

(7)   Non-human Antecedent
       (a) The *cat* [*which* [___ is bothering you at night]] is a tabby.
       (b) She finished the *book* [*which* [I had lent ___ to her]].
       (c) They bought a *house* [*which* [I could live in ___]].
       (d) *She just loves *people* [*which* [___ flatter her]].

The relative pronoun *which* is invariable. It is used for NPs which are subjects, as in (7)(a), and objects, as in (7)(b) and (c). In informal styles of English, *who* is also invariable, occurring both as subject (6)(a) and object (6)(b) and (c).

   In styles of English that are markedly formal, however, the form *who* is used only if the relative pronoun is subject of its clause, while *whom* is used when it is an object, as in (8).

whom = him
if him can
stand in
then you
would use
whom not
who

(8)   Formal English (Prescribed)

     (a)   Subject   The man [*who* [___ left]] is my brother.

     (b)   Dir Obj   He is a man [*whom* [I love ___ dearly]].

     (c)   Prep Obj   A man [*whom* [we can rely on ___]].

     (d)   PP   A man [on *whom* [we can rely ___]].

In (8)(d) WH-movement has moved the preposition *on* along with the NP$_{WH}$, a phenomenon which is also markedly formal and discussed further in 1.4.

1.2   The Relative Pronoun whose

The relative pronoun *whose* is used when the WH-word stands for a NP in the genitive functioning as a determiner, as in (9).

whose = his
if his can
stand when you
use whose
not who!

(9)   (a)   The man [*whose* help [I need ___ *his/whose?*]] is in the hospital.
         cf. I need [the man's] help.

     (b)   The woman [*whose* house [I'm painting ___]] has strange
         taste. cf. I'm painting [the woman's] house.

     (c)   The children [*whose* families [___ are poor]] get free lunches.
         cf. [The children's] families are poor.

Though *whose* is the genitive form of the pronoun *who* and thus would be expected to be restricted to human antecedents, we can find it used of non-human NPs as well, as in (10).

(10)   (a)   This was an idea [*whose* time [___ had come]].

     (b)   They constructed a sentence [*whose* presuppositions [___ were
         false]].

     (c)   She owns a house whose dimensions are astounding.

The diagrams in (11) show the stages in the derivation of (9)(a). Note that WH-movement cannot move the genitive NP *whose* alone; it moves the larger NP in which it is a constituent.

(11)   (a)   Before WH-movement

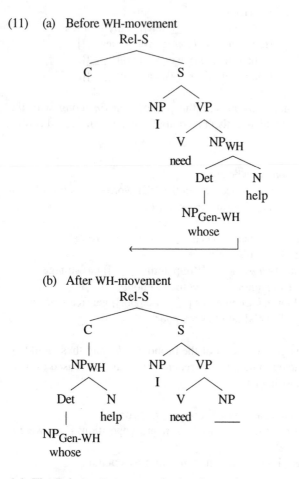

(b)   After WH-movement

1.3 The Relative Pronouns where, when, why

The relative pronouns *where*, *when*, and *why* function as adverbials, as in (12) - (14). The derivation of (12)(a) is given in (15).

(12)   Adverbial—Place Phrase (PlP)
       (a)   I saw the place [*where* [you put the beer ___]].
       (b)   We saw the house [*where* [George Washington lived ___]].
       (c)   The town [*where* [I was born ___]] is in Maine.

(13)   Adverbial—Time Phrase (TP)
    (a)   Good Friday is the day [*when* [Christ died ___]].
    (b)   The only time [*when* [I am free ___]] is Sunday.
    (c)   I don't know much about the year [*when* [I was born ___]].

(14)   Adverbial—Reason
    (a)   I know the reason [*why* [you're here ___]].
    (b)   The reason [*why* [I've asked you here ___]] will soon be
        revealed.

(15)   (a)   Rel-S

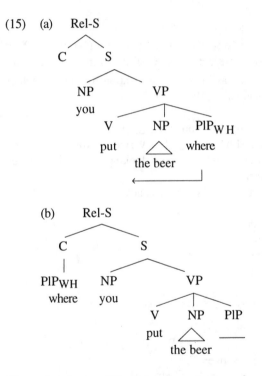

    (b)   Rel-S

The antecedents of the relative pronouns *where* and *when* must be very general common nouns for place and time, while the only possible antecedent for *why* is the noun *reason*. The use of the antecedent followed by the adverbial relative pronoun often seems awkward, and these meanings are frequently expressed not as Rel-Ss, but as IQs or free relatives (a structure discussed in Section 4), as shown in (16) - (17).

(16)   (a)   Rel-S   The reason [*why* [I've asked you here ___]] will
                         soon be revealed.
       (b)   IQ   [*Why* [I've asked you here ___]] will soon be
                         revealed.

(17)   (a)   Rel-S   I saw the place [*where* [you put the beer ___]].
       (b)   Free Rel-S I saw [*where* [you put the beer ___]].

1.4 WH-Movement and Prepositional Phrases

When the Rel-S contains a NP_{WH} that is the object of a preposition, WH-movement can apply in two different ways. First, it can move the NP_{WH}, leaving the preposition behind, as in (18). A derivation for (18)(a) (which uses the pronoun *who*) is shown in (19).

(18)   (a)   I know the girl [who [you spoke to ___]].
       (b)   The street [which [I live on ____]] is very dangerous.
       (c)   The grandfather clock [which [you're looking at ____]] was made
             by my grandfather.
       (d)   They saw the kids [who [I gave the candy to ____]].

(19)   (a)   Before WH-movement

(19)   (b)   After WH-movement

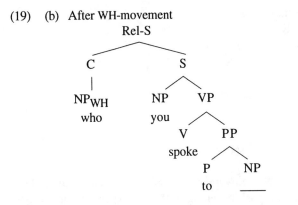

Second, WH-movement can move the PP, as in (20). A derivation for (20)(a) (which uses the pronoun *whom*, typical of this style of discourse) is shown in (21).

(20)   (a)   I know the girl [to whom [you spoke ____]].
        (b)   The street [on which [he lives ____]] is dangerous.
        (c)   The ideals [for which [we have fought ____]] have finally prevailed.
        (d)   They saw the children [to whom [she gave the candy ____]].

(21)   (a)   Before WH-movement

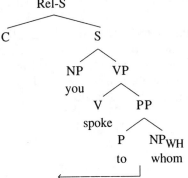

(21)   (b)   After WH-movement

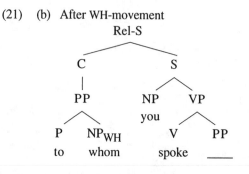

The two options for WH-movement are not stylistically equivalent, however. Moving the preposition along with the object is characteristic only of formal English, occurring more often in written than in spoken English. It must be accompanied by the pronoun *whom* (as opposed to *who*), also typical of formal English (e.g. *to whom you spoke* and never **to who you spoke*).

The movement of a preposition is an example of a more general phenomenon known as pied-piping. When the rule of WH-movement moves a relative pronoun, it is possible for the pronoun, like the Pied Piper of Hamlin, to carry other material along with it. This other material can be a NP or a PP of which it is a part. In the examples of (22) WH-movement has moved a NP which contains the NP$_{WH}$, as shown in the derivation for (22)(a), given in (23). (For detail on the internal structure of NPs, see Chapters 27 and 28.)

(22)   (a)   some books [the covers of which [I ruined ___]]
             cf. some books [which [I ruined the covers of ___]]
       (b)   associate professors [the majority of whom [we polled ___]]
       (c)   the shirt [the color of the stripes of which [I like ___]]
             cf. the shirt [which [I like the color of the stripes of ___]]

(23)   (a)   Before WH-Movement

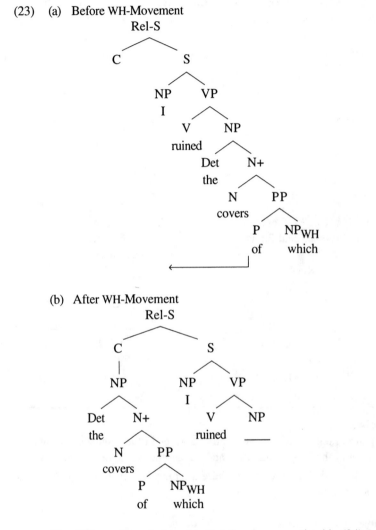

(b)   After WH-Movement

The WH-constituents found in Rel-Ss are summarized in (24).

collection of diagraming of pied piping.

(24) (a) WH-Constituent as NP   (b)   WH-Constituent as NP with
           who/whom, which   Determiner *whose*

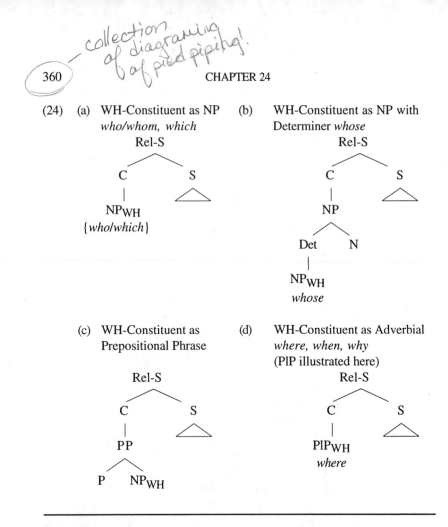

      (c) WH-Constituent as   (d)   WH-Constituent as Adverbial
           Prepositional Phrase   *where, when, why*
                                              (PIP illustrated here)

Exercise 1

Put square brackets around the relative clauses in the sentences below. For each, identify the XP$_{WH}$ and the S and put another set of brackets around the S. In each S, add a line to show where the missing constituent belongs and state its function.

Example: The fish which you ate was rotten.
          [which [you ate __]]
          The XP$_{WH}$ is a NP, the direct object of the verb *ate*.

1. The man who I married is very handsome.
2. The picture which you're looking at was painted by my grandfather.
3. The children who are playing on the playground now should come in.
4. Do you know the student whose house we visited?
5. We need a person on whose help we can rely.
6. We went to the place where he was buried. — *this has a Pass VP up to you if you want to diagram fully*
7. They saw the kids who I gave the candy to.
8. I hate the guy who you married.
9. The building in which I live is on Rock Street.
10. I went to see the teacher who had given me an "A."
11. I went to see the student who I had given an "A."
12. Sally taught a girl whose father owned a ranch.
13. We should buy books which children can read.
14. We should buy books the titles of which children can pronounce.

Exercise 2

Give derivations for the relative clauses in Exercise 1. A derivation shows the stages of a clause before and after the application of WH-movement, as in (23).

Exercise 3

Construct at least two sentences containing relative clauses with a relative pronoun that is a genitive NP. Construct at least two sentences with relative clauses in which the the relative pronoun is a genitive NP that is a determiner in an NP that is the object of a preposition that is fronted by WH-movement.

Exercise 4

As discussed in the chapter, the relative pronoun *who* is used for human antecedents and the pronoun *which,* for nonhumans. What happens if the antecedent is a conjoined NP that is both human and nonhuman, as in (1) and (2)? Which relative pronoun do you use? Circle one and discuss your choice.

1. She read only about people and things which / who amused her.
2. They dreamt of the places and people which / who they would meet.

Exercise 5

It is not always clear whether an antecedent is human or nonhuman. Which relative pronoun would you use in each of the following? Circle one and discuss your choice.

1.   There's not a team in town which / who can beat the Mighty Ducks.
2.   I serve on a committee which / who handles complaints.
3.   The baby which / who had been abandoned was taken to the hospital.
4.   I have a precious cat which / who likes to sit in my lap and be petted.

Exercise 6

One sometimes encounters sentences like the following (from Rudin 1986). In light of what has been said about WH-movement, describe what is odd or unexpected about them. Find additional examples of this phenomenon.

(1)   Linguists can reconstruct a ... parent language from which
these sister languages were created from.
(2)   We did underestimate the margin by which Ronald Reagan won by.
(3)   [This is a] phenomenon to which I refer to as a split subject.
(4)   At least 300 years ago a mug was a cup of which to drink out of.

---

2. RELATIVE CLAUSES WITH COMPLEMENTIZER *THAT*

A second type of relative clause has slightly different properties from WH-relatives. These structures have *that* in complementizer position, as in (25), and are accordingly called that-relatives.

(25)   (a)   The man [that left] is my brother.
        (b)   The book [that I just finished reading] was great.
        (c)   He is a man [that we can rely on].
        (d)   We're looking for a place [that we can store our books].

4.1 The Internal Syntax of That-Relatives

Like WH-relatives, that-relatives have two constituents, a C and an S. The C is the complementizer *that*, an invariant particle usually pronounced as unstressed [ðət], while the S is a clause that is missing a constituent.

Though the complementizer *that* is not a WH-word, it is assumed that this structure comes from the application of WH-movement. The word *that* is moved from a position within the clause to complementizer position, leaving behind a gap.

The missing constituent of a that-relative can be a NP or an adverbial, as in (26), where the position of the gap is indicated with a line.

(26) Missing Constituent is an NP
    (a) The man [that [___ left]] is my brother.
    (b) The book [that [I just finished reading ___]] was great.
    (c) He is a man [that [we can rely on ___]].

(27) Missing Constituent is an Adverbial
    (a) We're looking for a place [that [we can store our books ___]].
    (b) They called at a time [that [I was not at home ___]].
    (c) This is the reason [that [I lied to you ___]].
    (d) I cook chicken the way [that [Aunt Betsy cooks it ___]].

The missing NP is a subject (26)(a), a direct object (26)(b), or a prepositional object (26)(c). The missing adverbial can be an adverbial of place, time, reason, or manner. The last of these is *not* possible with relative clauses formed by WH-movement. The internal structure of a that-relative is shown schematically in (28).

(28) Rel-S

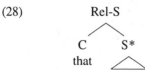

*S is missing an NP or Adverbial (of place, time, reason, or manner)

4.2 Deletion of the Complementizer that
As was the case with the complementizer of that-Ss (Chapter 20), the complementizer of that-relatives is frequently deleted, as shown in (29). (The position of the deleted complementizer is indicated by "Ø".)

(29) (a) The book [Ø [I just finished reading ___]] was great.
(b) He is a man [Ø [we can rely on ___]].
(c) We're looking for a place [Ø [we can store our books ___]].

Deletion of *that* is generally not possible when the missing constituent is in subject position, as in (30) and (31).

(30) (a) The man [that [___ left]] is my brother.
(b) *The man [Ø [___ left]] is my brother.

(31) (a) The book [that [___ is sitting on the table]] is worth reading.
(b) *The book [Ø [___ is sitting on the table]] is worth reading.

In a tree diagram, the position of the complementizer is shown, even when it is omitted, as shown in (32), the diagram for (29)(b).

(32)

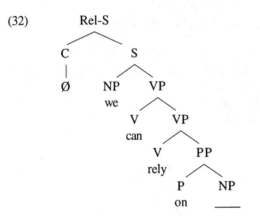

In many treatments of English grammar, the word *that* is considered a relative pronoun and not an invariant particle. However, such an analysis obscures the similarity between that-relatives and nominal that-clauses (cf. Chapter 20) and complicates the statements that need to be made about relative pronoun choice and the conditions under which a relative clause can have a zero complementizer. Here *that* is considered to be a complementizer which, like the WH-words of WH-relatives, can occur in the position of a subject, object, or adverbial (of time, place, reason) and is moved to C position by WH-movement, leaving behind a gap. Unlike the WH-words, it can also occur in the position of a manner adverbial, and it can be deleted.

Exercise 7

Draw a tree diagram for the relative clauses in each of the following sentences.

1. I know the guy that kissed my sister.
2. Let's write about the woman that they elected president.
3. They proposed a plan Susan will object to.
4. Kathy laughs just the way her mother laughed.
5. Patrick wanted to see the play Patricia wanted to see.
6. This is behavior I will not put up with.

Exercise 8

Are the numerous possibilities for the C position of relative clauses presented in the chapter equally frequent? In a text of one page, put square brackets around all the restrictive relative clauses (see Chapter 28). Circle the constituent in C position (including instances of deleted *that*) and calculate the percentage of clauses with relative pronouns (*who, which, whose,* or *whom*) as opposed to *that*. How often is *that* deleted? What implications do your conclusions have for teaching relative clauses?

Exercise 9

1. The missing NP in a WH-Rel-S can be an indirect object. Is this possible in a that-Rel-S as well? Give evidence for your answer.

2. The missing constituent in a WH-Rel-S can be a prepositional phrase (cf. *the friend* [*on whom* [*I rely* ___]]). Is this possible in a that-Rel-S as well? Give relevant sentences as evidence for your answer.

Exercise 10

In this chapter it was noted that treating *that* as a relative pronoun greatly complicates statements about relative pronoun choice and omission of *that*. Pick one of these two phenomenon and state it assuming that *that* is *not* a relative pronoun and then restate it assuming that *that* is a relative pronoun. Compare the two statements.

---

3. THE EXTERNAL SYNTAX OF RELATIVE CLAUSES

Relative clauses modify nouns, as in (33). In terms of structure, they combine with a noun (or N+) to form a N+, as shown schematically in (34). As noted in Chapters 14 and 20, a N+ is a constituent larger than a noun, but smaller than a NP. N+s combine with determiners to form NPs, as in (35). (On NP modification, see Chapter 28.)

(33) (a) The *girl* [who you kissed] is my sister.
      (b) We question the *data* [on which this theory is based].
      (c) The *man* [that left] is my brother.
      (d) The *city* [where I went to school] is very dangerous.

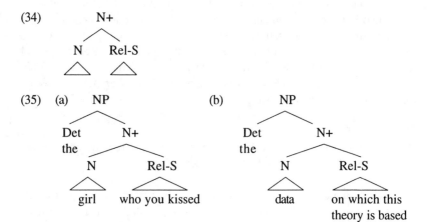

(34)   N+
          /   \
        N   Rel-S

(35) (a)   NP   (b)   NP
           /   \   /   \
        Det   N+   Det   N+
        the   /   \   the   /   \
              N   Rel-S   N   Rel-S
            girl who you kissed   data on which this
                                            theory is based

Relative clauses do not modify proper nouns or personal pronouns, as in the ungrammatical (36) and (37). Because they have unique reference, they do not usually allow restrictive modification of any sort. (On restrictive and nonrestrictive modifiers, see Chapter 28.)

Activities can be used with durational phrases which express how long the activity lasted.

(18) (a) Suzie laughed for ten minutes.
    (b) The children are playing outside for the afternoon.

3.3 States
States obtain. They don't take place in time like events; they simply are. Every piece or phase of a state is like every other one because the situation a state describes is viewed as constant, involving no change or development over time. In other words, states aren't "doing," but "being" or "existing." Unlike events, states do not have built-in end points. This lack of boundary results in the fact that they extend naturally in time, as in (19).

(19) (a) She is kind.
    (b) They felt cold when they were in Alaska.
    (c) We own a house in Florida.
    (d) That child loves her mother.

Like activities, states cannot be used with the test frames for events, as shown by the ungrammatical sentences in (20). They can be used with durational phrases, as in (21).

(20) (a) *How long did it take her to be kind?
    (b) *It took that child two hours/two years to love her mother.

(21) (a) They felt cold for the whole afternoon.
    (b) We owned a house in Florida for five years.
    (c) That child has loved her teacher all year.

A summary of the differences between the three types of lexical verbs is given in the chart below.

	EVENTS	ACTIVITIES	STATES
Take place	Yes	Yes	No
Have end points	Yes	No	No
Occur in frame: "it took [duration phrase] to…"	Yes*	No	No
Occur in frame: "for [duration phrase]"	No**	Yes	Yes

*Yes for most event verbs, but not for momentary event verbs.
**No for event verbs when they are in nonprogressive aspect (see Chapter 17).

Note that a single verb may be used to depict more than one of these meanings. Whether a verb can be used as an event verb, an activity verb, or a state verb will depend not only on the lexical verb itself, but also on the subject, direct object, and other aspects of the linguistic and extra-linguistic context.

(22) (a) I ate dinner.   an event   (+ end point)
      (b) I ate peas all day.   an activity   (- end point)

(23) (a) I knew the city very well.   a state
      (b) Suddenly I knew why she had been lying.   an event
           (Here *know* is a synonym of *realize*, a momentary event verb.)

In the next section we return to the uses of the present tense and see how they interact with the classification of verbal meanings into events, activities, and states.

In addition to functioning as subjects, that-Ss function as complements of both verbs and adjectives, as shown in (23) and (24).

(23)   Verbs with that-S complements
      (a)   My children *believe* [that there is a Santa Clause].
      (b)   The student *denied* [that she had cheated on the test].
      (c)   The officer *told* me [that I was about to be arrested].
      (d)   My mother *warned* me [that I shouldn't talk to strangers].

(24)   Adjectives with that-S complements
      (a)   You seem *disappointed* [that your opponent lost the election].
      (b)   They are *afraid* [that you might cheat them].
      (c)   I am *confident* [that you will pass this course].

Not all verbs and adjectives are subcategorized for that-S complements, as shown in the ungrammatical sentences of (25).

(25)   (a)   *I *eat* [that it is good].
      (b)   *The children *talked* [that they were afraid].
      (c)   *Mary is *intelligent* [that she gets good grades].
      (d)   *Your daughter is *insecure* [that you don't love her].

Once again, whether a verb or adjective occurs with a that-S complement must be listed in its subcategorization frame, as in (26). Some verbs combine with a that-S alone, while others take both a NP and a that-S.

(26)   (a)   Verbs: *believe, deny*   [_____ that-S]
      (b)   Verbs: *tell, warn*   [_____ NP that-S]
      (c)   Adjectives: *disappointed, afraid, confident*   [_____ that-S]

The number of verbs subcategorized for that-Ss is quite large; the number of adjectives is comparatively small, and many of them are derived from verbs (e.g. *alarmed, amused, disappointed, frightened*). In the tree diagrams given below, the internal structure of the clause part of the that-S is abbreviated with a triangle.

(27) (a)

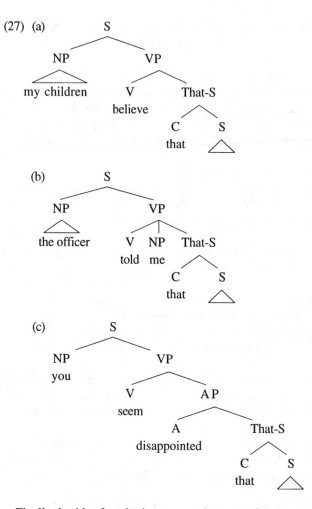

Finally, besides functioning as complements of verbs and adjectives, that-Ss function as complements of nouns as well, as in (28).

(28)   (a)   The *fact* [that he's lying] is obvious.
       (b)   The *belief* [that the world was flat] was held by many people.
       (c)   Some people are of the *opinion* [that grammar is boring].

(10)   Conjuncts
    (a) *In addition,* these words have no meaning.
    (b) *In conclusion,* the study of grammar is awfully complicated.
    (c) *In other words,* it is hard work.

Semantically, conjuncts indicate how the clause is to be connected to other linguistic material. For instance, from the conjunct in (10)(a) we are to understand that the clause is supplementary information, while in (10)(b) we are to understand the clause as a conclusion to some preceding discussion. A list of subcategories of conjuncts with examples is given in the appendix.

The chart in (11) summarizes the types of adverbials. (Adverbials which are complements have not been discussed here; see Chapters 10 and 12.)

(11)

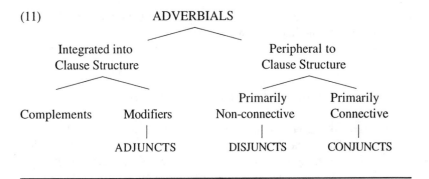

Exercise 1

Draw square brackets around each adverbial, note its syntactic category (Adv, PP, NP, CP), and indicate the constituent that it modifies.

Example: Susan lost her purse in the mall.
Answer: Contains the adverbial [in the mall].
          It is a PP that modifies the VP *lost her purse.*

1.   We bought a radio at Circuit City.
2.   To our amazement, the store was empty.
3.   After we left the store, we saw a movie.
4.   Our neighbors had dinner in an expensive restaurant last Saturday.

5.   Unfortunately, the food was terrible and the waiter was rude.
6.   Obviously, they were upset, but in addition, the manager seemed
      unconcerned about their bad experience.
7.   To everyone's surprise, their car stalled on the freeway at 1:00 a.m.
8.   The next day they sent a letter of complaint to the owners and
      described their experience in some detail.

Exercise 2
Draw tree diagrams for the sentences in Exercise 1. Use triangles for NPs
and other phrases and clauses that do not contain adverbials (as in (3)).

Exercise 3
Describe the ambiguity in the following sentences.

1.   The spy gave the stolen goods to the man on the train.
2.   The police shot the woman with the rifle.

---

2. ADVERBS AND OTHER WORD CLASSES

Of the parts of speech of traditional grammar, adverbs are the most
problematic, largely because there is more diversity among words called
adverbs than in the other word classes. The "class" has become to some
extent a wastebasket because words that do not fit elsewhere have been
dumped into it. As a point of reference, it may be useful to begin with a list
of words often identified as adverbs, given in (12), which shows typical
semantic subsets.

(12)   (a) time   *now, yesterday, soon, later, recently*
       (b) frequency   *often, frequently, always, seldom, rarely*
       (c) place   *here, there, abroad, downtown, northward*
       (d) manner   *slowly, carefully, skillfully*
       (e) means/   *chemically, manually, mechanically,*
            instrument   *microscopically, surgically*
       (f) modal   *perhaps, possibly, probably, necessarily*
       (g) connecting   *however, moreover, nevertheless, so, thus*

SUMMARY:
THE UNITS OF GRAMMAR

1. **WORD CLASSES**   **SOME SUBCLASSES**

Verb	lexical, auxiliary, modal auxiliary
	transitive, intransitive, ditransitive ...
Noun	proper, common; count, noncount
Adjective	gradable, nongradable
Adverb	place, time, manner ...
Intensifier	amplifer, downtoner
Focusing word	
Preposition	transitive, intransitive (= particle)
Conjunction	
Article	
Demonstrative	
Complementizer	
Interjection	
Proform	pronoun, WH-expression,
	proverb, proplace phrase ...

2. **PHRASES**   **SUBTYPES**

VP	verb phrase	InfVP, PassiveVP
NP	noun phrase	
AP	adjective phrase	
PP	prepositional phrase	
CP	complementizer phrase	
PIP	place phrase	
TP	time phrase	

41

3.   INTERNAL SYNTAX OF CLAUSES

	Complementizer	Clause	Form
Basic Clause	(none)	NP	VP
That-S	that	NP	VP
Inf-S	for	NP	InfVP
Gerundive	(none)	NP_{Gen}	$VP_{PresPart}$
WH-S	WH-phrase	S	

(C = XP, a phrase containing WH-expression;
S is missing a phrase of the same
syntactic category as XP)

4.   EXTERNAL SYNTAX OF CLAUSES

independent	(function as a sentence)
nominal	(function as an NP)
adverbial	(function as an adverbial)
relative	(function as a modifier in an NP)

5.   FUNCTIONAL CATEGORIES

Within phrases:	head, complement, modifier, determiner, intensifier
Within clauses:	subject, verb, object, predicate NP, adverbial

Most members of the class of verbs also have a present participle, formed by adding /ing/ to the base, and a past participle, formed for regular verbs by adding /d/ to the base. For irregular verbs, the past participle is formed in a number of different ways, often involving vowel changes and/or suffixation of /en/.

(6)	Present participle		*walk-ing*	*kiss-ing*
	Past participle	regular	*walk-ed*	*kiss-ed*
		irregular	*swum*	*ridden*

2. A CLOSER LOOK AT VERB FORMS

When we take into account all the forms of both regular and irregular verbs, as well as the different ways that verb forms are used, we must posit for English a system with six different forms, three finite, and three nonfinite, as shown in the chart on the following page.

The distinction between finite and nonfinite verb forms is an important one. A finite verb form is the head of a finite VP and only finite VPs function as the predicates of basic clauses (see Chapter 3). That is, finite VPs combine with NPs to form basic clauses.

(7) (a) VPs with finite verb forms   → Basic Clause
          walks to school   He walks to school.
          swam two miles   Sally swam two miles.
          rode on an elephant   She rode on an elephant.

     (b) VPs with nonfinite verb forms → Not a Basic Clause
          walking to school   *he walking to school
          swum two miles   *Sally swum two miles
          ridden on an elephant   *she ridden on an
                                               elephant
          be quiet   *the baby be quiet

Nonfinite VPs have a variety of uses discussed below.

CHAPTER 8

VERB FORMS

	FINITE			NONFINITE		
	Past	Present		Base	Present Participle (-*ing* form)	Past Participle
		3rd Sg Present	General Present			
	1	2	3	4	5	6
A	walked laughed	walks laughs	walk laugh	walk laugh	walking laughing	walked laughed
B	wrote took	writes takes	write take	write take	writing taking	written taken
C	put cut	puts cuts	put cut	put cut	putting cutting	put cut
D	could might	can may	can may	—	—	—
E	was/were	is	(**)	be	being	been

**See discussion of Row E below.

Row A has examples of regular verbs and Rows B - E, different groups of irregular verbs. Considering Rows A - D, we see that for most verbs, the six forms are not completely distinct. For all verbs in English (but the verb *be* in Row E) there is no phonetic difference between forms 3 and 4 (between the general present form and the base form). These two have collapsed into one phonetic form, a process known as syncretism.

All regular verbs (as well as some irregular verbs) also show syncretism between forms 1 and 6 (the past tense form and the past participle form) (see Row A). In addition, the irregular verbs in Row C show syncretism between

As discussed in the previous section, NPs also combine with verbs to form VPs. Examples of these NPs, known as direct objects, are given in (15).

(15) Verb   NP Direct Object
      kissed   her son
      love   their parents
      bake   an apple pie
      destroy the city

NPs combine with prepositions to form prepositional phrases.

(16) Preposition NP
      in   the house
      for   her husband
      on   the ball

(14) - (16) demonstrate three of the most common functions of NPs: They are used in the construction of clauses, of verb phrases, and of prepositional phrases. In later chapters, we will discuss other functions of NPs as well as the external syntax of all major phrase types.

2. TESTS FOR MAJOR PHRASE TYPES

Grammatical analysis requires that we be able to identify the syntactic category of any phrase. One obvious way to identify a phrase is by the word class of its head: If the head is a verb, we have a verb phrase. If the head is an adjective, we have an adjective phrase, etc. But what if we don't know which word is the head? What if we don't know what word class the head belongs to? What if the word in question is sometimes a verb and sometimes a noun? When in doubt about the word class of the head, it is also possible to identify a phrase by some aspect of its external syntax. A few simple tests using this means are presented in this section.

2.1 Verb Phrases

One test for a verb phrase is that it combines with an NP to form a clause. We can see how this works as a test as follows: Assume that in (17)(a) and (b) we have phrases of an unknown type. If we add NPs to these phrases, we get clauses, as in (17)(c) and (d). We can conclude, therefore, that the "unknown" phrases in (17)(a) and (b) are VPs.

(17)   ???
    (a) [destroyed the city]
    (b) [liked children]

       Noun Phrase + ???
    (c) the enemy [destroyed the city]
    (d) my mother [liked children]

Now assume that in (18)(a) and (b) we have phrases of an unknown type. If we add NPs to them, we do not get clauses, as shown by the ungrammatical combinations in (18)(c) and (d). We conclude provisionally that the unknown phrases in (18)(a) and (b) are not VPs.

(18)   ???
    (a) [destruction of the city]
    (b) [fond of children]

       Noun Phrase + ???
    (c) *the enemy [destruction of the city]
    (d) *my mother [fond of children]

2.2 Adjective Phrases

There is one syntactic frame that serves as a good test for an adjective phrase: APs (and only APs) combine with the verb *seem* to form a VP. Because the phrases of (19)(a) - (c) combine with *seem*, as shown in (19)(d) - (f), we conclude that they are APs.

(19)   ???
    (a) [fond of children]
    (b) [able to manage]

A summary of the types of multi-word verbs introduced in this chapter is given in the chart below (based on Quirk 1985:1161).

CLASSIFICATION OF MULTI-WORD VERBS

	Verb	Direct Object	Par	Prep	Prep Object
PHRASAL VERB					
Intransitive	turn	—	up	—	—
Transitive	turn	someone	down	—	—
PREPOSITIONAL VERB					
Intransitive	care	—	—	for	someone
Transitive	ply	someone	—	with	something
PHRASAL-PREPOSITIONAL VERB					
Intransitive	put	—	up	with	someone
Transitive	fix	someone	up	with	someone

Exercise 2

Identify each multi-word verb and figure out whether it is a phrasal verb or a prepositional verb, a transitive verb or an intransitive verb, and draw a tree diagram for the sentence. (Use triangles for NPs.)

1. We should write up the results of our investigation.
2. Susan really gets around.
3. Fortunately, this parka will protect you from the snow.
4. The accountant looked over the receipts from his client's trip.
5. A surly elderly man waited on us last night.

Exercise 3
Use each of the following multi-word verbs in a sentence. Then classify it using the table above.

1.   strip (someone) of (something)
2.   look forward to (something)
3.   show up (= "appear")
4.   put (someone) up to (something)
5.   hold (someone) off
6.   get over (an illness) (= "recover from")

Exercise 4
Draw tree diagrams for the following sentences. Use triangles to abbreviate the NPs and PPs, but draw out the other constituents.

1.   The label is wearing off.
2.   The student put the teacher down.
3.   My sister will care for our aging mother.
4.   The girls blamed the problem on the boys.
5.   The car thieves let the police in on their little secret.
6.   She played up to her boss.
7.   We congratulated them on their good fortune and thanked them for their cooperation.
8.   They gave up, but we are going through with it.
9.   Jacob doesn't get along with anyone.

Exercise 5
Look over the examples of phrasal prepositional verbs given in (24) and (25). Which word is the preposition and which one the particle? Give reasons for your answer.

Exercise 6   For Discussion
We have identified six different types of multi-word verbs. These types are not equal in size. Which category do you think has the largest number of verbs? Which category do you think has the smallest? Why should this matter to an ESL teacher?

Exercise 7

How does the analysis of multi-word verbs presented in this chapter compare to the treatment in books for ESL students? Pick one or two grammar books for ESL students and analyze the presentation. Write a one-page comparison.

---

4. POSTSCRIPT

In addition to the six types of multi-word verbs given above, there is one further type, a hybrid that shows some characteristics of prepositional verbs and some characteristics of phrasal verbs. The examples in (27) show that these verbs are prepositional, because the object must follow the preposition, even when it is a pronoun.

(27) (a) I hadn't seen Joan for months, but yesterday I *ran into* her.
      (b) My son had the flu, and it took weeks to *get over* it.
      (c) The bus stopped, and the old man *got on* it.

However, these verbs have the stress pattern of phrasal verbs. If you pronounce the examples of (27), you will notice that the preposition receives the main stress. We say: *I ran* INTO *her* and not *I* RAN *into her*.

Hybrid multi-word verbs are extremely common. A list of them is given in the appendix to this chapter.

APPENDIX OF MULTI-WORD VERBS

This appendix contains some examples of verbs in each of the categories discussed in the chapter. A blank line indicates a required NP.

PHRASAL VERBS (Verb + Particle)
Intransitive

> break down ("cease to function"), cheer up ("get happy"), clam up ("become silent"), come to ("recover"), get back ("return"), get up, give up ("surrender"), go off ("explode"), hang up ("end telephone conversation"), pass away ("die"), pass out ("faint"), throw up ("vomit"), turn up ("appear"), wear off ("fade")

Transitive

> bring __ up ("rear"), call __ back, call __ off ("cancel"), call ___ up ("telephone"), check ___ off, keep ___ up, make ___ up ("invent"), pick ___ out, pick ___ up ("begin"), point ___ out, put ___ down ("insult"), rule ___ out, take ___ up ("discuss"), turn ___ on/off/out/down/up (lights), take ___ out ("date"), turn ___ down ("reject")

PREPOSITIONAL VERBS (Verb + Preposition)
Intransitive

> agree on ___ , argue with ___ , believe in ___ , call on ___ , care for ___ , count on ___ ("rely on"), dispose of ___ , go with ___ ("date steadily"), hit on ___ ("discover accidentally"), look at ___ , run for ___, stick to ___ ("persist"), tell on ___ ("tattletale")

Transitive

> add ___ to ___ , blame ___ for ___ , blame ___ on ___ , congratulate ___ on ___ , deprive ___ of ___ , explain ___ to ___ ply __ with ___ , thank ___ for __

PHRASAL-PREPOSITIONAL VERBS (Verb + Par + Prep)
Intransitive

> check up on ___ , come up with ____ , feel up to ___ , fill in for ___ , get away with ___ , go in for ___ , go through with ___ , keep on with ___, play up to ___ , put up with ___, run out of __

(35)

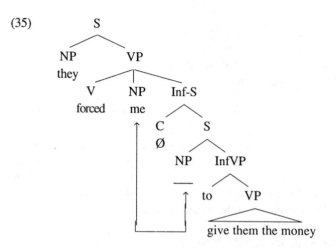

Verbs in the *force* class seem superficially similar to those in the *want* class, but for several reasons they are assigned a different syntactic structure. Compare (35) to (29)(b). We consider *force*-class verbs to be transitive verbs that are subcategorized for Inf-Ss that are always reduced because, unlike *want*-class verbs, they never occur with the complementizer *for*.

(36) (a) *They forced [for me to give them the money].
           *They forced me [for him to give them the money].

Adverbials and parentheticals also work differently with these two subclasses. With a *force*-class verb, they follow the direct object, as in (37). With a *want*-class verb, they precede the Inf-S, as in (38).

(37) (a) They forced me, after some time, [to give them the money].
      (b) *They forced, after some time, me [to give them the money].

(38) (a) I want, and I'm sure they do too, [for you to succeed].
      (b) *I want you, and I'm sure they do, too, [to succeed].

Subcategorizations of the three subclasses of verbs discussed here are given in (39). Additional discussion and further examples are presented in the appendix to this chapter.

(39)   (a) *Want* class   [_____ Inf-S]
      (b) *Try* class   [_____ Inf-S*]
      (c) *Force* class   [_____ NP Inf-S*]
         *The Inf-S must be reduced.

Exercise 7

In each of the following sentences, there is a verb or adjective subcategorized for an Inf-S subject or complement. Identify whether the verb is a member of the *want*, *try*, or *force* classes. If the Inf-S is reduced, indicate how the missing subject of the infinitive is to be understood—is it co-referential to the subject of the main clause or the direct object or is it generic?

1.   The children promised to be good.
2.   They arranged for Bert to take the test early.
3.   My teachers urged Bert to go on to college.
4.   This student deserves to get an "A."
5.   To care for small children requires a great deal of energy.
6.   We remembered to lock the front door.
7.   Your boss would love for you to arrive on time.
8.   The star prepared to make a grand entrance.
9.   The bank gently reminded them to pay their mortgage.
10. It is important to follow directions.

Exercise 8

Give tree diagrams for each of the following sentences, abbreviating the internal structure of NPs. Show all the structure of the Inf-S, even if it is reduced.

1.   The children will promise to be good.
2.   The teachers prefer for Molly to attend the conference.
3.   The teachers chose Molly to attend the conference.
4.   We want you to lock the door.
5.   We remembered to lock the front door.
6.   We need to learn to lock the front door.
7.   It is important to follow directions.
8.   The eager student struggled to understand a minor grammar point.

22
GERUNDIVES

LIKE THAT-CLAUSES and infinitive-clauses, gerundives also have the internal structure of a clause and function as nominals within another clause. The gerundives in square brackets in (1) are subject, direct object of a verb, and complement of a preposition.

(1)　(a)　[Peter's singing in the shower] disturbs us. *subject*
　　　(b)　We hate [Suzie's whining about everything]. *DO of verb*
　　　(c)　That mother is concerned about [her son's receiving an *complement of* "F" in grammar class]. *a prep*

In this chapter we will explore the special properties of gerundives, which have a Janus-like quality. Looking inward they are clauses, but outward they are noun phrases.

1. THE INTERNAL SYNTAX OF GERUNDIVES

In (2) - (4) gerundives are paired with corresponding finite clauses in the present tense.

(2)　(a)　Gerundive:　Peter's singing in the shower
　　　(b)　Finite S:　Peter sings in the shower

(3)　(a)　Gerundive:　Suzie's whining about everything
　　　(b)　Finite S:　Suzie whines about everything

(4)　(a)　Gerundive:　her son's receiving an "F" in grammar class
　　　(b)　Finite S:　her son received an "F" in grammar class

The subject of a gerundive is in a special form known as a genitive, formed by adding the suffix /-s/ to an NP. (Variants of the suffix are discussed in Chapter 30.) Personal pronouns have irregular genitive forms (*my, your, her, his,* etc.), in which there is no separate genitive suffix. The head of the VP is a verb in present participle form. Tree diagrams are given in (5). Note especially the labels given to the morphology of the gerundive.

(5)   (a)

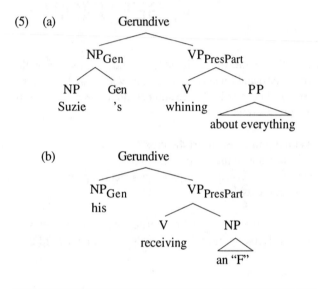

(b)

Exercise 1
Draw tree diagrams for the gerundives.

1. Hazel's raving about her kids
2. your brother's living in Washington
3. the committee's having appointed Margaret chairman
4. someone's playing the five-string banjo
5. her complaining to the principal about the teacher

Exercise 2
Use the gerundives in Exercise 1 in sentences and identify the function of the gerundives in each sentence.

(30)

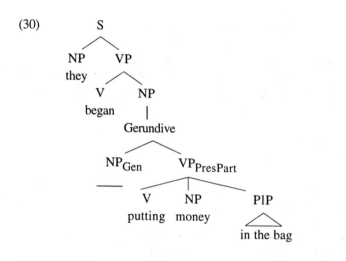

Exercise 8

The appendix to this chapter contains a list of verbs subcategorized for a gerundive. Identify at least five which are subcategorized for a reduced gerundive and give evidence for your answer.

Exercise 9

Some verbs are subcategorized for both an Inf-S and a gerundive. Considering the sentences below, would you say they are equivalent? Can you identify any difference in meaning?

(1)   (a) We forgot locking the door.
        (b) We forgot to lock the door.

(2)   (a) I like driving this car.
        (b) I like to drive this car.

(3)   (a) We regret missing the meeting.
        (b) We regret to inform you that we'll miss the meeting.

4. GERUNDIVES AND INFINITIVES

Inf-Ss often express unfulfilled events, which are hypothetical or in the future. In contrast, gerundives often express events which actually took place. This characterization can be invoked to explain differences in sentences like those of (31).

(31) (a) I remembered turning off the iron.
      (b) I remembered to turn off the iron.

The gerundive in (31)(a) refers to an event of turning off the iron which took place prior to the time of remembering, as shown on the time line in (32).

(32) ——————— X ———————————— X ———→
            turn off the iron   remember

The Inf-S in (31)(b), on the other hand, refers to a potential event of turning off the iron, one that is in the future with respect to the remembering and may at the time of the utterance still be unfulfilled, as shown in (33).

(33) ——————— X ———————————— X ———→
           remember   turn off the iron

The difference is even more striking with the verb *forget*. The gerundive in (34)(a) refers to a real, fulfilled event of packing; hence, we have the film. The Inf-S in (34)(b), however, refers to an unfulfilled event of packing; hence, we have no film.

(34) (a) We didn't know we had brought the extra film.
          We forgot packing it.
      (b) We didn't have any extra film. We forgot to pack it.

Try is also subcategorized for both gerundives and Inf-Ss, as in (35).

(35) (a) The sauce was too bland. We tried adding pepper, but that didn't help much.

(5)   (a) It bothers me that Sam snores.
        (b) Does it bother me that Sam snores?

(6)   (a) It is noteworthy that she won the contest.
        (b) Is it noteworthy that she won the contest?

In sentences (4)(b), (5)(b), and (6)(b) the rule of inversion has applied, inverting the pronoun *it* with the first auxiliary. Since *it* inverts, it must be the subject. Not only is *it* in the position we expect of the subject, it is also treated as the subject by the rule of inversion.

2. THE POSITION OF THE THAT-CLAUSE

Second, consider the that-S. Though it is a subject in (1)(a), (2)(a), and (3)(a), in the corresponding (b) sentences, it has been shifted into the verb phrase. More specifically, it forms a VP with the VP with which it combined to form a clause. This is shown in the tree diagrams in (7), where the VPs have subscripts to help distinguish them. The that-S forms a clause with VP_1 in ((7)(a)). When shifted into the predicate, it combines with VP_1 to form a new VP, labelled VP_2 in (7)(b).

(7)   (a)   (b)

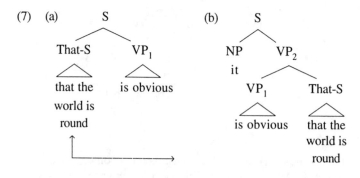

If the VP with which the that-S combines contains an auxiliary, there will be more than one VP node in the sentence. The that-S forms a constituent with the auxiliary and its VP, the VP with which it combined to form a clause, as shown in (8).

(8)   (a)   S   (b)   S

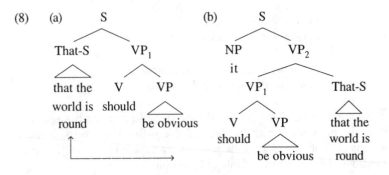

We cannot simply say that the that-S shifts to the end of the sentence. In sentences like (9), which contain an adverbial clause that modifies the entire sentence, the that-S shifts to the end of the VP, the position described above. This is shown in (10).

(9)   (a)   [That Sam snores] bothers me because I'm a light sleeper.
       (b)   It bothers me [that Sam snores] because I'm a light sleeper.

(10) (a)   S   (b)   S

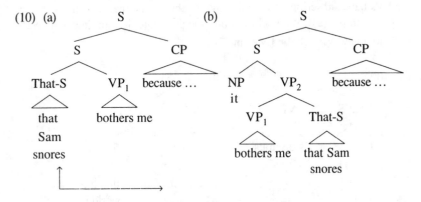

It is important to stress that the shifted that-S is not a complement, even though it is within the VP, a syntactic position in which we expect to find complements. The verbs and adjectives in these sentences are subcategorized for that-S subjects, and not for complements. We call the shifted that-S a "pseudocomplement."

(36)   (a)   *Mary Brown who you kissed is my sister.
       (b)   *Almanzo Wilder who left is my brother.
       (c)   *Chicago where I went to school is very dangerous.

(37)   (a)   *He who left is my brother.
       (b)   *We who help you should be paid.
       (c)   *They who were late were punished.

We should note in passing that restrictive relative clauses can, under very special circumstances, modify personal pronouns, as in (38). They also modify indefinite pronouns, as in (39). Because pronouns are NPs and not Ns, the combination of a relative clause and a pronoun presents complications for the syntax of modifiers that we will not consider here.

(38)   (a)   *He* who laughs last laughs best.
       (b)   Good things come to *he* who waits.

(39)   (a)   Do you know *somebody* [who can fix cars]?
       (b)   He won't believe *anything* [that you tell him].
       (c)   She gave *everything* [she owned] to the museum.

NPs of all types, and constituents of other syntactic categories as well, can be followed by *nonrestrictive* relative clauses. Nonrestrictive clauses are parenthetical expressions which provide extra information about the NP. They are set off from the rest of the sentence by commas in writing and pauses plus a drop in pitch in speaking, as in (40). Nonrestrictive relative clauses are very different from restrictive clauses syntactically and semantically and are not discussed further here.

(40)   (a)   John, who just left, is my brother.
       (b)   Chicago, where I live, is a very dangerous city.
       (c)   The aging English professor, who had forgotten his notes again, cancelled class.

It is possible for more than one (restrictive) Rel-S to modify the same noun, as in (41). These "stacked relatives" differ from relative clauses that happen to contain a relative clause, as in (42). Compare the tree diagrams in (43).

(41) (a) The picture [that you bought yesterday] [that you want to
         sell now] is missing.
     (b) The woman [who arrived late] [who kept interrupting the
         speaker] was very rude.
     (c) We enjoyed the chocolate [that you gave us] [that you said was
         from Switzerland].

(42) (a) The woman [who was reading a book [that I wanted to borrow]]
         suddenly disappeared.
     (b) We bought the picture [that was for sale in the gallery [that was
         going out of business]].
     (c) They saw a play [that had been written by a linguist [who was
         living in New Zealand]].

(43) (a)   Stacked Rel-Ss

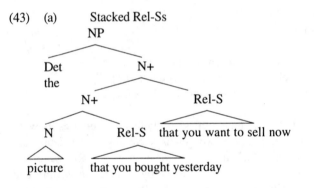

(b)   A Rel-S that contains a Rel-S

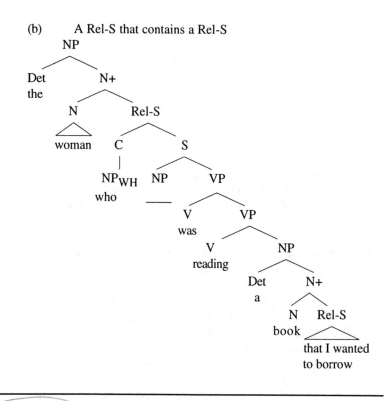

Exercise 11

Draw tree diagrams for the following sentences using triangles to abbreviate the internal structure of relative clauses, unless they contain a relative clause.

1.   They published the article that Charlie co-authored.
2.   The women who know your work recommended that you be hired.
3.   A man I don't know left a message I can't read.
4.   The article you wrote last year that was published in LI confuses the students who try to read it.
5.   They saw a play that had been written by a linguist who was living in New Zealand.
6.   I met with the student who passed the exam that Sonja failed.

7.   The chair tried to contact the student that you failed that had filed a
      complaint.
8.   Chris visited the museum you told us about that had an exhibit of
      rare photographs.

Exercise 12

Examine the following sentences. Can the relative clauses be accounted for
by the rules discussed in this chapter? Why or why not?

1.   A woman walked in who was carrying two small children.
2.   A bomb exploded that had been left on the doorstep.
3.   A little girl disappeared who had been shopping with her mother.

Exercise 13

Examine the following sentences. Can the relative clauses be accounted for
by the rules discussed in this chapter? Why or why not?

1.   They left the party suddenly, which surprised the host.
2.   They sent her obscene letters, which we thought was disgusting.
3.   We learned that the Prime Minister had been assassinated,
      which saddened us all.

---

4. FREE RELATIVE CLAUSES

In the last section of this chapter we turn very briefly to a constituent type
often associated with relative clauses, called a free relative clause. Free Rel-
Ss do not modify NPs, but function as independent constituents within
clauses. In (44) they are NPs and in (45), adverbials of place and time.

(44)   (a)   We read [what you wrote].
       (b)   They are grateful for [what we give them].
       (c)   You are [what you eat].
       (d)   [What help you gave] was appreciated.

(45)   (a)   Take that back [where you found it].
       (b)   We will stop [where we stopped last time].

(c) I'll come [when I'm ready].

Internally, free Rel-Ss, like other WH-Ss, are composed of a WH-constituent and a clause missing a constituent of the same syntactic category. The WH-constituent must contain a WH-word from the restricted subset possible in a free relative (*what, when, where* or any WH-word with the suffix *-ever*).

Externally, free Rel-Ss do not have the distribution pattern of subordinate clauses. They are not like Rel-Ss, because, as noted, they do not modify nouns. They are not like nominal clauses (that-Ss or IQs), because they are not part of the subcategorizations of words (i.e. their occurrence does not depend on particular words in the sentence). When in subject position (as in (44)(d)), they do not undergo extraposition.

Free-Rel-Ss have the same possibilities of occurrence as their WH-constituents: If the WH-constituent is a NP, the free Rel-S occurs in NP positions. If the WH-constituent is a PlP or a TP, the free Rel-S occurs in PlP or TP positions, etc. For this reason, we consider the WH-constituent to be the head of the construction and assign to free Rel-Ss a structure reminiscent of that assigned to gerundives. Inside, they are WH-clauses, but outside, they belong to the same syntactic category as the WH-constituent, shown schematically in (46) (with the category labels of the Rel-S and WH-constituent in bold).

(46) (a)   NP   (b)   PlP

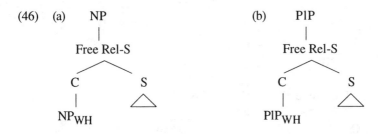

Free Rel-Ss in subject position occur with singular or plural verbs, depending on the WH-constituent, as in (47). This is further evidence for the claim that the WH-constituent is the head and that free Rel-Ss are not Ss, but NPs.

(47) (a) [What you donated] *was* appreciated.
     (b) I'm sure that [whatever valuables you donated] *were* appreciated.
     (c) [Whatever food you serve] is going to please your guests.
     (d) [Whatever tidbits you serve] are going to please your guests.

Tree diagrams for the free-Rel-Ss in (44)(a), (47)(a), and (45)(c) are given
in (48).

(48) (a)

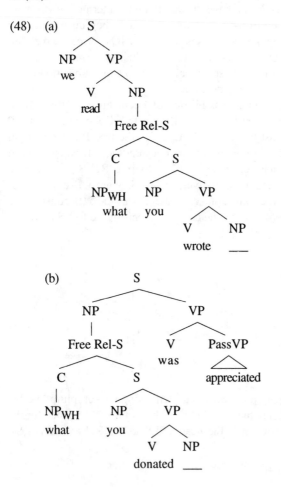

(48) (c)

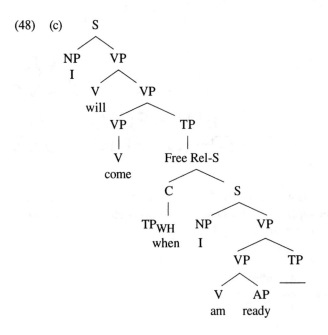

25

SENTENCE FORMS AND SENTENCE FUNCTIONS

IN TRADITIONAL APPROACHES TO ENGLISH GRAMMAR, it is customary to distinguish three types of independent clauses: declaratives, interrogatives, and imperatives. These are illustrated in (1) - (3).

(1)　Declaratives
　　(a)　The sun is shining.
　　(b)　You can swim very well.
　　(c)　They ate chocolate cake.

(2)　Interrogatives
　　(a)　Is the sun shining?
　　(b)　Can you swim?
　　(c)　Who left?
　　(d)　What did they eat?

(3)　Imperatives
　　(a)　Open the door.
　　(b)　Pass the salt, please.
　　(c)　Turn this assignment in tomorrow.

Some writers include a fourth sentence type as well, called an exclamative.

(4)　Exclamatives
　　(a)　How pretty she is!
　　(b)　What slobs they are!
　　(c)　What nice teeth you have!

The division of sentences into declaratives, interrogatives, imperatives, and exclamatives is based first and foremost on their form. Each of these sentence types is characterized by specific syntactic properties. In addition, each can be correlated to some extent with a pragmatic function, i.e. in terms of what speakers use it to do.

In this chapter we explore the form and function of the four sentence types, beginning with declaratives, as the basic sentence type, and continuing with imperatives and exclamatives. Because interrogatives are considerably more complex than the others, we discuss them last.

Exercise 1

State the syntactic properties of each of the four sentence types. Take the structure of the declarative as basic and describe the others in terms of it.

Exercise 2

What pragmatic function is associated with each of the four sentence types? That is, what does a speaker typically use each of them for?

---

1. DECLARATIVES

In a declarative, all of the subject precedes all of the VP, as shown in (5). (As a result of some syntactic processes such as the preposing of adverbials (not discussed here), this description is not true of all declaratives.)

(5)

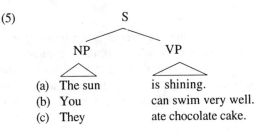

(a)	The sun	is shining.
(b)	You	can swim very well.
(c)	They	ate chocolate cake.

In all treatments of English grammar, declarative sentences are considered the basic sentence type and the others are described in terms of them.

The primary function of declarative sentences is to convey information. They are used to make statements about the world; they express propositions that can be evaluated as either true or false. For example, the proposition expressed in (5)(a) at the time you are reading this is either true or false. You could look out a window and determine its truth for yourself.

2. IMPERATIVES

2.1 Form

Imperatives show two deviations from the structure of a basic clause: The head of the VP is always a base form and there is typically no subject NP (but see below). Imperatives can also occur with the politeness marker *please,* most often initially or finally. Positive imperatives are given in (6) and negative imperatives in (7). The negatives show an additional peculiarity in that they have the auxiliary *do,* even when another auxiliary is present, as in (7)(d).

(6)   (a)   Open the door.
        (b)   Pass the salt, please.
        (c)   Turn this assignment in tomorrow.
        (d)   Please be quiet!

(7)   (a)   Don't move!
        (b)   Please don't whine so much.
        (c)   Don't close the window; it's too hot in here already.
        (d)   Don't be obnoxious.

It is often pointed out that the unexpressed subject of an imperative is understood as the second person, i.e. *you,* which can be demonstrated with reflexive pronouns. In non-imperatives, a reflexive is co-referential with the subject, as in (8). (The pronoun and its antecedent are in italics.) In imperatives, a reflexive is always *yourself* or *yourselves,* showing co-reference with an understood *you,* as in (9).

(8)   (a)   *I* gave *myself* a break.
        (b)   *She* gave *herself* a break.

(c) *They* gave *themselves* a break.

(9)   (a) Give *yourself* a break.
      (b) Consider *yourself* one of the family.
      (c) Please don't be so hard on *yourself.*

Though typically subjectless, imperatives *can* have an overt subject. Sometimes imperatives with subjects are used to express strong irritation or insistence, as (10)(a) and (b). At other times, they are used merely to make it clear who the intended addressee is, as in (11)(a), or to make a contrast among addressees, as in (11)(b).

(10) (a) You be quiet!
      (b) You mind your own business!
      (c) You take the book.
      (d) Don't you fret. We'll have this fixed in no time.

(11) (a) You over there bring your paper up to the desk.
      (b) You be Portia, and I'll be Hamlet.

Occasionally, NPs other than *you* appear as the overt subject of an imperative. As in (12)(a) - (c), they are often indefinite pronouns.

(12) (a) Nobody move.
      (b) Somebody please open this door for me.
      (c) Don't anybody panic. There's enough ice cream for everyone.
      (d) Parents with children come to the front now.

Imperatives with overt subjects remain distinct from declarative sentences because the head verb is a base form.

2.2 Function

Unlike declaratives, imperatives are not used to make statements. They do not express propositions and are neither true nor false. Imperatives are used, rather, to order, request, advise, warn, or suggest some course of action to an addressee, as illustrated in (13). In more general terms, they are used to elicit some kind of behavior. While speakers use declaratives to describe the world, imperatives are an attempt to change it.

(13) (a) Order: Open the door.
      (b) Request: Pass the salt, please.
      (c) Advise: Register early.
                        Take three aspirins and go to bed.
      (d) Warn: Watch out for that car!
      (e) Suggest: [Your picture is awfully dark.]
                        Try adding some light blue over here.

Though imperatives are neither true nor false, they *are* subject to certain appropriateness conditions. Imagine, for instance, a new employee uttering an imperative of (14) to his supervisor.

(14) (a) Be quiet.
      (b) Go away. I'm busy.
      (c) Put these papers away.
      (d) Bring me some coffee.

The new employee would be violating one important condition on the successful use of an imperative, namely that it requires some degree of authority of the speaker over the addressee. Using an imperative is a demonstration of authority. Sometimes the speaker has authority by virtue of his or her position, as with a supervisor over an employee, a teacher over a student, or a parent or adult over a child. At other times, the speaker may "acquire authority" by virtue of the immediate situation, as in an emergency or because of special knowledge or experience. Four degrees of authority are outlined below.

If the authority of the speaker vis-à-vis the addressee is unclear or in question, an imperative will be odd, inappropriate, or, very probably, rude. Fortunately, an imperative is only one of many linguistic expressions that can be used to get people to do things. It is the most direct of these expressions, lying at one end of a continuum from direct to indirect, as shown in (15).

DEGREES OF SPEAKER AUTHORITY

Speaker has authority over addressee by virtue of position

1. Greatest authority: Speaker holds a higher rank in a military
                          or military-like system
    Forward march!   Order
    Attack! Fire!   ↓

2. Great authority: Speaker is parent, teacher, boss,
                          leader, chairman, doctor, ...
    Go to bed!   ↓
    Finish this letter before you leave, please.   Request
    Now break into small groups.   ↓
    Try adding some blue here.   Suggestion
                                                            ↓

Speaker has authority by virtue of the situation

3. Some authority: Situation is an emergency or
                          speaker is giving advice   ↓
    Watch out!   Warning
    Stop! A car is coming!   ↓
    Take an aspirin and lie down if you don't feel well.   Advice
    Lock your car when you park in the city.   ↓
    Register early to get the best classes.

4. Polite authority: Speaker is host of addressee

    Come in and sit down.   Invitation
    Help yourself.   ↓
    Have some coffee.   Offer
                                                            ↓
    Have a nice trip.   Good
    Take care.   wishes

---

(15) (a) Open the door.
     (b) Please open the door.
     (c) Open the door, would you?
     (d) Will you (please) open the door?
     (e) Would you (please) open the door?
     (f) Can you open the door?
     (g) Could you open the door?
     (h) I'd appreciate it if you could open the door.
     (i) I'd appreciate your opening the door, if you don't mind.
     (j) I wonder if you would / could open the door.
     (k) Should we open the door?
     (l) It's awfully hot in here, isn't it?   (i.e. a hint that
         something is wrong that opening the door might fix.)

Note what happens as we go from the curt, direct command expressed by the imperative in (15)(a) to the overly polite, indirect hint of (15)(l). In this progression, the speaker gradually distances herself from the request itself. The language becomes less confrontational and more indirect, and as it becomes more indirect, it becomes easier for the addressee to reject the request. The effect of this distancing is politeness. It is achieved by specific syntactic devices, which are summarized in (16).

(16) (a) A shift in sentence type (from imperative to
         interrogative; from interrogative to declarative)
     (b) A shift in tense from present to past.
     (c) The addition of the politeness marker *please*.
     (d) A shift from asking the addressee to perform an action to
         asking about his/her ability to perform the action to
         merely hinting about a course of action.

Exercise 3

Below are some odd, perhaps even ungrammatical imperatives. Can you state the appropriateness condition that they violate?

1.   *Be ten years old.   [uttered to a seven-year old]
2.   *Be thinner.   [uttered to an overweight patient]
3.   *Have a house.   [uttered to a homeless person]

4. *Like spinach.   [uttered to a child at dinner]
5. *Know French.   [uttered to a student in French class]

Exercise 4

Negative imperatives like those in (7) use either the contraction *don't* or the uncontracted sequence *do not*. Can you use an overt subject with both forms? Give evidence for your answer.

Exercise 5

Above it was said that the verb of an imperative must be the base form. Provide evidence for this claim.

Exercise 6

As discussed, using an imperative assumes a certain kind of relationship with the addressee. Consider the following imperatives and list either specific people or categories of people with whom you could use each of them. Make another list of people with whom you could not use them.

1. Be quiet.
2. Do the dishes.
3. Pass the salt.
4. Give me a ride.
5. Lend me $10.00.

Exercise 7

Construct a sequence like that in (15) for some other commonly requested action, like e.g. one of those in Exercise 6.

Exercise 8

Sentences like those below are sometimes called first-person imperatives. Describe their form and function.

1. Let's discuss this calmly.
2. Let's go to the movies.
3. Let's all be very quiet.
4. Let's not get upset.

Exercise 9

Consider the italicized clauses in the sentences below. Do they have the structure of imperatives? Do they have the function of imperatives? Explain your answers. Provide one paraphrase for the sentences of (1) and another for those in (2).

(1) (a) *Clean up your room,* and I'll take you to the movies.
     (b) *Mow my lawn,* and I'll give you $ 5.00.
     (c) *Take one more step,* and you're dead.

(2) (a) *Don't move,* or I'll shoot.
     (b) *Give me your wallet,* or I'll blow your head off.
     (c) *Hang up the phone now,* or you'll be grounded.

---

3. EXCLAMATIVES

Exclamatives are a relatively rare sentence type. They have the structure of a WH-clause in which the WH-element is restricted to either *how* or *what.*

(17) (a) How pretty she is!
      (b) How clever you are!
      (c) How kind of you!

(18) (a) What slobs they are!
      (b) Oh, Grandmother, what nice teeth you have!
      (c) What nerve!

When used in exclamatives, the words *how* and *what* are intensifiers (Chapter 4.2.1). *How* serves as an intensifier of an adjective or adverb. As shown by the paraphrases in (19), it corresponds to an amplifier, conveying that there is a very high degree of the property expressed by the adjective or adverb.

(19) (a) How pretty she is!
           Used to convey: She's *extremely* pretty.
      (b) How clever you are!
           Used to convey: You are *very* clever.

The intensifier *what* combines with an indefinite NP, as in (20). This intensifier shows the same syntactic pattern as the degree word *such*: The NP has the determiner *a* if the head noun is a singular count noun and the determiner zero if the head noun is plural or noncount.

(20) (a) *What* a fascinating book that was!
      (b) It is *such* a fascinating book.
      (c) *What* slobs they are!
      (d) They are *such* slobs.

The intensifier *what* of exclamatives has a distinctly different pattern from interrogative *what*, which functions as a determiner or modifier in a NP. While exclamative *what* combines with a NP, interrogative *what* combines with a N or N+, as shown in (21) and in the tree diagrams of (22).

(21) (a) What book did you read?
      (b) *What a book did you read?

(22) (a) Exclamative *what*   (b) Interrogative *what*

Exclamatives often are reduced to only the WH-constituent, as in (23).

(23) (a) How pretty!
      (b) How kind of you!
      (c) What a fascinating book!
      (d) What slobs!
      (e) What nerve!

Exclamatives constitute a restricted class of sentences which have an emotive function. They are used to express a high degree of an emotion such as amazement, surprise, delight, disbelief, displeasure, or outrage.

Exercise 10

In this section it was claimed that exclamatives have the structure of a WH-clause. For each of the following exclamatives, give a corresponding declarative. In effect, this means to undo the effects of WH-movement and substitute a different intensifier for *how* or *what*. Identify the function that the WH-constituent has in the corresponding declarative.

1. What a jerk he was!
2. How lovely you look!
3. What confusion followed!
4. How quietly she talks!
5. What a fancy car you drive!
6. How silly you must have thought I was.

Exercise 11

The sentences below are a second type of exclamative. Describe their properties, including their syntax and special intonation pattern.

1. God, was I angry!
2. Boy, am I ever hungry!
3. Have things ever been happening!
4. Wow, was it ever raining!

---

4. INTERROGATIVES

The typical function of interrogatives is to elicit information, and English has developed a number of different ways to do this. In this section we look at four interrogatives, which differ both in form and in the kinds of information they elicit (i.e. in the answers they anticipate).

4.1 Yes-No Questions

Yes-no questions are formed from corresponding declaratives by the rule of inversion. They typically have rising or fall+rising intonation.

(24) (a) Is the sun shining?
      (b) Can you swim?
      (c) Have they finished the project?
      (d) Did Peter the Great die in 1753?

As discussed in Chapter 9, inversion moves the first auxiliary out of the clause it is in to form a constituent with that clause, as illustrated in (25).

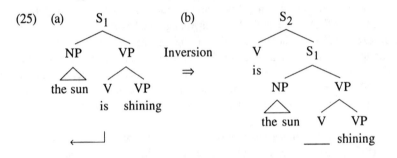

Yes-no questions, as the name implies, seek an answer which is either "yes" or "no." The speaker wants to know whether the proposition expressed by the sentence is true or not. Positive yes-no questions, like those in (24), are neutral, in that they anticipate neither "yes" nor "no." The form of the question itself doesn't indicate any particular expectation on the part of the speaker.

Negative yes-no questions, like those in (26), are not neutral. Depending on the context, they are used when speakers expect a particular response, either positive or negative.

(26) (a) Isn't this fun?
      (b) Isn't she awful?
      (c) Can't Wanita swim?
      (d) Don't you like chocolate?

Speakers frequently use negative yes-no questions to elicit *positive* agreement. For example, if two people are at the circus together, one might utter (26)(a) to seek confirmation of her belief that it is indeed fun. The speaker expects that the addressee will agree and the form of the question itself anticipates "yes" as the answer. Or someone might mutter (26)(b) to a friend about a misbehaving child in a store. The speaker seeks confirmation of her belief that the child is awful, anticipating "yes" as an answer. In such contexts, the speaker of a negative yes-no question expects a positive answer. Note that the addressee is, of course, free to disagree and could disappoint the expectation by answering "no."

Speakers also use negative yes-no questions to elicit a *negative* response; e.g. when the speaker holds a positive belief and then comes to doubt it. The speaker then utters a negative yes-no question, seeking a negative response to confirm the recently-formulated negative belief.

For example, suppose the speaker believes that the addressee likes chocolate and serves her a piece of delicious chocolate cake. Suppose the addressee doesn't eat it eagerly, but picks at it politely. The speaker might utter (26)(d), anticipating a negative which would confirm her recently-formulated negative belief. The steps in this process are outlined in (27).

(27) (a) Speaker holds a positive belief: Addressee likes chocolate.
      (b) Speaker comes to doubt this belief: Addressee doesn't eat a
                                                piece of chocolate cake.
      (c) Speaker formulates a   Addressee doesn't like
           negative belief: chocolate.
      (d) Speaker seeks confirmation
           of negative belief with a
           negative yes-no question: Don't you like chocolate?
      (e) Anticipates a negative response: No, I don't.

Similarly, if a speaker believes that Wanita is a good swimmer, but then sees her paddling clumsily around in the kiddie pool, she might utter (26)(c). The negative question expects a negative answer, conveying at the same time the information that the answer is somewhat surprising for the speaker.

A summary of the facts about negative yes-no questions is given below. In terms of both form and function, negative yes-no questions show a close affinity to tag questions, discussed in Section 4.4.

NEGATIVE YES-NO QUESTIONS

CONTEXT	RESPONSE EXPECTED
Speaker seeks confirmation of a positive belief	Yes
Speaker seeks confirmation of a surprising negative belief	No

Responding to yes-no questions. There is a dialect difference in English which concerns the response to negative yes-no questions. In one dialect, the response to a negative question is the same as the response to the corresponding positive. For example, if the addressee knows that Wanita can swim, the exchanges in (28) might take place. The answer is positive, regardless of whether the question is positive or negative. But if the addressee knows that Wanita *cannot* swim, the answer is negative, regardless of the form of the question, as in (29).

(28) Given: The addressee knows that Wanita knows how to swim.
           Response is positive.
    (a)   Q. Can Wanita swim?
          A. Yes, Wanita can indeed swim.
    (b)   Q. Can't Wanita swim?
          A. Yes, she can swim.

(29) Given: The addressee knows that Wanita cannot swim.
           Response is negative.
    (a)   Q. Can Wanita swim?
          A. No, she can't.
    (b)   Q. Can't Wanita swim?
          A. No, she can't.

In this dialect, the negative in the question has no effect on the answer; the response has to do with the content of the question (in this case, Wanita's ability to swim).

In a second dialect of English, the addressee answers positive and negative questions differently. The presence of the negative in the question has an influence on the response, as shown in (30) and (31).

(30) Given: The addressee knows that Wanita knows how to swim.
               Response is positive to a positive question and negative to
               a negative question.
    (a)   Q. Can Wanita swim?
            A. Yes, Wanita can indeed swim.
    (b)   Q. Can't Wanita swim?
            A. No, she can swim.

(31) Given: The addressee knows that Wanita cannot swim.
               The response is negative to a positive question and positive
               to a negative question.
    (a)   Q. Can Wanita swim?
            A. No, she can't.
    (b)   Q. Can't Wanita swim?
            A. Yes, she can't swim.

This dialect difference is a frequent source of confusion to native speakers of English and presents formidible problems to non-native speakers as well.

Exercise 12

Give tree diagrams for the following yes-no questions, indicating their structure before and after the rule of inversion has applied. (The relevant structures are discussed in Chapter 9, Section 2.)

1. Should we turn the paper in?
2. Shouldn't they be quiet?
3. Don't you like fish?
4. Will those students show their parents their report cards?
5. Could the woman who left three children at the stadium claim them?
6. Was George Washington the first president?

Exercise 13

Construct a scenerio for at least one of the negative yes-no questions below, including whether the speaker expects a positive or a negative response. If the scenerio expects a negative response, sketch out the steps in the process to that response, as was done in (27).

1. Don't you have red caviar?
2. Haven't you seen *Star Trek*?
3. Wasn't the test difficult?
4. Don't you like Hitchcock movies?
5. Isn't champagne good with chocolate?

Exercise 14

Examine your own pattern of answering yes-no questions and determine which dialect you speak.

4.2 Content Questions

Content questions, also known as WH-questions, are similar to yes-no questions in that they do not express propositions and, thus, cannot be judged to be true or false. Content questions are used, rather, to *elicit* information. The speaker of (32)(a), for instance, is asking for identification of the subject; the speaker of (32)(b), of the direct object, and so on. Content questions typically have falling intonation.

(32) (a) Who left?
    (b) Who did you kiss?
    (c) What did you bake this in?
    (d) Where did you stay?

In terms of structure, content questions are WH-clauses, clauses in which the rule of WH-movement has applied. As discussed in Chapter 23, this rule moves a constituent containing a WH-word to complementizer position, leaving behind a gap, as shown in (33) and the tree diagrams of (34).

(33) (a) Who [___ left]?
    (b) Who [did you kiss ___]?

you bake this in ___]?
d you stay ___]?

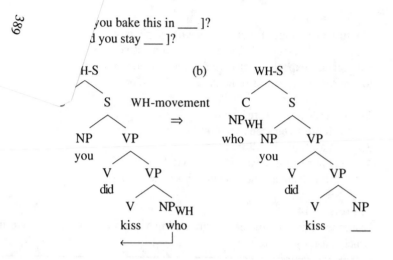

(34)(b) (*who you did kiss*) is not yet a grammatical question in English because the rule of inversion must apply in the formation of this and many content questions. The effects of inversion are shown in (34)(c).

(34) (c)

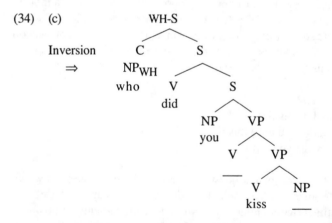

Inversion does *not* apply if the WH-constituent is the subject NP, as in (35). A tree diagram for (35)(b) is given in (36).

(35) (a) Who [___ left]?
    (b) Who [___ told you that]?
    (c) What [___ is bothering you]?
    (d) Whose mother [___ is going to come with us]?

(36)

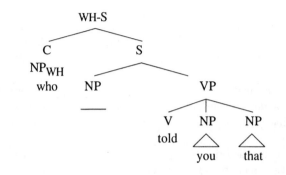

Interrogative pronouns. The WH-constituent in a content question contains one of the WH-expressions known as interrogative pronouns. The choice of pronoun depends on the syntactic category of the constituent being questioned, as listed in (38). Examples follow.

(38) (a) To question an NP   Interrogative Pronoun
        human referent: *who / whom*
        non-human referent: *what*
    (b) To question a constituent within an NP
        genitive determiner: *whose*
        other determiner: *what, which*
        modifier: *what kind of, which*
        quantity expression: *how much, how many*
    (c) To question an intensifier or degree: *how*
    (d) To question an adverbial
        of place: *where*
        of time: *when, how long,*
                                 how often
        of manner: *how*
        of means: *how*
        of reason: *why*

(39) To question an NP   NP answer
      (a) Who left?   *Mom*
      (b) Who told you that?   *Sam*
      (c) What is bothering you?   *the weather*
      (d) What did you bake this in?   *a coffee can*

(40) To question a genitive determiner   NP answer
      (a) Whose mother is going to come with us?   *John's mother*
      (b) Whose book are you reading?   *Susan's book*

(41) To question another determiner   NP answer
      (a) What book do you want?   *that book*
      (b) Which boy did you have a crush on?   *this one*

(42) To question a modifier   NP answer
      (a) What kind of house did she buy?   *a large one*
      (b) Which dress do you like?   *the red one*

(43) To question a quantity expression   NP answer
      (a) How many boyfriends does she have?   *five*
      (b) How much wine have you brought?   *two bottles*

(44) To question an intensifier   AP answer
      (a) How red was it?   *very red*
      (b) How smart is she?   *quite smart*

(45) To question an adverbial   Adverbial
      (a) Where did you stay?   *at a hotel*
      (b) When did he leave?   *yesterday*
      (c) How long was he gone?   *three hours*
      (d) How did she sing yesterday?   *beautifully*
      (e) How will you get there?   *by train*
      (f) Why are you laughing?   *because it's*
                                                          funny

In conclusion, a summary of the steps involved in content question formation is given in (46).

(46) (a) A piece of information is missing from the sentence.
           It is expressed with an interrogative pronoun.
      (b) WH-movement applies, moving the WH-constituent to
           complementizer position.
      (c) Inversion applies, unless the WH-constituent is the subject.

No WH-movement. Finally, note the existence of sentences in which a
WH-constituent has *not* undergone WH-movement. Such sentences are
sometimes used when more than one constituent of the sentence is being
questioned at the same time, as in (47).

(47) (a) Ms. Sawyers told which policeman whose secret?
      (b) Who told you about what new boy in town?
      (c) What have you hidden where?

Sometimes sentences without WH-movement are not true questions in that
they are not used by speakers to elicit information, but to convey surprise or
disbelief. They accomplish this by requesting that the addressee supply or
repeat the "astonishing" part of the sentence, as in (48). These are
sometimes called echo questions.

(48) (a) You did WHAT??
      (b) They went WHERE??
      (c) She likes WHO??

Finally, sentences without WH-movement are often commonly used to elicit
information in a teaching situation, as in (49).

(49) (a) World War II began in what year?
      (b) 2 + 2 equals what?
      (c) In a passive sentence the subject NP appears where?

Like those of (48), these sentences are not true questions, which are sincere
requests for information, because the speaker already knows the answer.
Such questions are asked to determine if the *addressee* knows the answer.

Exercise 15

For each of the following content questions, draw a vertical line between the two constituents of the WH-clause (C and S), identify the syntactic category of the phrase in C, add a blank line showing where it was located in the S prior to WH-movement, and identify its function.

Example: Who told you that?

who | _____ told you that

Missing constituent is an NP, the subject of the clause.

1.   Who gave you the answers?
2.   What have you eaten?   DO
3.   Which car did they steal?
4.   What are you looking at?____
5.   How smart are you?
6.   Who are you going to give this to?___
7.   Where did they put the beer?___
8.   Whose mother will bring the food?
9.   How many books did they read?___
10.   Whose garage will they store the books in?___
11.   What will you name the baby?___
12.   When is the play going to end?___

Exercise 16

Draw tree diagrams for each of the following sentences, showing their structures before and after the rules of WH-movement and inversion have applied.

1.   What have you eaten?
2.   Who are you looking at?
3.   How smart are you?
4.   Who told them to lie?
5.   Whose mother will bring the food?
6.   Where did they put the beer?
7.   What will you name the baby?
8.   When is the play going to end?

Exercise 17
Identify the one major constituent of the sentence that cannot be questioned with a content question. (Hint: Look over the interrogative pronouns in (38) to see what is *not* listed.)

Exercise 18
The sentences below demonstrate a special property of WH-movement in English. Draw tree diagrams for these sentences showing their structure *before* the application of WH-movement. Indicate with an arrow the effect of WH-movement and describe the special property of WH-movement.

1. Who did Sally say that Jane kissed?
2. Which box did you think Peter put the books in?
3. Where did Peter think that Susan said that Martin hid the money?

Exercise 19
Consider the sentences below. Do they pose a problem for content question formation as formulated in (46)? Why or why not? In answering, consider their syntax as well as what they are used for.

(1) How come Daddy doesn't like fish?
(2) How come you don't like grammar?
(3) How come it's so hot in here?

4.3 Alternative Questions
An alternative question is a minor type of interrogative in which the speaker elicits a choice from the addressee. Syntactically, an alternative question is characterized by inversion plus a conjoined constituent in which the alternatives are listed. There is a rising intonation on all alternatives but the last one.

(50) (a) Would you like coffee or tea?
     (b) Are they coming by train or by plane?
     (c) Do you want chocolate, vanilla, or strawberry?

(d)   Are you going to the beach or the mountains on your vacation?
(e)   Does she live in Arlington, Fairfax, or D.C.?

Alternative questions have the syntactic form of yes-no questions, in that the rule of inversion applies, but there are the following differences: Although a yes-no question seeks an answer of "yes" or "no," it would be inappropriate to answer an alternative question with *either* "yes" or "no." An alternative question asks the addressee to name one of the suggested alternatives. The two types of interrogatives also have different intonation patterns: A yes-no question has a rising intonation pattern, with one rise on the tonic, usually at the end of the question. An alternative question has a separate rise on each alternative, except for the last one, where there is a fall, indicating that the list of alternatives is complete. Pronounce the sentences of (50) outloud and note the intonation pattern.

There is a second type of alternative question, which is composed of two separate questions, a content question followed by an elliptical list of alternatives, as in (51).

(51)   (a)   Which ice cream would you like? Chocolate, vanilla, or
             strawberry?
       (b)   Where does she live? Arlington, Fairfax, or D.C.?

Any positive yes-no question can be turned into an alternative question by adding *or not?*

(52)   (a)   Are you coming?
       (b)   Are you coming or not?

Although one could answer (52)(a) with only a "yes" or "no," that option is not available for (52)(b), which requires the addressee to name one of the alternatives, as shown in (53).

(53)   Q: Are you coming or not?
       (a)   *Yes.
       (b)   *No.
       (c)   Yes, I'm coming.
       (d)   No, I'm not coming.

4.4 Tag Questions

The most familiar type of tag question in English consists of a declarative followed by an abbreviated question as in (54).

(54) (a) Mary's pregnant isn't she?
      (b) Wanita can swim, can't she?
      (c) You've seen *Star Trek*, haven't you?
      (d) He doesn't like chocolate, does he?

The properties of the tag itself are given in (55).

(55) (a) It contains a pronoun whose antecedent is the subject NP of the declarative.
      (b) It contains the first auxiliary verb from the declarative or, if none, the dummy auxiliary *do*.
      (c) Inversion applies.
      (d) The tag has opposite polarity of the declarative. (If the declarative is positive, the the tag will be negative; if the declarative is negative, the tag will be positive.)
      (e) There is rising intonation.

This type of tag question is used to elicit agreement, similar to a negative yes-no question (see 4.1). Also like negative yes-no questions, tag questions are not neutral, in that the speaker anticipates the kind of agreement, either positive or negative, and this determines the form of the tag. For instance, if the speaker expects a positive response (i.e. "yes"), the statement will be positive and the tag negative. If the speaker thinks that Mary is pregnant and seeks confirmation (i.e. seeks positive agreement), she would use a *negative* tag in anticipation of a *positive* response, as in (56).

(56) The speaker believes: Mary is pregnant.
      Speaker seeks: Positive agreement
      Speaker uses negative tag: Mary's pregnant, isn't she?
      Anticipates response: Yes, she is.

On the other hand, if the speaker expects a negative response (i.e. "no"), the statement will be negative and the tag positive. For example, if the speaker thinks that Mary is not pregnant and seeks confirmation, she would use a *positive* tag in anticipation of a *negative* response, as in (57).

(57)   The speaker believes: Mary is not pregnant.
       Speaker seeks: Negative agreement
       Speaker uses positive tag: Mary's not pregnant, is she?
       Anticipates response: No, she isn't.

The tag questions discussed here have rising intonation and are genuine questions in which the speaker elicits confirmation of the statement in the main clause. Note that they are only one of several types of tag constructions in English.

Tag questions are often problematic for ESL speakers because functionally similar constructions in many other languages consist of a frozen, i.e. unchanging tag, for example French *n'est-ce pas* or German *nicht wahr*. Learners sometimes latch onto a frequent English tag and overuse it.

5. SUMMARY

In this chapter we have examined the form and function of declarative, imperative, exclamative, and interrogative sentences in English. Whereas declaratives have the structure of basic clauses, in which the subject precedes the VP, which is finite, the others show various differences. Imperatives typically lack a subject and have a VP headed by a base form, while exclamatives are WH-clauses (with *how* or *what*). Interrogatives are the most well-developed sentence type, and we looked at four different interrogatives: yes-no questions, content questions, alternative questions, and tag questions. Though there are other differences, all four are characterized by the rule of inversion.

Each sentence form is associated with a typical function. Declarative sentences are used to convey information, imperatives are used to order or request some course of action, and exclamatives have an emotive function. Interrogatives, generally speaking, are used to elicit information. The form of the interrogative itself encodes the kind of information being sought: A yes-no question elicits either "yes" or "no" and a content question seeks a specific piece of information which is named in the WH-constituent. An alternative question is used to elicit a choice from a list of possible answers, while a tag question seeks agreement from the addressee.

Though there is a *typical* function for each of the sentence forms, it would be a mistake to conclude that linguistic form determines pragmatic function. For example, although sentences with interrogative form are typically used to elicit information, this is by no means always the case. Consider the question, "What do you think you're doing?" uttered by an irritated mother to a child engaged in some undesirable activity. It is unlikely that the mother wishes to elicit information; she probably intends to elicit a change in behavior instead. In this case, a sentence with interrogative form is used with the function of an imperative.

Finally, note that there are *other* types of sentences in English as well. We have chosen in this chapter to present only the most important ones. Their forms and typical functions are summarized below.

NAME	FORM	TYPICAL FUNCTION
Declarative	NP VP	Convey information
Interrogative	Inversion	Elicit information:
Yes-no	Inversion	"yes" or "no"
Content	WH-clause +/- inversion	specific "missing" information
Alternative	Inversion + conjoined XP	a choice of alternatives
Tag	Inversion in tag	agreement
Imperative	No subject NP V is base form	Elicit behavior
Exclamative	WH-clause with *how, what*	Express an emotional extreme (delight, disbelief, outrage ...)

Exercise 20

As discussed in 4.3, alternative questions have a rising intonation on all alternatives but the last one, which is pronounced with a fall. It is possible, however, to pronounce the last alternative with a rising intonation instead. Pronounce the following questions first with a fall on the last alternative and then with a rise. How do they differ? (Hint: What does the speaker assume? What is the speaker asking? What kind of answer does the speaker anticipate?)

(1)   Do you want coffee or tea?
(2)   Do you want cream or sugar?
(3)   Would you like a cookie or a piece of candy?
(4)   Do you want a window seat or an aisle seat?

Exercise 21

Sentences like those below have become quite common in informal, spoken American English. Discuss their structure and their function. Can you observe any restrictions on the use of *or what?*

(1)   Is he cute, or what?
(2)   Is this a hard course, or what?
(3)   Can she cook, or what?

Exercise 22

The tags below are different from those discussed in 4.4. Describe their form and function.

(1)   You can beat me, can you
(2)   He's making threats, is he
(3)   So we're stupid, are we

Exercise 23
A minor sentence type in English is exemplified below. Describe its
syntactic form and its function.

(1)   Why not go to France this summer?
(2)   Why not have pizza for supper?
(3)   Why not give up tennis and learn to swim?

Exercise 24
As noted at the end of the chapter, the form of a sentence does not determine
its function. Find at least five examples of sentences not used in their
"typical" function.

UNIT VI

UNPACKING THE NOUN PHRASE

THE VARIETY AND COMPLEXITY OF NOUN PHRASES is greater than that of any other constituent of English. The different pieces that make up NPs and the way they fit together are taken up in the chapters of Unit VI.

Each and every noun phrase has a head noun, the only obligatory constituent, and we begin in Chapter 26 with a focus on nouns. Topics of discussion include their defining properties, the distinction between common nouns and proper nouns, plural forms and number agreement, and, finally, the count-noncount distinction. NPs require more structure than other phrases, and it is necessary to refer to an intermediate level of structure, larger than a noun, but not quite an NP, that we call N+. Nouns and their complements form N+s.

In the next two chapters we turn to NP modifiers. In Chapter 27 we look at the properties of adjectives and adjective phrases, while in Chapter 28 we discuss various postmodifiers.

In Chapter 29 we explore the complex topic of determiners with focus on different constituents that function as determiners and some complex issues involving reference. Chapter 29 concludes with a worksheet on a special sentence type known as existential sentences.

In Chapter 30, we conclude with genitive noun phrases. Among other things, they function as determiners within noun phrases.

403

26
NOUNS

THE CLASS OF NOUNS is the largest word class in English, containing tens of thousands of members. It is an open class, with daily additions of new words that serve as names for everything from new products in the supermarket to advances in technology.

In the first section of this chapter we examine the grammatical properties of nouns and two important subclasses. The second section focuses specifically on singular and plural nouns and on number agreement in English. Finally, in the last section we look at some differences between count and noncount, or mass, nouns.

1. A DEFINITION FOR NOUNS

The core members of the class of nouns share the following properties.

1.1. Morphology

Inflectional properties. Many nouns have singular and plural forms, as shown in (1) and discussed more fully in Section 2.

(1)   Singular   Plural
       book   books
       girl   girls
       boy   boys
       bus   buses
       church   churches
       child   children

It is often said that nouns have possessive forms, too, but the so-called "possessive suffix" attaches to noun phrases, not to nouns (see Chapter 30).

Derivational properties. There are many rules which create nouns from members of other word classes, a few of which are illustrated in (2).

(2)   (a)   Suffixation of *-er*   Verb   ⟶   Noun
                                           write   writer
                                           work   worker
                                           build   builder
                                           smoke   smoker

       (b)   Suffixation of *-ment*   Verb   ⟶   Noun
                                           amuse   amusement
                                           enjoy   enjoyment
                                           judge   judgement
                                           state   statement

       (c)   Suffixation of *-ness*   Adjective ⟶ Noun
                                           firm   firmness
                                           hard   hardness
                                           fair   fairness
                                           loud   loudness

Other derivational rules apply only to nouns, creating new words from existing nouns, as shown in (3).

(3)   (a)   Suffixation of *-ish*   Noun   ⟶   Adjective
                                           girl   girlish
                                           boy   boyish
                                           child   childish
                                           book   bookish

       (b)   Suffixation of *-like*   Noun   ⟶   Adjective
                                           child   childlike
                                           teacher   teacherlike
                                           war   warlike

(c) Conversion of noun to verb

Noun	$\longrightarrow$	Verb
bottle		bottle
package		package
cap		cap
can		can

1.2 Syntax

Nouns function as the heads of noun phrases. As seen throughout this book, NPs have many functions. Among others, they combine with VPs to form clauses, with Vs to form VPs, and with Ps to form PPs, as shown in (4). (The NPs are in square brackets, the head nouns in italics.)

(4) (a) [The *memory*] was lost.
     (b) We recorded [that *donation*].
     (c) She is very serious about [her *faith*].

Like verbs and adjectives, some nouns are subcategorized for complements, which are most often PPs or that-Ss. The combination of a noun and its complement forms a constituent larger than a noun and not yet a NP that we call N+. Examples are given in (5), with tree diagrams in (6). (The head nouns are in italics and their complements in square brackets.)

(5) (a) *memory* [of her childhood]
     (b) *donation* [to UNICEF]
     (c) *faith* [in people]
     (d) *argument* [with the police] [about guns]
     (e) *fact* [that I like grammar]

(6) (a)   (b)

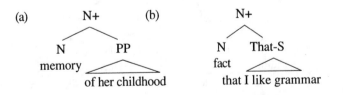

Unlike the case with verbs, complements of nouns are always optional, and most nouns do not occur with complements at all, as shown in (7), where the NPs are in square brackets, the head nouns italicized.

(7)   (a) [The *child*] cried.
       (b) [A *woman*] gave [the *apple*] to [my *sister*].
       (c) [Some *cats*] hid behind [the *house*].

The subcategorizations for the nouns in (5) and (7) are given in (8) and (9).

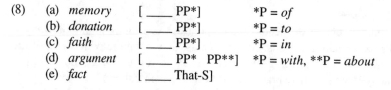

(8)   (a) *memory*   [_____ PP*]   *P = *of*
       (b) *donation*   [_____ PP*]   *P = *to*
       (c) *faith*   [_____ PP*]   *P = *in*
       (d) *argument*   [_____ PP* PP**]   *P = *with, **P = *about*
       (e) *fact*   [_____ That-S]

(9)   *child, woman, apple, sister, cat, house*   [_____]

Nouns or N+s combine with determiners to form noun phrases, as in (10). (Determiners include articles, demonstratives, and genitive noun phrases, as discussed in Chapter 29.)

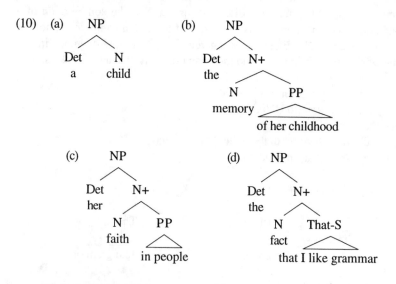

Not all nouns combine freely with determiners, however, and traditionally two subclasses have been identified, common nouns and proper nouns.

1.3 Common Nouns and Proper Nouns

A common noun is typically used to denote a member of a set; e.g. the noun *child* denotes a member of the set of children, the noun *tree*, a member of the set of trees. Common nouns are core members of the class of nouns and, as such, show the full range of noun properties: They have singular and plural forms, as in (1), and combine with both definite and indefinite determiners, as in (11), where the determiners are in italics.

(11)   Definite Determiner
        (a) *the* memory of her childhood
        (b) *the* fact that I like grammar
      Indefinite Determiner
        (c) *a* memory from her childhood
        (d) *some* facts about grammar

In addition, only common nouns are subcategorized for complements (see (5)) or occur with restrictive modifiers (see Chapter 28).

Proper nouns, on the other hand, are typically used to refer to unique entities. They are the names of specific people, places, months, holidays, books, courses, and so on, as in (12). In writing, they are always capitalized.

(12)   (a) Alice
        (b) President Alberta Mudwater
        (c) Oregon
        (d) Orchard Street
        (e) December
        (f) Thanksgiving Day
        (g) English 785

When used to refer to unique entities, proper nouns are always definite and show no determiner contrast. Most proper nouns do not ever occur with a determiner, although some require one, the definite article *the*, as in (13).

(13)   (a) Never a Determiner   Oregon   *the Oregon
                                       Peter   *the Peter
                                       Christmas   *the Christmas
       (b) Always a Determiner
            (the definite article *the*)   *Hague   The Hague
                                           *Andes   the Andes
                                           *4th of July the 4th of July

Proper nouns (as typically used to refer uniquely) also show no contrast
between singular and plural. Most are always singular; a few are plural, as
can be seen in the number agreement in (14).

(14)   (a) Always Singular   Oregon   *Oregons
                                       Boston   *Bostons
                                       Susan   *Susans
       (b) Always Plural (note verb agreement)
            The Smiths *is / are rich.
            The Andes *is / are very high.
            The Florida Keys *is / are lovely.

   Although we typically use proper nouns to refer, we sometimes use them
like common nouns to denote members of a set, as in (15).

(15)   (a) *Shakespeares* are not a dime a dozen.
       (b) Atlanta is the *Chicago* of the South.
       (c) Everyone seems to know a *Mary Smith*.
       (d) I knew Jack Kennedy and you're no *Jack Kennedy*.
            (Lloyd Bentson to Dan Quayle, Vice Presidential debates, 1988)

In (15), the proper nouns in italics are used to denote people or places with
the characteristics of their usual referents. For example, in (15)(a)
Shakespeares is used to denote "authors like Shakespeare," while in (15)(b)
Chicago is used to denote "a city with the characteristics of Chicago,"
possibly, "a large industrial city." Because they are *not* used to refer
uniquely, but to denote members of a set, they have all the properties of
common nouns. That is, they have singular and plural forms and can, indeed
must, occur with determiners.

In a somewhat different atypical use of a proper noun, the unique entity that the proper noun refers to is broken down into a number of different pieces or phases, as in (16).

(16)   (a)   in the *Russia* of 1917
       (b)   the *Paris* I like
       (c)   the young *Shakespeare*
       (d)   in the *English 785* that I taught last spring

In (16)(a) *Russia* is not being used to refer to a unique entity, but to stand for the country during one specific historical periods, as though there were a set of Russia's each corresponding to a different historical period. Similarly, in (16)(c) *Shakespeare* is not being used to refer to Shakespeare, a *unique* person, but to stand for this person at different times in his life. As in the atypical use discussed above, the proper nouns here are also used to refer to members of a set (the set of Russia's, the set of Shakespeares), and, therefore, have the properties of common nouns (e.g. singular and plural forms, determiner contrast, restrictive modification).

Exercise 1

Note the proper nouns in the following sentences and discuss the meaning conveyed by each one.

1.   Mom, a Doctor Jones called you this afternoon.
2.   You should meet my brother-in-law. He's a real John Wayne.
3.   How the city had changed in the years of her absence! The New York of her youth was quieter, cleaner.
4.   A: I once met John Lennon.
     B: Do you mean THE John Lennon?!!
5.   My husband's a regular Woodie Allen.
6.   I haven't read *The Times* today. Do you have a *Times*?
7.   John Smiths are a dime a dozen.

Exercise 2

Is it possible to predict which proper nouns occur with a determiner? Note the following patterns, add some examples of your own to the lists, and make any generalizations you can.

Always a Determiner		Never a Determiner
1.	the Andes	*Andes	Mt. Elbrus
	the Rockies	*Rockies	
2.	the Bahamas	*Bahamas	Isle Royal
	the Keys	*Keys	Key West
3.	the Smiths	*Smiths	Peter Smith
	the Johnsons	*Johnsons	Merideth Johnson
4.	the Red River	*Red River	Cripple Creek
	the Ohio River	*Ohio River	Sugarloaf Run

Exercise 3

Which of the following words are singular and which are plural? In each case, give a reason for your answer.

1. face	6. shelf	11. AIDS
2. box	7. news	12. jeans
3. legs	8. people	13. data
4. paper	9. pen	14. linguistics
5. tweezers	10. sheep	15. police

Exercise 4

For most nouns, the plural is formed in a regular way by adding a suffix to the noun. This suffix has several orthographic variants and three phonetic variants. What are the phonetic variants and what is their distribution? What are the orthographic variants? If necessary, consult a good reference grammar of English.

Exercise 5

List four *irregular* ways to form the plural in English, with a few examples of each, consulting a reference grammar if necessary.

---

2. SINGULAR, PLURAL, AND NUMBER AGREEMENT

Most common nouns have two forms, a singular and a plural (*table—tables, book—books*). The plural is formed for regular nouns with the suffix /-s/ (phonetic variants [-əz], [-s], and [-z]). There are a number of irregular plural markers, such as ablaut (*foot—feet*) or the suffix /-en/. In addition, a small number of nouns have a 'zero plural,' in which the singular and plural forms are identical, as in (17) and (18).

(17) (a) Singular: I like this *sheep*.
     (b) Plural: I like these *sheep*.

(18) (a) Singular: Look at that *fish*! He's got green eyes!
     (b) Plural: Look at those *fish*! They are waving at us!

If we consider nouns with both singular and plural forms to be "variable nouns," we need to recognize two types of invariable ones.

Invariably *singular* nouns do not have plural forms, as in (19). They name entities that cannot be counted (**one water*, **two waters*, **three furnitures*, **one sincerity*, *two sincerities*) and are known as noncount, or mass, nouns (see Section 3).

(19) (a) Singular: This *furniture* is very old.
     (b) Plural: *These *furnitures* are very old.

Invariably *plural* nouns do not have singular forms, as in (20). This small group includes collectives (*police*, *cattle*) and summation plurals; i.e. tools, instruments, and articles of clothing that have two equal parts, such as *scissors, pliers, (eye) glasses, pants*.

(20) (a) Singular: *The police has filed a report.
     (b) Plural: The police have filed a report.

Though the form of these nouns is invariable, it is nonetheless important to know whether they are singular or plural, for this will determine their agreement patterns.

Subject-verb agreement. In English a verb in the present tense shows agreement with a subject that is third person and singular. (As discussed in Chapter 8, agreement is shown with a special form of the verb.) This rule provides evidence for the categorization of nouns into variable and invariable groups, as shown in (21) - (23). (The verb forms are in italics.)

(21) Variable
    (a) Singular: The table *wobbles*.
    (b) Plural: The tables *wobble*.
    (c) Singular: The sheep *is* grazing.
    (d) Plural: The sheep *are* grazing.

(22) Invariably Singular
    (a) The water *runs* / **run* through this pipe.
    (b) This furniture *has* / **have* to be repaired.

(23) Invariably Plural
    (a) My glasses **is* / *are* foggy.
    (b) Your pants **has* / *have* grass stains on the knees.

   Noun-determiner agreement. In English some determiners show agreement with the noun they combine with. For example the demonstratives *this* and *that* occur only with singulars, while *these* and *those* occur with plurals. (The determiners are in italics.)

(24) Variable
    (a) Singular: I don't like *this* table.
    (b) Plural: I don't like *these* tables.
    (c) Singular: Look at *that* deer!
    (d) Plural: Look at *those* deer!

(25) Invariably Singular
    (a) I can't drink *this* / **these* water.
    (b) I want to buy *this* / **these* furniture.

(26) Invariably Plural
    (a) I can't see through **this* / *these* glasses.
    (b) You should let out **that* / *those* pants.

   Subject-predicate NP agreement. Some predicate noun phrases show number agreement with a subject NP, as in (27).

(27) Variable
    (a)   This man is *a professor.*
    (b)   These men are *professors.*
    (c)   *These men are *(a) professor.*
    (d)   The deer is *a doe.*
    (e)   The deer are *does.*

(28) Invariably singular
    (a)   Water is *a good thing* to drink when you're thirsty.
    (b)   *Water is / are *good things* to drink when you're thirsty.

(29) Invariably plural
    (a)   *Scissors is / are *a good thing* to use for cutting.
    (b)   Scissors are *good things* to use for cutting.

Antecedent-anaphor agreement. Finally, many pronouns show number agreement with their antecedents, as in (30). (Both the antecedent and pronoun are in italics.)

(30)   (a)   *The table* is dirty. Will you wash *it* off?
          (b)   *The tables* are dirty. Will you wash *them* off?
          (c)   *The sheep* is grazing. Please keep an eye on *it.*
          (d)   *The sheep* are grazing. Please keep an eye on *them.*
          (e)   *Your furniture* is ready. Do you want to pick *it* up?
          (f)   *My glasses* are foggy. Will you clean *them* for me?

When the antecedent is singular (*table, sheep, furniture*) a singular pronoun *it* is required. When it is plural (*tables, sheep, glasses*), a plural *they* or *them* is required.

Exercise 6
Find the one determiner in the list below that occurs *only* with noncount nouns and divide the rest into three groups: those that require a singular head noun, those that require a plural, and those that occur with nouns of both types. Give evidence for your classification.

a, a dozen, all, a few, a little, another, both, each, either, every, few, fewer, less, little, many, much, neither, no, one, several, the, three, we, your

Exercise 7

Circle the verb form you would use in the following sentences. If both are possible, discuss any difference in meaning.

1. The Washington Bullets ___ a team the city can be proud of.

    (is / are)

2. The Redskins ___ to eat barbequed ribs before every game.

    (likes / like)

3. None of the speakers at the ceremonies ___ wearing hats.

    (was / were)

4. The committee ___ decided to postpone discussions temporarily.

    (has / have)

5. Neither Mrs. Gore nor any of her assistants ___ to attend
    the rally to raise money for MTV.   (plans / plan)

6. According to a recent survey, out of every dollar an American spends
    on food, thirty-six cents ___ spent at restaurants.   (is / are)
    (From Azar 1989:142)

7. All of the furniture ___ broken.   (has / have)

8. All of the students ___ turned their papers in.   (has / have)

9. One-half the population of Virginia ___ with the proposed
    gun control measure.   (agrees / agree)

10. Every one of those politicians, as expected by the voters in their
    home states, ___ ready to vote for Proposition 73.   (is / are)

11. The majority of my friends ___ supporters of Perot.   (was / were)

12. The majority still ___ Perot.   (supports / support)

Exercise 8

Tag questions require antecedent-anaphor agreement. In each of the following sentences, give the tag question, then underline the word (or words) in the subject noun phrase that determines the choice of pronoun in the tag.

1. During the inaugural parade the police were everywhere, _____?

2. The President and his wife looked very nice on Inauguration
    Day, _____?

3. Ten percent of the crowd carried protest signs, _____?

4. Twenty percent of the population of Arlington can
    speak Spanish, _____?
5. Either Dan Rather or the people in the White House Press Corps will
    attend tomorrow's press conference, _____?
6. The Gang of Four should be discredited, _____?
7. The Silent Majority can no longer be silenced, _____?
8. Of the homeless in Washington, the great majority have drug
    problems, _____?

Exercise 9

Exercises 7 and 8 contain constructions that pose problems for the rules of
number agreement, many of which are discussed in handbooks, style
manuals, and reference grammars. Consult one reference book on number
agreement and determine if the rules given there describe your usage.

---

3. COUNT AND NONCOUNT (MASS) NOUNS

On the basis of facts like those in Section 2, the subclass of common nouns
has traditionally been further subdivided into two groups: count nouns,
which are variable, and noncount nouns, which are invariably singular.

3.1 Count and Noncount Nouns

Count nouns are used to denote discrete, individuated entities, which have
borders or boundaries. They have singular and plural forms and can be
counted, as in (31). Count nouns can be concrete (*noodle, table, child*) or
abstract (*idea, fact*).

(31) (a) one noodle, two noodles, twenty noodles
      (b) one child, five children, seven children
      (c) one idea, two ideas, three ideas

Noncount nouns, on the other hand, name unindividuated entities, which
are not perceived as having borders or boundaries. They seem to flow or
extend continuously, and since they don't name discrete entities, they cannot
be counted, as in (32). They can also be concrete (*rice, furniture*) or abstract
(*sincerity, truth*).

(32) (a) *one rice, *two rices, *twenty rices
      (b) *one furniture, *two furnitures, *ten furnitures
      (c) *one sincerity, *two sincerities, *seven sincerities

The difference between count and noncount nouns is not due to any difference in the objects or abstract notions they denote. Both noodles and rice come in individual pieces, but only the former is a count noun. The difference is due, rather, to the lexical meaning of the words themselves: The meaning of count nouns *includes* individuation, while that of noncount nouns does not.

Count and noncount nouns combine with different determiners and quantity expressions. For instance, only *singular* count nouns occur with determiners *a/an* or *each*, while only *plurals* occur with numbers greater than *one* or with *many*. Only *noncount* nouns occur with the determiner *much*. These restrictions are shown in (33) - (35) and summarized in the chart below.

(33) (a)   a girl that I know
      (b) *a girls that I know
      (c)   each boy that I know
      (d) *each boys that I know

(34) (a)   two noodles, three tables, many children
      (b) *two rice, *three furniture, *three furnitures, *many water

(35) (a)   much water, much rice
      (b) *much noodle, *much noodles

Although it is usual to consider nouns as either count or noncount, many words can be used as both, often with a predictable relationship between the two. For instance, most noncount nouns can be used as plural count nouns with the meaning "types of" or "kinds of," as in (36), where *wines* means "types of wine" and *breads,* "types of bread."

(36) (a) At the tasting there were five wonderful *wines*.
      (b) The Heidelberg sells many lovely *breads*.

COMBINATORICS OF NOUN CLASSES

DETERMINERS	COUNT		NONCOUNT
	SINGULAR cat	PLURAL cats	furniture
The number *one*; determiners *a/an*, *each, every, either, neither*	√	---	---
Numbers *two, three, four* ... determiners *these, those*, *a few, several, many*	---	√	---
Determiner *much**	---	---	√
Determiners unstressed *some/any*	---	√	√
Determiners *this, that*	√	---	√
Determiners *the, no*, genitive NPs	√	√	√

*The word *much* is restricted to non-affirmative contexts (i.e. negatives and questions).

A more restricted set of noncount nouns, those that name a food or drink, may be used as count nouns meaning "a unit" or "a serving."

(37)　(a)　Noncount　　I like *coffee.*
　　　(b)　Count　　　Can you give me two *coffees*, please?
　　　(c)　Noncount　　Do you eat *chocolate*?
　　　(d)　Count　　　Have a *chocolate.*

In the other direction, the names of animals are count nouns, while the food product from the animal is a noncount noun.

(38)　(a)　Count　　　Go buy a chicken and two baby lambs.
　　　(b)　Noncount　　I like to eat chicken, but not lamb.

(39) (a) Count   Look at those three big fish!
      (b) Noncount   I can't eat much fish.

Though these uses are lexicalized, virually any count noun can be used in
a noncount way if we imagine a process or activity which has destroyed its
natural borders, as in (40).

(40) (a) He has egg on his tie.
      (b) Eek! There is mouse all over your shoe.

Finally, the relationship between a count noun and a phonologically
similar noncount noun is sometimes relatively idiosyncratic, as in (41).

(41)		Noncount	Count
	cloth	a yard of cloth	four cloths for cleaning
	pain	too much pain	a pain in one's ear
	TV	too much TV	two large TVs
	ballet, opera	he loves ballet	many long ballets
	light, sound		
	taste, smell	too much light	the bright lights
	grammar	grammar is fun	a grammar of an exotic
			language of the Caucasus
	history	some history	a detailed history of Paris

3.2 Individuating Noncount Nouns

Although a noncount noun is used to denote an unindividuated mass, there
are numerous ways to talk about a discrete part of that mass. For example,
if we want to talk about bread, we could use a word that names a specific
quantity (*one pound of bread*) or a specific "unit" (*slice, loaf, crust,* or
crumb). In English different expressions are used to individuate noncount
nouns.

Units of measure. Units of measure individuate noncount nouns by
specifying measurable quantities of them, as listed in (42). Units of measure
are not restricted to noncount nouns, of course, and are often used with
plural count nouns (e.g. *three pints of strawberries, a ton of bricks*).

(42)

Dimension	Measure	Noncount Noun
length	a foot of	waterfront
	a yard of	cloth
	a mile of	cable
area	an acre of	land
volume	a cup of	sugar
	a pint of	whiskey
	a gallon of	wine
weight	an ounce of	butter
	a pound of	sugar
	a ton of	mulch

Words for "type of." Three very general terms (*type, kind, sort*) individuate noncount nouns by picking out a particular type, as illustrated in (43). These can also be used with count nouns as well (e.g. *two types of berries*).

(43) (a) I'm looking for a rare *type* of rice.
      (b) Please try this new *kind* of wine.
      (c) We had a special *sort* of experience in Paris.

Partitives. Partitives individuate noncount nouns by denoting very specific units of the thing in question. For a given entity, there are often idiosyncratic partitives, as, for instance, for the noncount noun *bread*, which has the partitives *loaf, slice, crust,* and *crumb.* Most partitives are used with a relatively limited number of noncount nouns, as shown in the sample in (44).

(44) (a) a *bar* of chocolate, soap, iron
      (b) a *grain* of sand, salt, rice, corn, truth
      (c) a *slice* of bread, bacon, cake, meat
      (d) a *stick* of chalk, celery, butter, dynamite
      (e) a *loaf* of bread, pound cake

A few partitives such as *bit* and *piece* are very general, being used to individuate a large number of different noncount nouns, as in (45).

(45)   (a)   a *bit* of cake, fruit, trouble, fun, news ...
       (b)   a *piece* of bread, cake, fruit, advice, luck ...

3.3 The Syntax of Units of Measure and Partitives

Units of measure, words for types, and partitives are themselves common nouns that take complements which are expressed as PPs with *of*. The noun and its complement form an N+, as shown in (46).

(46)   (a)   (b)

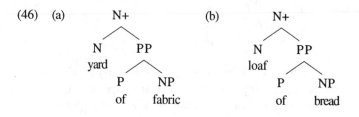

These N+s, like all N+s, combine with determiners to form noun phrases, as in (47).

(47)   (a)   (b)

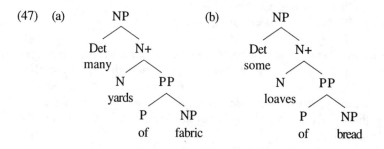

As is clear from the tree diagrams, the head of the noun phrase is *not* the noncount noun (*fabric* or *bread* in (47)), but the unit of measure, type word, or partitive (*yards* and *loaves*). It is the number of this word that determines the number of the noun phrase and corresponding agreement, as shown in (48) - (50) (the agreeing verbs are in italics). If the noncount noun were relevant to agreement, these verbs would all be singular.

(48)   (a)   One *yard* of fabric *is* not enough.
       (b)   Three *yards* of fabric *were* ruined.

(49) (a) A rare *type* of cheese *was* served.

     (b) Several rare *types* of cheese *were* served.

(50) (a) One *loaf* of bread *is* stale.

     (b) Some *loaves* of bread *are* moldy.

Exercise 10

For each of the English nouns below, state whether it can be used as a count noun, as a noncount noun, or both, giving relevant examples. If both, characterize the difference in meaning, if possible.

1. information	5. idea	9. life
2. iron	6. glass	10. aspirin
3. cake	7. data	11. pill
4. lamb	8. brick	12. thread

Find five more examples of English nouns which occur as both count and noncount. Use them in sentences and discuss what differences in meaning you perceive, if any.

Exercise 11

For each partitive below, give a number of nouns that it is used with. Then name five other partitives and some nouns they typically occur with.

1. a blade of	5. a sheet of
2. a block of	6. a speck of
3. a drop of	7. a word of
4. a strip of	8. a dose of

Exercise 12

Give a partitive that could be used with each of these nouns.

1. coal	5. guilt
2. passion	6. clothes
3. courage	7. meat
4. dirt	8. evidence

Exercise 13

Some plural nouns occur with expressions that name collectives, like those for groups of animals. Give the collective expressions for each of the nouns below. Then name five other collective expressions. How does the semantics of a partitive differ from the semantics of a collective?

1. birds	3. geese	5. fish
2. dogs	4. lions	6. sheep

Exercise 14

As Exercises 11 - 13 show, there is an idiosyncratic (i.e. unpredictable) relationship between a noun and the typical partitive or collective expression it is used with. What consequences does this have for learners of English?

Exercise 15

Draw tree diagrams for the following noun phrases.

1. this stalk of celery
2. several kinds of advice
3. a cup of sugar
4. every pound of clay
5. those crumbs of bread
6. your bit of fun

Exercise 16

Discuss the errors in the following sentences, using concepts discussed in this chapter.

1. *Can you give me informations?
2. *My sister has no interest on her new job.
3. *They have bought many new furnitures for their new house.
4. *My teacher assigns much books to read.
5. *Oh, what a good news!
6. *His hair are grey.
7. *The people in your country is a great people.
8. *Will you please give me advices?

27
ADJECTIVES AND ADJECTIVE PHRASES

ADJECTIVES FORM A LARGE, open word class. Semantically, most adjectives express attributes, which are, among other things, dimensions, shapes, colors, qualities, or other characteristics. For instance, the adjectives *big* and *little* express the dimension of size; the adjectives *good* and *bad,* the quality of goodness.

In the first section we present a definition for adjectives that derives from their major morphological and syntactic properties. In the second, we look at the internal syntax of adjective phrases and, in the third, at their external syntax. In the fourth section we consider some subgroups which are relevant to the order of prenominal adjectives, discussed in Chapter 28.

1. A DEFINITION FOR ADJECTIVES

The core members of the adjective class have the following properties.

1.1 Morphology
Inflectional morphology. Many adjectives can be compared, and for some of these, the comparative and superlative are expressed by inflectional suffixes, /-ɚ/ and /-ɛst /.

(1)		Absolute	Comparative	Superlative
	(a)	big	bigger	biggest
	(b)	red	redder	reddest
	(c)	nice	nicer	nicest
	(d)	noisy	noisier	noisiest

For other adjectives, the comparative and superlative are formed analytically, by the use of the words *more* and *most*.

(2)   Absolute   Comparative   Superlative
     (a) bored   more bored   most bored
     (b) famous   more famous   most famous
     (c) beautiful   more beautiful   most beautiful

Derivational morphology. There are a number of productive rules which create new adjectives from other word classes, as shown in (3).

(3)   (a) Suffixation of *-able*   Verb $\longrightarrow$ Adjective
                                         read   readable
                                         wash   washable
                                         think   thinkable

      (b) Suffixation of *-ful*   Noun $\longrightarrow$ Adjective
                                         faith   faithful
                                         hate   hateful
                                         joy   joyful

      (c) Suffixation of *-ic*   Noun $\longrightarrow$ Adjective
                                         atom   atomic
                                         cone   conic
                                         idiot   idiotic

      (d) Suffixation of *-y*   Noun $\longrightarrow$ Adjective
                                         dirt   dirty
                                         noise   noisy
                                         wealth   wealthy

Because the suffixes *-able, -ful, -ic,* and others typically are found with adjectives, they help in part to identify a word as an adjective. There are also derivational rules which apply to adjectives, as in (4).

(4)   (a)   Suffixation of -*ize*

Adjective	$\longrightarrow$	Verb
American		Americanize
legal		legalize
modern		modernize

    (b)   Suffixation of -*ly*

Adjective	$\longrightarrow$	Adverb
nice		nicely
quick		quickly
slow		slowly

    (c)   Suffixation of -*ness*

Adjective	$\longrightarrow$	Noun
kind		kindness
nice		niceness
thick		thickness

1.2 Syntax

Adjectives are the heads of adjective phrases and function most often as modifiers of common nouns, as in (5), or complements of linking verbs, as in (6). (The adjectives are in italics.)

(5)   (a)   Do you know that [*little*] boy?
    (b)   I saw a [very *funny*] play last night.
    (c)   We just witnessed a [rather *ugly*] incident.

(6)   (a)   Your child is [quite *talented*].
    (b)   Jason is [extremely *smart*].
    (c)   That mother seems [overly *fond* of her children].

As noted in Chapter 2, the ability to occur with *seem* is taken as a test for an AP. The syntax of APs is discussed further in Sections 2 and 3.

2. THE INTERNAL SYNTAX OF ADJECTIVE PHRASES

In addition to an adjective, the head of the phrase and the only obligatory element, an adjective phrase may contain an intensifier or a complement.

2.1 Intensifiers
A gradable adjective (see Section 4 below) may combine with an intensifier ('Int'), as in (7) and (8). As discussed in Chapter 4, intensifiers express degree and either amplify or diminish the quality expressed by the adjective. The adjective and intensifer form an adjective, as shown in (9).

(7)   Intensifiers that amplify the degree
       (a) *extremely* smart
       (b) *really* big
       (c) *terribly* sorry about the accident

(8)   Intensifiers that diminish the degree
       (a) *barely* polite
       (b) *slightly* upset about the grade
       (c) *somewhat* big for an ant

(9)   (a)   A   (b)   A

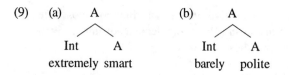

              Int   A   Int   A
            extremely smart   barely   polite

2.2 Complements
Some adjectives are subcategorized for an optional complement, as in (10), where the adjectives are in italics and the complements in square brackets.

(10)   (a) I am [*ashamed* [of you]].
       (b) We are [quite *delighted* [about your promotion]].
       (c) Don't be [so *angry* [at me]].
       (d) Are you [*satisfied* [with the results of the experiment]]?

Like these, many adjectives take PPs as complements, most often with the prepositions *of, about, at, on, to,* or *with*. Subcategorizations of these adjectives are given in (11) and tree diagrams in (12). Note that the adjective and its complement form an adjective phrase.

(11) (a) *ashamed*   [_____ PP*]   *P = *of*
      (b) *delighted*   [_____ PP*]   *P = *about*
      (c) *angry*   [_____ PP*]   *P = *at*
      (d) *satisfied*   [_____ PP*]   *P = *with*

(12) (a)

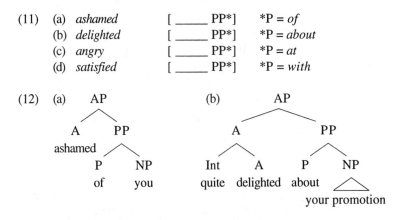

A smaller number of adjectives are subcategorized for that-Ss or Inf-Ss (most often reduced infinitives), as in (13). Subcategorizations are given in (14) and trees in (15).

(13) (a) They were [*thankful* [that we could help them]].
      (b) Bill is [very *sure* [that everyone likes him]].
      (c) We are [terribly *sorry* [to hear about your problems]].
      (d) Your patient is [*reluctant* [to undergo the procedure]].

(14) (a) *thankful, sure*   [_____ that-S]
      (b) *sorry, reluctant*   [_____ Inf-S]

(15) (a)

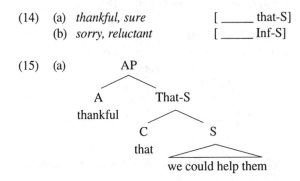

(15)   (b)

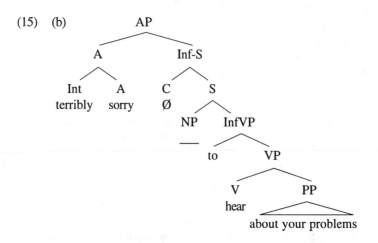

Although these complements are optional, a few adjectives *require* a complement, like *fond* in (16).

(16)   (a)   They are *fond* of chocolate.
       (b)   *They are *fond*.

Some adjectives occur with many different complements, like *afraid* in (17). Its multiple subcategorization frames are listed in (18).

(17)   (a)   PP   I am [*afraid* [of heights]].
       (b)   That-S   They are [*afraid* [that we won't arrive on time]].
       (c)   Inf-S   We are [*afraid* [to go home alone]].
       (d)   None   The baby is [*afraid*].

(18)   *afraid*   [___ PP*], [___ that-S], [___ Inf-S], [___]
                         *P = of

Finally, note that many adjectives, particularly ones that describe concrete properties, never occur with complements.

(19)   (a)   She is *big*.
       (b)   The river is very *wide*.
       (c)   The barn was painted *red*.

If an adjective phrase contains both an intensifier and a complement, the adjective first combines with the intensifier, which then combines with the complement to form an AP, as shown in (20).

(20)

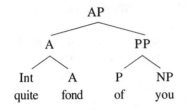

Exercise 1

The comparative and superlative for some adjectives are formed with inflectional suffixes and for others, with the words *more* or *most*. How do you know which to use for any given adjective? Consult a good reference grammar of English, if necessary. Be sure your answer can account for the following forms.

Absolute	Comparative
real	*realer
small	smaller
tiny	tinier
torn	*torner
yellow	yellower

A very small number of adjectives have irregular comparative and superlative forms. List them, consulting a reference grammar if necessary.

Exercise 2

Put square brackets around the APs in the following sentences, circle each adjective, and give its subcategorization frame (as it is used here). Note whether the complement is optional or obligatory.

1. My younger sister is nervous about the fate of the lost child.
2. We are astonished that you feel angry about the last race.
3. Are you aware of the trouble I have gone to for that stupid person?

4.   This girl is good at math, but hopeless at writing.
5.   Our latest plans are contingent on the President's cooperation.
6.   Sue was unhappy that we had stayed home.
7.   The committee is not eager to meet with the disappointed applicants.
8.   Are you familiar with the binding conditions of this contract?
9.   The chicken seems ready to eat.
10.   The Secretary was furious that the chief officer had misled the press.
11.   Small children left unattended are liable to get into trouble.

Exercise 3
Draw a tree diagram for the adjective phrases.

1.   These parents are proud of their son.
2.   The team is surprisingly close to a solution.
3.   My sister is eager to finish the project.
4.   Sue was rather unhappy that we had missed her party but glad that the
      other guests had been able to come.
5.   I am quite aware of these problems.
6.   This girl is good at math, but hopeless at writing.
7.   Sam is extremely embarrassed to have arrived so late.
8.   The Secretary was furious with the chief officer and her staff.

Exercise 4
Compare the sentences in (1) and (2), which contain adjectives followed by
reduced Inf-Ss. For each one, state how the subject of the reduced Inf-S is
understood. How do the sentences in (1) differ from those in (2)?

(1)   (a) We are powerless to stop them.
      (b) They are most anxious to help us.
      (c) Everyone is eager to see this movie.
      (d) She is certain to win the prize.
      (e) We are inclined to help them.

(2)   (a) Most people are easy to fool
      (b) My mother will be hard to convince.
      (c) The harpsicord is quite difficult to play.
      (d) My husband is impossible to please.
      (e) This problem was really tough to solve.

Exercise 5

The adjectives below take PP complements. Determine which prepositions each one requires, noting that more than one preposition may be possible. Compare List A with List B.

List A: *aware, brilliant, busy, certain, conscious, dependent, free, friendly, grateful, impatient, nervous, positive, sad*

List B: These are derived from verbs.
accustomed, amazed, amused, convinced, depressed, disturbed, excited, frightened, pleased, shocked

Do adjectives have to be subcategorized for the prepositions they occur with? Is the preposition a predictable aspect of their syntax or does it have to be learned separately for each adjective? What relevance does the answer to this question have for learners of English?

Exercise 6   For Discussion

Learners of English often use the wrong preposition for the complement of adjectives, perhaps because adjectives are usually learned first without complements. Would it be more sound pedagogically to introduce the complement at the same time as the adjective (e.g. teaching [*angry at* NP] and not just [*angry*]? Why or why not? Regardless of teaching order, develop some strategies to get the learner to focus on the preposition. (Hint: Consider English constructions which "leave" the preposition in sentence-final position and then develop classroom activities which require use of those constructions.)

Exercise 7

Compare the sentences in (1) with those in (2) and state a principle to account for the ungrammatical ones.

(1)   (a)   My neighbor is extremely angry at me.
        (b)   The student was very happy about the test.
        (c)   The customers were satisifed with the sale.
        (d)   We were hesitant to lie about the incident.

(2) (a) *I'm afraid of the angry at me neighbor.
     (b) *The happy about the test student went out to celebrate.
     (c) *Stores always like satisfied with the sales customers.
     (d) *We praised the hesitant to lie children.

---

3. THE EXTERNAL SYNTAX OF ADJECTIVE PHRASES

Adjectives and adjective phrases have a number of functions. Adjectives are often used as premodifiers of nouns, as in (21). The adjective (possibly with an intensifier) combines with a noun to form an N+, as shown in (22).

(21) (a) Do you know that [[*little*] boy]?
      (b) I saw a [[very *funny*] play] last night.
      (c) We just witnessed a [[rather *ugly*] incident].

(22) (a)   N+   (b)   N+

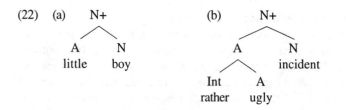

More than one adjective can premodify the same noun, as in (23). These combinations are assigned the minimal structure shown in (24).

(23) (a) a large, mean dog
      (b) a tall, dark, inquisitive stranger
      (c) a strong, disturbing memory of her childhood
      (d) a rather fat, extremely anxious teacher

(24)   (a) NP   (b)   NP

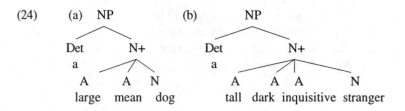

If the modified noun has a complement, as in (23)(c), the adjective(s) combines with the constituent formed by the noun and its complement (a N+).

(25)

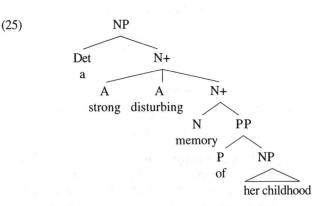

In prenominal position we find adjectives, but not adjective phrases. If APs were allowed, we should expect to find an adjective with a complement prenominally, but that is not possible, as shown in the ungrammatical sentences of (26).

(26) (a) *I'm afraid of the [*angry* [at me]] neighbor.
      (b) *The [*happy* [about the test]] student went out to celebrate.
      (c) *Stores always like [*satisfied* [with the sales]] customers.
      (d) *We praised the [*hesitant* [to lie]] children.

Adjective phrases serve as complements of either linking verbs or complex transitives, as in (27) and (28), with tree diagrams in (29). Though these positions call for APs, remember that APs can be realized as a single adjective or as an adjective plus complement.

(27) AP as complement of a linking verb
      (a) The child [is [quite *smart*]].
      (b) This coffee [tastes [*bitter*]].
      (c) That teacher [seems [*fond* of her children]].

(28) AP as complement of a complex transitive verb
    (a) We [painted the house [*red*]].
    (b) They [considered him [extremely *stupid*]].
    (c) We [find your attitude [quite *irritating*]].
    (d) The committee [judged him [highly *qualified* for the job]].

(29) (a)   (b)

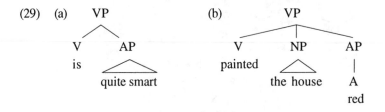

Though most adjectives can appear either prenominally or in complement position, a small number can appear *only* in complement position, including three that describe health (*well, ill,* and *faint*) and most of those that have the prefix *a-* (*ablaze, adrift, afraid, alive, alone, ashamed, asleep, awake, aware*).

(30)   (a)   This child is *well*. That child is quite *ill*.
      (b)   *The *well* child returned to school; the *ill* child stayed home.

(31)   (a)   The house was *ablaze*. The owners were *afraid*.
      (b)   *The *afraid* owners cried as they looked at the *ablaze* house.

Adjective phrases also function occasionally as postposed modifiers of nouns. Postposed APs have a literary flavor and usually contain complements or are otherwise complex, as in (32). Most APs that consist of a single adjective are excluded from this position. Like all postposed modifiers, postposed APs combine with a noun (or N+) to form an N+, as in (33).

(32)   (a)   We were beseiged by [some people [*eager* to impress us]].
      (b)   [A man [*angry* about the outcome of the elections]] filed an official complaint.
      (c)   She detected [a mistake [*typical* of beginners]].
      (d)   He was a president [both popular and long suffering].

(33)

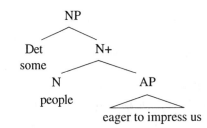

NP
Det   N+
some
    N   AP
  people
        eager to impress us

Postposed position is the only possible one for modifiers of pronouns, as shown in (34).

(34) (a) We want [something [*different*]] for dinner tonight.
      (b) I'm looking for [somebody [very *tall*]].
      (c) Please report [anything [*unusual*]] to us at once.

Finally, APs can be sentence adverbials, a function sometimes called absolutive. Adverbial adjective phrases have various semantic functions: They are commonly used to provide further information about a noun phrase (as in (35)(a)), to give a reason for a particular action (35)(b), or to express a contingency or condition. For example, the APs of (35)(c) state the conditions under which the speaker drinks coffee and beer; they can be paraphrased with clauses, "when it is hot" and "when it is cold."

(35) (a) [*Nervous*], she opened the letter.
      (b) [*Tired* of her son's nagging], the old woman turned her hearing aid off.
      (c) I drink my coffee [*hot*] and my beer [*cold*].

(36)

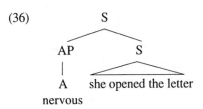

S
AP   S
|
A   she opened the letter
nervous

Exercise 8
Draw tree diagrams for the following sentences.

1.   Everyone was afraid of the angry soldiers.
2.   The committee considers the proposal extremely likely to result in a good product.
3.   This precious child is extremely protective of her sweet little kitten.
4.   She detected a mistake typical of beginners.
5.   Upset and insulted, she stormed out of the room.
6.   We made a rather generous donation to Reed College.
7.   They are looking for someone honest and reliable.
8.   It will be hard to locate a judge experienced in these technical matters and impartial to the legal profession.
9.   The surprisingly thorough preliminary investigation made me quite nervous that they would discover more serious violations.

Exercise 9
Above it was claimed that *well, faint, alone, ashamed, awake,* and *aware* occur only in complement position. For each adjective, provide evidence to support this claim.

Exercise 10
When more than one AP modifies the same noun, is it possible to predict the order they occur in? Note the patterns in (1) and (2) and then construct five NPs of the types described in (3) and (4). Using your examples, what generalizations can you make about the ordering of prenominal adjectives?

(1)   (a)   a tall red building
       (b)   *a red tall building

(2)   (a)   a friendly, elderly Persian tourist
       (b)   *a Persian friendly tourist
       (c)   ?an elderly friendly tourist

(3)   A noun that denotes an inanimate object modified by two or three adjectives from these categories: color, shape, size, age, or condition (e.g.

new, dirty, cracked, etc.)

(4)   A noun that denotes a human being modified by two or three adjectives from these categories: nationality, age, size, intelligence, personality trait (e.g. *friendly, introverted, pleasant,* etc.).

Exercise 11
In the following sentences put the *whole* adjective phrase in square brackets and identify what is unusual about it.

1.   I don't know any nice children to play with.
2.   They have a larger house than yours.
3.   Do you know of a more lovely city than Washington?
4.   Which is the best wine to drink with stew?
5.   Everyone says that Jack Lemon is the most suitable actor for
       the part.
6.   The easiest way to get to Fairfax from here is to take Route 66.

Exercise 12
Some adjectives are ambiguous, and occasionally, one of the meanings is restricted to either prenominal or complement position. Consider the following sentences, characterize the meanings of the adjectives in italics, and note any restrictions on their occurrence.

(1)   (a)   An *old* friend stopped by to see you.
       (b)   Your friend is quite *old.*

(2)   (a)   The patient said that he feels quite *faint.*
       (b)   *We gave some medicine to the *faint* patient.
       (c)   The patient let out a *faint* cry.

(3)   (a)   An *angry* silence filled the room.
       (b)   *The silence was *angry.*
       (c)   The customers were very *angry.*

(4)   (a)   The doctors are *certain* that you are mistaken.
       (b)   *The *certain* doctors are suing you.
       (c)   A *certain* doctor is suing you.

(5)   (a)   The child was very *sorry* that she had lied.
       (b)   ?The *sorry* child made a sincere apology.
       (c)   The child made a *sorry* attempt at apology.

---

4. ADJECTIVE SUBCLASSES

In order to more fully describe the syntactic behavior of adjectives, it is helpful to recognize a number of subclasses. In this section we distinguish between core and peripheral adjectives and identify several adjective subclasses.

4.1 Core Adjectives
Core members of the class of adjectives are both premodifiers of nouns and complements of verbs. They are either gradable or nongradable, a semantic distinction which has syntactic consequences.

Gradable (core) adjectives. Gradable adjectives express attributes that one can have more or less of, like size, beauty, or strength. It is because they are gradable that such adjectives have comparative and superlative forms and can be intensified, as in (37). (Intensifiers are in italics.)

(37)   (a)   Your house is [*really* big].
       (b)   Her dress is [*very* lovely].
       (c)   The children seem [*extremely* tired].

When we use a gradable adjective, we invoke a scale, and often opposite ends, or poles, of the scale are named by pairs of adjectives called polar opposites, as in (38).

(38)   Scale   Ends of Scale Named by
                                    Polar Opposites
       (a)   Scale of size: *big*   *little*
       (b)   Scale of age: *old*   *young*
       (c)   Scale of beauty: *beautiful*   *ugly*
       (d)   Scale of depth: *deep*   *shallow*
       (e)   Scale of friendliness: *friendly*   *unfriendly*

An interesting feature of polar opposites is the way they work in questions. In a neutral question about size, for example, one in which there are no prior assumptions about the size of the object in question, we use *big*, as in (39)(a), and not *little*, as in (39)(b).

(39) (a) Neutral question: How big is the house?
      (b) Not neutral: How little is the house?

Saying (39)(b) is not neutral means that it can only be asked if there is a prior context or assumption on the part of the speaker which establishes that the house is at the little end of the size scale. We pronounce the two questions differently, as well: In neutral questions like (39)(a), primary stress is generally on the adjective (*big*). (The speaker is asking where the house lies on the size scale.) In questions using its polar opposite, like (39)(b), however, primary stress can be on the verb (*is*). (The speaker assumes that the house is little and is asking about the degree to which it is little; i.e. where the house lies on the little end of the size scale.)

Because the word *big* can be used in questions about size without prior context or assumptions, we refer to it as the neutral, or unmarked, member of the pair. The word *little*, on the contrary, because it requires a special context to be used in a question about size, is considered the marked member. Many polar opposites work like *big* and *little*.

(40) (a) Neutral question: How old is your mother?
      (b) Not neutral: How young is your mother?

(41) (a) Neutral question: How deep is this pool?
      (b) Not neutral: How shallow is this pool?

The difference between unmarked and marked adjectives can also be seen in the fact that the unmarked adjective is often used to name the scale itself, as in (38)(c) - (e). And, thirdly, note that the unmarked adjective is the one used in measure phrases, as in (42)(a).

(42) (a) Unmarked: five years *old*   six feet *deep*
      (b) Marked: *five years *young*   *three feet *shallow*

Nongradable (core) adjectives. Many nongradable adjectives are extremes, words which denote qualities at one extreme of a scale. For example, the word *gigantic* denotes an extreme of *big*. Something that is gigantic is very, very big, so big that it is off the size scale, if you will. Extremes resist being treated as gradable and are usually quite odd when compared or used with intensifiers, as in (43). Other extremes are given in (44).

(43) (a) Her house is *gigantic*. ?It's even more *gigantic* than yours.
      (b) ?That elephant is very *gigantic*.
      (c) ?That tax break is extremely *minute*.

(44) (a) Extreme of *beautiful*:   *gorgeous*
                                          ?more gorgeous, ?very gorgeous
      (b) Extreme of *good*:   *fabulous*
                                          ?more fabulous, ?very fabulous
      (c) Extreme of *happy*:   *ecstatic*
                                          ?more ecstatic, ?extremely ecstatic

A smaller number of nongradable adjectives are absolutes. They express attributes that one cannot have more or less of, but which (strictly speaking) apply in an all or nothing way, such as *dead, eternal,* or *unique*. Absolutes are not gradable because their meanings do not invoke a scale; hence they cannot be compared or used with intensifiers, as in (45). Some adjectives considered to be absolutes are listed in (46).

(45) (a) This is an *eternal* flame. ?*That flame is more *eternal*.
      (b) ?Your solution is rather / extremely *unique*.

(46) Absolutes
      (a) *unique, perfect, correct, right, true, false*
      (b) *infinite, eternal, endless, ultimate*
      (c) *dead, alive, pregnant, ideal*

Speakers do not always agree about the meanings of words, and there is considerable disagreement about some absolutes. A particularly salient example is the word *unique*: Although prescriptivists insist that it names an absolute quality that cannot be compared (for them *more unique* is ungrammatical), many speakers use it as a gradable adjective meaning "very unusual" (for them *more unique* is fine).

A third group of core adjectives is derived from past participles. Though some are gradable, most are nongradable, and, because of their position within the NP (discussed in Chapter 28), we consider them one of the nongradable subtypes.

(47) Nongradable
  (a) an *expired* passport
  (b) some *frozen* shrimp
  (c) a *broken* promise
  Gradable
  (d) some very *wilted* lettuce
  (e) two rather *swollen* feet

4.2 Peripheral Adjectives

Peripheral members of the adjective class appear *only* in prenominal position, do not express attributes (at least not in the ordinary sense), and are not gradable. They are closely linked to other syntactic categories. One group is related to verbs; a peripheral adjective can be created from the present participle of virtually any verb, as in (48). (Of course, not all adjectives of this form will be peripheral; cf. *a stunning dress.*)

(48) (a) the *sleeping* children
  (b) a *singing* mailman
  (c) some *complaining* students
  (d) a *drooping* flower
  (e) a *rotting* piece of meat

A small number of peripheral adjectives express adverbial categories.

(49) (a) Place: *urban* problems, a *rural* lifestyle, *upstairs* neighbors
  (b) Time: my *former* neighbor, an *old* teacher, the *late* dean,
        past mistakes, the *present* dilemma, *future*
        generations, *eventual* solutions, *occasional* showers
  (c) Manner: *hard* worker, *big* eater, *heavy* smoker,
        sound sleeper, *rapid* calculations

A third group of peripheral adjectives has the semantic function of intensifiers (see Chapter 4). Some amplify, conveying the extent to which the noun applies to the referent and answering questions like, "To what extent?" or "How much of a ...?" In (50)(a), for instance, the phrase *a complete fool* conveys the degree to which Bozo was a fool, answering the question, "How much of a fool was Bozo?"

(50) Intensifying adjectives
    (a) Bozo was a *complete* fool.
    (b) They are *firm* / *fast* friends.
    (c) That was *utter* nonsense!
    (d) I've lost my *entire* life savings. That's the *whole* truth.

Other intensifying adjectives convey emphasis or certainty about the applicability of the noun to its referent. These words are closely related to the subclass of adverbials that express conviction (see the appendix to Chapter 4), as shown in the paraphrases in (51) and (52).

(51) (a) He is a *certain* winner.
    (b) I know for *certain* he is a winner.
    (c) *Certainly*, he is a winner.

(52) (a) That was a *sure* sign.
    (b) I am *sure* that was a sign.
    (c) *Surely*, that was a sign.

(53) Intensifying adjectives that convey emphasis or certainty
    (a) a *certain* (=sure) winner, a *real* hero, a *true* friend
    (b) *sheer* stupidity
    (c) *plain* nonsense, an *outright* lie, a *clear* failure, a *sure* sign

Focusing words. A fourth, rather small group of peripheral adjectives has the semantic function of focusing words. They restrict the reference of the noun they occur with. The main ones are listed in (54).

(54) (a) a *certain* person, a *particular* person, a *specific* idea
      (b) his *chief* excuse, the *main* problem, the *principal* effort
      (c) the *exact* answer, the *very* person for the job
      (d) the *only* help, the *sole* relief, a *mere* pittance
      (e) the *same* child

4.3 Numerals

A final class of adjectives consists of numerals, i.e. the cardinal numbers and a small number of quantity expressions (including *many* and *few*). These words combine with count nouns and, like other adjectives, can occur with determiners, as in (55). Other quantity expressions of English (*all, both, some*) are not adjectives, but determiners, as discussed in Chapter 29.

(55) (a) [The *two* white shirts] are both dirty.
      (b) I am tired of hearing about [your *many* problems].
      (c) After that, she was deserted by [the *few* friends she had].

The subclasses of adjectives (except for numerals) are summarized in the chart below. These subclasses are important not only for understanding the contribution that adjectives make to the meaning of an NP, but also for describing the order of prenominal adjectives, discussed in Chapter 28.

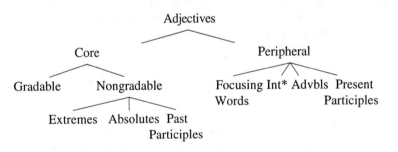

*Intensifers

Exercise 13

Pick ten of the following adjectives and put them into one of the subclasses discussed above, giving evidence for your answer. Beware of adjectives that have more than one meaning.

happy	despondent	eternal	retired	retiring	girlish
knowing	grown	pregnant	apoplectic	extreme	dead
brilliant	unique	high	acting	pure	divine
crying	American	present	sincere	unanimous	frozen
precise	square	clean	scalding	cute	petrified

Exercise 14

Give the polar opposite of each adjective, if there is one. Then, for each pair, determine which is the unmarked one, if either. In each case, give some evidence for your answer. Finally, find at least three other polar opposites and determine which member of the pair is unmarked.

1. pretty
2. smart
3. happy
4. loved

5. good
6. illegal
7. cold
8. wonderful

9. thin
10. high
11. late
12. dirty

13. near
14. short
15. moral
16. narrow

Exercise 15

Adjectives derived from past participles can be formed from transitive verbs, as in (1), and from *some* intransitives, as in (2). They cannot be derived from other intransitives, as in (3). What is the factor that differentiates the intransitive verbs in (2) from those in (3)? (Hint: The answer involves semantic roles, discussed in Chapter 5.)

(1)   an *opened* door, my *hurt* feelings, a freshly *painted* chair,
        the *printed* page, a *broken* promise

(2)   *wilted* lettuce, *fallen* leaf, *collapsed* tent, *burst* pipes,
        rotten railings, *sprouted* wheat, *swollen* feet, *expired* passport

(3)   **run* man, **coughed* patient, **swum* contestant,
        *flown pilot, **cried* child, **exercised* athlete,
        *sung artist, **yawned* student, **laughed* clown

28

NOUN PHRASE MODIFIERS

CHAPTER 27 DEALT WITH adjectives, commonly defined as words that modify nouns. Adjectives are not the only type of modifier, however, for constituents of nearly every syntactic category can modify a noun. In the first section of this chapter, we continue our discussion of adjectives by considering the ordering of prenominal adjectives. In Section 2, we take up the issue of restrictive versus nonrestrictive modification, and in Section 3, examine some familiar constituents in their role as postmodifiers and also introduce one new constituent. In Section 4, we explore some issues that arise in cases of multiple modification.

1. COMPOUND NOUNS AND MULTIPLE PRENOMINAL ADJECTIVES

A noun may be premodified by one, two, or even three adjectives, though more than three is unusual. The existence of ungrammatical sequences like those in (1) - (2) provides evidence that the order is not completely free, but subject to certain restrictions.

(1) (a) the same wilted lettuce   *the wilted same lettuce
     (b) a particular tall building   *a tall particular building
     (c) the overweight former coach   *a former overweight coach
     (d) the only two white shirts   *the only white two shirts

(2) (a) a tall red building   *a red tall building
     (b) a small, musty room   *a musty small room
     (c) a friendly, elderly tourist   ?an elderly friendly tourist
     (d) a kind capable nurse   ?a capable kind nurse

447

Before turning specifically to ordering, however, we need to look at compound nouns. The ubiquitous nature of compounds and the fact that compound nouns often contain words with the superficial form of adjectives is potentially confusing for the issue of adjective ordering.

Like all compounds, compound nouns are lexical units that consist of two independent units, either of which can be a compound itself, resulting in potentially very long strings, as in (3) - (4). Each part is binary, however, as shown in (5). (Note that a compound noun, in spite of its internal complexity, is still a noun, labelled "N" in the tree.)

(3)   (a)   car seat
       (b)   [car seat] company
       (c)   [[car seat] company] meeting
       (d)   [[[car seat] company] meeting] chairman

(4)   (a)   history library
       (b)   [history library] staff
       (c)   [[history library] staff] party
       (d)   [[history library] staff] [holiday party]
       (e)   [[[history library] staff] [holiday party]] announcement

(5)   (a)   (b)   (c)

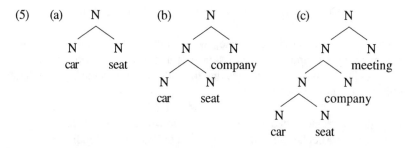

The compound nouns above and in (6) are composed of nouns, but compounds can also be composed of an adjective and a noun, as in (7) - (8), though these are somewhat less frequent.

(6)   Noun - Noun compounds
       (a)   brick house
       (b)   stone wall
       (c)   apple pie

    (d) eye doctor
    (e) divorce lawyer
    (f) drama teacher

(7)   Adjective - Noun Compounds
    (a) high tide
    (b) strong box   (for jewels)
    (c) green tea   (from Ceylon)
    (d) hard roll   (fresh from the bakery)
    (e) wet suit   (worn by divers)

(8)   Denominal Adjective - Noun Compounds
    (a) atomic particle
    (b) linguistic argument
    (c) electrical appliance
    (d) musical clock
    (e) polar freeze
    (f) American attack

Compounds, which are formed in the lexicon, are distinguished from syntactically-formed constituents by the fact that the individual units of the compound cannot be inflected or modified. For example, the adjectives in (7) - (8) cannot be compared or intensified. If we should attempt to make a comparative or add an intensifier, the combination loses the specialized sense of the compound, as in (9).

(9)   (a)   The diver wore a wet suit.   (may be a compound)
     (b)   The diver wore an extremely wet suit.   (not a compound)
     (c)   I have a strong box.   (may be a compound)
     (d)   You have a stronger box.   (not a compound)

Similarly, the nouns in (3) - (6) cannot be individually inflected for number. The expression *stones wall* is ungrammatical even though a wall is made of many stones. Only the whole compound may be plural (if the head is a count noun) (as in (10)).

(10)   (a)   *stones wall   stone walls   (more than one [stone wall])
       (b)   *apples pie   apple pies   (more than one [apple pie])

The individual nouns of a compound may not be modified, either. Any premodifiers are understood as modifying the entire compound, as in (11).

(11)   (a)   *[cheap brick] house
             (Not possible in the meaning that the bricks are cheap.)
       (b)   *[small stone] wall
             (Not possible in the meaning that the stones are small.)
       (c)   *[messy divorce] lawyer
             (Not possible in the meaning that the lawyer only deals with messy divorces.)

(Of course, a compound may be *formed from* a modified element that is itself a compound, such as *red brick* or *crab apple.*)

The rules that form compound nouns in English are extremely general and productive, but beyond the scope of this book. Suffice it to say that a compound enters the syntax as an unanalyzed unit and that, regardless of the number of individual words that make up a compound noun or their syntactic category, the compound has the node label "N." The ordering tendencies to which we now turn do not apply within compounds.

Any description of the ordering of prenominal adjectives must be stated in terms of the adjective subclasses introduced in Chapter 27 and summarized in the chart below. There is also a subclass of numerals which is not included on the chart.

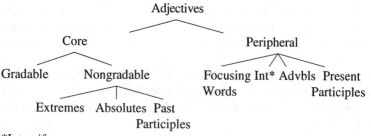

*Intensifers

Adjectives from the first two peripheral subclasses (focusing words and intensifiers) always precede core adjectives, while adjectives from the last two (adverbials and present participles), follow. If a core adjective is preceded by both a focusing word and an intensifier, itself a rare occurrence, the focusing word will precede. These patterns are shown in (12) - (14).

(12) Focusing word or intensifier before core adjective
    (a) You served the *same wilted* lettuce to me last night.
    (b) A *certain mysterious* person called on my neighbor.
    (c) They agreed to meet at the top of a *particular tall* building.
    (d) That's the *whole painful* truth.

(13) Focusing word before intensifier (rare)
    (a) You are the *only complete* fool I know.
    (b) They are the *same perfect* strangers I was talking about.
    (c) They are the *exact fast* friends I was talking about.
    (d) Those women are the *chief strong* supporters of this candidate.

(14) Core adjective before adverbial or present participle
    (a) the *overweight former* coach
    (b) a *polite heavy* smoker
    (c) the *adorable sleeping* children
    (d) a *large rotting* piece of meat

When more than one *core* adjective modifies the same noun, there is a tendency to order them according to semantic subsets. For instance, adjectives that express more subjective qualities (*kind, generous, lovely*) generally appear before those that express less subjective ones, like size or shape (*large, short, pudgy*). A numeral, if present, occurs first. A typical ordering is shown in (15), with examples in (16).

(15) (a) numeral   (*one, two, 30, 100; many, few*)
    (b) emotive, evaluative, or subjective quality
                 (*nice, kind, sweet, pretty, friendly, important, ...*)
    (c) size   (*large, small, tiny ...*)
    (d) shape   (*round, square, fat, slender ...*)
    (e) condition   (*musty, dirty, dilapidated, healthy, tired ...*)

    (f)   age   (*old, young, ancient ...*)
    (g)   color   (*red, green, blue ...*)

(16)   (a)   a lovely old painting
       (b)   a lazy overweight housekeeper
       (c)   the two tall narrow cupboards
       (d)   a small square green box
       (e)   a weird-looking violet-colored flower
       (f)   the many complicated ancient riddles

It should be stressed that except for the numerals, which must appear first, the list of adjective subclasses in (15) is not to be understood as a rigid ordering that must be followed, but, rather, as a description of frequently-found combinations. It represents the fact that speakers have come to expect information about the attributes of people and things to come in a certain order. It is not that the order cannot be altered, but that when it is, something special is conveyed.

Exercise 1
Give tree diagrams for these compound nouns.

1.   sidewalk hotdog vendor
2.   electrical outlet cover
3.   atomic bomb
4.   solar generator station commander
6.   community college baseball umpire's association president
5.   history library staff holiday party announcement

Exercise 2
Collect five examples of NPs containing more than one prenominal adjective. Do they follow the ordering presented above? If not, describe the way in which they do not conform. (Be careful to distinguish between prenominal adjectives and adjectives that are part of a compound noun.)

---

2. RESTRICTIVE AND NONRESTRICTIVE MODIFIERS

All modifiers have the function of providing more information about the noun being modified. But in addition, some modifiers have a restrictive function, while others are nonrestrictive. Restrictive modifiers provide information that is necessary for identifying the NP. They restrict what the speaker intends it to refer to, as in (17). (Restrictive modifiers are in square brackets.)

(17) (a) All students [who wrote a paper] were excused from the exam.
     (b) The class collected money for our neighbors [left homeless by the floods last spring].
     (c) The women [with children] were asked to leave.

The modifier in (17)(a) (*who wrote a paper*) is used to restrict the number of students that were excused to only those that had written a paper. The restrictive modifier in (17)(b) is necessary in order to understand which neighbors were given money. The restrictive modifier in (17)(c) identifies which women were asked to leave; it restricts the number only to women with children. The sentences convey different meanings without the restrictive modifiers, as shown in (18).

(18) (a) All students were excused from the exam.
     (b) The class collected money for our neighbors.
     (c) The women were asked to leave.

Nonrestrictive modifiers, on the other hand, provide information that is not necessary for identifying the NP. They do not restrict what it is intended to refer to, but merely provide additional information about it, as in (19).

(19) (a) Mrs. Amanda Johnson, [who has agreed to chair the new committee], will now give us a progress report.
     (b) I'm moving to Chicago, [which is the largest city in Illinois].
     (c) The [beautiful] Princess Diana was seen at the races yesterday.

In (19)(a) the nonrestrictive modifier (*who has agreed* ...) provides additional information about the NP *Mrs. Amanda Johnson*, but is not necessary to help identify her. Similarly, in (19)(c) the adjective *beautiful* is a nonrestrictive modifier that serves to provide additional information about the NP *Princess Diana,* but is not necessary to identify her. Nonrestrictive modifiers are like asides, incidental information that the speaker supplies about the referent of the NP.

In (19), nonrestrictive modifiers are used with proper nouns, a very frequent use. They may be used with common nouns as well, if the referent of the NP was previously established in the discourse or can be understood to be unique. In (20) the nonrestrictive modifiers are in square brackets.

(20)   Nonrestrictive Modifiers with Common Nouns
   (a)   I'd like you to meet my [wonderful] mother.
   (b)   This is my son, [whom I'm very proud of tonight].
   (c)   Secretary to teacher: A student called you today, and
         someone else left this book for you. The student, [who was
         very agitated], wants you to give him an extension on his
         paper.

A man uttering (20)(a) does not use the modifier *wonderful* to help identify the referent of *my mother* because the NP has only one possible referent. The speaker uses the modifier to supply additional information about her. In (20)(c), a student is introduced in the discourse and so the nonrestrictive modifier used with *the student* (the Rel-S, *who was very agitated*) is not intended to be used to identify the student, but merely to supply further information about him. In brief, the additional information provided by the nonrestrictive modifier may be interesting or even important, but is not intended by the speaker to help identify the referent of the NP.

There are several properties that are used to mark nonrestrictive modifiers. Nonrestrictive modifiers which *follow* the head noun are set off by commas in writing and by a drop in pitch in speaking. In this they are much like parenthetical expressions. Also like parentheticals, they can be omitted without affecting the structure or the meaning of the rest of the sentence. Nonrestrictive relative clauses are WH-Ss; that-relatives are not used in this function.

Nonrestrictive modifiers which *precede* the head noun never receive contrastive stress. This distinguishes them from restrictive modifiers, which can, and often do, receive contrastive stress. By virtue of the fact that they are restrictive, necessary for the identification of the referent, there is a built-in contrast between the restrictive modifier that is mentioned and other possibilities. These facts about stress can be seen in (21)(a) (with a nonrestrictive, unstressed modifier) and (21)(b) (with a restrictive and stressed modifier). (Stress is indicated with small capitals.)

(21) (a) Nonrestrictive: I'd like you to meet my wonderful wife.
      (b) Restrictive: ?I'd like you to meet my WONDERFUL wife.

Under ordinary circumstances, a person can have (at most) one wife, and therefore the NP *my wife* has a unique reference. NPs with unique reference do not occur with restrictive modifiers, however, which leads to the oddness of (21)(b). It requires an interpretation in which the speaker has at least two wives, one of which is characterized as *wonderful*. For this reason, proper nouns, which also have unique reference, are never used with restrictive modifiers, as in (22).

(22) (a) *John with a big smile   (contrast: a man with a big smile)
      (b) *extremely cute Sally   (contrast: an extremely cute baby)

We will have nothing further to say about nonrestrictive modifiers. In the remainder of this chapter, as we look at modifiers that follow the noun and at multiple modification, we will be considering only *restrictive* modifiers.

Exercise 3
The modifiers in the sentences below could be restrictive or nonrestrictive. First describe the meaning that would be conveyed by each if the modifier is understood as restrictive and then, if it is nonrestrictive. (Since nonrestrictive relative clauses are set off with commas, you will have to add them when considering that reading.)

1. The students [who had passed the test] were given gold stars.
2. She hired a nurse to take care of her children [who had pneumonia].
3. I'm going to visit my [elderly] parents.
4. We should paint the [dirty] walls.

Exercise 4
In the sentences below, proper nouns are used with restrictive modifiers (in square brackets), although in general, they occur only with nonrestrictive ones. Discuss the meaning conveyed.

1.   The Kathy [who lives on Evergreen] called you last night.
2.   The Chicago [that I knew as a graduate student] is much different from the Chicago of today.
3.   I was visited by a [very witty] [young] Einstein.

---

3. NOUN PHRASE POSTMODIFIERS

We use the term postmodifier for a constituent that follows the noun it modifies. Relative clauses, one type of postmodifier, were discussed in Chapter 24. A Rel-S combines with a noun to form a N+, as in (23).

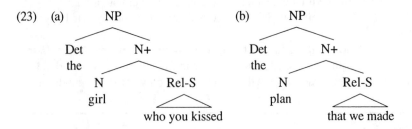

All other postmodifiers have the same pattern: They follow the noun and form with it an N+, as shown schematically in (24)(a) and contrasted with premodifiers in (24)(b).

3.1 Prepositional Phrases
The most common postmodifiers are prepositional phrases, which are three or four times more frequent than other types. PPs functioning as postmodifiers show the same range of meanings as other PPs do, expressing

circumstantial information and semantic roles (see Chapter 5, Section 4), as in (25) and (26). (The PP modifiers are in square brackets.) Tree diagrams are given in (27).

(25) Circumstantial Information
    (a) Place: the book [on the table], a party [on the beach]
                 the trip [to Key West], the way [out]
    (b) Time: a party [at midnight], three days [before her wedding]
    (c) Means: our trip [by train]
    (d) Reason: his death [from an overdose]

(26) Semantic Roles
    (a) Agent: this book [by Noam Chomsky]
    (b) Source: a ring [from Jim]
    (c) Benefactive: a present [for Mother]

(27) (a)   NP   (b)   NP

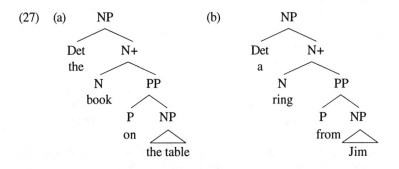

Note that NPs with PP postmodifiers can be paraphrased by sentences in which the PPs are complements of the linking verb *be*, as in (28). This possibility is important for distinguishing among postmodifiers, as discussed below.

(28) (a) The book is [on the table].
     (b) The party is [at midnight].
     (c) Our trip was [by train].
     (d) Her death was [from an overdose].
     (e) This ring is [from Jim].

3.2 Nonfinite Verb Phrases

Both passive verb phrases, which are headed by past participles, and verb phrases headed by present participles can function as noun modifiers, as in (29) and (30), with corresponding tree diagrams in (31).

(29)   Passive Verb Phrase
    (a)   I don't know the student [assigned by the teacher to this group].
    (b)   A team [beaten badly by the Redskins] flew home yesterday.
    (c)   Some books [stolen from the library] were finally recovered.

(30)   Verb Phrase Headed by a Present Participle
    (a)   The student [sitting next to me] is stupid.
    (b)   That girl [running down the street] seems pretty scared.
    (c)   The people [demonstrating in Times Square] are crazy.

(31)   (a)   (b)

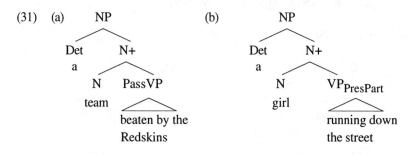

Most postmodifiers that are VPs can also be paraphrased by sentences in which they are complements of a linking verb, as in (32).

(32)   (a)   The student was [assigned by the teacher to this group].
    (b)   Some books were [stolen from the library].
    (c)   The student was [sitting next to me].
    (d)   That girl is [running down the street].

3.3 Adjective Phrases and Adverbs

Less common postmodifiers include APs in (33) and adverbs in (34). These also can be paraphrased by sentences with *be*, as in (35). (APs consisting of a single A cannot usually be postposed.)

(33) (a) It was a play [very popular in the 1940's].
     (b) The assassin was a man [angry about the outcome of the election].
     (c) He was a president [both popular and long-suffering].

(34) (a) The path [back] was covered with snow.
     (b) The walk [home] was very unpleasant.
     (c) The branch office [downtown] was unexpectedly closed.
     (d) The trip [abroad] will be postponed.

(35) (a) The play was [very popular in the 1940's].
     (b) The president was [both popular and long-suffering].
     (c) The branch office is [downtown].
     (d) The trip will be [abroad].

3.4 With-phrases

With-phrases differ from other postmodifying PPs in the meaning they convey. They are not paraphrased by sentences with *be*, but by those with *have*, as in (36).

(36) (a) a girl with a problem   *A girl is with a problem.
                                    A girl has a problem.
     (b) the student with a smile on her face
             *The student is with a smile on her face.
             The student has a smile on her face.
     (c) That child has a song in her heart.
     (d) The mother has a baby sitting in her lap.
     (e) A client has a valuable picture signed by Picasso.

Tree diagrams in (37) show the internal structure of postmodifying PPs with the preposition *with*.

(37)   (a)   N+   (b)   N+

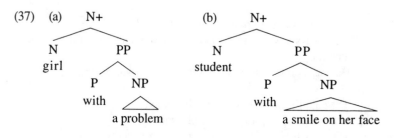

3.5 Postnominal Genitive NPs

A final constituent of the NP, one which we have not yet discussed at all, is
a postnominal genitive (PNG), shown in (38). PNGs are not modifiers, but
postposed determiners (discussed further in Chapter 30).

(38)   (a)   A friend [of Ivan's] called last night.
       (b)   The flood ruined a picture [of my mother's].
       (c)   I lost a book [of my sister's].
       (d)   She will do a report on an invention [of Edison's].

PNGs differ syntactically from PPs in that the complement of the
preposition *of* is not an ordinary noun phrase, but one in a special form
called the genitive, marked by the suffix /-s/. The genitive marker is attached
to an NP, as shown in the diagram in (39). (See Chapter 30.)

(39)

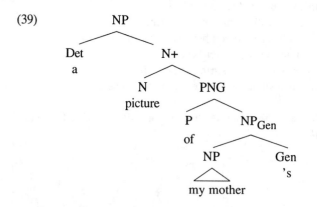

Postposed PNGs and PPs differ semantically as well, as shown by the
glosses in (40) and (41). (The PPs are complements.)

(40) (a) PNG   a picture [of my mother's]
           Gloss   The picture belongs to my mother.
      (b) PP   a picture [of my mother]
           Gloss   My mother is portrayed in the picture.

(41) (a) PNG   an invention [of Edison's]
           Gloss   The invention is credited to Edison.
      (b) PP   the invention of the light bulb
           Gloss   The "content" of the invention is the light bulb.

In summary, the constituents that function as modifiers of nouns are listed in (42). Remember that all postmodifiers exhibit the same external syntax, as in (24)(a). (PNGs, which are not modifiers, are not included.)

(42) Relative clause   a student [who was late to class]
      PP   a student [in the front row]
      Pass VP   a student [assigned by the teacher to this group]
      $VP_{PresPart}$ a student [sitting next to me]
      AP   a student [extremely fond of grammar]
      Adverb   the way [home]

Exercise 5
In the following sentences, underline each common noun, put each postmodifying phrase in square brackets, and identify its syntactic category.

1. The man over there sent my older sister a present wrapped in purple paper with silver stripes.
2. The new teacher in this school can't read the messy writing of a friend of ours named Mabel.
3. The house on the corner that was for sale was bought by some people from South America who have three kids.
4. A little boy with a stain on his shirt gave me a ticket to the new exhibit showing at the museum downtown this month.
5. A very strange couple from Toledo sitting behind us at the game last night got into a huge fight over some popcorn they bought.

6. I took the seat on the end by the back door because the girl that I hired to babysit had to go home at 10:00.
7. A student of Peter's recommended a book about syntax written by a linguist from Holland.

Exercise 6
Give a tree diagram for each noun phrase given below, using a triangle to abbreviate the internal structure of APs and PNGs.

1. the boys on the bus
2. the traffic downtown
3. your rather polite refusal
4. an idea of my uncle's
5. a house with ghosts living in the attic
6. the house owned by their clients
7. those students studying in the library by the park
8. a letter faxed to the president and leaked to the press
9. some children in the school cited by the Health Department
10. a large donation to the organization with friends in the White House

Exercise 7
Some postmodifying VPs headed by a present participle can be paraphrased by progressive sentences, as in (1). Can all postmodifying VPs be paraphrased in this way? In your answer, consider sentences like those in (2).

(1) (a) the student sitting next to me
     (b) The student is sitting next to me.

(2) (a) the dog barking at you
     (b) a statue standing at the entrance to the park
     (c) a delicious dessert consisting of chocolate and fruit
     (d) the children living on our block
     (e) a person knowing a lot about chemistry
     (f) a woman resembling your mother

Exercise 8

If a single common noun is modified by both a PP and a Rel-S, are there restrictions on the order in which they occur? Give examples to support your answer. (Be sure that the relative clause modifies the common noun in question and not a common noun within the PP.)

4. MULTIPLE MODIFICATION

A single noun may have more than one postmodifier, as in (43) and (44).

(43) (a) a man [from Russia]
      (b) a man [from Russia] [with a wart on his nose]
      (c) a man [from Russia] [with a wart on his nose] [named Ivan]
      (d) a man [from Russia] [with a wart on his nose] [named Ivan]
           [who sleeps in class]

(44) (a) a picture [in the study]
      (b) a picture [in the study] [painted by Picasso]
      (c) a picture [in the study] [painted by Picasso] [depicting a guitar
           player]
      (d) a picture [in the study] [painted by Picasso] [depicting a guitar
           player] [that I got at a garage sale]

Modification is a process of constructing a description that is increasingly restrictive, with each modifier narrowing down the set of "objects" that could fit the description. This process is recursive. The noun and the first modifier form a N+, and each successive modifier combines with the N+ to form a N+, as shown in (45). (It often helps to "read the tree" from the bottom up.)

(45)   (a)

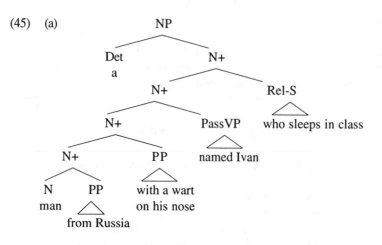

The order of postmodifiers is quite flexible, as shown in (46) and (47). It depends on *how* the speaker chooses to narrow down the description. There is a tendency to place PP postmodifiers closer to the head, with nonfinite VP postmodifiers following them, but this ordering is only a preference. The one clear restriction involves relative clause postmodifiers; they must come after the others, as shown in the ungrammatical sentences of (48). (Remember that we are considering only *restrictive* postmodifiers.)

(46)   (a)   a man [with a wart on his nose] [named Ivan] [from Russia]
       (b)   a man [from Russia] [named Ivan] [with a wart on his nose]
       (c)   a man [named Ivan] [with a wart on his nose] [from Russia]

(47)   (a)   a picture [in the study] [depicting a guitar player] [painted by Picasso]
       (b)   a picture [depicting a guitar player] [painted by Picasso] [(hanging) in the study]

(48)   (a)   *a man [who sleeps in class] [from Russia]
       (b)   *a man [from Russia] [who sleeps in class] [named Ivan]
       (c)   *a picture [that I got at a garage sale] [in the study]
       (d)   *a picture [in the study] [that I got at a garage sale] [painted by Picasso]

In terms of the ordering of postnominal constituents, PNGs and complements are closest to the noun, as in (49) and (50), where they are in square brackets. If both are present, PNGs tend to precede complements, as in (51).

(49) (a) a friend [of Ivan's] named Sasha.
      (b) *a friend named Sasha [of Ivan's]

(50) (a) the king [of Greece] with a large following
      (b) *the king with a large following [of Greece]

(51) (a) a picture [of Peter's] [of my family]
      (b) *a picture [of my family] [of Peter's]
      (c) the assumption [of the judge's] [that he is guilty]
      (d) *the assumption [that he is guilty] [of the judge's]
      (e) a donation [of our neighbors'] [to UNICEF]
      (f) *a donation [to UNICEF] [of our neighbors']

The existence of both premodifiers and postmodifiers leads to questions about their interaction as well. Consider (52) and (53), where the NPs in (c) have two modifiers and are ambiguous.

(52) (a) a tall man
      (b) a man from Russia
      (c) a tall man from Russia

(53) (a) the blue picture
      (b) the picture painted by Picasso
      (c) the blue picture painted by Picasso

The ambiguity arises because the NP can be constructed in two different ways, each conveying a different meaning, as shown in the trees for (52)(c) in (54).

(54)   (a)

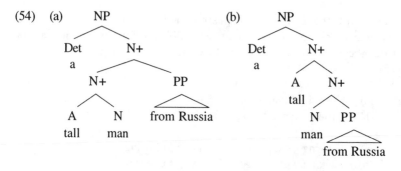

Here, as above, the ordering depends on how the speaker chooses to narrow down the description. In a conversation about, for instance, a conference of tall men from various countries, a speaker could use (52)(c) to pick out a tall man who was from Russia (as opposed to a tall man from France, Spain, Poland, etc.). An N+ with this meaning would be formed by first combining the noun with the A *tall* to form the N+ *tall man*. That is to say, the set of tall men is given, and this set is further restricted by the postposed modifier *from Russia*. This meaning is represented in the constituent structure in (54)(a).

On the other hand, in a conversation about a delegation of men from Russia, a speaker could use (52)(c) to pick out from this delegation a man who was particularly tall (as opposed to a man from Russia who was short or fat or articulate, etc.). an N+ with this meaning would be formed by first combining the noun with the modifier *from Russia* to form the N+ *man from Russia*. That is to say, the set of men from Russia is given, and further restricted by the preposed modifier *tall,* a meaning represented in the constituent structure in (54)(b).

In summary, noun phrases with multiple modifiers are built up in incremental stages, with modifiers added one at a time. Each modifier (after the first) combines with an N+ to form successively larger N+s. The effect of this process is a stacking of modifiers, hierarchically, within an NP. The order in which restrictive modifiers are combined with a noun, though extremely flexible, is not irrelevant. It depends crucially on the meaning the speaker wants to convey.

Finally, when analyzing sentences, keep in mind that most postmodifying constituents discussed here function as modifiers of VPs and complements of verbs as well. It is important therefore to pay special attention to the interpretation of such constituents (in particular, PPs and nonfinite VPs). In some sentences, a constituent may be interpreted in more than one way, and the possibility of ambiguity arises.

For instance, (55) is ambiguous because the PP *with the rifle* may be understood as a postmodifier of the noun *woman* ("the woman is holding the rifle") or as a modifier of the VP *shot the woman* ("they used the rifle to shoot the woman"). The two readings have different constituent structures, shown in (56).

(55)   The police shot the woman with the rifle.

(56)   (a)   S   (b)   S

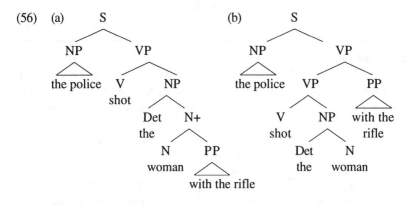

Sentence (57) is also ambiguous.

(57)   I want the landscape painted by Mrs. Jones.

The PassVP *painted by Mrs. Jones* may be understood as a postmodifier of the noun *landscape* (the speaker wants a landscape that was painted by Mrs. Jones). In this reading the subcategorization for *want* is [___ NP], as shown in (58)(a). Or the PassVP may be interpreted as a complement of the verb *want* (the speaker wants to have, i.e. cause, Mrs. Jones to paint a landscape). The subcategorization for *want* is [___ NP PassVP], as in (58)(b).

(58) (a)

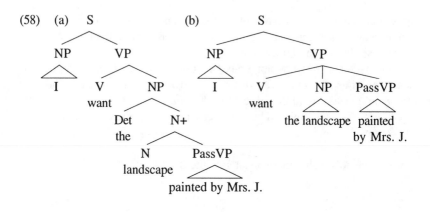

Exercise 9

Draw a tree diagram for each of the NPs below. Draw a diagram for each meaning of the ambiguous NPs in 8-9. (Use a triangle to abbreviate the internal structure of relative clauses unless they contain a relative clause.)

1. those editors from New York that don't know your work
2. those editors from a town I never heard of
3. a friend of Ivan's named Sasha
4. a picture of Peter's of my family lost in the fire
5. a woman in my class on grammar writing a dissertation on modifiers
6. a list of the poems that were published in this journal
7. a list of the poems that was published in this journal
8. a list of the poems that were published in the journal that was left in the library
9. the photograph of the beautiful Caucasian carpet that is hanging in the living room

Exercise 10

The following NPs have two readings. Give a context in which each might be natural and a tree diagram that corresponds to each reading.

1. a young woman from Kentucky
2. the blue vase on the table

Exercise 11

The pronoun *one* can be used in place of a repeated N+. In each of the following sentences, identify the N+ that the pronoun *one* stands for.

1. I bought a blue hat, and Mary bought a red one.
2. I bought a blue hat with a feather, and Mary bought a red one.
3. I bought a blue hat with a feather, and Mary bought one with a bow.
4. My sister wrote a long story about the Civil War, while my brother wrote a short one.
5. My sister wrote a long story about the Civil War, while my brother wrote one about Pearl Harbor.
6. The girls read a boring story about nurses, but the boys read an exciting one.
7. The girls read a boring story about nurses, but the boys read one about whales.
8. I prefer the blue vase on the table, but mother prefers the one on the floor.
9. I prefer the blue vase on the table, but mother prefers the red one.

Exericse 12

Give a tree diagram for these sentences, two diagrams if the sentence is ambiguous. (You may need to review the structure for adverbial modifiers of VPs in Chapter 4.)

1. The neighbors sold the trunk in the basement.
2. The neighbors locked the trunk in the basement.
3. I spied the beautiful princess looking out the window.
4. We got the dog certified by the Royal Lab Society.
5. The boys attacked the girls with kisses.

Exercise 13

In this chapter numerous claims are made about the ordering of modifiers. After reviewing the claims, examine a narrative passage of a page or so underlining each common noun and putting square brackets around all modifiers. Note the ordering of multiple modifiers and discuss the claims in light of what you find.

29

DETERMINERS

THIS CHAPTER deals with two of the most complex topics in English grammar, determiners and the definite-indefinite distinction. No area of English is more difficult for learners than the use of determiners in general and the articles in particular. Errors like those in (1) are common.

(1) (a) *Most people live in big family.
     (b) *What time do you go to the school?
     (c) *My father is doctor.

In (1)(a) an indefinite article (*a*) should be present but isn't, while in (1)(b), the definite article (*the*) is present, but shouldn't be. In order to understand such errors, we must first examine the different types of determiners and then consider the ways in which NPs are used.

We begin in Section 1 with a discussion of determiners and the formal properties of definite and indefinite NPs. We consider how NPs are used by speakers, looking in Section 2 at specific referring NPs and in Section 3 at describing NPs and generic NPs. We conclude in Section 4 with a discussion of some well-known problem areas of article use in English.

1. DETERMINERS AND THE DEFINITE-INDEFINITE DISTINCTION

An NP headed by a count noun must have a determiner. It is always the initial constituent of the phrase, combining with a N or N+ to form an NP, as shown schematically in (2).

(2)   (a)   NP   (b)   NP

         Det   N   Det   N+

In the examples throughout this book, the determiners have been articles, demonstratives, or genitive pronouns, but they may come from other syntactic categories as well, including genitive NPs of all types, some personal pronouns, and certain quantifiers.

Because the determiner "determines" whether an NP is definite or indefinite, determiners are accordingly divided into definite and indefinite subclasses. Definite determiners are listed in (3), with examples in (4).

(3)   Definite determiners
      (a)   The definite article: *the*
      (b)   Demonstratives: *this, that, these, those*
      (c)   Genitive NPs:
            Genitive pronouns   *my, our, your, his, her, its, their*
            Other genitive NPs   *the spy's, the teachers', that car's*
                                                    this smart student's, those girls', etc.
      (d)   Personal pronouns: *we/us, you*
      (e)   Definite quantifiers: *all, every, each, most,*
                                                     both, either/neither

(4)   (a)   *the* members, *the* delegation, *the* law firm
      (b)   *this* small sum, *that* blue car, *those* crazy people
      (c)   *my* sister, *your* favorite proverb, *his* time, *their* money
            the spy's secret, *that car's* exhaust fumes, *those girls'* mothers
      (d)   *we* teachers, *you* students, *us* girls, *you* boys
      (e)   *all* voters, *each* dog, *most* furniture, *both* cars, *either* arm

While most definite determiners combine freely with any common noun, the demonstratives *this* and *that* are restricted to nouns in the singular, the demonstratives *these* and *those* and the personal pronouns to nouns in the plural, and each of the quantifiers to particular subclasses of nouns (e.g. *each* and *every* to count nouns in the singular) (see Chapter 26, Section 3).

The indefinite determiners are listed in (5). As with the definite determiners, some are restricted to certain subclasses of nouns. Examples follow in (6).

(5) Indefinite determiners
    (a) The indefinite articles:
             With singular count Ns   *a/an*
             With plural count or noncount Ns   Ø (zero)
    (b) Genitive (indefinite) pronouns: *someone's, anyone's*
    (c) Indefinite quantifiers: *some* (unstressed),
                                                 SOME, ANY,
(stressed)

                                                 several, enough, no,
                                                 **any, *much*
        *Non-affirmative contexts only (e.g. negatives, interrogatives)

(6)   (a)   *a* delegation, *a* law firm, *a* tall building, *a* sick cat
              some members, *some* dogs, *some* water, *some* furniture
              Ø members, Ø dogs, Ø water, Ø furniture
       (b)   *someone's* car, *anyone's* books
       (c)   *some* [sm̩] *books, SOME* [sʌm] *people, several* songs,
              enough water, *no* cats, not *any* water, not *much* rice

A word should be said about the *two* indefinite articles listed in (5). With
singular count nouns we use the indefinite article *a* [ə] (with the variant *an*
[ən] (or [æn]) if the following word begins with a syllabic sound). With
plural count nouns and noncount nouns, we use the indefinite article Ø (a
zero article).

(7)   Singular count nouns—indefinite article *a*
       (a) They bought [a book] at Border's.
       (b) There is [a stain] on our new tablecloth.
       (c) I saw [a quarter] on the floor.
       (d) We bought [a new sofa].

(8)   Plural count nouns and noncount nouns
       Indefinite article Ø (zero article)
       (a) They buy [Ø books] at Border's.
       (b) [Ø Good students] do their homework on time.
       (c) This machine takes [Ø quarters].
       (d) In that store they sell [Ø furniture].
       (e) You have [Ø jelly] all over your face.

We posit a zero indefinite article Ø to account for the fact that whenever an NP headed by a common noun lacks an overt determiner, the NP is understood as indefinite. That is, we use the zero article as an indicator of indefiniteness. It should be shown when diagramming NPs, as in (9).

(9)

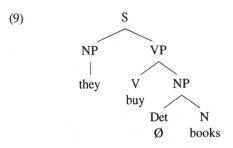

A potential for confusion arises with respect to the two indefinite quantifiers spelled <some>, which are used with plural count nouns and noncount nouns. Unstressed *some,* pronounced [səm] or [sm̩], is used to convey a specific, indefinite, small quantity as in "a few" or "a little bit." In some contexts it seems more or less equivalent to a zero article, as in (10), but in others, the two are not interchangeable, as shown in (11).

(10)　(a)　They bought [some / Ø books] at Border's.
　　　(b)　We got [some / Ø quarters] to do the wash.
　　　(c)　They spilled [some / Ø wine] on the new tablecloth.
　　　(d)　Put [some / Ø jelly] on my sandwich, please.
　　　(e)　Do you want [some / Ø coffee]?

(11)　(a)　[Good students] do their homework on time.
　　　(b)　*[Some [sm̩] good students] do their homework on time.
　　　(c)　 I like [Ø fish].
　　　(d)　*I like [some [sm̩] fish].
　　　(e)　 This desk is made of [Ø hardwood].
　　　(f)　 This desk is made of [some [sm̩] hardwood].

Stressed *SOME* [sʌm] (written here with small caps to distinguish it), on the other hand, conveys that part of a (larger) group is involved. NPs with stressed *SOME* can often be paraphrased "some, but not all," as in (12). (Note that *some* has other senses, not discussed here.)

(12)   (a)   I like [*SOME* fish], but I can't stand tuna.
       (b)   [*SOME* people] like opera, but others don't.
       (c)   [*SOME* parts of the country] received over two feet of snow.

The quantifier *any* also has stressed and unstressed variants. Unstressed *any,* used with plural count and noncount nouns, occurs in non-affirmative contexts such as negative and interrogative sentences and conveys "some" or "even the smallest amount," as in (13).

(13)   (a)   Did they buy [*any* books]?   They didn't buy [*any* books].
       (b)   Do you have [*any* money]?   We don't have [*any* money].
       (c)   Is there [*any* jelly] on my sandwich?
             There isn't [*any* jelly] on your sandwich.

Stressed *ANY,* used with singular or plural nouns, occurs in positive sentences, such as (14), where it conveys that the statement would be true for any members of the group named by the NP.

(14)   (a)   [*ANY* ESL teacher] will tell you that articles are difficult to
             learn.
       (b)   This word will be given in [*ANY* dictionary].

In addition to the determiners listed above in (3) and (5), WH-clauses are marked by a determiner that is a WH-word (*whose, which, what*). (See Chapter 23, Section 2 and Chapter 25, Section 4.2.)

(15)   (a)   [Whose mother] died?   John's mother.
       (b)   [Which car] do you want?   That one.
       (c)   He knows [what bus] he was supposed to take.

Finally, note that some of the quantifiers listed above have a more complex syntactic structure than indicated here, in that they can combine not only with a N or N+, but also with a PP or an NP, as in (16). Still other quantifiers, not listed above, are even more complex, in that they consist of a determiner and quantity expression (e.g. *a lot of, a few, a little* "a small amount") as in (17).

(16) (a) all [of the voters], each [of the dogs], most [of the furniture]
(b) several [of the songs], much [of the rice], enough [of the water]
(c) all [the voters], all [the furniture], both [the cars]

(17) (a) a lot [of the furniture], a few [of the children]
(b) a little [water], a little [furniture]
(c) Also: a couple of, a number of, a great deal of

And yet other English quantifiers (*many, few, little* "not much") are not determiners at all because they combine with a determiner, as in (18). These words have the syntactic behavior of cardinal numbers, shown in (19) and belong to the class of numerals discussed in Chapter 28.

(18) (a) I invited [Ø many people] to the party.
(b) [The many students] who passed the test are excused from class.
(c) [Ø Few people] could answer this question.
(d) [Those few people who participated] found the workshop useful.
(e) We have [Ø little hope] that she will be found alive.
(f) [The little joy] they had in their lives was at holiday time.
(g) We would be happy to share [the little food] we have.

(19) (a) I invited [Ø ten people] to dinner.
(b) [Those two students] should stay after class.
(c) I will give you [Ø five reasons] for this decision.
(d) [My five reasons] are as follows.
(e) [These three students] want to see you.

In addition to exhibiting such syntactically diverse behavior, quantifiers also make complex contributions to meaning. Because their syntax and semantics are beyond the scope of this chapter, we will concentrate below on NPs with determiners that are not quantifiers.

When the head of an NP is a common noun, the definiteness of the NP depends on the determiner. If the head of an NP is not a common noun, however, the definite-indefinite distinction is borne by the head of the phrase itself. Noun phrases whose head is a proper noun (i.e. a noun used by a speaker to refer to a unique entity) are always definite, as are NPs composed of a personal or demonstrative pronoun (*I, you, she, they; this, that,* etc.). Noun phrases with an indefinite pronoun (*someone, something, anything, no one,* etc.) are, as their name indicates, indefinite. Thus, proper nouns and pronouns have inherent or "built-in" definiteness. It is for this reason that they do not occur with determiners. (As noted in Chapter 25, some proper nouns do have a definite article, e.g. *The Andes,* but in such cases the article is required and unchanging, and not itself a marker of definiteness.)

The major markers of definite and indefinite NPs are summarized below. Having thus identified their form, we turn in the next three sections to explore the different meanings that they are used to convey.

		DEFINITE NP	INDEFINITE NP
Determiner			
	Articles	the	a / an, Ø
	Demonstratives	this, that, these, those	
	Genitive NPs	my, your, their, the car's	someone's, anyone's
	Personal pron	we/our, you	
	Quantifiers	all, every, each	some, SOME, ANY,
		most, both, ...	several, enough, no,
		either/neither	any, much
Noun		proper noun	
Pronoun		personal	indefinite
		demonstrative	

Exercise 1

Put a circle around the definite NPs and a square around the indefinites.

Beware of NPs with a zero (indefinite) determiner.

1. I have three sisters. The oldest one is a nurse. She is a member of the local nurses' union and was once the president of that organization. Since an office like that is very time-consuming, she didn't run for re-election so that she could spend more time with her children.

2. Mom, a Dr. Jones called you this afternoon. The doctor said the test results were not yet available and that his assistant would send you a report. Someone from his office will contact you soon about the bill and several other matters. You should call his office next week and make an appointment to see him.

3. Some people in my neighborhood have voiced opposition to the proposal for a new shopping mall. The head of the city council objects to their tactics and says that we taxpayers should be more supportive of the mayor's development plan. We believe taxpayers have a responsibility to make their views known on this issue.

Exercise 2
The definite article *the* is pronounced [ðə] or [ðij]. Read the noun phrases below and determine which form you could use in each. If you can, make a generalization about the distribution of the two forms in your dialect and test your generalization on other noun phrases.

1. the time
2. the hour
3. the angel
4. the angry child
5. the mess

6. the initial shock
7. the union
8. the idiot
9. the snake
10. the evening breeze

Exercise 3
Though normally unstressed, the definite article is occasionally stressed (indicated here with small capitals). Discuss the meaning it conveys in the following sentences.

1. A: Oh, look! There's John Kennedy.
   B: Do you mean THE John Kennedy?

2.   We've decided that you're THE woman we've been looking for!
3.   The dance will undoubtedly be THE event of the semester.
4.   Maureen's is THE place to go for great food.

Exercise 4

Read the following passage out loud and note your pronunciation of *some*
and *any*. Put a circle around each instance of unstressed *some* and
unstressed *any*.

Some teenagers are very rude. Ask any parent. At the movies last night
some kids wanted some candy, but didn't want to wait in line. They gave
some money to a friend of theirs in line in front of me. The manager saw
them and told them they couldn't buy any food without waiting in line.
Some of them got mad, but the rest apologized and later one even bought
me some popcorn. I am glad that at least some people believe in common
courtesy. I don't have any patience with line-cutting and any well-mannered
person will agree with me.

Exercise 5

The complex syntax of quantifiers presents formidable problems for learners
of English. Pick four quantifiers mentioned in the chapter and work out the
details of their syntax by answering the following questions. Present your
findings in a way that would be accessible to a learner of English.

1.   Is it a determiner or does it combine with determiners?
2.   If it is a determiner, is it definite or indefinite?
3.   Which syntactic categories does it combine with: N or N+, PP, NP?
4.   Which subclasses of Ns does it combine with: singular count, plural
      count, noncount?

---

2. REFERRING NOUN PHRASES

Before we can consider the conditions under which speakers use definite and
indefinite NPs, we need to have some understanding of the terms reference,
referring NP, and referent. Reference is the relationship between a linguistic

expression and something in the world (the real world or an imaginary one). A referring NP is one used by a speaker to refer, i.e. to point to persons, objects, concepts, etc. that she is talking about, while the person(s), object(s), etc. are the referents (of the referring NP). Referring NPs can be definite or indefinite, singular or plural, as in the examples in (20), where the referring NPs are in square brackets.

(20) (a) [Peter Jones] got married.
      (b) [That blue car in the No Parking Zone] belongs to [a friend of mine].
      (c) [The idea he proposed] was ridiculous.
      (d) [Some boys in our school] got into trouble with [the principal].

The speaker of (20)(a) uses the definite NP *Peter Jones* to refer to a specific individual with the name "Peter Jones." That individual is the referent of the NP. The speaker of (20)(b) uses the definite NP *that blue car in the No Parking Zone* to refer to an object and the indefinite NP *a friend of mine* to refer to an individual. Because of their pointing function, referring NPs serve as a link between the language and the world (real or imaginary).

2.1 Definite Referring NPs

When a speaker uses a definite referring NP, he conveys that he has a specific referent in mind and that he expects the addressee to be able to identify it from the clues provided. The addressee, on hearing a definite NP, must find the intended referent, perhaps by searching the immediate context or by examining the general knowledge that she and the speaker share. The successful use of a definite NP relies heavily on the assumption of shared knowledge. There is a tacit assumption (on the part of the speaker) that there is only one thing (or one set of things) that can "satisfy" the NP, which is associated in some clear way with the context.

For example, when a speaker utters (21), he conveys that he has a specific dog in mind and has provided what he thinks is sufficient information for the addressee to identify it. That is, he assumes the addressee will know or be able to figure out which dog, of all the possible dogs in the world, he has in mind.

(21)   Will you walk [the dog]?

This characterization of definite NPs, stated in terms of speaker expectations and assumptions about the addressee, makes it clear that the distribution of definite NPs (including the definite article) is not as much a matter of grammar (language form), as it is of pragmatics (language use). For this reason, it is not possible to give precise rules (such that a nonnative speaker might follow) for when to use a definite NP. The best we can do is to consider some typical situations in which reasonable native speakers use definite NPs as opposed to indefinite ones. In these situations speakers generally expect addressees to be able to identify the referents (of the definite NPs), and they can, therefore, serve as guidelines for nonnatives. (This list is not exhaustive.)

The referent is in the linguistic context. The referent of a definite NP is often something that was mentioned earlier in the discourse. In (22)(a), for example, the speaker introduces a dog by means of an indefinite NP, but continues to refer to it with definite NPs (given in square brackets). This phenomenon is called direct anaphoric reference because the indefinite NP *a funny-looking dog* serves as an anaphor to the definite NPs *it* and *that dog*.

(22)   (a)   I saw a funny-looking dog today. [It] had white fur and a
                  long red tail. I wonder who [that dog] belongs to.
         (b)   The bride wore a white dress and a long lace veil. I liked
                  [the dress] but thought [the veil] was tacky.
         (c)   I surveyed 45 Senators. [The Senators] all told me that
                  they earned too much money.

The referent is *implied* by something in the linguistic context. The referent of a definite NP is often not mentioned directly, but can be implied by something which is. Examples of this phenomenon, called bridging (or indirect anaphoric reference), are given in (23), where the definite NPs sanctioned by bridging are in square brackets.

(23)   (a)   We went to a new restaurant last night. [The food] was great,
                  but [the service] was lousy.
         (b)   Peter wanted to buy a car, but he couldn't afford [the insurance].
         (c)   Our daughter is in college. [The tuition] is outrageous.

Because of the general knowledge about restaurants that is shared by most speakers of English, once a restaurant has been introduced into the discourse, as in (23)(a), the existence of other things can be taken for granted, including the food, the service, the ambiance, the prices, the bar, the entertainment, etc. A speaker may bridge (and assumes that the addressee can bridge) from an established entity to things which can be assumed from it. Thus, she uses a definite NP [the food] because she expects that the addressee will be able to identify which food she has in mind (viz. the food in the restaurant just mentioned). Bridging thus involves both anaphoric reference and general knowledge.

The referent is present in the immediate context. A reasonable speaker assumes that an addressee can identify a referent that is, so to speak, right in front of them. Though the NP *the blackboard* has many possible referents, in a particular classroom, the speaker of (24)(a) can assume that the addressee can identify the intended referent and will know that she means the blackboard in the classroom in which they are located. This expectation is conveyed with a definite referring NP. (Only the most uncooperative addressee would respond to (24)(a) with the question, "Which blackboard? Do you mean the blackboard in this room?")

(24) (a) In a classroom: Write your name on [the blackboard].
      (b) In a living room: How do you like [the sofa]?
      (c) In any room: Would you turn on [the light]?
      (d) To someone reading a book: Is [that book] any good?
      (e) Pointing to a computer part: What's [this thing]?

The referent is located in *any* context shared by speaker and addressee. Shared contexts include, but are not limited to, a shared household (25), workplace (26), neighborhood, city (27), or country (28). In a large city, for instance, a speaker might reasonably assume that an addressee could identify such things as the mayor, the city council, the metro, the shopping district, the airport, and so on; thus speakers refer to all these things with definite NPs, as in (27). Even though there is more than one president in the world, there is only one in the situation shared by an American speaker and addressee located in the U.S., so a speaker can reasonably assume the addressee can identify the referent in (28)(a) as the president of the U.S.

(25)   (a)   Will you walk [the dog]?
       (b)   Someone has to clean [the bathroom].
       (c)   [The TV] is broken.

(26)   (a)   Be careful! [The boss] is in a bad mood.
       (b)   [The xerox machine] is broken.
       (c)   I'll meet you in [the cafeteria].

(27)   (a)   [The mayor] has just submitted a new budget.
       (b)   How do I get to [the airport]?

(28)   (a)   [The President] held a press conference today.
       (b)   My daughter wants to join [the army].
       (c)   [The French ambassador] went to [the State Department].

The notion of a context which speaker and addressee share extends to the world itself and general knowledge about stages in human history, science, etc. For example, even though there are many moons in the universe, there is only one in the general situation shared by speaker and addressee, i.e. in proximity to the earth. Hence, it is reasonable for the speaker of (29)(a) to assume that the addressee can identify the referent of the definite NP as the moon that revolves around the earth. Similarly, we use definite NPs for entities such as *the sun, the clouds, the stars, the sky, the universe.*

(29)   (a)   Several spaceships have landed on [the moon].
       (b)   Name a country that is located near [the equator].
       (c)   Oil spills are damaging [the environment].

Finally, a speaker may use a definite NP if the NP has only one possible referent. For instance, in (30), the referents of the definite NPs in square brackets are understood to include all the individuals (or objects) who meet the description; i.e. each description in (30) has only one possible referent. As a result, it is reasonable for a speaker to assume that the addressee can identify it. In other words, the speaker in such cases provides the necessary clues to the referent by giving a definite description that specifies it uniquely.

(30) (a) I gave "A's" to [the women in my class].

    (b) [The president of Tivali, a small island in the Pacific] held a press conference yesterday.

    (c) I went on vacation with [the family that lives next door].

    (d) You can get it at [the store on 34th street].

    (e) [The blue car in the No Parking Zone] belongs to me.

When the speaker uses the definite description *the women in my class,* he conveys that he has a specific set of women in mind and that he has given the addressee sufficient criteria to identify the set. If there is no prior context (linguistic or situational) that establishes a subset of women in the class as the referent, the addressee is justified in assuming that the speaker means the entire set (i.e. all the women in the class). (Consider the possible reaction of the addressee if she were to later meet a woman who had received a B in the class. Surely she would be justified in being surprised, if not irked for having been misled.)

Similarly, if a speaker responds to the question, "Where can I buy a lottery ticket?" with (30)(c), she conveys by the use of a definite NP that she has a specific referent in mind (i.e. a specific store) and that she believes she has given the the addressee sufficient criteria to identify it from the clues provided. The addressee, on the other hand, is justified in assuming that the speaker has given enough information to identify the referent and might reasonably conclude that the speaker means that there is only one referent, only one store on 34th street.

Finally, descriptive NPs like those in (31) occur *only* with a definite article and never with an indefinite one. They are always definite because they have only one possible referent in all contexts because of the meaning of the words *first, last, next,* and *fastest* (or any superlative). It would be bizarre to respond to (31)(a) with a question about the referent such as, "Which first flight on March 3, 1995, do you mean?"

(31) (a) the first flight on March 3, 1995

    (b) the last sentence of the third chapter of *Madam Bovary*

    (c) the next issue of *Time Magazine*

    (d) the fastest runner in the world

2.2 Failed Reference

As discussed above, the use of a definite referring NP involves expectations and assumptions on the part of the speaker about the addressee vis-à-vis the context. The speaker assumes that she has given the addressee sufficient information to identify the referent from the clues provided, often involving assumptions about shared context, general knowledge, etc. It is sometimes the case, however, that the speaker's assumptions about what is sufficient for the addressee are not accurate. When the speaker miscalculates in this way, communication goes awry. The addressee is unable to locate the intended referent, and we have an example of failed reference. In clear cases of failed reference, the addressee might seek clarification, as in (32). (Note that in reference repairs, WH-words are stressed.)

(32)   (a)   Teacher to Aide: Do you have [the papers]?
         (b)   Aide: WHAT papers?

The speaker of (32)(a) has one set of papers in mind and in using a definite description conveys that she believes that there is sufficient criteria for the aide to be able to identify it. This is a mistaken assumption, however, because the addressee must ask for clarification. This is the nature of failed reference: The speaker miscalculates, and the addressee fails to identify the intended referent of the definite NP. If the communicative failure is recognized, some sort of linguistic repair may be in order.

(33)   (a)   A: (Thinking that there is only one store on 34th street.)
                     You can get it at [the store on 34th street].
         B: (Knowing there are several stores on 34th street.)
                     WHICH store?
         (b)   A: (Temporary guest at B's house who took a phone message
                     from Dr. Jones.)
                     [Your doctor] called today.
         B: (Regularly seeing a podiatrist, an obstetrician, and a
                     psychiatrist.)
                     Which one?
         (c)   A: (Smiling and gesturing around the room which he has just
                     redecorated.)
                     How do you like [it]?
         B: WHAT?

When presented with a question like (33)(c), an addressee (who doesn't know or remember that the speaker redecorated), must search the context for a possible referent of *it* (does the speaker mean the walls, the carpet, the arrangement, the furniture, the smell, the fact that he cleaned the room for a change, etc.?).

At first glance, example (34) also looks like a case of failed reference in that the child seems not to be able to identify the dog that the mother has in mind.

(34) (a) Mother to Child: Have you walked [the dog]?
      (b) Child: WHAT dog?

However, in an ordinary household with a single dog, this supposed instance of failed reference represents a different kind of failure. The child refuses to expend any effort to locate the referent, but immediately asks for further clarification. Thus the communicative failure is due to singularly uncooperative linguistic behavior on the part of the child, and not to any unreasonable or incorrect assumptions on the part of the mother.

In conclusion, in the successful use of a definite noun phrase, the addressee correctly identifies the specific thing(s) that the speaker has in mind. If the addressee is not able to identify the intended referent, we have a case of failed reference. This surely happens much more often than we realize.

2.3 Indefinite Referring NPs

Having spelled out some of the conditions under which a speaker uses a definite referring NP, we can say simply that a speaker uses an indefinite NP when she does not feel there is justification for using a definite one. That is, she uses an indefinite NP if she has something specific in mind that she would like to refer to, but it has not been established in the discourse and she does not feel she can assume that the addressee can identify it from the NP itself, the context, general knowledge, or other shared experience.

A major use of indefinite referring noun phrases is to introduce something into the discourse. In (35)(a), for example, the speaker has no reason to believe that the addressee can identify a particular conversation that she has had, so she uses an indefinite NP to introduce it. Similarly, each of the bracketed indefinite NPs in (35) is being used to introduce something.

(35) (a) I had [an interesting conversation] today.
      (b) There was [some jelly] on the carpet. Does anyone know
           how it got there?
      (c) Dad, [someone] called you this morning. She said she
           would call back later.
      (d) Mama, [a man with a suitcase] followed me home today.
      (e) I'm looking for [a book], but I can't find it.

Indefinite NPs, as well as definite ones, have other functions, which we will
take up in the next section.

Exercise 6
Choose one of the following events or objects and name at least five things
that can be bridged from it. Then write a paragraph introducing the event or
object in the first sentence and using as many of the bridged NPs as you
can. Do you use definite NPs to refer to them?

a wedding, a ball game, a party, a country, a book, a picture, a computer

Exercise 7
Pick two of the following contexts, and, assuming that a speaker and
addressee share them, list eight things that a reasonable speaker could
assume the addressee could identify.

a classroom, a hotel, a picnic, a library, a university, a trial, an election

Exercise 8
What would the probable referent of the definite NP in (1) be if the speaker
and addressee are in the same city? If the speaker is in Kansas and the
addressee in Texas?

(1)   How is [the weather]?

Exercise 9
Discuss the difference in meaning between the (a) and (b) sentences below,
making reference to speaker assumptions.

(1)   (a) The house on the corner is for sale.
       (b) A house on the corner is for sale.

(2)   (a) I heard it from the girl in my class.
       (b) I heard it from a girl in my class.

(3)   (a) The students in this class are smart.
       (b) Students in this class are smart.
       (c) Some students in this class are smart.
       (d) SOME students in this class are smart.

Exercise 10
Pay close attention to conversations around you and to those on radio and TV. Identify any instances of failed reference and write out a description of them.

---

3. DESCRIBING AND GENERIC NOUN PHRASES

3.1 Describing NPs
Sometimes NPs are not used to refer, but to describe. NPs in predicate position are usually describing ones. Recall that predicate positions include the complements of linking verbs (36) and of complex transitives (37) (see Chapters 10 and 12). (The describing NPs are in square brackets.)

(36)   (a) Mozart was [a great composer].
       (b) Her only daughter became [a Supreme Court Justice].
       (c) Mr. Bradshaw is [(the) secretary of the PTO].
       (d) Kim Kennedy was [(the) captain of the team].

(37)   (a) Scholars consider him [an important figure of the 20th century].
       (b) They elected her [(the) chairman of the Duval Commission].

The predicate noun phrases are nonreferring because they are not used to refer to, i.e. to pick out, an individual. They are used to describe the individual referred to by the subject (in 36) or object (in 37). For instance the phrase *a great composer* does not refer to any individual; it describes an individual already referred to, namely the composer we all know by the name of Mozart. The speaker of (36)(a) uses the referring NP *Mozart* to pick out a particular individual and the nonreferring NP *a great composer* to say something about him.

Describing NPs are either definite or indefinite. An indefinite describing NP, as in (36)(a) and (b) and (37)(a) conveys that the description is not unique. For example, in uttering (36)(a), the speaker describes Mozart as a great composer, but leaves open the possibility that there are other great composers as well. A definite describing NP, however, conveys that there is only one individual (in the relevant domain) who fits the description. In uttering (36)(c) the speaker describes Mr. Bradshaw as *the secretary* and conveys that he is the only one in the relevant domain, the PTO.

In (36)(c) and (d) and (37)(b) the definite article is in parentheses because definite describing NPs can appear with or without the determiner, with no clear difference in meaning. Both the definite article and the absence of an article convey that the description is unique; i.e. that only one person meets the description. This absence of article is similar to the absence found with proper nouns, which are also determinerless and definite. It should not be confused with the zero article posited above (Ø) that signals an indefinite NP.

Although nonreferring noun phrases are often predicate NPs, they may appear in other syntactic positions as well, as shown in (38). The speaker of (38)(a) is not referring to a particular house, but merely describing one.

(38)   (a)   I would like to have [a clean house].
      (b)   Larry doesn't have [a job].

Because NPs can be used referentially as well as descriptively, it is not always clear how a particular NP is being used. Sometimes ambiguity results, as in (39).

(39)   (a)   John wants to marry [a Norwegian].
      (b)   I'm looking for [a child who speaks Estonian].
      (c)   Sally plans to buy [a cheap Mercedes Benz].

In uttering (39)(a) a speaker could be using the NP *a Norwegian* to refer to a particular person named Sonya who lives in Trondheim. Or, she could be using the NP to describe the kind of person John hopes to marry, someone he has not yet found. In this case, the NP *a Norwegian* is not used to refer, but only to describe the hypothetical object of John's desire. Perhaps he likes tall, blonde, blue-eyed women with Scandinavian accents.

3.2 Generic NPs

Generic statements are used to express typical properties of a class. The NPs in such sentences are used to refer to the class as a whole and not to specific members of the class. In form, the head of a generic NP is most often a plural count noun or a noncount noun, and the determiner is zero. The generic NPs in (40) are in square brackets.

(40) (a) [Ø Cats] have claws.
      (b) [Ø Cockroaches] are widespread.
      (c) [Ø Bears] hibernate in the winter.
      (d) [Ø Vinegar] makes a good spot remover.
      (e) [Ø Coffee] is grown in Brazil.

Generic statements are different semantically from universal statements, which are used to express essential or criterial properties. As shown in (41), NPs in universal statements most often have the same form as generic NPs, and it is often hard to tell them apart.

(41) (a) [Ø Cats] are mammals.
      (b) [Ø Pediatricians] treat children.
      (c) [Ø Water] is a liquid.
      (d) [Ø Pork] comes from pigs.

The generic statement in (40)(a) says it is typical for cats to have claws, and is consistent with the possibility that there are cats which do not (ones that are genetically deformed or have been declawed, for instance). On the other hand, the universal statement in (41)(a) is necessarily true of all cats. It would not be possible for there to be even one cat of which it is not true. Note that the difference between these two kinds of statements does not follow from the form of the NP, but from our knowledge of cats. People who know about cats can identify statements about them as definitional, (and universal), or merely typical (hence generic), though with respect to some properties they might sometimes disagree.

Generic NPs with zero determiner are used to identify the class as an undifferentiated whole. They contrast with generic NPs with an indefinite article, as in (42), which pick out any representative member of the class.

(42)   (a)   [A dog] is man's best friend.
       (b)   [A lawyer] makes lots of money.
       (c)   [A cockroach] carries germs.
       (d)   It's illegal to carry [a gun] without a permit.

Generics of this type are not used with predicates that name properties of the species as a whole, such as *be endangered, be extinct*, as in (43).

(43)   (a)   *A polar bear is not an endangered species. (Cf. Polar bears ...)
       (b)   *A mammoth is extinct. (Cf. Mammoths are extinct.)
       (c)   *A cockroach is widespread.

These two forms of generic NPs are less formal in tone than the third one which has a definite article and a singular count noun, as in (44).

(44)   (a)   [The Englishman] loves his garden.
       (b)   [The daffodil] is a lovely spring flower.
       (c)   [The kidneys] are located on either side of the body.
       (d)   [The telephone] and [the computer] are indispensible to [the modern businessman].
       (e)   My daughter plays [the flute].

These generic NPs indicate that the class is represented by a typical specimen. Generics of this form are widely used in technical and scientific writing, but only of certain classes of things, including well-defined sets of human beings, plant and animal species, organs of the body, and complex inventions, including musical instruments (a usage which is not formal).

Generic NPs with the definite article occur with a count noun in the plural in only two cases: with nouns that name nationalities and with NPs that have an adjective as head. Generic NPs with this form are used to refer to groups of people.

(45) (a) [The Japanese] eat raw fish.
     (b) [The Danes] smoke too much.
     (c) [The rich] get richer and [the poor] get poorer.

A summary of article use in generic NPs is given in the table below.
Note in particular that the generic use of noncount nouns allows only the
zero article.

TYPE OF NOUN	Zero Article	Indefinite Article	Definite Article
Count N singular	—	a camel	the camel*
Count N plural	books	—-	the Danes**
			the rich**
Noncount N	vinegar	—-	—-
The class is represented as:	an undiffer-entiated whole	any represen-tative member	a typical specimen

*Only possible with certain classes of nouns. They are always singular.
**Only possible with certain nouns that name nationalities and certain
adjectives. They are always plural.

Exercise 11
For each noun phrase in square brackets below, identify whether it is
referring, describing, or generic.

1.   [Dogs] not allowed.
2.   I don't like [dogs].
3.   I don't like [your dogs].
4.   [The dog] is [a mammal].
5.   [The lion at the zoo] gave birth to [a new cub].
6.   [The lion] is king of [the jungle].
7.   I'm looking for [a good book to read]. Can you recommend one?

8.   A: What are you doing?
      B: I'm looking for [a book], but I can't find it.
9.   [Her husband] is studying to be [an architect].
10.   [Germans] like to drink [beer].
11.   Did you see [those Germans]? [They] were speaking Japanese.
12.   We need to put the papers through for [a new ESL teacher].

Exercise 12

The following sentences contain predicate NPs with no determiner. Why are the sentences in (a) ungrammatical, but those in (b) grammatical?

(1)   (a) *My Aunt Chris is nurse.
       (b) My sister Barbara is head nurse of pediatrics for Mass General.

(2)   (a) *That guy is singer with a rock group.
       (b) That woman is lead singer for Kalebi.

Exercise 13

Pick a short passage of several paragraphs and highlight occurrences of the definite article *the*. Circle those which introduce a referring NP. Can the referent be recovered via one of the mechanisms discussed in Section 2.1? Identify any uses of the definite article which are *not* accounted for by the treatment of definite NPs in this chapter.

Exercise 14

Pick a passage of several paragraphs. Put square brackets around each NP and state whether it is referring, describing, or generic. For referring NPs, specify whether the reference is definite or indefinite. For each instance of a definite referring NP, can the referent be recovered via one of the mechanisms discussed in Section 2.1?

Exercise 15

Write a short description of the ambiguity of (39)(b) or (39)(c).

Exercise 16

Describe the difference in meaning between the bracketed NPs with a definite article and those without one.

(1)   (a)   My neighbor volunteers at [the school].
       (b)   My neighbor goes to [school].

(2)   (a)   Every day I walk past [the church].
       (b)   Once a week I go to [church].

---

4. RESIDUAL PROBLEMS

In this section we discuss some problematic areas of article use that pose
particular difficulties for learners of English. We divide them into contexts
where no article is allowed, though one might be expected and is often
incorrectly added by nonnative speakers, and those in which the definite
article is required, though the conditions for its use seem not to be met.

4.1 Singular Count Nouns with No Article

A generalization given above is that an NP headed by a singular count noun
must have an overt determiner (except when used in definite describing
NPs). The zero article is used only with plural count nouns and noncount
nouns. There are, however, a number of circumstances in which a singular
count noun appears to occur without an article.

   Institutions of life and society. A number of nouns that name
institutions of life or society are used without an article, as in (47).

(47)   (a)   She went to [prison].
             She is in [prison].
       (b)   She goes to [college].
             She is at [college].
       (c)   My husband went to [sea].
             My husband is at [sea].
       (d)   David went to [class].
             David is in [class] now.

(47)(a) cannot be used about guards or cooks who work in a prison, but only
about a person who is in a specific role vis-à-vis the institution, namely, a

prisoner. Thus, the phrase *in prison* does not convey that someone is in a particular location, but that she is in a specific relationship to the institution, with the noun *prison* naming an abstract institution that is a noncount noun and not a concrete location that is a count noun. Some evidence that it is noncount comes from the fact that it lacks a plural form (**She is in prisons*). The lack of determiner, rather than being exceptional, follows from the fact that *prison*, in this sense, is a noncount noun.

A similar argument could be made for any of the nouns without articles in (47). For example, if someone is at college, she is in a particular institutionally-defined role, the role of college student. One couldn't say (47)(b) about a college professor or librarian on campus. In this expression the noun *college* is a noncount noun that names an abstract institution and not a count noun that names a concrete location. The lack of article follows from the fact that it is noncount, as shown by the lack of a plural (**She is at colleges*).

These nouns are also nonreferring. They can't be used to pick out a specific prison or college, for example, and they can't be modified (**she is at near-by college*). Modification is only possible if one uses the related count noun, thereby requiring a determiner (*she is at a near-by college*).

Means of transportation and communication. When nouns that name means of transportation and communication occur as objects of the preposition *by,* they are used without an article, as in (48).

(48) (a) We came by [bus], but will leave by [plane].
     (b) I prefer to travel by [train].
     (c) We communicate regularly by [fax] and [phone].

The explanation offered above for lack of an article applies here as well. Though the nouns *bus, train, phone,* and so on, may be used as count nouns, in the sentences of (48) they are noncount. They denote abstract and noncount means of transportation and communication, and not specific (concrete and countable) objects or instruments. Plural forms are not possible. For instance, one can't use *bus* in the plural in a sentence like (48)(a) even if several buses are involved (**We came by three buses*).

Other common expressions with no article, which pose common problems for learners, are listed below.

(49) (a) Times of day and night
           at dawn, before morning, by noon, after nightfall ...
      (b) Seasons
           Spring has arrived! Winter is gone.
      (c) Meals as institution
           We eat dinner at 8:00. Please have breakfast with us.
           Lunch is at 1:00.
      (d) Idioms (frozen pieces)
           We walked [hand in hand].
           We don't see [eye to eye].
           We travelled [mile upon mile].
           They act like [husband and wife]
           He took [advantage] of her.
           Also: face to face, cheek to cheek, back to back, hand to mouth

4.2 Nouns with the Definite Article

As discussed above, using a definite referring NP should convey that the
speaker has a specific thing in mind and assumes the addressee can identify
it. There are, however, a number of circumstances in which the use of a
definite article doesn't seem to follow this guideline, as in (50).

(50) (a) I was listening to [the radio].
      (b) They took [the train].
      (c) My neighbors often go to [the theater].

Speakers using an NP of (50) would not necessarily expect the addressee to
locate a specific radio, train, or theater. For instance, (50)(a) does not convey
that the speaker has a specific radio in mind (whether one means by this a
specific instrument or a specific radio station). It is not an instance of failed
reference if the addressee wishes to inquire further, as in (51).

(51) (a) Which radio were you using?
      (b) Which station were you listening to?

Similarly, in (50)(c) the NP *the theater* does not refer to a specific building
or to a specific theater company, but is perfectly consistent with a situation
in which the neighbors attend plays in a number of different places.

What is the referent of these NPs? They do not stand for specific, concrete objects or locations, but for specific abstract institutions. The speaker uses the NP *the radio* in (50)(a) to refer to a specific institution within mass communication (cf. similar uses of *the paper* or *the news*). The speaker uses *the theater* in (50)(c) to refer to the cultural institution of the theater (cf. also *the movies, the opera, the ballet*). In using a definite NP the speaker is assuming that the addressee can identify the shared cultural institutions *radio, theater,* etc. and not specific instruments or locations that deliver them.

Like *theater* and *radio*, many nouns have both count and noncount senses. Otherwise seemingly paradoxical uses of the definite article with a count noun can often be explained by realizing that a different, noncount sense is involved. The examples of (52) contain definite NPs, but the speaker does not (necessarily) use them to refer to specific locations that he expects the speaker to be able to identify.

(52)   (a)   Mom went to [the store].
       (b)   In the summer we spent two weeks at [the beach].
       (c)   I have to go to [the doctor's].

Exercise 17
Above, the lack of a determiner was discussed with respect to expressions such as *by train*. Name three other means of transportation and three methods of communication. Use them in sentences and note whether a determiner is allowed or not allowed.

Exercise 18
Consider the following examples and describe the (abstract) institution conveyed by each bracketed noun phrase. It may help to consider situations in which one could use the sentence and those in which one could not.

1.   I'll see you in [court].
2.   We always go to [church].
3.   She is in [kindergarten].
4.   The baby is in [bed].

Exercise 19

Whether a count noun can be used as a noncount in the institutional sense discussed in this chapter is conventionalized in that not every noun can be used in this way. This fact accounts for two well-known differences between British and American usage shown below. Discuss the use of articles in each of these.

1. American English: My mother is in [the hospital].
   British English: My mother is in [hospital].

2. American English: She's at [the university].
   British English: She's at [university].

Exercise 20

The names of diseases seem to show a bewildering variety of patterns with respect to the article used and whether the noun is singular, plural, or noncount. Add eight to ten diseases to the appropriate column in the table. Which column has the most members? Can you make any generalizations about the grammar of disease? (Parentheses indicate that *the* is optional.)

ARTICLES AND DISEASES

a/an SG NOUN	the SG NOUN	(the) PL NOUN	Ø NONCOUNT
a cold	the flu	the mumps	cancer

Exercise 21

Explain why the sentences in parentheses are ungrammatical.

1. I once had a dog. Her name was Poppy. She always came when I called her. She was a good dog.   (Not *She was the good dog.)

2. Do you know Mr. Peters? He teaches science at Swanson. He's a great teacher.   (Not *He's the great teacher.)

Exercise 22

Each of the following sentences contains an error in article use. Discuss the errors using concepts introduced in this chapter.

1.   *Most people live in big family.
2.   *After the school I go home and eat.
3.   *I don't have brother.
4.   *You are serious!?   You are pulling the leg.
5.   *My father is doctor.
6.   *The life is difficult.
7.   *She got very mad at the Donald.
8.   *It's the human nature to change.

THE EXISTENTIAL CONSTRUCTION

IN THIS WORKSHEET we explore the properties of the special sentence type in English illustrated in (1).

(1)   (a)   There's a mouse in the bathtub.
         (b)   There was a man on the balcony.
         (c)   There are some students in the ballroom.
         (d)   There are many unsolved problems in linguistics.

Before we proceed, however, it is necessary to distinguish the word *there* found in (1), called "existential *there*," from a different word *there*, the locative *there* in (2).

(2)   (a)   There's Romeo! He's on the balcony.
         (b)   There's just the man we've been looking for.
         (c)   The mouse is over there.

Pronounce (1) and (2) out loud, and notice the phonological difference between them. Existential *there* is unstressed, while locative *there* receives primary or secondary stress. Locative *there,* which has the function of an adverbial of location, could be accompanied by pointing. One would not accompany existential *there* by pointing. In the remainder of this worksheet, we consider only existential *there*.

1. THE SYNTACTIC FUNCTION OF EXISTENTIAL *THERE*

What is the syntactic function of existential *there*? There are a number of ways to argue that a particular word or phrase has a particular syntactic function. For example, if you consider the data in (3) - (5), there might come to mind an important clue about the function of existential *there*. What is the relevance of these sentences?

(3)   (a) They were late.
        (b) Were they late?

(4)   (a) That note was written by Susan.
        (b) Was that note written by Susan?

(5)   (a) There was a mouse in the bathtub.
        (b) Was there a mouse in the bathtub?

The argument implicit in (3) - (5):

Step 1.   Yes-no questions are formed in English by applying the rule of
            inversion. (Review the rule of Inversion if you need to.)
Step 2.   In sentence (3)(b), existential *there* has been inverted with the
            first auxiliary.
Step 3.   The fact that *there* inverts with the first auxiliary is an argument
            that it is a _____.

   A similar argument can be constructed for the data in (6) and (7), which
represent two additional ways to demonstrate the function of *there*.
Examine the data and write out the two arguments in steps, as above.

(6)   (a) Rodney was eating an octopus, wasn't he?
        (b) It's raining, isn't it?
        (c) Bill kissed Harriet, didn't he?
        (d) Last Saturday was a great day, wasn't it?
        (e) There is a mouse in the bathtub, isn't there?

(7)   (a) Susan said that the guy from Ohio was happy, and so he was.
        (b) Harriet said that the Orioles won, and so they did.
        (c) Frank said that Lacy would be elected and so she was.
        (d) Joe said that there was a mouse in the bathroom and so there
             was.
        (e) The principal said that there were students in the ballroom and so
             there were.

   In conclusion, since existential *there* behaves like a _____, it must be a _____.

1. RESTRICTIONS ON EXISTENTIAL CONSTRUCTIONS

1.1 Restrictions on the Verb
In all the examples given above, the verb was a form of *be*. There seem to be other verbs which can appear with existential *there,* however. Make a list of as many as you can and determine if the verbs have anything in common syntactically or semantically. Examine your list carefully, and there might come to light some interesting facts. If looking at grammatical sentences does not help, examine ungrammatical ones like those in (8), which illustrate verbs that do not occur in the existential construction. Consider the subcategorization frames of these verbs and of the verbs in existential sentences. Consider the semantic subclasses (i.e. events, activities, or states). Think carefully, and there might emerge a new fact about the existential construction.

(8)   (a)   *There laughed two men in the room.
       (b)   *There danced two mice in the bathroom.
       (c)   *There sang some men an aria from Aida.
       (d)   *There ate peanut butter two small children.

The verb in an existential construction must be _____.

1.2 Restrictions on the NP Following there
There appears also to be a restriction on the type of NP which follows existential *there.* Look over the examples given thus far and the following ungrammatical sentences and see if you can make any generalizations.

(9)   (a)   *There was Romeo on the balcony.
       (b)   *There was the boy in the ballroom.
      (c)   *There wasn't the bear in sight.
      (d)   *There weren't those cars in the parking lot.

The NP following existential *there* must be _____.

Although this NP is not the syntactic subject (the word *there* is the subject, as shown in (2), it is understood or interpreted as the subject. In a rephrasing of an existential sentence it would appear as the subject, as in (10)(b). For these and other reasons as well, we will refer to the NP following the verb in an existential sentence as a "pseudosubject."

(10) (a) There is a mouse in the bathtub.
      (b) A mouse is in the bathtub.

2. THE SYNTAX OF EXISTENTIAL CONSTRUCTIONS

In all the existential sentences given thus far, the VP contains, besides the verb, a noun phrase and a place phrase, an adverbial indicating a location. (In some cases the "location" is understood abstractly and/or metaphorically, as in *there are problems in your solution.*) We assume that all three constituents are sisters, members of the same VP, and accordingly assign existential sentences the syntactic structure in (11).

(11)

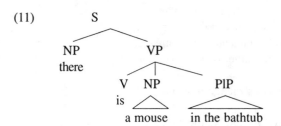

The sentences of (12) show that existential constructions can contain other types of phrases as well as place phrases. Identify the constituents in square brackets.

(12) (a) There is a stranger [lurking behind that bush].
      (b) There is a statue of Washington [standing in the center of the park].
      (c) There was one team [beaten by the Redskins last year].
      (d) There was a rare book [stolen from the library yesterday].

Occasionally, an existential sentence has only an NP as part of the verb phrase, as in (13). Such sentences describe existence.

(13)   (a)   There is a Santa Claus.
    (b)   There is a God.

Tree diagrams for (12)(a) and (12)(c) are given in (14).

(14)   (a)

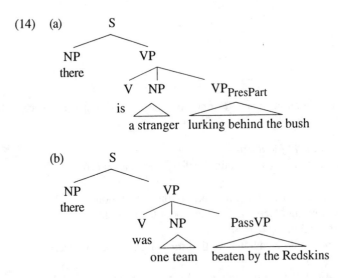

We can sum up the syntactic properties of the existential construction as follows:

1.   The subject NP is existential *there*.
2.   The VP contains an intransitive verb of existence or coming into existence plus an indefinite NP (the pseudosubject) plus either a place adverbial, VP headed by a present participle, a passive VP, or (rarely) nothing.

(15)

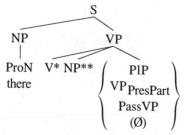

Conditions:
*The verb must be intransitive and describe existence or coming into existence.
**The NP must be indefinite.

2.1   Complication 1: Auxiliaries
Existential sentences can also contain auxiliary verbs, as in (16).

(16)   (a)   There have been some mistakes in the calculations.
    (b)   There might emerge a new fact about the existential
        construction.
    (c)   There should be a letter waiting for you at the post office.

We assume that the VPs of the existential sentences are as shown in (15),
but that there may be auxiliary verbs intervening between the special subject
NP and VP of existential sentences. A tree diagram for (16)(a) is given in
(17).

(17)

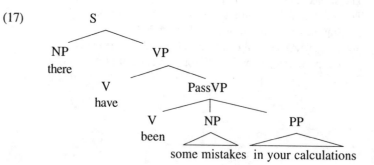

2.2 Complication 2: Verb Agreement

Existential sentences show an additional complication when it comes to verb agreement (see Chapter 26). Examine (18) - (20) and note the difference between the (a) and (b) sentences. Are the (c) sentences are grammatical or ungrammatical in your dialect of English? If they are ungrammatical, can you say why?

(18) (a) There is a bird living in my attic.
      (b) There are birds living in my attic.
      (c) *There is birds living in my attic.

(19) (a) There was an accident on the Beltway last night.
      (b) There were five accidents on the Beltway last night.
      (c) *There was five accidents on the Beltway last night.

(20) (a) There seems to have been a serious error on my tax return.
      (b) There seem to have been several serious errors on my tax return.
      (c) *There seems to have been several serious errors on my tax return.

Although not all speakers of English agree with these grammaticality judgements, those that do have a verb agreement rule with the following stipulation: In existential sentences, the verb agrees with the pseudosubject and not with the subject.

Exercise 1

State a version of verb agreement for existential sentences that works for speakers who accept all the sentences in (18) - (20).

Exercise 2

Give tree diagrams for the following sentences.

1.   There is a mouse in my bathtub.
2.   There must have been a thief hiding in the bushes.
3.   There have been some miscalculations made here.
4.   I believe there was too much salt in the soup.

30
GENITIVE NOUN PHRASES

IN THIS CHAPTER we conclude the study of NPs with a closer look at genitive NPs. As seen in the previous chapter, genitive NPs function as one type of definite determiner, but they have other functions as well. We begin in Section 1 with a discussion of their internal syntax, considering in particular the forms of the genitive suffix. After examining their different functions in Section 2, we turn to the meanings of genitive NPs in Section 3. Finally, we discuss some conditions that govern the alternation between the genitive as a prenominal determiner or a postposed *of*-phrase.

1. THE INTERNAL SYNTAX OF GENITIVE NPS

Genitive NPs are NPs which have the suffix /-s/, usually written <'s>, as shown in (1). The genitive NPs are in square brackets.

(1)　(a)　[The teacher's] car broke down.
　　　(b)　[The teacher of music's] car broke down.
　　　(c)　Everyone was amazed at [the teacher from Key School's] denunciation of the new proposal.

If the NP ends with the head noun, as in (1)(a), the genitive suffix is attached to the noun, a fact which has misled people to analyze it as a noun suffix. However, the suffix is in fact attached to the last word of the NP, e.g. a complement in (1)(b) or postmodifier in (1)(c).

The genitive suffix has three phonetic variants: [-əz] following sibilants, [-s] following voiceless segments, and [-z] elsewhere. It is realized as zero (i.e. is not pronounced) when it is added to a phrase-final noun with a regular plural suffix, in which case it is written only as an apostrophe, as in (2).

506

(2)   (a)   We cleaned up [the boys'] mess after they left.
             (The mess was made by the boys.)
       (b)   [Those busses'] brakes began to screech.
             (The brakes of those busses.)

Note that the regular genitive suffix /-s/ is used if the suffix is added to a
phrase-final noun with an irregular plural (one that does not end in /-s/),
including nouns with zero plural (see Chapter 26) (cf. *the fish's skeletons,
the children's excuses*).

   Personal pronouns are irregular in that they have two different genitive
forms, as shown in (3), neither of which has a separate genitive suffix. The
forms in (3)(a) are used if the genitive NP is either a determiner in an NP
which has a head noun or the subject of a gerundive; these are sometimes
called weak forms. The pronouns in (3)(b), known as strong forms, are used
in other contexts, where the pronoun is the only constituent of the NP (see
(4)(d) and Section 2). (Note that *its* does not have a strong form.)

(3)   (a)   Weak: my, our, your, his, her, its, their
       (b)   Strong: mine, ours, yours, his, hers, theirs

Also lacking an isolatable genitive suffix is the WH-word *whose.*

   As noted in Chapter 22, we assign genitive NPs a structure in which the
suffix combines with an NP, as in (4). Genitive pronouns are shown with
no internal structure, as in (4)(c) and (d), with the missing structure in (4)(d)
indicated with a blank line.

(4)   (a)   (b)

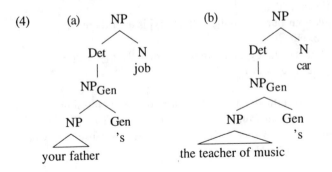

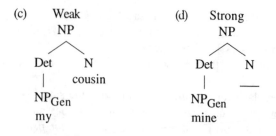

2. THE EXTERNAL SYNTAX OF GENITIVES

2.1 Genitive NPs as Definite Determiners

As shown in all examples thus far and discussed in Chapter 29, genitive NPs function as definite determiners within NPs. In using a genitive determiner, the speaker conveys that she has a specific entity in mind and that she believes the addressee can identify it through its relationship to the (referent of the) NP expressed in the genitive. (See Section 3.)

Genitive determiners may also occur in the syntactic position of an NP without an expressed head noun, as in (5), where the free-standing genitives are in square brackets. Recall that this context calls for the strong forms of the personal pronouns, as in (5)(c) - (d).

(5)   (a) My vacation house is in France. [Mary's] is in Belgium.
             cf. [Mary's vacation house]
       (b) Your idea had potential, but [Jason's] was more practical.
             cf. [Jason's idea]
       (c) I think your purse is in the hall. [Hers] is over there.
             cf. [her purse]
       (d) His flights of fancy are more imaginative than [yours].
             cf. [your flights of fancy]

Often this is a case of ellipsis: a specific noun (or N+) is missing and can be unambiguously filled in from context. In the sentences of (5), full NPs could have been used, but would have been redundant because they would contain a repeated noun (or N+).

Free-standing genitive determiners often occur in predicate position following a linking verb. In this position, the use of a head noun is not only redundant, it is awkward, at times bordering on ungrammatical. In some sentences, is it not even possible to specify what the head noun might be, as in (6)(d) - (f).

(6) Free-standing   With head noun

(a) The house is [Mary's].   Mary's house

(b) The idea was [Jason's].   Jason's idea

(c) That purse is [hers].   her purse

(d) Everything in this room is [mine].   ?my things, ?my stuff

(e) Three loaves of bread and two pounds of apples are [Joe's].
?Joe's three loaves of bread and two pounds of apples
?Joe's bread and apples

(f) Will you be [mine]? Oh, baby, I'm [yours].

It is also not clear what the head noun would be when the free-standing genitive refers to a location such as a residence, an institution, a public building, or a place of business. In such uses, known as local genitives, it is only understood that a location is intended.

(7) (a) They're going to [Betty's] tonight. ?apartment, ?house, ?cafe

(b) She went to [St. Patrick's].   ?church, ?cathedral, ?school

(c) Pam took him to [the doctor's]. ?office, ?clinic, ?hospital

(d) I got this at [Mr. Appleby's].   ?grocery, ?drug store, ?bar, ?cabin

The genitive of personal pronouns cannot be used in this way.

(8) (a) My friends are going to Sally's for dinner.

(b) *My friends are going to hers for dinner.

(c) *Whose are you going to?

(d) I had a fever and they took me to the doctor's.

(e) *I had a fever and they took me to his.

Genitive determiners are not the *only* determiners that can occur in the syntactic position of an NP without an expressed head noun, as shown in

(9). In tree diagrams for free-standing determiners, the position of the
unexpressed N (or N+) is indicated with a blank line (like in (4)(d)), as
shown in (10).

(9)   (a)   Pat prefers these flowers, but Mike likes [those].
        (a)   Of her students, [most] study pretty hard.
        (b)   I've had enough coffee. Have you had [enough]?

(10)   (a)   (b)

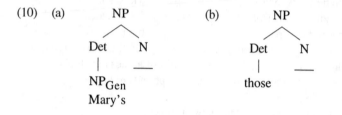

2.2 Postnominal Genitives (PNG)

As noted, if the genitive NP is in determiner position of an NP, the NP is
definite. However, if a speaker wants to express one of the meanings
conveyed by the genitive (see Section 3), but does not feel that the
conditions for the use of a definite NP are met or has reason to use a
different definite determiner (e.g. *this* or *that*), she has recourse to a
construction known as a postnominal genitive: The genitive NP is
expressed as the complement of the preposition *of* and positioned after the
head noun. The PNG construction frees up the determiner slot, so to speak,
which can then be filled by a different determiner. Compare the NPs in (a)
(which have preposed genitive determiners) with the NPs in (b) (which have
PNGs). (The genitives and PNGs are in square brackets.)

(11)   (a)   Genitive as determiner: We went to visit [Kim's] uncle.
        (b)   Genitive in PNG: We went to visit an uncle [of Kim's].

(12)   (a)   Genitive as determiner: [Pat's] house is for sale.
        (b)   Genitive in PNG: That house [of Pat's] is for sale.

In brief, speakers use PNGs when they want to express the relational
meaning of the genitive, but have reason to use a different determiner.

(13)   (a)   (b)

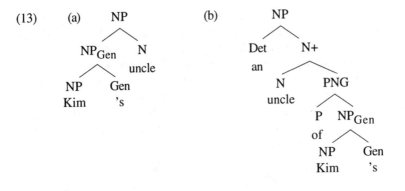

2.3 Subjects of Gerundives

As noted in Chapter 22, genitive NPs are used to express the subject of a gerundive. The weak forms of the personal pronouns are used here.

(14)   (a)   [[The child's] crying about everything] is very annoying.
        (b)   I dislike [[my sister's] taking charge of these matters].
        (c)   [[Her] complaining to the principal] caused a scandal.

These three positions are structurally the same, and we can summarize by noting that genitive NPs are the left-most constituent of an NP. The presence or absence of rest of the NP will determine which form of the personal pronoun must be used.

2.4 Genitives as Modifiers

Finally, genitives can function as modifiers, as in (15), where the genitives are in italics.

(15)   (a)   I sent my daughter to [that famous [[*girl's* school] in Kentucky]].
            that famous school for girls in Kentucky
        (b)   He walked back to [the newly-raked [*pitcher's* mound]].
            the mound for a pitcher
        (c)   I checked out [those three [[*children's* books] you recommended]].
            those three books for children

Genitive modifiers are distinct from genitive determiners in that the modifiers are not the leftmost constituent of an NP. In (15), the modifiers are preceded by a determiner and even another modifier. For instance, as shown by the bracketing, in (15)(a) the word *that* functions as a determiner of the N+ *famous girl's school in Kentucky* and is not a determiner within a genitive NP determiner. The adjective *famous* modifies *girl's school* (or *girl's school in Kentucky*) and not just *girl's* (i.e. it is the school that is famous, not its students). The modifying genitive and noun form a compound noun, as shown in in (16).

(16)

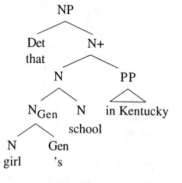

Note that the modifying genitive is a *noun*, not an NP, another distinction between genitive modifiers and genitive determiners, which are always (full) NPs. Consistent with this fact, genitive modifiers do not generally contain determiners or other modifiers, unless the genitive noun itself is a compound noun. The sentences of (17) are ungrammatical in the interpretations indicated by the bracketing.

(17) (a) *that [famous girls'] school in Kentucky
      (b) *that [girls with problems'] school in Kentucky
      (c) *the [left-handed pitcher's] mound
      (d) *the [three children's] books
           (cannot mean "the books of three children")

In (17)(a), the intended interpretation indicated by the bracketing could be paraphrased *that school for famous girls*. (The intended interpretation might be possible if one analyzes the expression *famous girls* as a compound noun.)

Many compound nouns with genitives are idioms, i.e. expressions with specialized, often unpredictable meanings. They must be listed in the lexicon and learned individually. A small sample is given in (18).

(18) (a) teacher's pet   ("favorite of the teacher")
      (b) cat's cradle   (a child's game)
      (c) dog's life   ("slavish existence")
      (d) women's movement   ("feminism")
      (e) men's room   ("bathroom for men")
      (f) old wives' tale   ("superstitious folklore")
      (g) Montezuma's revenge   ("diarrhea")

3. MEANINGS OF THE GENITIVE DETERMINER

A genitive (whether prenominal, free-standing, or in a PNG) expresses the fact that there is a relationship between the (referent of the) NP in the genitive and (the referent of) the head noun: The referent of the head is identified in terms of its relationship to (the referent of) the genitive. For example, in *your father's job*, the head noun *job* is identified as the one connected in some way to your father (the job he currently holds, the job he is advertising, the type of job he has or had, etc.). The relationship between the head noun and the genitive NP is vague and must be calculated by the addressee from the context and other clues.

In the phrase *Jill's book* , the book is identified by its relationship with Jill, but the nature of that relationship is unspecified: The book may be one she owns, one she wrote or is reading or is holding, or one she gave a report on in class yesterday, and so on. In using a genitive determiner, the speaker conveys that she has a specific book in mind and that she believes the addressee can identify it through its relationship to Jill.

In spite of this inherent vagueness, though, we can mention a few meanings commonly expressed by the genitive. First, the genitive NP may possess or own the head noun as in (19). The fact that genitive NPs are called possessives in many grammars is evidence of the frequency and salience of this meaning.

(19)   (a)   [Jody's] car   "the car which Jody owns"
       (b)   [that student's] pen   "the pen that belongs to that student"
       (c)   This money is [theirs].   "the money that belongs to them"

If we interpret possession in a very broad sense, we might include the
relationships of (20) (where the entity "possessed" is a human being), (21)
(which involve kinship), or (22) (which involve an attribute or behavior).

(20)   (a)   [my] new baby   "the new baby that I have"
       (b)   [that woman's] boss   "the boss that she has"
       (c)   [Professor Lao's] classes   "the classes that she teaches, i.e. has"

(21)   (a)   [Susan's] brother
       (b)   [the car mechanic's] mother-in-law
       (c)   [your] wife

(22)   (a)   [the president's] courage
       (b)   [the GOP's] policies
       (c)   [her] enthusiasm
       (d)   [their] happiness

Although we speak of possessing a car or a pen, as in (19), it would be odd
to paraphrase the genitives in (20) - (22) with expressions of possession (cf.
?the brother possessed by Susan, ?the policies possessed by the GOP).
   It makes even less sense to characterize other meanings expressed by the
genitive as possessive. For instance, the genitive NP and head often express
a whole-part relationship (the genitive being the whole, the head noun the
part), as in (23).

(23)   (a)   [the patient's] left arm
       (b)   [Yale's] English Department
       (c)   [the computer's] CPU
       (d)   [the earth's] surface

The genitive NP may name the origin or source of the head noun,
particularly when the noun is a product or creation as in (24).

(24) (a) [the student's] excuse   "the excuse given by the student"
      (b) [the leader's] orders   "the orders issued by the leader"
      (c) [the prisoner's] story   "the story told by the prisoner"
      (d) [his] complaints   "the complaints made by him"
      (e) [Robbins'] "Fancy Free"   "the ballet created by Robbins"

Genitives are also found in measure expressions as in (25); the majority of
these express time, as in (26).

(25) (a) the lion's share
      (b) a dollar's worth

(26) (a) a moment's hesitation
      (b) an hour's delay
      (c) three weeks' time
      (d) a year's work
      (e) the evening's reading
      (f) a lifetime's effort
      (g) a hard day's night

Finally, when the head is a deverbal noun, the genitive may be understood
as either the subject or the direct object of the related verb.

(27)   Genitive NP as Subject   Corresponding S
      (a) [your sister's] laugh   your sister laughs / laughed
      (b) [Mother's] complaint   Mother complained
      (c) [the dog's] death   the dog died
      (d) [the Pope's] denunciation   the Pope denounced St. Nick
           of St. Nicholas

(28)   Genitive NP as Direct Object
      (a) [my family's] support   x supports my family
      (b) [the man's] murder   x murdered the man
      (c) [St. Nick's] denunciation   x denounced St. Nick

Because of the inherent vagueness discussed above, the genitives in (28)
could also be understood as subjects. That is, (28)(c) could be understood

either as St. Nick's denunciation of some unnamed person or as someone's
denunciation of St. Nick.

4. GENITIVE DETERMINER VERSUS PP WITH *OF*

The relational meanings expressed by the genitive determiner can also be
expressed by a postposed prepositional phrase with *of*, as in (29).

(29)   Genitive Determiner   Postposed PP
       (a)   [the city's] problems   the problems [of the city]
       (b)   [Asia's] development   the development [of Asia]

Note that a postposed of-phrase is different from a postnominal genitive
(PNG). A postposed of-phrase has an ordinary NP as its complement,
whereas a PNG has a *genitive* NP (as discussed in 2.2).

   Considering the alternation between a genitive determiner and a postposed
of-phrase, in many cases the two expressions seem equally acceptable, as
shown in (30) and (31).

(30)   Genitive NP
       (a)   [the university's] tenured professors
       (b)   [the newspaper's] editorial policy
       (c)   [the auditorium's] seating capacity
       (d)   [Australia's] indigeneous languages
       (e)   [the computer's] popularity

(31)   Postposed PP
       (a)   the tenured professors [of the university]
       (b)   the editorial policy [of the newspaper]
       (c)   the seating capacity [of the auditorium]
       (d)   the indigeneous languages [of Australia]
       (e)   the popularity [of the computer]

If the genitive is a personal name, however, the prenominal form is much
preferred, as in (32).

(32)   Prenominal genitive   Postposed PP
     (a) [Marcello's] new car   ??the new car [of Marcello]
     (b) [Sophia's] syntax paper   ??the syntax paper [of Sophia]

The preposed genitive is also said (Quirk 1985:1277) to be preferred if the genitive is a common noun denoting a person or a higher order animal. The postposed of-phrase is said to be prefered if the genitive denotes a lower animal or inanimate, as in (33) and (34).

(33)   Prenominal genitive   Postposed PP
     (a) my sister's new baby   ?the new baby of my sister
     (b) the woman's smile   ?the smile of the woman
     (c) the policeman's badge   ?the badge of the policeman
     (d) the cat's dinner   ?the dinner of the cat

(34) (a) ?the worm's diet   the diet of the worm
     (b) ?the house's roof   the roof of the house
     (c) ?the car's wheels   the wheels of the car
     (d) ?the issue's complexity   the complexity of the issue

However, these differences are not due to the nature of the referent of the NP, but to the fact that NPs of this type are more likely to be specific and known to both speaker and hearer and hence, definite. They are more likely to be given in the discourse context (see below). Though (34)(a) with preposed genitive seems odd, the same NP is acceptable with a little context, as in (35).

(35) If you had a pet worm, you would worry about the worm's diet and spend money on its shelter.

As (35) shows, syntactic and discourse factors also influence the position of the genitive. In terms of syntax, there is a preference to put a longer or syntactically more complex constituent in second position. As a result, if the head noun has modifiers or a complement, making the N+ constituent longer or more complex than the genitive determiner, the prenominal genitive will be preferred.

(36)   N+ is longer or more complex—prenominal genitive preferred
        (a)   [the young artist's] unexpected collapse from extreme fatigue
        (b)   ?the unexpected collapse from extreme fatigue [of the young
              artist]

(37)   (a)   [that woman's] new convertible with a silver stripe and white
              leather interior
        (b)   ?the new convertible with a silver stripe and white leather
              interior [of that woman]

On the other hand, if the genitive NP is longer or more complex than the
N+ (the head noun and its complements and modifiers), the postposed PP
construction, which puts it second, will be preferred.

(38)   Genitive is longer or more complex—postposed PP preferred
        (a)   ?[my friend who had been studying for a year in Germany's]
              return
        (b)   the return [of my friend who had been studying for a year ...]

(39)   (a)   ?[that talented young artist from Prague's] collapse
        (b)   the collapse [of that talented young artist from Prague]

Discourse factors involve the relative communicative value of the two
units, there being a general tendency to put more important information or
new information toward the end of the phrase. Thus, when the information
in the N+ is new or considered more important, the prenominal genitive is
favored, as in (40)(a) and (41)(a). But, when the information in the genitive
determiner is new or relatively more important, the postposed of-phrase is
favored, as in (40)(b) and (41)(b).

(40)   (a)   A Senator was interviewed by the committee. [The Senator's]
              initial answers to the questions were unclear.
              (*Senator* is old information; *answers* is in focus.)
        (b)   Many people were questioned by the committee, but the answers
              [of the Senator from Florida] were most revealing.
              (*Senator* is new information and in focus.)

(41) (a) What have *you* been up to? Last week *I* went to [my best
            friend's] wedding.
            (*Wedding* is new information, in focus, and given second.)
      (b) Do you like weddings? Last week I went to the wedding [of my
            best friend from college].
            (*Wedding* is old information and given first; *best friend* is
            new information and given second.)

Exercise 1

When the genitive suffix is added to nouns that end in [-z], speakers do not
agree on how to write or pronounce it. Turn the following phrases into NPs
that have genitive determiners. Note what orthographic and phonetic forms
you use. Compare your usage with that of other students or with a reference
grammar of English.

1.   a car owned by Dr. Jones
2.   a novel written by Dickens
3.   a woman who is the wife of Charles
4.   the office occupied by Professor Burns
5.   a play written by Euripides
6.   the birth of Jesus

Exercise 2

Discuss the meaning conveyed by the genitive NPs.

1.   my sister's neck
2.   the chairman's office
3.   the doctor's dilemma
4.   my cousin's wedding
5.   Kim Bartlett's rejection
6.   Bausch's first novel
7.   the university's early admissions program
8.   the Bullets' defeat
9.   three month's effort
10. their next door neighbor's oldest daughter
11. her generosity
12. Apple's new chairman

13.   her neighbor's new coat
14.   the school's application for accreditation

Exercise 3

Draw tree diagrams for the NPs in square brackets, paying special attention to the genitives.

1.   [The teachers' decision] was that we should order [a teacher's manual].
3.   I don't like her. She's [a real Daddy's girl].
4.   Look at [my Daddy's new car].
5.   We're going to [Mabel's boyfriend's sister's house] for Thanksgiving.
6.   Everyone enjoyed their visit to [Georgia and Alfred's cabin on Lake George].
7.   [Mable's car] is white, but [mine] is blue.

Exercise 4

Identify the structural and semantic differences between the NPs in each set below. Why is (1)(c) grammatical, but (2)(c) not?

(1)   (a)   Andy's picture
      (b)   a picture of Andy's
      (c)   a picture of Andy

(2)   (a)   Susan's assignment
      (b)   an assignment of Susan's
      (c)   *an assignment of Susan

Exercise 5

Figure out which determiners can occur as a free-standing determiner, using the lists of determiners in (3) and (5) of Chapter 29.

Exercise 6

In a passage of a page or so, put brackets around all the genitive NPs and state their meanings as precisely as you can. Identify any PNGs or postposed of-phrases.

SELECTED BIBLIOGRAPHY

Alexander, D. and W.J. Kunz. 1964. Some classes of verbs in English. Bloomington, Indiana: Indiana University.

Austin, J. L. 1965. How to do things with words. Cambridge, Massachusetts: Harvard University Press.

Azar, Betty. 1984. Basic English grammar. Englewood Cliffs, New Jersey: Regents Prentice Hall.

Azar, Betty. 1989. Understanding and using English grammar. Englewood Cliffs, New Jersey: Prentice Hall Regents.

Bailey, Charles-James N. 1984. Markedness-reversal and the pragmatic principle of "reading between the lines in the presence of marked uses." Papiere zur Linguistik 31.43-100.

Bailey, Charles-James N. 1984. How can grammar be learned if the "present tense" is neither present nor a tense? Arbeitspapiere zur linguistik 21.228-45.

Baker, C. L. 1989. English Syntax. Cambridge, Massachusetts: The MIT Press.

Bierwisch, Manfried. 1967. Some semantic universals of German adjectives. Foundations of Language 3.1-36.

Bland, Susan Kesner. 1988. The present progressive in discourse: grammar versus usage revisited. TESOL Quarterly 22.53-68.

Bolinger, Dwight. 1968. Entailment and the meaning of structures. Glossa 2.119 - 127.

Bolinger, Dwight. 1971. The phrasal verb in English. Cambridge, Massachusetts: Harvard University Press.

Bridgeman, Loraine I., Dale Dillinger, et al. 1965. More classes of verbs in English. Bloomington, Indiana: Indiana University.

Celce-Murcia, Marianne and Diane Larsen-Freeman. 1983. The grammar book. Rowley, Massachusetts: Newbury House Publishers.

Comrie, Bernard. 1976. Aspect. Cambridge, England: Cambridge University Press.

Davison, Alice. 1980. Peculiar passives. Language 56.42-66.

Fraser, Bruce. 1976. The verb-particle combination in English. New York:

Academic Press.

Frodesen, Jan and Janet Eyring. 1993. Grammar dimensions. Boston, Massachusetts: Heinle & Heinle.

Gorden, David and George Lakoff. 1971. Conversational postulates. Chicago Linguistic Society 7.63-84.

Green, Georgia. 1974. Semantics and syntactic regularity. Bloomington, Indiana: Indiana University Press.

Green, Georgia. 1982. Colloquial and literary uses of inversions. Spoken and written language, ed. by Deborah Tannen, 119-153. Norwood, New Jersey: Ablex.

Hook, J. N. 1981. Two-word verbs in English. New York: Harcourt Brace Javonovich.

Huddleston, Rodney. 1984. Introduction to the grammar of English. Cambridge, England: Cambridge University Press.

Johnson, Ben. 1641. English grammar.

Leech, Geoffrey N. 1987. Meaning and the English verb. New York: Longman.

Lehrer, Adrienne. 1985. Markedness and antonymy. Journal of Linguistics 21.397-429.

Levi, Judith N. 1978. The syntax and semantics of complex nominals. New York: Academic Press.

Levin, Beth. 1993. English verb classes and alternations. Chicago, Illinois: The University of Chicago Press.

Lily, William and John Colet. 1970. A short introduction of grammar, 1549. English linguistics, 1500-1800; a collection of facsimile reprints, ed. by R. C. Alston. Menston, England: The Scholar Press, Ltd.

Longman Dictionary of Contempory English. 1987. Essex, England: Longman.

McCawley, James D. 1971. Tense and time reference in English. Studies in Linguistic Semantics, ed. by Charles Fillmore and D. Terence Langendoen, 97-113. New York: Holt, Rinehart and Winston, Inc.

McCawley, James D. 1979. Lexicography and the count-mass distinction. Adverbs, vowels, and other objects of wonder, 165-173. Chicago: University of Chicago Press.

McCawley, James D. 1981. Everything that linguists have always wanted to know about logic. Chicago: University of Chicago Press.

McCawley, James D. 1988. The syntactic phenomena of English. Chicago: University of Chicago Press.

McCawley, Noriko Akatuska. 1973. Boy, is syntax easy. Chicago Linguistic Society 9.369-77.

Mourelatos, Alexander P. D. 1981. Events, processes, and states. Syntax and semantics 14, ed. by Philip Tedeschi and Annie Zaenen, 191-212. New York: Academic Press.

O'Grady, William, Michael Dobrovolsky, et al., Eds. 1997. Contemporary linguistics. New York: St. Martin's Press.

Oosten, Jeanne van. 1984. On the nature of subjects, topics and agents: A cognitive explanation. Berkeley: University of California dissertation.

Pinker, Stephen. 1994. The language instinct. New York: HarperCollins.

Quirk, Randolph, Sidney Greenbaum, et al. 1985. A comprehensive grammar of the English language. New York: Longman.

Riddle, Elizabeth. 1986. The meaning and discourse function of the past tense in English. TESOL Quarterly 20.267-286.

Robinson, Barbara. 1989. Focus; an ESL grammar. New York: St. Martin's Press.

Rudin, Catherine. 1986. Changing the rules: "Extra" prepositions in relative clauses. Chicago Linguistic Society 22.277-85.

Sadock, Jerrold M. 1972. Speech act idioms. Chicago Linguistic Society 8:329-39.

Sapir, Edward. 1985. Grading: a study in semantics. Selected writings of Edward Sapir in language, culture and personality, ed. by David G. Mandelbaum, 122-49. Berkeley, California: University of California Press.

Schiffrin, Deborah. 1981. Tense variation in narrative. Language 57.45-62.

Vendler, Zeno. 1967. Verbs and times, 97-121. Ithaca, NY: Cornell University Press.

Sources for Text Examples

Carroll, Lewis. 1980. The annotated Alice. New York: C. N. Potter.

Connell, Evan S. 1992. Review of Secrets of the Pyramid by Sidney Kirkpatrick. Washington Post Book World, November 8.2

Grove, Lloyd. The men who won't be president. Washington Post, November 3, 1992.C1+6.

Hemingway, Ernst. 1961. The Snows of Kilimanjaro. New York:

Macmillan.

Joyce, James. 1962. Dubliners. New York: The Viking Press.

Laxalt, Robert. 1966. Basque sheepherders, lonely sentinels of the American west. National Geographic, June 1966.870-888.

Lockhart, Robin Bruce. 1986. Reilly: ace of spies. New York: Dorset Press.

Marsh, Ngaio. 1966. Killer dolphin. Boston: Little Brown.

Sayers, Dorothy. 1969. Hangman's holiday. New York: Avon Books.

Taylor, Paul. 1993. For South Africans, the big fear is crime. Washington Post, April,.A1+11.Title.